MOROCCAN NOIR

PUBLIC CULTURES OF THE MIDDLE EAST AND NORTH AFRICA

Paul A. Silverstein, Susan Slyomovics, and Ted Swedenburg, *editors*

MOROCCAN NOIR
Police, Crime, and Politics in Popular Culture

Jonathan Smolin

Indiana University Press

Bloomington & Indianapolis

This book is a publication of

Indiana University Press
Office of Scholarly Publishing
Herman B Wells Library 350
1320 East 10th Street
Bloomington, Indiana 47405 USA

iupress.indiana.edu

Telephone orders 800-842-6796
Fax orders 812-855-7931

© 2013 by Jonathan Smolin

All rights reserved

No part of this book may be reproduced or utilized in any form or by any means, electronic or mechanical, including photocopying and recording, or by any information storage and retrieval system, without permission in writing from the publisher. The Association of American University Presses' Resolution on Permissions constitutes the only exception to this prohibition.

♾ The paper used in this publication meets the minimum requirements of the American National Standard for Information Sciences—Permanence of Paper for Printed Library Materials, ANSI Z39.48-1992.

Manufactured in the United States of America

Library of Congress Cataloging-in-Publication Data

Smolin, Jonathan, author.
 Moroccan noir : police, crime, and politics
in popular culture / Jonathan Smolin.
   pages cm. — (Public cultures of the Middle East and North Africa)
   Includes bibliographical references and index.
   ISBN 978-0-253-01057-5 (cloth : alk. paper) — ISBN 978-0-253-01065-0 (pbk. : alk. paper) — ISBN 978-0-253-01073-5 (e-book) 1. Police—Morocco. 2. Police in popular culture—Morocco. 3. Crime in popular culture—Morocco. 4. Mass media and crime—Morocco. 5. Police in mass media. 6. Crime in mass media. 7. Mass media policy—Morocco. I. Title. II. Series: Public cultures of the Middle East and North Africa.
   HV8268.3.A2S66 2013
   306.280964—dc23

2013019514

1 2 3 4 5 18 17 16 15 14 13

for Jessica

The behavior of the police is the real proof of a country's democratization.

Khalid Jamaï, former editor-in-chief of *L'Opinion*

Our antecedents . . . go back to crime fiction more than crime fact.

John Douglas, one of the first serial-killer profilers

The most important preoccupation of the police establishment during the past years is indisputably its image among the public.

Mohamed Lemzabi, *Police Magazine*

Contents

Preface	xi
Acknowledgments	xv
Note on Transliteration, Translation, and Style	xvii
Introduction: State, Mass Media, and the New Moroccan Authoritarianism	1
1 Police on Trial: The Tabit Affair, Newspaper Sensationalism, and the End of the Years of Lead	14
2 "He Butchered His Wife Because of Witchcraft and Adultery": Crime Tabloids, Moral Panic, and the Remaking of the Moroccan Cop	47
3 Crime-Page Fiction: Moroccan True Crime and the New Independent Press	80
4 Prime-Time Cops: Blurring Police Fact and Fiction on Moroccan Television	124
5 The Moroccan "Serial Killer" and CSI: Casablanca	157
6 From Morocco's 9/11 to Community Policing: State Advertising and the New Citizen	201
Epilogue: "The Police Are at the Service of the People"	235
Notes	239
Bibliography	261
Index	277

Preface

I BEGAN WORKING ON this book over a decade ago, when I lived in Fez. While shopping at a local bookstore, I discovered a wonderful new literary form—the Moroccan Arabic police novel. Modern Arabic literature is rich in narrative experimentation but there is little genre fiction. Considering the highly negative image of the police in Arab society, it should come as no surprise that novelists ignored police fiction. In fact, by the late 1990s, the Arabic police procedural did not even exist outside Morocco. And that made the novels that I discovered in my local bookstore that much more interesting. What was happening in Morocco that led writers to depict a cop as a sympathetic figure at the center of a novel? Why did the genre exist in Arabic in Morocco but nowhere else in the Middle East or North Africa?

As I read these novels, I began noticing a connection between them and the crime articles in Morocco's new independent press. Like the novels, the crime stories in the country's highest-circulation newspaper at the time typically took the perspective of the police and used fictional narrative techniques to depict real-world criminal investigations. It hardly seemed like a coincidence that police fiction was emerging in Moroccan Arabic newspapers only a year or two after it first appeared on bookstore shelves. I immediately wanted to know why journalists of the new independent press had decided to narrate the details of real-life crime and punishment in a style that seemed consciously to mimic the country's new police novels.

I became even more interested in the link between the police novels and the increasingly commercial mass media when I discovered that the television stations were making movie versions of the novels. Novels have a very limited readership throughout the Arab world and Morocco is no exception. Selling only a few thousand copies makes a novel a bestseller. By producing the police novels for the small screen—and in Moroccan, not Standard Arabic—the television stations made police fiction accessible to millions across the country. Moreover, the police movies, with their taboo themes and modernist audiovisual techniques, represented a striking break from the conservative television programming of previous decades. After seeing police fiction in novels, newspapers, and now television, I asked myself why it was suddenly becoming so popular in Morocco in the early 2000s. Why was police fiction spreading so quickly in the mass media? And what was the connection between these new images of the police in popular culture and large-scale changes taking place in the mass media and politics at the time?

These questions set me on a long and challenging investigation into the development and spread of mass media images of the police in contemporary Moroccan society and their connection to transformations in the nature of authoritarianism in the country. I immediately found myself in the role of a detective, chasing down leads, searching for evidence, and finding unexpected connections. And I quickly found that it would not be easy. After discovering that the novels emerged in an atmosphere of growing sensationalism and state involvement in the depictions of crime and punishment in the press, I went in search of back issues of newspapers that would allow me to trace the development of this new kind of reporting. I went to newspaper headquarters in Casablanca and Rabat but I discovered that most did not keep complete organized archives.

I then went to the national library, *al-Maktaba al-Wataniyya li-l-Mamlaka al-Maghribiyya*/Bibliothèque Nationale du Royaume du Maroc (BNRM) in Rabat, which collected most newspapers in the country. As in any archive, it took a tremendous amount of time to locate issues that I needed and to find ways to copy the sheer volume of articles that I wanted. Each chapter in this book is based on thousands of newspaper articles and it was an ongoing challenge to collect such an enormous amount of material for analysis. Issues that could not be located during one research trip turned up during the next, while issues that I had read previously went missing. Rules about copying or photographing newspaper pages changed from time to time, further delaying the collection process. Moreover, all of the newspapers that I worked with were only available in the form of paper copies, not microfilm, and were commonly organized in stacks, not bound volumes. This added considerably to the time it took to go through years of issues, as I needed to handle physical copies of each day's paper to search for material instead of simply scanning microfilm or flipping through bound volumes. Considering that the BNRM was the only place in the world where most of my source material could be found, I spent many months there spread out over the span of years working with their collection, navigating the process of accessing and copying articles from several decades of newspapers. In the history that I present in each chapter, I seek to give readers a sense of what it was like to follow many of the cases that I discuss as they unfolded, weaving each chapter of this book from thousands of newspapers that took years to collect and analyze.

The tabloids that I discuss in chapter 2 presented unique challenges. As is the case with tabloids around the world, it is exceedingly difficult to find back issues of Moroccan crime tabloids, since they are typically discarded and not considered worthy of archiving. I was never able to locate old issues in used newspaper and magazine markets, despite their popularity in Morocco during the 1990s. Najib Skir, the editor of the main tabloids in Morocco, generously gave me access to his personal collection of back issues but there were significant gaps in their coverage that did not permit me to verify some of his assertions about the history of the tabloids in the country. After four years of working at the BNRM and making repeated requests, I managed to uncover a largely complete collection of the tabloids, both before and after the pivotal Tabit Affair, as the staff was in the process of moving their newspaper collection to a new building. Without this incredible stroke of good luck, it would have been impossible to offer the history of the tabloids in chapter 2 and to be able to discuss the full scope of their coverage. When I returned to the BNRM in spring 2012, however, I discovered that they had discarded their collection of crime tabloids. Thankfully, I had already taken hundreds of photographs of the tabloid covers and articles for reference.

Finding copies of the police television movies was another adventure altogether. I was able to track down all of the directors and many of the actors that I discuss in chapter 4 but most did not have copies of their movies. In Morocco, television movies are not for sale and the stations control their distribution. The stations rarely give copies of the movies to anyone, even to the movie stars and directors. For this reason, it took a number of years to collect copies of the several dozen police movies that have appeared in Morocco since the early 2000s. In some cases, official requests were fruitful. In others, I had to wait for the movies to re-air on television so that either friends or I could record them. Only in recent years have many of these movies appeared for sale in pirated copies in the souks or streamed on websites.

One of the most significant challenges was collecting the material for the GUS advertising campaign, which I discuss in chapter 6. I bought most issues of *Police Magazine* when they appeared on the newsstands but several key early issues eluded me. It took many months to track these down. In addition to checking regularly at a number of newsstands in Rabat, Casablanca, and Fez over the span of a year, I went to the police headquarters in Rabat to request these issues. I was able to meet with one of the highest-ranked police officials in the country, but my request was denied. Eventually, though, my persistence at the newsstands paid off, as a newspaper seller with deep connections was able to locate the missing material that I needed. As for the television advertisement that I analyze in chapter 6, I managed to secure a copy directly from Boomerang, the firm that commissioned it, after several visits. Without this material, I would not have been able to write chapter 6, which plays a pivotal role in the central argument of this book.

I felt at moments that my ability to write this book hinged on whether I would be fortunate enough to find a particular movie, magazine, or newspaper issue. Simply collecting the material for any one chapter took an enormous amount of time and persistence. At times, I very much envied researchers who could access their primary material in well-organized libraries and bookshops. Fortunately, I was able to spend a significant amount of time in Morocco during the period that I cover in this book, immersing myself in Arabic popular culture, including newspapers, magazines, television programming, and advertising. This allowed me to follow many of the events that I discuss as they happened and to collect the material that I needed as it appeared, adding to my excitement in undertaking this book and helping me through difficult periods.

This work focuses on the way mass media ephemera reflect and engage political and social change. While relying on this material presented me with significant challenges, it also gave me unique opportunities for offering new perspectives on contemporary Arab culture, society, and politics. I hope that my source material and method will lead to renewed interest in using neglected media sources for analyzing contemporary Arab society and encourage reevaluation of the life of popular culture in today's Middle East and North Africa.

Acknowledgments

I AM GRATEFUL TO many people and organizations for their support while I undertook this project. I composed the initial draft of the manuscript during a year of research in Rabat thanks to a generous Fulbright-Hays Faculty Research Abroad Fellowship from the U.S. Department of Education. This year of research and writing provided me with the opportunity to reconceptualize aspects of this work and to collect source materials that were necessary for completing this manuscript. It also allowed me to renew old contacts and establish new ones that would prove essential for finishing this book.

At Dartmouth College, I am grateful for the Walter and Constance Burke Research Initiation Award, which provided extremely valuable resources for research and travel. The Dickey Center for International Understanding also generously helped fund two research trips and supported this work through their Manuscript Review Program. I would like to thank Christianne Hardy Wohlforth and all of my readers—John Entelis, Susan Gilson Miller, Lynn Higgins, Rebecca Biron, Dennis Washburn, James Dorsey, and Jennifer Fluri—for their valuable feedback and suggestions. The reviewers for Indiana University Press also provided extremely useful comments and ways to improve the manuscript. Rebecca Tolen, Sarah Jacobi, June Silay, Eric Levy, and the staff of Indiana University Press provided expert guidance on editing and preparing this manuscript for publication. Anthony Helm, head of digital media and library technologies at Dartmouth College, generously helped produce the images for this book.

I would like to thank Katharine Conley, associate dean of the humanities at Dartmouth during the time I drafted this manuscript, for her support during the research and writing stages of this book. Her successor, Adrian Randolph, has generously supported this book through its completion. I am also grateful to the Graduate School of Arts and Sciences, Moroccan Studies Program, and the Department of Near Eastern Languages and Civilization, all of Harvard University, for providing opportunities for regular travel to Morocco to collect material in the early stages of this project when I was a graduate student.

Many colleagues helped at various stages of research and writing. In particular, I would like to thank Dale Eickelman, Lynn Higgins, Kevin Reinhart, Dennis Washburn, Mary Jean Green, Susan Blader, James Dorsey, Gerd Gemünden, Dirk Vandewalle, Jeff Ruoff, Silvia Spitta, Allen Hockley, Hussein Kadhim, and George Demko for their support, comments, and suggestions. Roger Allen, Susan Slyomovics, Kamal Abu Deeb, Carol Bardenstein, Valérie Orlando, and Paul

Heck helped me think through various aspects of this work. I would also like to thank Leonard Wood for his comments and encouragement.

During my time in Morocco, I was extremely fortunate to meet and spend time with most of the people whose work I discuss in this book. I would like to thank Najib Skir, Hafid Benkmil, Adil Fadili, Hassan Rhanja, Abdelmajid Hachadi, Hadin Saghir, Abderrahim Ariri, Rachid El Ouali, Mehdi Sebti, and Miloudi Hamdouchi for meeting with me to discuss their work. Najib Skir and Abderrahim Ariri provided me with valuable source material for this project. I would also like to thank Ahmed Abdessalam Bekkali, Yassin Adnan, and Hassan Bahraoui for discussing aspects of this work. The staff of the Bibliothèque Nationale du Royaume du Maroc—Saad Charkaoui, Sidi El Mokhtar El Alaoui, and the assistants in the periodical room—were extremely helpful over the years. I would like to thank them in particular for accommodating my repeated requests to access an ever-growing amount of material. The staff of the newspapers *al-Ahdath al-Maghribiyya* (Moroccan Events) and *al-'Alam* (Banner)/*L'Opinion* generously allowed me to access their archives. I would also like to thank Mitchell Cohn, Saadia Maski, Salwa Jaafari, and Farah Chery-Medor during my Fulbright year in Rabat as well as Chris Strenta, Cynthia Dudzinski, Erin Bennett, Robyn Hadlock, Aarron Clough, and Gérard Bohlen for their administrative help. Salwa Jaafari provided me with the audiovisual material that I discuss in chapter 5. I also owe a debt of gratitude to Amine, Si Mohamed, Rachid, Nezha, Aïcha, Brahim, and Rubio.

This book would not have been possible without the help and support of several people in particular. I would first like to thank Bill Granara for guiding my development as a researcher, writer, and scholar. Bill has always pushed me to think about this work in new and exciting ways. I would also like to thank Susan Gilson Miller for welcoming me into the Moroccan Studies Program at Harvard and for her generous intellectual support over the years. Abdelilah Hamdouchi and his family offered kind hospitality during my stays in Rabat. He was always eager to exchange ideas about this work during my many visits. I would also like to thank Diana Abouali for her support, enthusiasm, and sense of humor over the years.

Last but not least, I want to thank my family for their encouragement, especially during my extended research periods in Morocco. Without my parents, this work would not have been possible. My in-laws, Barb and Alan, were also a wonderful source of support, especially in the final editing stages. My son Noah, who arrived just as I was working through the final edits, was a wonderful source of inspiration. Finally, I would like to dedicate this book to my wife Jessica, who gave me the daily encouragement, support, and enthusiasm I needed to follow through on what seemed at times like an unending investigation.

Note on Transliteration, Translation, and Style

I USE BOTH FRENCH and Arabic transliterations of Moroccan words and names in this book. When an author writes in Arabic, I transliterate their name and the title of their work with a simplified transliteration system based on the one used by the *International Journal of Middle Eastern Studies*. When an author writes in Arabic but has a commonly used name in French transliteration, I use the French spelling in the text but an Arabic transliteration in the notes and bibliography. If an author writes in French, I use the French spelling of their name instead of an Arabic transliteration. Throughout this work, I adopt standard French spellings of Moroccan names when discussing characters in various texts (e.g., Mohamed, not Muhammad; Bouchra, not Bushra; Lahcen, not al-Hasan). I also leave the standard transliterations of proper nouns and well-known names in their French form instead of transliterating them from Arabic (e.g., Ibn Rochd Hospital instead of Ibn Rushd Hospital, Hamidou Laânigri instead of Hamidu al-'Anikri).

In order to aid the reader, I have translated all titles from Arabic. When discussing a newspaper, novel, or television film, I transliterate the name of the work when I first mention it and use the English translation afterward. While I translate French when discussing a work in this book, I have not translated French titles in the notes or bibliography. In translating passages for this book, I have sought to match the register of the original language as much as possible. All translations are my own. As for style, I follow the *Chicago Manual of Style* throughout this work.

MOROCCAN NOIR

Introduction
State, Mass Media, and the New Moroccan Authoritarianism

On the morning of December 17, 2010, a vegetable seller named Mohamed Bouazizi covered himself in gasoline and set himself ablaze in the Tunisian town of Sidi Bouzid. Just an hour earlier, the local police had harassed Bouazizi, demanding bribes to allow him to continue selling his vegetables. Fed up with years of abuse by the police, Bouazizi went to the local governor's office to complain. After officials ignored him, Bouazizi, desperate to have his voice heard, went into the street and committed his act of self-immolation, a stunning form of public protest against systematic corruption, repression, and injustice. Despite the attempts of doctors to save him, Bouazizi eventually died from his wounds on January 4, 2011.

Few knew it at the time but Bouazizi's protest hit a deep nerve. While Tunisia had experienced significant economic liberalization during the previous twenty years, the country's political elite maintained legitimacy largely through the intimidation, violence, and coercion of the security forces. By the start of 2011, Tunisians still lived in a heavy-handed police state that crushed freedom of expression, public protest, and acts of dissent. The police, in their various administrative forms, were widely feared for their systematic repression and human rights abuses. Despite the dangers involved in expressing public dissent, Bouazizi's self-immolation inspired massive street protests against the regime of Tunisian president Zine El Abidine Ben Ali, who had ruled the country since 1987. Demonstrations expanded exponentially as Bouazizi's death unleashed long-simmering anger over years of abuse. On January 14, 2011, to the shock of many observers, the Ben Ali regime crumbled in the face of these protests and the disgraced dictator fled to Saudi Arabia to avoid accountability for his years of rule.

On January 25, 2011, street protests erupted in Cairo that would quickly lead to the ousting of another long-standing dictator, Hosni Mubarak. No doubt, the Tunisian revolution served as an inspiration. But there is an even more specific connection between the initial Egyptian protests and the events in Tunisia that has been largely overlooked. Bouazizi set himself on fire because of years of police abuse and repression. As in Tunisia, the Egyptian police were widely known for their corruption and human rights violations. For decades, the regime had used the various police divisions as a means to crush dissent, silence opposition, and intimidate the public. Despite widespread and long-standing disgust at the repression of the security forces, Egypt had a national holiday in which the public was expected to celebrate their police for maintaining the nation's stability. The protests in Egypt that would bring down the Mubarak regime began on January 25, the holiday known as "National Police Day," as a mass expression of anger and outrage against decades of police abuses.

Police repression is an experience that binds people throughout the Arab world, not just Egyptians and Tunisians. After the anticolonial movements of the 1940s and 1950s, post-independence leaders consolidated their grip on power by using the police to arrest, detain, and torture those viewed as a potential threat to their authority. This included anyone who represented significant opposition to the regime and, possibly, their friends and family. From leftist intellectuals, academics, and journalists to Islamist radicals, members of the political opposition, and ordinary citizens, people across the political and socioeconomic spectrum in the Arab world have experienced the authoritarianism of the state through the medium of police violence, intimidation, and corruption. Because of this shared experience, the police, in their different divisions, came to symbolize not only state-authorized violence, as in democratic societies, but also the lawlessness, repression, and human rights abuses of authoritarianism across the region. As Peter K. Manning writes, "The police are the most common symbol of governmental authority in everyday life."[1] In the Arab world, police, authoritarianism, and state became intertwined in the post-independence period. It should therefore come as no surprise that the police—with all of their symbolic value—could serve as the spark that ignited the recent Tunisian and Egyptian revolutions.

In Morocco, the link between the police and state authoritarianism is just as strong. As in other countries in the region, police repression emerged in Morocco immediately after independence. After Hassan II became king in 1961, he widened the use of the security forces to crush dissent, arresting some five thousand people in 1963 alone. Only two years later, the police and other security forces brutally suppressed widespread riots in Casablanca, killing hundreds and detaining thousands. When Hassan II faced two coup attempts, the first in 1971 and the second in 1972, the police arrested thousands of opposition members, detained them without trial, and used torture to extract "confessions" to political crimes.[2] This period of grave human rights violations, which lasted from the early 1970s until the early 1990s, is known as *sanawat al-rasas, les années de plomb,* or the Years of Lead. During these decades, secret detention centers such as the notorious Derb Moulay Chérif in Casablanca were used to hold and abuse prisoners, few of whom ever received a trial. Those who did were tried in farcical mass hearings. Freedom of expression was severely restricted during these years and fear of the police spread through society.

While state power was far from absolute or total during the Years of Lead—among other acts of resistance, riots erupted in cities like Casablanca and Fez in the 1980s and early 1990s—political contestation withered in this period, as engaging in something as simple as handing out leaflets could have dire consequences. Thousands faced arbitrary arrest, torture, and unlimited detention. Others simply disappeared, some only for having questionable associates or being in the wrong place at the wrong time. Moreover, the abuses of the police and security forces were not the only forms of state violence that existed in Moroccan society during this period. As Abdellah Hammoudi has shown, authoritarianism in Morocco also functioned through symbolic violence, the internalization of fear and subservience, and patronage systems.[3]

The police in Morocco were founded in 1956, right after independence. Known administratively as *al-Idara al-'Amma li-l-Amn al-Watani/Direction générale de la sécurité nationale* (DGSN), the police are organized into a number of divisions, such as the Criminal, Border, and Royal Police, as well as the Secret Police, known officially as *al-Idara al-'Amma li-Muraqabat al-Turab al-Watani/ Département de sécurité territoriale* (DST).[4] Other elements of the security apparatus include the Auxiliary Forces, or *al-Quwwat al-Musa'ida/Forces auxiliaires*, which fall under the control of the Ministry of the Interior, and the Gendarmerie, or *al-Darak al-Malaki*, a subunit of *al-Quwwat al-Musallaha al-Malikiyya/ Forces armées royales* (FAR), also known as the Moroccan military. While these administrative distinctions are important for understanding the organization of power within the security forces, they were not necessarily significant to the wider public. The members of these divisions, in real-world interactions, have represented the public's direct contact with state authoritarianism since independence. In general terms, this book uses the word "police" to refer broadly to the armed agents of state control who maintained authoritarian rule within the country through intimidation, coercion, and violence as well as their administrative management and directorate. When discussing the police more specifically, especially after the early 1990s, this book uses the term to refer to the uniformed officers and plainclothes detectives of the DGSN who interact directly with the public.

Starting in the early 1990s, after decades of police abuse during the Years of Lead, the *makhzen*, or Moroccan state, began renegotiating its strategies for maintaining the public's consent to its authority, moving away from violence and coercion to ensure social cohesion.[5] This took place in the context of political liberalization in other Arab regimes, in what has been called a transition to "new" or "durable" authoritarianism in the region.[6] There have been a number of theories about what motivated the shift away from physical repression in Morocco. One is that King Hassan II was sick and began to soften the repressive nature of the regime in order to ensure a smooth transition to his son, Mohamed VI, who became king in 1999. Another is that international pressure in response to its human rights record forced the Moroccan regime to end systematic repression of the population and seek out new forms of social control. Also, the end of the Cold War and the first Gulf War—as well as local factors, such as drought—put significant socioeconomic pressures on the palace that could have led it to reconsider its methods of achieving stability. Regardless of these possibilities, in the early 1990s, the state began to clear the air and set off on an evolutionary path away from the repression of the Years of Lead. As Antonio Gramsci and Louis Althusser have argued, no regime can survive simply through violence and coercion, whether physical or psychological.[7]

Many of the changes in Morocco since the early 1990s have been examined, such as economic policy, political contestation, and human rights, among others.[8] Nonetheless, the transformations that have taken place in the mass media—and the Arabic mass media in particular—remain one of the most understudied aspects of contemporary Moroccan society.[9] Since the early 1990s, the Moroccan mass media have become increasingly commercial, catering to the widest possible audience in the country by focusing on a variety of previously taboo subjects, sensational representations of crime and punishment the most prominent among them. During this time, the state fostered these new media, providing them with source material on which to base their narratives of police justice in the new era. This book examines the intersections between the state and sensational mass media that led to the production and dissemination of new police images, which were intended to serve as markers for the broader public of the changing nature of authoritarianism in the country. Through these images of the police—the linchpin of state power—the state attempted to reposition the public in its relationship with state authority, turning away from coercion and violence to public relations and opinion management in an attempt to maintain its legitimacy in an evolving era. The mass media, through the contradictory, contentious, and oftentimes ambiguous ways that they intersected with the state in the new era, offer a new framework for understanding the changing nature and mechanics of authoritarianism in the country during the past twenty years.

The origins of this media revolution lie in the notorious Tabit Affair. In early 1993, Hajj Mustapha Tabit, a high-level police commissioner in Casablanca, was arrested for abducting and sexually assaulting over five hundred women, crimes that he recorded on more than one hundred videotapes. The trial was a watershed moment because a police official—a direct symbol of state authoritarianism, someone presumed to be above the law and beyond criticism—was made publicly accountable for horrendous crimes. The trial also broke the taboo against criticizing the police in the press as journalists were permitted to cover the scandal in a largely unrestrained way, giving birth to sensationalism in the Moroccan media. The new sensationalism challenged the state and humiliated the police. It also attracted a massive audience of non-elite readers to the press for the first time, demonstrating that the mass media could cater to the broader public, despite illiteracy rates in the country of at least 50 percent.[10] The shocking trial—because of its press coverage, among other factors—signified to the wider public that the Years of Lead were finally coming to a close.

One reason why the Tabit Affair attracted such attention was because of the highly restrained and restricted nature of the mass media in the country during the decades before the trial. As of the early 1990s, Morocco's printed press consisted of about a dozen major daily newspapers, all of which were sponsored by political parties, the government, or the state. Every significant political organization published separate French- and Arabic-language dailies in which they expressed partisan views on social, economic, cultural, and political issues, not general news or information for the public. *al-Ittihad al-Ishtiraki* (Socialist Union), the Arabic newspaper of *al-Ittihad al-Ishtiraki li-l-Quwwat al-Shaʿabiyya/Union Socialiste des Forces Populaires* (USFP), and its earlier incarnation, *al-Muharrir* (Liberator), served as the mouthpiece for the main political opposition in the country during the Years of Lead. *Al-ʿAlam* (Banner), the Arabic newspaper of *Hizb al-Istiqlal*, the Independence Party, offered a more accommodating and less confrontational nationalist platform. As of the early 1990s, these two newspapers had the highest circulations in the country. There were no independent dailies until the late 1990s but a variety of independent weeklies appeared as early as the 1960s. These included elite Francophone magazines like Zakya Daoud's *Lamalif* and Arabic political rumor weeklies, which the well-known journalist Mustapha Alaoui published.[11] Satirical weeklies written mostly in Moroccan colloquial Arabic, such as Mohamed Filali's *Akhbar al-Suq* (Market News) and *al-Usbuʿ al-Dahik* (Laughing Week), also emerged in the 1980s.[12]

The daily press as a whole catered to the educated elite, taking a largely pedantic perspective on the sponsoring organization's political platform. In addition to party news and analysis of political, economic, and social issues, the daily press printed highbrow cultural and literary reports and debates, almost exclusively by or about party members. State and political propaganda during these years was heavy-handed and transparent. Newspapers featured few of the characteristics of media sensationalism, such as simplified and vivid language, striking photographs, and a focus on the private lives of individuals, all elements that draw in a large and diverse readership in countries around the world. The daily press therefore ignored the massive semiliterate public or readers who desired nonpartisan, lively general interest news and entertainment from newspapers.

As for television, the public had highly limited contact with small-screen programming before the 1990s. There was only one station, the state-owned Moroccan Radio and Television, commonly known as RTM, or the "First" channel, which was founded in 1962. The Ministry of the Interior—not the Ministry of Culture—directly supervised its operations. It broadcast for several hours a day, showing a mix of royal speeches, governmental activities, readings of the Quran, news reports, and some foreign movies and television series, mostly from the Middle East or France. There were few local programs during these years. Among those produced were talk shows about cultural affairs, music performances, and the rare television movie or miniseries, all of which presented a strongly positive, idealized image of society. With its headquarters in the center of Rabat, a short walk from the palace, ministry headquarters, and main military complex, RTM has always been perceived as the direct domain of the state and palace, another means by which to control the public. In stark contrast to the widespread repression and abuses of the Years of Lead, the country appeared in the post-independence mass media as a land of widespread security and strong moral and social bonds. From its beginnings, television served as a medium for disseminating state propaganda and an extremely conservative image of culture, society, and politics.[13]

The emergence of sensationalism in newspapers during the Tabit Affair attracted broad and diverse audiences to the media for the first time in the country's history. But it also created deep tensions between state, press, and public. While the state saw the Tabit case as a way to initiate long-awaited reforms of the police and clear the air after decades of repression, it was unprepared for the degree of public anger that the scandal unleashed, leading to what Gramsci has termed a "crisis of authority."[14] During and immediately after Tabit's trial, the press challenged the legitimacy of not only the police but also the state. Moreover, thanks to the trial coverage, the public became emboldened to challenge the police publicly. After the trial, the state needed to find a way to transform its brand of authoritarianism and make it amenable to public demands for reform. The state also had to demonstrate to the public that it could be compatible with respect for human rights, freedom of expression, and the rule of law, all demands that the trial brought to the forefront.

The sensationalism with which the press covered the Tabit Affair set an important precedent for the changes that would take place in the Moroccan media after the early 1990s. With the trial complete, the state initiated a highly sophisticated, dynamic, and at times contradictory engagement with the mass media. In particular, the state began fostering and interfacing with new forms of sensational media in order to produce and disseminate new images of the police for the wider public. Just as the police maintained the authoritarian state during the Years of Lead, they would once again serve as a vehicle for state attempts to achieve stability and social cohesion. Instead of using the police for violence and repression, the state would turn to generating and circulating new images of the police in society, recognizing the direct link between police and authoritarianism for the public. These new images, which recast the police as the symbol of the rule of law and respect for human rights in post–Years of Lead Morocco, worked to redefine the relationship between state and police as well as their relationship with the public. Moreover, these images were intended to serve as signposts for the public that state authority was in the process of reform and that the country was turning the page on its authoritarian past and entering a new era of rule of law. By collaborating on producing and disseminating these new images of the police in the media, the state acknowledged the importance of public opinion and worked to make its authority responsive to public demands for change after decades of fear and coercion.

New media forms—tabloids, true-crime articles in the independent daily press, television cop thrillers, and even police advertising—soon emerged and interfaced with the state to transform official source material into a wide variety of sensational representations of police investigations, circulating them to the broader public.[15] These new sources used a number of strategies to make the police appear sympathetic, encouraging the public to identify with the police as they investigated crime and applied justice in a new era of respect for the rule of law and human rights. In producing these images, each media source sought to blur the lines between fact and fiction, to break down the boundary between representation and reality, in order to improve the image of the real-world police and recast them in the guise of their media counterparts. The state fostered this media environment not simply to end the public's fear of the police but also to persuade the wider public to see authority on terms defined by the state in the new era. By repositioning the public in their relationship with the police, the state sought to renegotiate its authority and legitimacy, producing, or what Althusser has termed "interpellating," a new citizen for the new Morocco.[16]

The media, interfacing with the state, may have constructed and disseminated these messages but there is no way to know exactly how the public interpreted them. One trend in cultural studies is to assume that the media have a predictable effect on an undifferentiated public and can easily manufacture their consent to the dominant ideology. An influential text in this approach is Max Horkheimer and Theodor Adorno's essay "The Culture Industry: Enlightenment as Mass Deception," in which they argue that entertainment businesses, through the industrialization of culture, work to submit the public to capitalist ideology and make them docile.[17] Horkheimer and Adorno claim, "The more strongly the culture industry entrenches itself, the more it can do as it chooses with the needs of consumers—producing, controlling, disciplining them."[18] Another influential writer depicting the public as powerless and easily manipulated is Jürgen Habermas, who argues that the mass media in the twentieth century was transformed from a medium of contesting state authority to a vehicle for the economic and political elite to manage public opinion by suppressing dissent through entertainment.[19]

The Moroccan public is not homogenous or docile. They are not the dupes commonly depicted in studies of media effects on society. The audiences for the sensational media in Morocco are highly diverse, ranging from elite to non-elite, and spread across the literacy spectrum, including well-educated, semiliterate, and illiterate. They are largely urban—the Moroccan media display a strongly urban bias—but media texts, such as newspapers, radio, and television programming, easily circulate to rural areas of the country as well. Moreover, there is a multiplicity of reader positions and audiences for one media source easily shift to others. Media texts also flow and circulate in Morocco in the background of daily social life, intersecting and competing with other elements for the attention of audiences. Despite the desire of the state to direct public perceptions through new images of the police, particular meanings from media texts cannot simply be imposed on audiences and interpretation cannot be easily managed and directed. These texts work through persuasion, suggestion, repetition, and invitation, not a simple top-down linear model of production and consumption with predictable results. While John Fiske perhaps overstates the subversive and ironic responses of audiences to popular culture, he has convincingly shown how the public is active, critical, resistant, and unpredictable in the way they receive and understand media texts.[20]

This book will examine the politics of representations of crime and police in Moroccan society after the early 1990s. While the media point at times to the response of the public to aspects of these texts, including moments of backlash and rejection, this book, unlike ethnographic works such as *Dramas of Nationhood* by Lila Abu-Lughod, will not track the immediate viewing environment of these media and their reception.[21] Instead, this book will examine the strategies and mechanics for how the increasingly sensational and commercial newspaper and television industries mediated a new relationship between state, police, and citizen, transforming the nature of authoritarianism in the country. Representations of the police in this new media environment appeared in a wide variety of forms and migrated from one medium to another, pointing to the intertextual relationship that developed between the various media during this period. Moreover, the repetition of these forms—an element that eventually made the once-terrifying police banal—demonstrates the far-reaching nature of the project of recasting the relationship between state and citizen. The multiplicity of representations and forms also points to the failings of the project, slippages of power, and anxieties and insecurities over its effectiveness. As John Fiske has argued, the diversity of audience positions make "ideology work so hard and insistently to maintain itself and its values."[22]

The history presented in this book demonstrates how the increasingly commercialized mass media can paradoxically serve the interests of authoritarianism in today's Middle East. Sensational and commercialized newspapers and television programming in Morocco draw wider and more diverse audiences than ever before, create new terrains for freedom of expression and engage broader public interests, especially compared to the restrained, paternalistic, and partisan media of the Years of Lead. At the same time, these new media developed a highly contradictory relationship with the state, which provided the raw material for their depictions of crime and punishment. Even though the new media look nonpartisan and appear like nonstate sources, they are still restricted and constrained by state concerns. The new style and content of the sensational and commercial press and television does not necessarily indicate a radical break in the tight link between the mass media and the state. Rather, it points to an evolving relationship between the two, one characterized by ambiguity, contradiction, and contestation in attempting to engage the widest possible audience and influence public opinion.

Morocco is not the only authoritarian environment in which the state interlinked with increasingly commercialized mass media to produce a highly contradictory and ambiguous media environment. Yuezhi Zhao, for example, has described how the Chinese press and television industries after 1992 have produced "the intertwining of Party logic and market logic."[23] Zhao shows how sensationalism can be used to make "hard ideological propaganda gentler, softer, and much more appealing."[24] Sensational media have flourished in China since the early 1990s because of the way they have transformed content in order to accommodate both state interests for innovative propaganda and public desires for a more daring and inclusive press and television. Michael Schudon, in discussing Zhao's work, explains that "the blend of state, independent, and commercial news media and the mixed pattern of ownership and control are so new that they do not even have names, let alone theories to explain them."[25] This book will add to the literature seeking to address these new media-state interfaces in an evolving authoritarian environment.

The rise in sensational newspapers and television programs in Morocco since the early 1990s demonstrate the complexity, dynamism, and contradictory nature of the country's commercial media and authoritarianism. The state fostered a nonpartisan sensational media environment to deliver its message of police reform to the broadest possible public. While there was an increasingly intimate relationship between the state and media during the 2000s, the state allowed nonstate players such as journalists, movie directors and television actors, newspaper publishers, and advertising firms to construct and circulate these images of the police on their behalf, a relationship that points to a paradox of agency. Nonetheless, while the state was the driving force behind the process, this is not a simple top-down story, neatly controlled by a few individuals. These transformations took place because, at times, they suited and benefitted broad diverse interests. Nonetheless, these texts are full of contestations, ruptures, and contradictions, as they demonstrate moments of dissent and renegotiation that show how the media were not as docile as the state would have liked. Journalists, publishers, and movie directors at times directly challenged the state, the pace of reforms in the country, and the status of the police. Moreover, these media actors clearly had an interest in building an audience for sales and this would occasionally come into conflict with the state's desire for media pliability.

As the state became more and more involved in the production of these images, it would increasingly lose its ability to manage the process. This shows how the changes in the media-state interface were far from linear and the outcome of this relationship was—and remains—uncertain and unpredictable. Nonetheless, the state's willingness to lose control of its message at times demonstrates the progressive nature of authoritarianism in Morocco during the past twenty years. Even though Marwan M. Kraidy addresses transnational Arab satellite television—and not the local national media that this book examines—he correctly notes, "As crude propaganda gives way to image management in an uncontrollable hypermedia environment . . . it becomes clear that Arab leaders are forced to enter the battle to define reality without guarantees that their version of reality would prevail."[26]

This book tracks the political trajectory of the past twenty years in Morocco as seen through watershed media events that have been largely overlooked by scholars outside the country, and traces the evolving state-media relationship in the shift away from the violence and coercion of the Years of Lead. Privileging typically neglected Arabic sources—popular culture ephemera such as tabloids, television programming, newspapers and magazines, and advertising—it examines the way this media-state interface constructed and disseminated sensational images of crime and punishment in an attempt to direct public perceptions of state authority in a new era that trumpeted human rights, freedom of expression, and the rule of law. Fusing media studies, sociology, and literary analysis, this book analyzes the cultural mechanics of an evolving authoritarianism, one that adapts and renews itself to unexpected challenges, new publics, and evolving political environments. By following the relationship between the state and media during the past twenty years, this book demonstrates the contradictions and contestations that are at the core of the changing nature of authoritarianism in Morocco. The state-media nexus described in this book presents, in the words of Abdellah Hammoudi, "a modern authoritarianism that remains entrenched in social and political life despite an unceasing struggle for change."[27]

Road Map

Each chapter in this book traces the emergence of new forms of sensational mass media, new images of the police, and new markers for the public that the nature of authoritarianism in the country was changing. Chapter 1 examines the Tabit Affair, showing how the unprecedented trial gave birth to mass media sensationalism in Morocco, smashed the taboo against the press's writing about the police, and undermined the position of the police in society. By allowing the case to go public, the state used the commissioner's crimes to clear the air after decades of abuse during the Years of Lead, marking a fundamental shift in the nature of authoritarianism away from repression and brutality. The trial and its sensational coverage in the press attracted a wide public of both elite and non-elite readers for the first time in the country's history. The scandal led to a crisis of authority, demonstrating the importance of public opinion to the state and setting the stage for radical new images of the police in society.

In the aftermath of the Tabit Affair, Arabic-language crime tabloids emerged on the newsstands in the fall of 1993, only months after the end of Tabit's trial. These tabloids used their shocking color photographs, arrest reports, and explicit headlines to reveal previously hidden truths in society and construct a widespread moral panic and terrifying crime wave that targeted the working-class and semiliterate public. Chapter 2 will trace how tabloid journalists—in collaboration with the state—constructed this radical new threat in order to present their enormous non-elite audience with a new image of the police as the sole safeguard against the spreading chaos. The tabloids used fear as a tool to begin the process of reconciling the broader public with the police after the Tabit Affair was over. Moreover, the tabloids mark a fundamental change in the relationship between state and media as they shifted the use of sensationalism from contesting state authority to attempting to influence and direct public opinion.

In 1998, the first independent daily newspaper, the Arabic-language *al-Ahdath al-Maghribiyya* (Moroccan Events), hit the newsstands and greatly transformed the country's press. Chapter 3 will examine how this newspaper invented a genre that I call Moroccan True Crime, which fused fictional narrative techniques from Arabic police novels with facts from real-world criminal investigations. Thanks to these true-crime articles, among other factors, *Moroccan Events* became the highest-circulation newspaper in the country, showing how commercialism in the daily press can fuse with state attempts to manage public perceptions and create sensational narratives of crime and punishment. Moreover, these texts attempted to make the public active participants in the process of criminal investigations, positioning them to see crime from the perspective of the police. As a result, the newspaper worked to blur the lines between real-world cop and the self-sacrificing, hard-working, and law-bound fictional detective. The state provided the newspaper with crime reports and other official material on which to base the true-crime articles, helping the newspaper disseminate a new model of the real-world cop that represented a total break from the Years of Lead and embodied the new era of human rights and the rule of law.

Just as fictional narratives of the police helped commercialize the press by making it responsive to a mass audience, they served as a vehicle for transforming the local television industry. In 2001, the two Moroccan television channels began producing police movies that targeted broad audiences thanks to their use of Moroccan Arabic, exciting plots, and taboo-breaking themes. While the best-known film actors in the country played the cops, directors shot the movies in real-world police stations and used actual police cars and props. Chapter 4 will show how these movies fused police fact and fiction, urging viewers to see real-world cops in the guise of movie actors and reinforcing the new intertextual image of the Moroccan police across the mass media to an audience of millions. Like the true-crime articles, the films invited the public to participate in the practice and function of state authority through narratives of police investigations. Thanks to their real-world sets, the films opened up recognizable police stations in cities like Casablanca and Rabat to the public eye, transforming them from sites of torture during the Years of Lead to sets of exciting cop movies.

Sensational and unexpected real-world crime challenges forced the state to become more involved in creating, managing, and disseminating images of the police for the broader public. The first of these challenges erupted when a serial killer suddenly appeared to be hunting victims in Casablanca in 2002. Serial murder was a form of criminality that the public presumed only existed in the West. Now, all of a sudden, bodies began appearing on the streets of the Moroccan economic capital and the sensational media stoked public fears—and contested the state—by depicting the police as incapable of catching the killer. Chapter 5 will trace how the media constructed the serial killer as an entirely new and uniquely modern form of criminality that appeared suddenly in the Moroccan context, causing a panic in the city and sending the press into competition for readers. The emergence of a serial killer disrupted state control of media police images but it also presented an opportunity to redefine the police and present them in a new role: by trumpeting new scientific units, crime labs, and forensic teams, the local mass media—together with the state—recast the police as "CSI: Casablanca" after the popular American television series. Building on Baudrillard's concept of the simulacrum, this chapter shows how Morocco's first "serial killer" was a sensational invention by the media and the state, a fabrication to present the public with a new rational and scientific image of the police for the age of technological modernity.

In 2003 another shocking new form of criminality once again discredited the Moroccan police, disrupting state management of the media and leading to a new crisis of authority. On May 16 of that year, suicide bombers struck Casablanca, killing forty-four people. In order to prevent another attack and soothe public fears, the state launched a new community-policing program accompanied by a massive multimedia advertising campaign to promote this new force to the broader public. Continuing the discussion of the simulacrum in the Moroccan context, chapter 6 shows how the advertising campaign, thanks to its television ads, magazines, billboards, and newspaper photographs, appropriated preexisting fictional images of the police in Moroccan society and mapped them onto real-world cops on the streets. Instead of leaving the construction of this new image to the press or television industry, the state took full control of the process in an attempt to interpellate a new citizen who would participate in community policing. The increasing blending of fiction and reality in the mass media during the previous decade—combined with the shocking danger of modern terrorism—made this fundamental shift in image manipulation possible. The community policing project, however, was eventually canceled, presumably because of the brutality with which its members treated the public. This chapter will argue, however, that the reasons for the project's end lie elsewhere: the state, through its unprecedented advertising campaign and demands for public action, revealed too clearly that the new police were a fabrication with no basis in local reality, failing in their attempt to interpellate a new Moroccan citizen.

The epilogue unpacks the well-known Moroccan slogan "The Police Are at the Service of the People," teasing out many of its meanings. It discusses how the state paid increasing attention to public opinion during the past twenty years, attempting to transform its brand of authoritarianism and make it responsive to public demands for change. It traces the mechanics of authoritarianism today, as the state and media industries—through mutually aligned and oftentimes contradictory interests in the new era—produced new images of the police with the aim of performing the disciplining work that violence and repression used to achieve in the old era. It shows how the new authoritarian environment in Morocco points to deep ambiguities, contradictions, and contestations in the evolving state-media nexus, emphasizing that there is no guarantee that these images will have the intended effect on the public and their perceptions of the state and the police, especially in the wake of the Arab Spring.

Finally, it is important to note that this book retells the story of sensational crimes that affected the lives of real people. While this book presents many cases of violence, abuse, and murder, it is analyzing the representations of these events, their dissemination in society, and their connection to larger political, cultural, social, and historical dynamics. This book does not attempt to examine the actual events or the accuracy with which the media reported on them. By discussing the sensationalization of violence, I in no way intend to downplay the suffering that real people experienced from these acts or the way these events painfully changed their lives. Rather, I seek to understand how sensational forms of mass media representation point to large-scale changes in society.

1 Police on Trial

The Tabit Affair, Newspaper Sensationalism, and the End of the Years of Lead

On the morning of February 3, 1993, two female university students entered the first instance court of Anfa, the most affluent district of Casablanca, to report a shocking and gruesome crime. They told the public prosecutor that a man claiming to be a police commissioner abducted them from the city streets the day before, held them hostage in his apartment, and videotaped himself and an associate sexually assaulting them for more than three hours. The two women said that before he finally let them go, the man took down the information from their identity cards and threatened them with retribution if they told anyone what had happened. Scared for their safety and the shame and scandal the incident would bring on them and their families, the two women reluctantly decided to keep quiet about the brutal crime. That morning, however, as they walked in the streets near the university, they saw the same man following them in his car. Terrified, the two ran off and managed to escape. It was at this point that they decided to go to the authorities and press charges, regardless of the consequences.

After listening to these horrific details, the Anfa public prosecutor's office immediately began investigating the case and called in the Gendarmerie—a security force known for their independence from the police—for help. The two students led investigators to the apartment of the suspect, who turned out to be Hajj Mustapha Tabit, a well-known and powerful police commissioner in the industrial district of Aïn Sebaâ-Hay Mohammedi in Casablanca. As the confident Tabit watched, the Gendarmerie searched his apartment and quickly found evidence that not only confirmed the two women's claims, but also proved that they had been the most recent in a very long line of victims. Investigators confiscated 118 carefully labeled videotapes that contained footage of Tabit and his associates committing hundreds of sexual assaults. They also recovered notebooks and computer files in which Tabit kept detailed information on his victims, including their address, profession, birthdate, and marital status. Although the state would soon charge him with abducting and raping 518 women and minors over a period of three years, Tabit's own meticulous recordkeeping, together with the videotape evidence, put the real number of victims at approximately 1,600.

The Tabit Affair, as the case would become known, was a moment of deep rupture in the country's history and culture. As one newspaper headline explained at the time, it was "the crime that profoundly shook Moroccan society in all its foundations."[1] The case, which was quickly labeled the country's "trial of the century," marked the first time that a high-ranking police official was arrested and brought to justice. As in other Arab regimes at the time, the police were the terrifying and brutal institution that operated above the law and maintained authoritarian rule in Morocco through repression. The public disgracing of a seemingly omnipotent commissioner deeply challenged and undermined the untouchable image of the police as an institution. Because the police were such a powerful symbol of the country's long decades of human rights abuses, the case served as a breathtaking spectacle for the entire public that the state was shifting its strategies of control away from physical violence and coercion. As one commentator poignantly explained after the commissioner's spectacular trial was concluded, the case represented "the fall of the Moroccan Berlin Wall and the end of fear."[2]

The Tabit Affair was also the first time that the press, which had operated under heavy censorship since independence, was free to write about the police, an institution considered utterly taboo. During the trial, journalists seized on this opportunity and invented a radical new form of local representation: mass media sensationalism. Although the global media during the 1990s employed sensationalism and a new tabloid style as a way to increase profits by expanding audience share, it would be used for an entirely different purpose in Morocco. The sensational coverage of the Tabit Affair was a tool that greatly expanded the space for image production in the country, bringing the broader public together from across the social spectrum to participate in the mass media for the first time in the country's history. During the decades since independence, Morocco's mass media had catered only to the highly educated members of political organization. The new sensationalism, which played up the taboo-breaking, scandalous, and, above all, sexual nature of the case, served as a powerful means to attract the entire public, regardless of education, social background, or class. In the process, the press used the crimes of the commissioner to launch an assault on the omnipotent and terrifying image of the police throughout Moroccan society.

Journalists employed the new sensationalism not simply to draw both the elite and the non-elite public to the press. For the first time, the press served as a vehicle for articulating the demands of the broader public for fundamental change. After decades of repression, newspapers gave voice to public desires for the rule of law and respect for human rights. By granting the press unprecedented freedoms in covering the trial and attacking the police, the state clearly wanted to use the case to clear the air after decades of repression, symbolically announcing to the wider public that the Years of Lead were finally coming to an end. At the same time, the case signaled that the nature of authoritarianism in society was changing as the state began shifting its strategies for social control away from repression and fear of the police in order to maintain social cohesion. Nonetheless, during the trial, journalists, in voicing the public's demands for political change, created an unexpected crisis of authority for the state and came to represent a threat to its stability.

Once the trial was complete, the state would respond to this crisis by reining in the press and stifling the new sensationalism in an attempt to diffuse the threat that the new public and mass media represented. Censorship, however, was no longer sufficient for ensuring social cohesion in the new era. The trial demonstrated for the state how sensational media coverage of crime and punishment could be used as an effective tool for communicating messages of political and social change to the broadest possible audience, a lesson that the state would put to use in the months after the trial as it began fostering and interfacing with new forms of sensational media, such as crime tabloids. The Tabit Affair is the beginning of a pivotal yet unexplored process—the symbiosis of state and sensational mass media in order to transform the nature of authoritarianism in the country.

Breaking the Police Taboo

Despite the unprecedented media storm and wide-scale public fascination that the Tabit Affair would soon command, the scandal broke in a brief anonymous article, innocuously placed in a small box on the bottom of the front page of the Arabic daily *al-Ittihad al-Ishtiraki* (the Socialist Union). It appeared on February 6, 1993, and read as follows:

> News is circulating urgently among security circles in greater Casablanca that one of the powerful officials in the regional police force of the Aïn Sebaâ-Hay Mohammedi district has been arrested because of his involvement in serious acts related to morals and honor, which the law punishes severely. The same news sources add that special authorities raided a house that the aforementioned official used to carry out his immoral crimes and seized evidence.[3]

With a hesitant tone and lack of detail, the anonymous journalist uses vague language to report on what appear to be rumors. The article states that a high-ranking police official in the large industrial district of Casablanca, Aïn Sebaâ-Hay Mohammedi, is under arrest but never identifies him. The alleged crimes are "related to morals," but the journalist never explicitly says what they are, why authorities raided the house, or what evidence they collected. This vague unattributed news brief about an ongoing criminal investigation, buried on the bottom of the page, appears initially as an unlikely first step in transforming the nature of authoritarianism in a modern Arab country.

When it appeared in early 1993, however, this article was shocking. During the country's long decades of authoritarianism, newspaper reports on ongoing criminal investigations, and especially the police, were considered taboo. There was no censorship committee that read articles before they were printed, but the state monitored the press closely. The minister of the interior also served as minister of communication, effectively linking the country's security apparatus to media censorship. When newspapers and journalists discovered that they had crossed the line, it was only after an issue had been seized from the newsstands. This could mean financial disaster for a paper, since it would lose the revenues for an entire day's issue. It could also lead the police to shut the newspaper down for an undetermined period, as happened many times during the decades after independence. Moreover, publishing a rogue article about the police and their activities could have grave consequences not only for the newspaper but also for the journalist and the people around them. As one journalist wrote anonymously once the trial got underway,

> Everyone knows that the authority of a police official makes him someone not to be discussed or openly commented on because his power is greater than that of the average citizen. Moreover, it is not even possible for the press in this country to write about his actions due to numerous considerations that make doing so dangerous for the author, newspaper, defenders of the party that publishes the newspaper, their families, and others. Everyone knows the many taboos in this country by practice, tradition, and experience—not only by law—just as everyone knows the consequences of breaking those taboos, by a little or a lot, such as arrests, fabricated charges, and trials without legal guarantees.[4]

For their safety and the well-being of those around them, reporters paid close attention to the "red lines." A careless article about the police or an ongoing criminal investigation could lead to the closing of a newspaper or worse.

Although party newspapers could certainly be critical of government policies, this was with the goal of promoting the agenda of the sponsoring political organization. As long as they did not touch on any of the major taboos—such as the status of the monarchy, the ongoing dispute over the status of the Western Sahara, or the role of Islam in society—limited political contestation was tolerated. Nonetheless, the party press almost always disseminated an image of Morocco that corresponded with the security interests of the state. A key element of authoritarian culture in Morocco during the Years of Lead was that the printed press presented the palace and security forces as being in complete control of the country, regardless of the political angle of the newspaper or its criticisms of socioeconomic issues. During these decades, the dominant image of the country in the press, regardless of party affiliation, was one of safety and security, strong social and moral values, peaceful interpersonal relations, and modest but growing prosperity.

Some articles during this period might appear to contradict this rule. For example, it is possible to find the occasional news report about police arrests in the Moroccan press during the Years of Lead, with a small mug shot or picture of a criminal standing next to stolen goods. These appear to show dangerous individuals who had been threatening the safety of a given neighborhood or city until the police stepped in and brought them under control. A closer look reveals that these articles were written directly from police reports, which authorities had given the journalist. Sometimes these articles were nothing more than the text of the police report. This means that the press would occasionally collaborate with the police in printing crime news, showing how the authorities arrested dangerous criminals and restored order. Well-known journalists like Aïcha Mekki and Hadin Saghir published stylized reports on criminal trials but only after a verdict was announced and suspects were punished.[5] Newspapers practically never published reports on crime during the Years of Lead before the culprit was arrested. The crime articles in the press before the early 1990s therefore show the strength of the police, rather than their weakness, and demonstrate how journalists cooperated with the state to reinforce this image to the public. Even when they printed these reports, the daily press was still disseminating an image of the police as wielding full control and authority over society, restoring order immediately after the presumably rare instances when the social bond was disturbed.

As in other authoritarian regimes, newspaper articles about unsolved violent crime and ongoing police investigations were highly sensitive. Publishing such an article would have been perceived as a direct challenge to the regime's legitimacy, strength, and ability to control the country. Printing this type of news would have been the equivalent of a political act, tantamount to claiming that the state and security services were weak, ineffective, and unable to control crime, a dangerous charge against a police force well known for repression, corruption, and systematic abuses of power. In addition to being closely monitored by the Ministry of the Interior and the police, journalists therefore practiced a form of self-censorship for their own survival that also reflected and helped disseminate the authoritarian nature of the state. The Moroccan press across the political spectrum—as well as the tightly controlled audiovisual mass media—expressed the control of the police and security services over society during the Years of Lead. It showed the public that there was little outlet to criticize or challenge the omnipotence of the police.

The authoritarianism of the Years of Lead, the country's strictly monitored mass media, and the power of the police that operated above the law and beyond criticism explain why the news brief from February 6, 1993, about the unnamed police commissioner was so shocking. The country had taken hesitant steps toward political and economic liberalization, starting in the late 1980s, thanks to international pressure on its human rights record, the end of the Cold War, and the desperate need for economic reform. Nonetheless, these changes had little effect on the lives of ordinary citizens and their relationship with the authoritarian state. The seemingly innocuous brief about the police commissioner, however, was a total break from the past. Not only did a newspaper print a front-page article about an ongoing criminal investigation, but the case itself centered on a high-level police commissioner who had been arrested for "immoral crimes." This hesitant report, buried at the bottom of the front page, therefore embodied a powerful nexus of taboos about a figure that symbolized decades of repression and represented a decisive step forward in the level of freedom of speech in the country. For the first time in memory, news appeared in the press that a police commissioner—not some low-level inspector—was under arrest. Even though the story broke in the *Socialist Union*—the main opposition newspaper at the time—and without clear attribution, it is certain that it came from a security official that gave permission to print the news, since the Ministry of the Interior tightly controlled the flow of all sensitive information to the press. This meant that the state wanted the information to go public. The brief anonymous article of February 6 therefore represented the beginning of a radical change in the public's relationship with the state and the police, as well as a striking improvement in freedom of expression in the media.

Despite the daring nature of the first article, news about the case did not appear again for another four days. Even though the brief from February 6 represented a tangible expansion in freedom of speech in the printed press, decades of fear, restrictions, and self-censorship made it impossible for journalists to throw caution to the wind. The unprecedented arrest embodied long-standing taboos, and journalists simply did not know how the red lines were shifting. Not surprisingly, the second article about the case, published on February 10, continued the same hesitation and lack of concrete detail, but it was certainly more daring than the first.[6] With the headline "Transfer of Security Official to Criminal Chamber in Casablanca," it appeared in the *Socialist Union* and included significantly more information about the charges against the commissioner, although it still did not name him or identify its sources:

> Judicial circles inside the court say that the charges against the commissioner are related to violating the public trust, rape, detaining a married woman, detention in order to commit rape, using violence against a public official, and incitement of depravity and rape. The same circles add that among the evidence present in the case are a collection of videocassettes on which the accused recorded his acts.[7]

The first sentence explains that the information is coming from the court—not police sources—and then quotes the legal language of the charges against the commissioner, a concrete element about the case that the first article lacked, including the explosive charge of rape. Together with the detailed headline revealing that the commissioner had been turned over to the criminal court, this article indicated to the public that he would actually be brought to trial for his crimes. The second sentence, however, adds a shocking new detail that the article on February 6 only alluded to: the videotapes. This suggested not only the potentially sensational nature of the evidence against the commissioner, but also that the state possessed concrete proof in the case. The videotapes signified that it would be difficult to bury the case since the trial would not simply become the word of a powerless victim against that of the mighty police. The presence of the tapes—and explicit acknowledgment of their existence—showed the public that the accusations would be substantiated with indisputable and spectacular evidence.

Now that the case appeared a second time—and the nature of the crimes began to come into focus—the press became increasingly emboldened. *Al-'Alam* (the Banner), the Arabic newspaper of *Hizb al-Istiqlal*, the Independence Party, finally entered the fray and printed its first article on the case the next day.[8] Instead of mimicking the restrained nature of the initial two articles in the *Socialist Union*, the *Banner* printed a bold headline in white letters against a black background that read "High-Ranking Police Commissioner in Morals Affair," emphasizing the position of the accused and the charges in the case.[9] The sub-headline of the article, however, highlighted the scandalous and lurid nature of his crimes: "Seizure of Videotapes with Depraved Live Images." Citing "what is circulating in some circles" as its source, the anonymous author claims that the commissioner "was trafficking in the honor of girls through filming them with a video camera in a depraved 'pornographic' method with his companions." The article also states for the first time that a large number of cassettes were seized as evidence from the commissioner's apartment.

It was one thing for the *Socialist Union*, the newspaper of the opposition party, to print reports about the arrested police official. But when the *Banner*, a conservative newspaper typically associated with allegiance to the palace and government, published the same information, this showed the public that the press would continue uncovering more and more information about the arrested police commissioner. Moreover, the author makes much more explicit the salacious and sensational nature of the crimes and the evidence against the commissioner, which was a stunning move for the press at the time and indicated to the public the enormous scale of the case. Since the Moroccan mass media were closely controlled and monitored during the decades leading up the trial, reporting on pornographic videotapes represented a total break from the past. More and more the police taboo in the printed press was beginning to crumble.

The next day, on February 13, after discussing the facts known about the case, Abdelmoula Tawhidi, a journalist writing for *L'Opinion*, the Independence Party's French-language newspaper, asked openly if the suspect "benefitted from a 'plot of silence,' with no one daring to denounce him."[10] For the public at the time, the atmosphere of fear and silence was the norm. Writing about it in the press, however, was a daring form of protest. Despite his inflammatory suggestion, Tawhidi ended his article with stale language well-known from the Years of Lead: "Justice will follow its course in order to clear the police and preserve them from suspicion, as they are a profession that is and must remain one of the most respectable." This kind of phrasing, full of fear and submission, shows that despite the audacious nature of the initial articles in the case, the taboo of the police was still very much present in the press by the end of the first week of covering the scandal. Even though he indicates that the commissioner was able to continue committing his crimes because of widespread fear of the police in society, Tawhidi praises the police establishment for its honorable position in society.

On February 16, ten days after the first article about the case, *L'Opinion* broke the names and background of the main defendants.[11] They were Hajj Mustapha Tabit, first-rank police commissioner and main defendant; a doctor who conducted operations to restore the virginity of Tabit's victims; two businessmen and a retired military officer who participated with Tabit in the assaults; and the video technician who set up and maintained the cameras in Tabit's apartment.[12] Three other commissioners, three detectives, and five police inspectors would soon be charged with burying complaints against Tabit or destroying case evidence. Among these inspectors was Tabit's personal driver, who was accused of seeking out, following, and abducting victims.[13] The same *L'Opinion* article also revealed the large number of victims involved in the case, not just the number of cassettes. Now that news about the case appeared in multiple party newspapers and the names of the defendants were printed, there was no turning back. Although it was widely assumed at first that, despite the initial coverage, the case would be buried because of its taboo nature, the appearance of the defendants' names in the press signified that the trial would proceed and that the wall of silence surrounding the police would finally fall.

The first session of what would soon be known as the "trial of the century" was held under unprecedented security on February 18, 1993, only two weeks after Tabit's arrest. Even though there was still little information in the press—and not a single mention of the case on television or radio—rumors about the trial had spread like wildfire. Huge crowds flooded the criminal court in Casablanca, as people hoped to witness the proceedings in person. Special security teams from the Gendarmerie guarded Tabit and his codefendants as they were brought before the public eye for the first time. Some thirteen victims also attended the initial session. Newspapers described how people across the country—of all socioeconomic backgrounds—were obsessed with the case and talked about nothing but Tabit's appalling crimes. With only a few articles and word of mouth, the case commanded widespread attention because of the shocking combination of sex, power, and political scandal. The possibility of seeing such a mighty figure, someone who crystallized the abuses of the Years of Lead, brought to justice and made accountable for his crimes attracted a massive audience to the case at this stage.

Now that the trial had begun and the defendants were paraded before the public, the press became increasingly emboldened. In its coverage of the first session, the *Socialist Union* printed an anonymous article on February 19 that explicitly connected the wide-scale nature of Tabit's crimes to the authority of his position. Although it was clear that Tabit's unlimited power as a police commissioner had provided him with the means and opportunity to continue committing his crimes and avoid punishment, no newspaper had stated this. Finally, the press began spelling out the obvious: "It is worth mentioning that Commissioner Tabit, for a number of his victims that presented complaints against him, proceeded to bury these charges due to his powerful influence."[14] The next day, the *Socialist Union* went even further when an anonymous journalist discussed the role of power, authority, and morality in the scandal. Trying to explain why the case attracted such unprecedented attention from all socioeconomic classes in the country, the author wrote, "We're before a dangerous decline of morals, a disgusting exploitation of power, and a scandalous case of corruption. . . . Is it possible for all of this to happen without the position of authority that the perpetrator occupies?"[15] The author then discusses the shocking elements of the case—pornography, silencing victims, and trafficking in sexual abuse—and states that these crimes were made possible because the main defendant was a police commissioner. It was the long-standing and embedded system of silence, abuse, and corruption that produced Tabit and his crimes.

The anonymous author continued: "Anyone who doubted it before now understands that the exploitation of authority is a phenomenon spread throughout the security services, a cancer eating away at the core of our country." This daring criticism of the police as an establishment represents a striking breakthrough in depicting the police in the media at the time. Although other newspapers and journalists would soon follow suit, this was the first instance of a journalist claiming that Tabit's crimes were not simply those of an individual but of an entire institution that operated above the law for decades. These articles therefore indicate a tremendous expansion of freedom of expression in the printed press. For the first time, journalists—despite writing anonymously—were tying the disgraceful and far-reaching crimes of a police commissioner to the decades-old silence and fear surrounding the police as an institution.

In his article published on February 20 in *L'Opinion*, journalist Nabil Arabi continues connecting Tabit's crimes to the police establishment as a whole. "The case stands a good chance of hitting other officials. The trial that is getting underway in Casablanca is not, in fact, only that of Tabit but also of institutional debauchery. Heads could fall."[16] In a stunning move, Arabi suggests that even higher-level officials in the police will be held responsible for Tabit's crimes. Like several others, he points to the role of fear and silence surrounding someone in Tabit's position. "No one could complain against the big commissioner who ruled the roost. He reduced his victims to silence." This element of silence connects the position of the press, for example, to the role of the police in Moroccan society during the Years of Lead. For Arabi, the fear and silence that dominated the image of the police created the circumstances that made Tabit's crimes possible. For the first time since independence, journalists began writing openly about the basic elements that constituted the regime's hold on power: fear and silence as well as the brutal and omnipotent police. These open discussions allowed journalists like Arabi to continue assaulting the taboo image that had controlled the press's treatment of the police for decades.

The next day, February 21, Nabil Arabi took his position even further. In a piece headlined "Has the Housecleaning Begun?" he argues that Tabit is an "extreme case of irresponsible officials who instead of taking care of order and applying the law are busy creating disorder and encouraging with their conduct the violation of the laws that govern society."[17] For Arabi, officials who conduct themselves like Tabit commit crimes against the nation and compromise its future. He calls for a cleansing of the police, the first of many such appeals that would appear in the press both during and after the trial. Such a move was unthinkable only three weeks earlier. Suggesting a housecleaning of the police on the front page of a newspaper would have led to horrible consequences for the journalist and publisher. Now, it represented another escalation in the public expansion of the freedom of the press as well as the rapidly deteriorating position of power and authority that the police occupied in society.

In its article on February 22, the *Socialist Union* continued the onslaught on the institutional and widespread nature of Tabit's crimes. The anonymous journalist begins by asking if the reason why people across the country are talking about the case is because Tabit is "an important official in the police . . . with all the mystery, secrets, and terror this word stirs up."[18] The author then poses the questions that would appear again and again throughout the trial: Why was Tabit free to operate for so many years? Who else knew about his crimes and will they be brought to justice too, regardless of their position? Will evidence in the case be suppressed as it was before he was arrested? The author ends by stating,

> The reality is that it's not possible to give this case a simple criminal or moral character. Rather, it's much more pervasive and universal. When an official in the police comes to do whatever he pleases in his area of authority, without anyone to stop him or keep him in check, we're entitled to say that the case has an obvious political nature that tangibly clarifies the deteriorated situation of civil and human rights in Morocco, the extent of corruption that is eating away at the core of the police establishment, and the amount of shameless complicity on a number of fronts to cover this corruption up.

For this anonymous journalist, the scale of the crimes does not simply implicate the actions of an individual or the institution of the police. Rather, it is a political case that demonstrates the status of individual rights and the rule of law in Moroccan society. At the same time, the author connects this to the police by stating that corruption is rotting its core since it was becoming increasingly clear that the establishment as a whole undertook a widespread cover-up to bury complaints against Tabit for years. Tabit's crimes therefore came to represent the magnitude of corruption in the institution of the police, the disgraceful state of human rights for ordinary citizens, and the lack of democracy in the country.

With this article, which appeared before the second session of the trial, the press had profoundly transformed how it treated the police. Gone was the silence and tangible fear of the Years of Lead and the hesitation of the initial articles on the case. It quickly became clear that the Tabit Affair was cutting to the heart of not simply the police establishment but the authoritarian system that had dominated the country for so long. By the time the trial resumed for its second session on February 23, the taboo surrounding the police and their status in society had been smashed in the press, creating a new terrain for representing both the police and the end of the old form of authoritarianism in the country. It also quickly became clear that the public was flocking to the press in unprecedented numbers. Although the stunning attack on the image of the police in society was certainly part of the reason for this attention, there were other factors as well.

A Drama for Ramadan

Massive public fascination with the case quickly led to skyrocketing newspaper circulations. Besides the open attack on the power and position of the police, an important factor in the public's increasing attention to the press was that the start of the second session of the trial coincided with the first day of Ramadan in 1993. During this month, Muslims across the Middle East and North Africa fast during the day and stay up late at night. It is a time of widespread religious participation and increased togetherness among family and friends, as well as of prayer and reflection. As the public followed the shocking trial and disgraceful crimes of Hajj Mustapha Tabit, many were fasting as part of the holy month and going to the mosque for prayer. The fact that the greatest criminal in the country's history had performed the pilgrimage four times was particularly disturbing as the public attempted to make sense of the scandal during Ramadan.

In addition to its religious dimension, Ramadan is a time when men typically spend long nights sitting in cafés, talking with friends and passing time reading newspapers. In order to cater to this audience, Moroccan newspapers often print month-long serials on a variety of topics, leading to a significant increase in circulations. The timing of the Tabit Affair, then, allowed the newly emboldened press to capitalize on what was already a time of increased sales. With the shocking crimes and tales of sex, power, and abuse at the center of the case, the Tabit Affair became the country's best-selling Ramadan serial, the real-life trial of the century that featured the first steps away from the brutal authoritarianism of the Years of Lead.

Another reason why the public turned to the press in such unprecedented numbers was because neither television nor radio ever mentioned the case during the trial. Considering the highly controlled nature of the audiovisual mass media in the country, this should not have been a surprise. In fact, some journalists in the press used the opportunity to criticize the state of television at the time. For them, it was not simply that television chose to ignore such a scandalous crime. Rather, by the early 1990s, the audiovisual mass media did not report any news that could be interpreted as social criticism, such as arrests, trials, divorce, and other matters that could attract a wide audience. For one anonymous journalist, this showed how television presented a "rosy image of life in a way totally disengaged from the reality of our country."[19] This author, writing as Tabit's trial was coming to a close, used the case to call for the audiovisual mass media to engage social matters and connect with the daily concerns of ordinary people.

The entire case was left to the printed press, which shows on the one hand that authorities did not believe that the press could reach a wide audience, indicating that the state did not anticipate the sensationalism with which the press covered the case and created a massive non-elite audience during the trial. On the other hand, it also proves that the state was not yet willing to grant the same level of freedom of expression to the highly conservative audiovisual mass media. The liberalization of television would come well after the Tabit Affair was over and will be discussed in chapter 4. Even the government did not mention the Tabit Affair until several days before the verdict. Moreover, government newspapers such as *al-Anba'* (the News) maintained complete silence on the case, operating as if the trial were not even taking place. Except for rumors and word of mouth, party newspapers like the *Socialist Union* and the *Banner* held a near monopoly on information about the case. This gave them not only an unparalleled audience but also a powerful level of credibility in covering the trial.

Despite the expanding freedom of the press and assault on the taboo of the police, the Tabit Affair featured an atmosphere of cover-up that appeared to reach up to the highest levels of the state, something that further fueled public fascination with the case. After the first day of the trial, the court decided to close the sessions to the public and press, allowing only victims, lawyers working the case, and state officials to attend the proceedings. Closing the sessions suggested that the state still had plenty to hide in the case, especially since the public had never been refused entry to a trial before. Moreover, the trial was full of incredible irregularities. It began only two weeks after Tabit was arrested and the defense reportedly was not permitted to see the state's case until after the first session, another unprecedented move. The trial was also held at breakneck speed, most days featuring two separate sessions, the second lasting until three or four o'clock in the morning. When the verdict was read on March 13, barely three weeks after the start of the trial, the press saw the frenzied pace as an attempt to bury even larger crimes surrounding the case.

This atmosphere of a cover-up was only strengthened when news spread that Tabit managed to convince officers to take him back to his apartment after the initial search to destroy material from a locked safe, leading many to wonder if the worst of the evidence against him would never be recovered. Moreover, Tabit inflamed speculation when he promised in court that he would "not go down alone" and insisted that the judges watch tape number 118.[20] Tabit's mysterious statements ratcheted up public speculation that the palace wanted to protect others implicated in the case. One of the police commissioners tried along with Tabit also told the court that he and the other commissioners were scapegoats and that he had "proof and names" of high-level officials who protected Tabit during his crime spree.[21]

It was in this charged environment that newspaper circulations began to rise during the first two weeks after Tabit's arrest and skyrocketed at the beginning of the trial and the start of Ramadan on February 23, quadrupling when the verdict arrived by mid-March.[22] By that time, printing presses in the country had long reached their capacity and broke down from overuse. Public demand for newspapers from people of all social backgrounds was so great that crowds fought at newsstands for copies when new issues arrived. The press reported that ambulant newspaper sellers feared for their lives as hostile crowds demanded the latest edition.[23] Many newsstand owners discovered that people were willing to pay inflated prices and even rented issues, with at least five to six people reading a single copy. The country had never seen anything like it before.

Sex, Lies, and Newspapers

The initial coverage of the case featured not only an assault on the police taboo, but also a growing sensationalism over the sexual nature of Tabit's crimes. During the Years of Lead, the country's party press had shunned any topic that was considered lowbrow or would arouse any kind of shock and excitement. Newspapers presented the world of their own elite and those whom they believed were sympathetic to their political and social platforms. Regardless of the coverage, the daily press used a highly educated, restrained, and sophisticated language. Moreover, the press downplayed any visual elements, such as photographs, that would help narrate events. This style effectively shut out of the press enormous segments of the public who were semiliterate or illiterate, some 50 percent of the country.

That changed with the initial coverage of the Tabit Affair. As the press began printing information about Tabit and his crimes, they also increased their attention to the sexual nature of the case, turning to sensationalism for the first time in the country's history. Once Tabit's name was released and journalists had access to the initial police report on the case, they took this information and began creating titillating descriptions and lurid narratives of his crimes. This sexual sensationalism both disgraced the high-level police commissioner and further assaulted the untouchable nature of the institution he represented. At the same time, the graphic and shocking sexual depictions drew in a semiliterate public eager for salacious details of the scandal and lurid news about the case. Although the politicized treatment of the police and the trial appealed to the typical elite audience of the party newspapers, it was this new sensationalism that attracted a massive readership from across the social spectrum during the trial. Throughout the history of the printed press, sensationalism has been used as a tool to expand audiences and the Tabit Affair proved that Morocco was no different, despite its low literacy rate. For the first time since independence, the party press threw aside their normal attention to good taste and employed a sensationalism that would entice the emotions and excitement of the entire public, regardless of socioeconomic background.

The first example of this sexual sensationalism appeared on February 19, when *L'Opinion* published an article by Nabil Arabi with the following headline in bold white letters against a black background: "Story of Two Students Who Exploded Scandal."[24] Arabi first details the scene at the initial trial session, calling Tabit "the 'hero' of the longest pornographic series ever made." Taking information from the statements submitted to the court on the first day of the trial, he narrates how Tabit picked up the two students who would later press charges with the Anfa authorities. Arabi describes how Tabit took them to his apartment, prayed in front of them, and then ordered one to undress. After he assaulted the first one, Arabi explains, Tabit did the same to the second, forcing them both to act out scenes from a pornographic video that he played for them. Arabi writes that a friend of Tabit soon arrived and assaulted the two again before finally letting them go.[25] The same narrative, taken from the victims' statement submitted at the court, also appeared in the Arabic newspaper the *Banner* on February 22. Never before had such a sensational story, centered on sex, violence, and police abuse, appeared in a Moroccan newspaper for the entire country to read.

With this precedent broken, journalists continued ratcheting up their sensational and lurid coverage of the case. In his next article in *L'Opinion*, provocatively entitled "Trial of Debauchery," Nabil Arabi presents a survey of graphic information about the case with increasingly sexualized language.[26] Among several examples of abuse, he cites one particularly egregious case. When a woman came to Tabit's office to apply for a passport to work in Saudi Arabia, he forced her to have sex with him in exchange for the document. Arabi explains how from that point on, Tabit controlled all of her movements between Casablanca and Jeddah as well as her bank account, and that while she was in Saudi Arabia, Tabit forced her to buy him a video camera, which he subsequently used to tape his assaults. Finally, Arabi writes that when she wanted to marry an American Muslim who lived in Saudi Arabia, Tabit took her to the doctor later charged in the case to have her virginity restored. Like the story of the two students who pressed charges at the Anfa prosecutor's office, this latest example served as a precursor for the language and narrative style that the press would employ once the trial got underway. Although these narratives were brief compared to what would soon emerge in the press, they set a striking precedent for gruesome language and sexual sensationalism in the Moroccan media.

As for the videos that mesmerized the public, Arabi in the same article provides a preliminary description of their content:

> Among the cassettes presented as evidence, one finds those on which there is a married woman, her twenty-year-old daughter, and her niece, whom Tabit deflowered; another married woman whom he abused in front of her young child; another married woman whom he mistreated horribly in front of her daughter; schoolgirls.... Always in the same way, each of them vaginally, then anally, and finishing in their mouths. Victims whom he leaves afterward for his accomplices.

The details that Arabi gives here were a total break with the past. Never before had the Moroccan press printed such graphic descriptions of sexual activity. Just as Arabi set a precedent for narrating specific instances of abuse, here he helped launch the press on its path of increasing sexual sensationalism. Although he is describing horrific crimes of rape, Arabi uses pornographic language to expand the reach of the press and attract wide segments of the public who would have been shocked to find such details in the daily press. Even though journalists would soon describe the contents of Tabit's videos in even more graphic terms, this article was a striking step forward in expanding the terrain of representation in the Moroccan press.

It is tempting to view the increasingly sexualized language in the coverage of the Tabit Affair as restricted to the local developments in the case. But Morocco was not the only country at the time that was experiencing a radical transformation in depictions of sexuality in the media. In the late 1980s and early 1990s, the mass media in the United States significantly expanded the use of sensational and sexualized language in mainstream sources. Although media critics typically point to the emergence of the tabloid television program *A Current Affair* in 1986 as the starting point for the increasing tabloidization of the United States mass media, it was the 1991 William Kennedy Smith trial that introduced explicit descriptions of rape and sexual language into mainstream sources such as the *New York Times* and the *Boston Globe*, in addition to the major television news outlets.[27] Although Smith was acquitted on all counts, the prosecution portrayed him as committing a series of rapes, and exploiting his position of wealth and status to commit his crimes. Because of its lurid, sexual, and voyeuristic qualities, the case attracted an enormous following both in the United States and abroad and likely served as a framework for the Moroccan press in their sexualized coverage of Tabit's rapes.

That same year, Clarence Thomas was nominated to replace Thurgood Marshall on the Supreme Court. His confirmation hearings were moving ahead smoothly until word spread that Thomas had sexually harassed a former co-worker named Anita Hill a decade earlier. Senators called Hill to testify and she recounted on live national television how Thomas had told her that his penis was of an enormous size, how he had described pornographic videos to her that included rape scenes, and how he had told her he had unusual sexual prowess, all elements that would appear nearly verbatim in the Moroccan media's coverage of the Tabit Affair. Although the Thomas case featured powerful issues of race, gender, and sexual harassment in the workplace, the mainstream television and print media seized instead on the graphic sexual language, disseminating it across the country on the nighttime news and front pages of the press. The Clarence Thomas hearings expanded the boundaries of acceptability for sexual language in the mainstream mass media in the United States. Thanks to the increasing globalization of the mass media in the early 1990s, it was only a matter of time before the limits of acceptability in sexual language and imagery would expand in other countries such as Morocco, which had been following the Thomas hearings with as much fascination as the United States.

Although the William Kennedy Smith trial and Clarence Thomas hearings raised important social issues, there was another mainstream case of sexual sensationalism in 1991 that had almost no news value but combined lurid language with titillating videotape evidence. A deputy sheriff in Florida named Jeffery Willets was arrested for taking money to arrange for men to have sex with his wife, Kathy, at their home. Jeffery also videotaped the sexual encounters and kept lists of her customers. In addition to the details of the case, their defense was sensational: the Willets' lawyer claimed that Kathy suffered from nymphomania and that her sexual activities represented a form of therapy. The case was soon picked up by mainstream sources, such as the *Washington Post*, the *Chicago Tribune*, and *Time* magazine, among others. The widespread media coverage focused on Kathy's apparent insatiable sexual appetite and the sensational videotapes, much like how the Moroccan press would later describe the Tabit Affair. According to David Krajicek, "It seems clear in retrospect that the two Florida cases from 1991—William Kennedy Smith and Kathy Willets—served as a watershed for media mores. An anything-goes ethos had elbowed aside self-restraint."[28] These cases not only established a new form of representation in the U.S. mainstream media but also helped establish the defining characteristic of what would famously be called the "tabloid decade"—the media's obsession during the 1990s with graphic sex, sensationalism, and lurid details of scandal.[29]

It should not be forgotten that another case from 1991 included powerful videotape evidence of police abuse—the Rodney King beatings. A motorist shot footage of the police brutally kicking and clubbing King as he lay on the ground. These images were disseminated around the world thanks to repeated television coverage of the incident and unleashed a firestorm of anger at the Los Angeles Police Department for years of alleged abuses in general and against African Americans in particular. Although the case could have opened up important public discussions of race and systematic police misconduct, the media focused instead on the shocking visual evidence of violence, using the incident to bolster television audiences because it appeared to be such a transparent example of police abuse caught on tape.

These various cases should be seen as the background for the developments in the Moroccan media during the Tabit Affair, which, like the cases in the United States, centered on shocking video evidence of police abuse, watershed sensationalism, and a sudden new explicit language in the mainstream media that was used to depict rape and sexual abuse. As journalists seized on the new freedom of speech that the case had brought to the press, they not only attacked the taboo of the police but also began employing this new form of representation that was circulating in the global media thanks to the precedent in the United States. Although the Moroccan press before the Tabit Affair avoided sensationalism to depict local news, it was not cut off from these developments in global media. The sensational cases from 1991 in the United States appeared in the Moroccan press at the time, though they were not front-page stories and were not serialized.

By early 1993, sexual sensationalism had become a form of representation that symbolized the latest developments in the global media. Its appearance in the local press—to describe local affairs—was a total break from the stuffy and restrained media language of the Years of Lead. It indicated not only a striking new direction for the local press but also that the country was becoming connected to the world through globalization. A similar process was happening in other countries emerging rapidly out of repressive authoritarianism. As Eliot Borensetin has shown, Russia experienced a parallel phenomenon in the early 1990s as decades of censorship in the Soviet media suddenly fell to the wayside and journalists quickly flooded the press with graphic narratives of sex and violence.[30] The same connection between tabloid journalism and political transition can be seen in South Africa, just as the apartheid era came to an end.[31]

Although journalists like Nabil Arabi began incorporating sexual sensationalism in their initial coverage of the case, this style began to expand significantly once the trial resumed on February 23 with unprecedented crowds and extreme security measures. The most important reason for this change is that during the second session, the judges decided to close the trial to the press and allow only lawyers working the case and victims into the court. The Gendarmerie then blocked the court building from enormous crowds, who, emboldened by the press coverage and rumors, broke into protests and impromptu chants about the scandal, accusing authorities of covering up the case and denying information to the public.

The fact that the trial was held largely in closed sessions only increased the public's fascination with the case and desire for more information. Because they were not permitted to attend the sessions until right before the verdict when the judges finally lifted the ban on the press, journalists scrambled to find other ways to provide the public with case details. Although their coverage did include basic events of the sessions—thanks to lawyers who leaked information to the press—journalists quickly found that there were plenty of shocking stories and word-of-mouth accounts surrounding the case that they could exploit to satisfy the desires of their audiences for more and more salacious details. Using bombastic headlines and shocking language, the press immediately focused on elements of cover-up, sexual sensationalism, and moral degradation. In particular, the newspapers sold the case to the public by narrating Tabit's crimes in gruesome detail and fetishizing his sexual prowess, much like the scandals in the United States during 1991, such as the William Kennedy Smith trial, the Kathy Willets case, and the Clarence Thomas hearings. These accounts also typically highlighted the way Tabit's colleagues in the police colluded to bury complaints against him, allowing Tabit to remain free to commit his crimes for years.[32]

In one example of these narratives, Nabil Arabi begins the account by stating that it was recorded on videotapes number 98 and 99, connecting his narrative to the explosive visual evidence.[33] In November 1992, Tabit approached a woman on the street as she walked home with her daughter and niece at eight o'clock in the evening. The woman recognized Tabit from when she had applied for a passport and realized that he was a police commissioner. Terrified, she followed his orders when he told them to get into his car. He reportedly took them to his apartment and told them that if they did not come in with him, he would arrest them for prostitution. Once he forced them into his apartment, Tabit slapped and kicked them. Nabil Arabi then explains,

> He pulled the mother into the bathroom where he ordered her to stay and keep quiet and then came back to undress the daughter and the niece, both of whom he abused in his way, deflowering the niece in the process. He then called the mother whom he abused next in front of her daughter, telling the latter to make his organ penetrate the same place were she was born. Each time one of his victims started to cry, he hit them and had them go wash their face before starting his barbaric acts again.

Arabi also describes how Tabit, during the lengthy assault, would respond to calls on his police radio. Once he finally let the three go at midnight, he made each take five hundred dirhams, as if they were prostitutes. According to Arabi, the next day the daughter had a mental breakdown and tried to commit suicide by swallowing two vials of barbiturates. She was saved, however, and rushed to the hospital, where doctors pumped her stomach. In the end, the three never pressed charges for fear of reprisal. Journalists focused on this case—and others in which Tabit assaulted multiple family members at the same time—to highlight the assaults that had the most shocking elements for an audience eager for more and more lurid details.

In addition to the horrifying tales of cover-up, collusion, and abuse, another sensational element of the trial coverage was Tabit's defense, which was leaked to the press despite the closed sessions. Before the trial even began, one of Tabit's parents told reporters that he was possessed by a perverted *djinn*, or spirit, which Tabit had unsuccessfully tried to exorcize many times by going to *fuqaha*, or traditional Moroccan witch doctors.[34] Although this initial explanation may seem bizarre, it would certainly have been credible to much of the ordinary public that was coming to the printed press for the first time during the Tabit Affair. Once the trial got underway, Tabit's lawyers demanded that he take a psychological examination, further suggesting that he was not in full control of himself. For his part, Tabit reportedly screamed out and rolled around on the ground in the courtroom in order to demonstrate that he was not sane.[35] Nonetheless, the request for an examination was denied.

These elements only hinted at what would come when the judges began interrogating Tabit on March 2. Tabit defended himself vigorously and confidently in a booming voice loud enough for journalists to hear from outside the courtroom. His defense featured two elements. First, he claimed that he suffered from a split-personality complex. The first personality—dignified, religious, and respectable—was what his coworkers, friends, and family saw and was his normal external appearance.[36] The second, he said, erupted from within and overwhelmed him when he saw a woman engaged in a moral disgrace, such as accepting money for sex or committing adultery. He told the court that he hated women because of what he called their "immoral nature" and that this drove him to punish them and "give them lessons."[37] He said that he expressed his disgust for women by having violent and sadistic sex with them. Tabit claimed that when he had sex, he became an entirely different person, losing consciousness and having no control over what he was doing. Considering the devalued position of psychology in Moroccan society, Tabit's public claim that he suffered from a split personality was completely unexpected.[38]

This aspect of Tabit's defense became a source of fascination in the press. Tabit's second wife, with whom he lived, told investigators before Tabit was interrogated in court that she had no knowledge at all about his criminal activities and that "she didn't notice at any point that he was psychologically sick or suffered from any kind of deficiency."[39] Moreover, the dual-personality defense provided a powerful explanation for how he could hide such abominable acts behind a respectable and pious outward demeanor. It was deeply disturbing that a Hajj, someone who had completed the pilgrimage, one of the five pillars of Islam, was able to commit such atrocities. As the press sensationalized Tabit's defense, it marked the first time that the public saw in the mass media the shocking disconnect between respectable external appearances and degraded inner realities. For decades, the press had avoided printing news of scandal, sensationalism, and moral depravity. The theme of how outwardly dignified and respectable appearances clash with hidden evil realities—and the terrifying dangers this created for society—would soon become a key trope of the printed press as it plunged into crime journalism after the trial. It pointed to how the new era uncovered hidden truths, exposing the sordid aspects of life that had been previously kept concealed from public view.

The second component of Tabit's defense was just as shocking. He flatly denied abducting women and rejected accusations that he exploited his position or authority in any way. He claimed that he never told a single woman that he was a police official or that he set up a network to abduct women from the streets. He admitted having sex with his victims, but said that he did not force a single one. Incredibly, Tabit argued that the women actually enjoyed having sex with him. As proof, he told the court repeatedly that they could be seen smiling on the videos, savoring what he was doing to them. He claimed: "I was always with whores that I'd round up in the streets. They came with me voluntarily. I never forced a single one. They were all consenting. You can see that on the tapes."[40]

Tabit admitted to being guilty of adultery and paying for sex, claiming to spend five thousand dirhams a month on prostitutes, roughly the equivalent of a monthly salary for an average white-collar worker.[41] Considering the meager official salary for police officers in the country, this detail only inflamed speculation that Tabit had earned enormous sums from issuing liquor licenses, protection money from establishments in his district, and even selling his videocassettes on the international black market. The court asked how he managed to acquire his fortune but Tabit refused to elaborate. He argued that prostitution was widespread and visible in the country, and that he did nothing different from what thousands of men did every day. To Tabit, the women he abducted and raped were simply prostitutes who enjoyed having sex because of their immorality.

Further inflaming the salacious nature of the case, the press seized on Tabit's defense—and the number of victims—and began describing him as having superhuman sexual abilities, something that generated a wide-scale fascination among the public. In much the same way as the mainstream U.S. media marveled at Kathy Willets' nymphomania during 1991–1992, the Moroccan press quickly became enthralled by Tabit's supposed sexual prowess. Early in the trial, for example, when the amount of victims became known, newspapers compared Tabit to Harun al-Rashid in the *Arabian Nights*.[42] One front-page blurb early in the trial announced the math behind Tabit's crimes with the following headline: "Three Victims Every Two Days."[43]

By the time Tabit was interrogated in court, the press had lost any inhibition in describing his sexual prowess. In his first coverage of Tabit's defense, Nabil Arabi wrote that Tabit had a "sexual fire."[44] In a subsequent article, Arabi marveled at Tabit's sexual abilities in a subsection provocatively entitled "A Scientific Curiosity." Arabi explained, "Tabit denied using any kind of medicine or drug to allow him to keep an erection for hours, the time that his relations with his partners, who could number up to six, would last. In one day, he'd sleep with four women at the same time and less than an hour later, two others, in frolics that could last three hours!"[45] As if the case had no connection to years of abductions and rape, here Arabi seems to take pleasure in describing Tabit's actions, boasting about his sexual adventures. Moreover, Arabi explains in the same article how Tabit told the court that his sexual obsession became stronger with age. "Since he was twenty years old, Tabit continued, the duration of his erections got longer and longer, reaching a record time when he was older than fifty! Also, Tabit concluded, he was never satisfied sexually." When the court asked him about a cassette that included forty-five sexual acts, Arabi reported that Tabit boasted he was "capable of doing even more without feeling the least fatigue or let-up." Although Tabit clearly encouraged this fascination with his sexual abilities, it was journalists like Nabil Arabi who disseminated it throughout the country. Commenting on the fact that Tabit could do this without any kind of drug or stimulant, Arabi wrote in what seemed to be an admiring tone, "We have to confess that no normal man, or even one of a constitution that surpasses the norms, can measure up to Tabit. . . . Is he a supernatural force?" Yet another part of the press's sensationalism, this element gave journalists an outlet to dramatize the sexual nature of Tabit's crimes, turning the highly descriptive narratives of the ways he would violate his victims into voyeuristic entertainment for the wider public.[46]

By this stage, the media frenzy surrounding the trial had dealt the police a crushing blow. What started as an attack on the status of the police during the Years of Lead turned into lurid and sensational narratives of cover-up, collusion, and sexual fetishization. The printed press had not only broken through the decades-old fear surrounding the police, but also managed to associate the entire establishment with the horrifying and scandalous crimes of the commissioner, turning the once terrifying institution into a source of sexual humor and fascination, humiliating them in the process. The fact that these narratives appeared in the printed press, which was under tight control throughout the Years of Lead, demonstrated to the public how fast the police were falling from their position of fear, power, and control in society and how radically the boundaries of acceptable language in the media were expanding. The next step in destroying the image of the police from the Years of Lead and attracting the broadest possible public to the press would come in the final hours of the trial as the videotapes were screened and journalists were finally allowed to return to court, just in time for the verdict.

Voyeurism and the Verdict

The session that ran from the night of March 11 into the early hours of the next morning was the most dramatic and charged of the trial. It began as some eleven victims gave testimony about the abuse they suffered as Tabit sat in court and listened. The victims now confirmed in their own words the horrific stories that had been circulating in the press for several weeks, giving stunning and graphic first-person testimonies. Their statements were so powerful that, as all of the party newspapers reported, the court scribe broke out in tears. The judges stopped the witness statements, however, when, as was reported in sensational terms in the press, one woman passed out after seeing Tabit in court and another collapsed on the witness stand during questioning and was rushed to the hospital.[47]

The victim testimonies were only a prelude for what would happen next. After much deliberation, the judges decided to screen an hour-long montage of the videotapes. It was the first time video in any form was used as evidence in a Moroccan court, and the material was explosive. Although the sessions were still closed to journalists, lawyers representing victims watched the montage in horror and emerged from the courtroom disgusted and outraged. As all of the party newspapers reported, one lawyer rushed out of the session to vomit while another passed out and was taken to the hospital. Other lawyers described to the various journalists camped outside the courtroom the scenes of brutality and sadism they witnessed, clearly contradicting the earlier pornographic fascination in the press and Tabit's claims that his victims were willing participants. The press in turn narrated these various sequences to readers in the most graphic and salacious language possible, reaching the most extreme level of sexual sensationalism during the trial.

Journalists set the stage by warning readers about their descriptions of the tapes. In a provocative article entitled "Incest, Defloration, Crude Sadism in Its Raw State," the anonymous journalist who covered the screening of the videos for *Libération*, the French newspaper of the Socialist Union, wrote, "The scenes were truly sadism in its raw state. I therefore invite sensitive readers to avoid reading the lines that follow. They risk harming their civilized values."[48] Before describing the horrific scenes of rape, this journalist again begged readers for forgiveness, warning them "not to read on." As for the *Socialist Union*, Noureddine Miftah, the main journalist covering the trial for the newspaper, first described the court scene briefly and then wrote, "It's very difficult for someone to rid themselves of all this burden and undertake their duty to inform the reader."[49] Miftah briefly detailed two scenes on the videos but then cut off his coverage, writing in underline print, "We apologize to our readers that we cannot permit ourselves to publish details of Tabit's acts." He described how the lawyers rushed out of the courtroom and that "what happened . . . was the equivalent of a horror movie, with real actors and a script from reality."

Although *Libération* quoted one of the lawyers as saying "words prove useless to describe the atrocity of the sexual acts that Tabit made his victims suffer,"[50] journalists predictably had no trouble finding sensational language to report on the tapes. Miftah's apology to his readers was clearly not an institutional decision since the anonymous author writing for *Libération*, which was published by the same political party as the *Socialist Union*, continued to describe the horrific scenes of sadism on the tapes in the most graphic terms. The newspaper provided lurid details of how Tabit brutally beat and tortured some twenty victims. These included narratives of how he assaulted two sisters at the same time as well as a mother, her daughter, and niece. The newspaper also described how Tabit assaulted a woman as she tried to cover the eyes of her four-year-old son, who was sitting next to her on the bed, but he pulled the boy toward them so "he could see well what he made his mother endure." In one scene, he continued to assault a woman after she passed out. In another, he used his gun to threaten and terrorize a victim. In most scenes, Tabit barked orders at the men under his command by radio as he assaulted his victims.

Both *Libération* and *L'Opinion* paid particular attention to the physical nature of the images in an effort to bring readers as close as possible to the horror of Tabit's crimes, spelling out the visual elements for readers. In an article with the bold front-page headline "Nightmarish: Tabit's Studio Was Site of Detention and Torture," Nabil Arabi wrote that these tapes included "scenes of an incredible atrocity: slaps, punches, blood, cries of pain, women begging the commissioner, kissing his hands and feet for mercy."[51] Arabi described in detail how Tabit beat his victims, causing them to bleed from their wounds, and how they vomited from disgust and horror. In his article published the next day, Arabi continued,

> We've talked a lot about pornography but it turns out that, after the videos were shown, they're something else. . . . Above all, they're horror films, scenes of rare violence, blood, excrement, torture, cries of pain, women, and terrified children. Nothing erotic. And a hideous torturer, without pity, bestial, barbaric, who tortured with his body and his penis, humiliating souls and destroying flesh. Acts of indescribable cruelty whose after-effects, moral as much as physical, will not easily heal.[52]

Judging from his enthusiastic description of Tabit's sexual abilities only days earlier, the videos must have come as quite a shock to Arabi. Although he seemed to expect titillation and eroticism from them, the reality of Tabit's violence and abuse overwhelmed the entertaining style that he had previously used to describe sex in the case. The press now employed its most graphic language to drive home the incredible brutality and violence of Tabit's actions. The most explicit was the anonymous journalist who wrote for *Libération*. In covering the tapes, the anonymous journalist repeatedly described the "blood flowing from the victims' torn up flesh."[53] This journalist detailed various assaults in the most extreme pornographic language used during the entire trial. Echoing the sexual descriptions in the mainstream U.S. media during the early 1990s, the Moroccan press at this stage showed how it lost any kind of inhibition.

Perhaps the most dramatic moment in the trial coverage came after the video montage was screened and the judges decided finally to open the sessions up to the press. At one thirty on the morning of March 12, journalists returned to the court, just in time for the closing arguments, final statements, verdict, and sentencing. This led to a landmark element in the trial coverage—the use of photographs, and not simply words, to narrate the trial proceedings. Since the press was barred from the court for almost all of the sessions—and the case never appeared on television—the public had no visual images of the country's trial of the century. For the educated, the description of Tabit's crimes and videotape evidence throughout the trial provided a highly graphic record of the case. Although the bold headlines and shocking narratives attracted an unprecedented audience and produced record circulation figures, the inability of the press to print courtroom photographs during the trial meant that the massive semiliterate and illiterate audience in the country would have only limited direct access to the scandal. No doubt, parts of the illiterate public had newspaper articles about the case read to them by friends and family. But their ability to follow trial coverage on their own was restricted due to the lack of visual elements in the press and the complete absence of the case in the audiovisual mass media.

Throughout the trial, the press did manage to print a few photographs, such as small images of the crowds outside the courthouse, the apartment building where Tabit committed his crimes, leaked case documents, and old shots of the codefendants. Now that the press was permitted in the court for the final hours of the trial, current photographs flooded the newspapers. As featured in figure 1, the press printed pictures not only of the crowded courthouse and trial hall but also of the lawyers, judges, and defendants, together with narrative captions. Because there were no previous images of the trial or current photographs of the defendants in the press, the sudden photographs commanded public attention. With bold headlines and stunning images of the last sessions, the final coverage of the trial in the press turned the public into voyeurs of scandal, crime, and cover-up for the first time in the country's history. The use of photographs in the last days of Tabit's trial, just as newspaper circulations hit their peak, stands as a watershed event for sensationalism and voyeurism in the Moroccan mass media. It was the first time that the press relied on both verbal and visual elements of sensationalism to draw in the broader public. This would have far-reaching consequences for the country as it heralded the end of the Years of Lead to the widest possible audience, not just the educated reading public. New forms of sensational mass media, in both visual and verbal elements, would serve as a powerful medium for the state as it sought to transform its authoritarianism and, consequently, its relationship with the ordinary citizen in the years after the trial.

At a quarter to four on the morning of March 15, 1993, barely six weeks after Tabit's arrest, the court announced the verdict. Tabit was sentenced to death and ordered to pay a total of 240,000 dirhams in restitution to his victims. It was the first time in Morocco's history that the death penalty was given to a security official. The court also ordered authorities to destroy the videotapes and seal off Tabit's apartment. His codefendants were given sentences ranging from two years to life in jail. The press headlines from that day screamed "Death for Tabit!" and newspapers printed a variety of pictures from the sentencing, including a series of shots of the disgraced Tabit refusing to look at photographers. The once powerful police were now symbolized by this notorious criminal, who, as seen in figure 2, was now slouched in disgrace between two guards, too ashamed to raise his head to the cameras. This image, which appeared on the cover of most daily newspapers, demonstrated to the entire country how the verdict had disgraced the police after decades of repression.

Abdellatif Jebru, one of the most important political commentators in the country, compared the Tabit Affair to the fall of the Berlin Wall, claiming that the tyranny Morocco experienced during the Years of Lead was finally coming to an end and that the country would now enter a new era of democratic reform.[54] Although his comparison was striking, Jebru did not clarify in the article what he meant by it. He would have been correct to claim that the trial ended decades of fear, humiliating the once powerful police through repeated sensational tales of sexual abuse, cover-up, and collusion. The case greatly expanded freedom of speech and led the press to call for a widespread cleansing of the entire police establishment. It also featured the birth of mass-media sensationalism and its use as a tool to bring down the once mighty police before the eyes of the entire country, elite and non-elite alike. Finally, it marked the emergence of a new kind of public for the mass media, one that cut across socioeconomic lines. The graphic sensationalism of the police's downfall during the Tabit Affair told the widest possible audience—people of all backgrounds—that the Years of Lead were finally coming to a close.

With the fall of the Moroccan Berlin Wall, however, the press was now in an unprecedented position. Although the country's most notorious criminal was found guilty and taken away to await execution, journalists did not know how the red lines were now shifting. Would they continue to use the new sensationalism as a political tool? Would the state crack down and end journalists' suddenly expanded freedom of speech? Would Morocco finally enter an age of open democratic debate? And what would happen to the new massive public for the media? Although Tabit's trial had ended, the transformation of the press was only beginning.

An Old Cop in a New Era

In the immediate aftermath of the trial, the image of the Moroccan police sank to new lows. The Tabit Affair disgraced police officers of all ranks, and people from across the social spectrum held them responsible for his acts. Because Tabit exploited his position as police commissioner to carry out his crimes—and his colleagues repeatedly buried complaints against him—the entire institution of the police, at the highest levels, appeared guilty of widespread abuses of power and corruption. This condemnation—and its sensational coverage in the press—emboldened the public to begin talking about the police openly, expressing their outrage and making the police a subject of open scorn and mockery. Crowds protested in front of the house of Tabit's parents, for example, and threw rocks at the police as they searched the property, an unthinkable act of outrage and protest only two months earlier. Jokes about the police also spread widely through society. One went as follows: "A Moroccan went into a police station and when he was asked what he wanted, he took out a videotape and said: 'I came to exchange this!'"[55] In this joke, the police station no longer inspired the fear and terror of the Years of Lead. Instead, it had become a video store renting pornographic tapes to the public. This kind of disrespect suggested that the new public that had formed during the trial was now openly challenging the status of the main source of state authority, the police.

Not recognizing the serious political threat that Tabit had created, both the government and the palace remained silent about the case through nearly the entire trial, leaving newspapers like the *Socialist Union* and the *Banner* to define the case for the public. On March 11, four days before verdict, the government finally issued a statement about Tabit. In it, the government first claimed that Tabit's acts were isolated and that the swift way with which he was brought to justice highlighted the rule of law in the country.[56] The statement emphasized that putting Tabit on trial for his crimes, despite the fact that he was a high-level police commissioner, demonstrated that no one in the country is above the law. Most importantly, the government claimed that Tabit's crimes were the actions of an individual and not the institution to which he belonged.[57] Responding directly to calls for a widespread firing of officials, the government attempted to absolve the police establishment of the commissioner's crimes:

> These acts that concern a police official are the behavior of an individual . . . and it goes without saying that individual conduct, whatever its seriousness

and misfortune may be, only its actor, actors, or participants can bear responsibility for it and it cannot reflect in any way the body to which he belongs or, more explicitly, soil its reputation. The government takes this opportunity to mention the integrity, devotion, good manners, self-sacrifice, and respect for the law with which are graced the police, whose services, both past and present, have earned it a good reputation that the actions of an individual cannot tarnish.

Despite the way the press repeatedly linked the Tabit Affair to institutional cover-up, human rights abuses, and the power of the police during the Years of the Lead, the government aimed to treat Tabit's crimes purely as an isolated case that had no effect on the larger establishment that he represented. Using the stale language of the Years of Lead, widely known in Arabic as *lughat al-khashab,* or the "language of wood" from the French phrase "la langue du bois," the government praises the police as an honorable institution with a glorious reputation that cannot be dirtied by the acts of any one person. This language suggests that the state still did not recognize the seriousness of the situation. This kind of wording would have been effective in silencing opposition during the Years of Lead, but it had little impact on the press in the new era of freedom of speech. Once the trial was complete, journalists simply ramped up their attack on the position of the police in society, becoming a vehicle for expressing public outrage after years of repression at the hands of the police and challenging them further.

For the next ten days, newspapers like the *Banner* and the *Socialist Union* printed daily editorials and interviews about the effects of Tabit's trial on society. These featured some of the most prominent writers and intellectuals in the country, such as Mohamed Choukri, Salah El Ouadie, Abdelkrim Ghallab, and others. The press as a whole repeatedly claimed that despite the verdict, the case remained open, and called for the state to investigate other cases and put an end to abuses of power. Speculation ran rampant that more officials would be arrested and that others, perhaps some even more powerful than Tabit, had been allowed to escape justice. The press used the case as a rallying cry for full democratic reform and a total cleansing of the police, arguing that Tabit represented the tip of the iceberg of a corrupt system and that only democracy would prevent future Tabits. The case allowed the press to put on its front pages the abusive relationships of power and authority in the country as well as the nature of the connection between citizen and police. Journalists also called for a full investigation into Tabit's activities and how they could have been concealed for so long. Others called for the police to reopen all of the cases in which Tabit made an arrest as well as for the police to investigate all of the bars and establishments in his district.

Some commentators claimed that the Moroccan press needed to become a tool to observe the political parties and government in order to protect the public against systematic abuses of power and corruption. Journalists also used the case to link Tabit's crimes to the country's long-standing experience of human rights abuses. The Tabit Affair—and its immediate aftermath—gave birth to heady days in the party press as journalists began openly envisioning what could be achieved if they continued down the path of freedom of expression. Just as with Watergate, "Tabitgate," which the case was also called, seemed to be giving birth to a new era in which the Moroccan press would become a tool to investigate abuses of power at the highest levels on behalf of the public interest.

The press at this point articulated the outrage of the public and their desire for deep reform. The Tabit Affair was not simply the first time that the entire public, elite and non-elite alike, participated in the press. It was also the first time that the press served as a vehicle for confronting and challenging the authority of the state. The case began with the police—the core of the authoritarian system—but expanded to include the nature of the state once the trial came to a close. As the crisis widened, the state became fully aware of broader public opinion and its demands for the first time. It was during the immediate aftermath of the trial that the case created a crisis of authority for the state. At the time when the scandal broke, the state was clearly ready to begin the process of change since it allowed the Tabit Affair to go public and granted a new level of freedom of expression in the press. But all this talk of true democracy and transparency quickly became too much and forced the state into crisis control.

First, the feared minister of the interior, Driss Basri, stepped in. Basri broke his silence about the case in a special meeting with the government panel for media oversight on March 26, 1993. There, he said that journalists had overstepped their bounds in covering the case and that he was bringing a number of legal charges to rein in their coverage.[58] For most, this threat to prosecute journalists showed not only that they had gone too far in challenging the state, but also that the possibility of a truly free press was in danger of coming to an end. News of this meeting did not appear in the *Banner*, and the *Socialist Union* did not mention it—or Basri's threats—again, suggesting that the reining in of the press was already underway and precluded any follow-up on the issue.

Next, King Hassan II addressed the situation the following day at the end of his speech on March 27, 1993. It was the first and only time he mentioned the Tabit Affair, though he did not actually name the disgraced police commissioner:

> Wisdom and good sense necessitate not passing over in silence a dramatic event that has come upon us. . . . I am not evoking it solely to talk about it because talking about it soils the mouth that evokes it and the hand that describes it. One day, an Arab poet told his sovereign about the behavior of a tribe: "The injustice of perverse beings among the people has created afflictions known by innocents." We are proud of our Moroccan police. Proud of them, yes. God is a witness to it. . . . Five or six men must leave their ranks, even though they have not been brought before the courts or justice. But I know who they are and they must leave. As for the modest policeman who stands on the public highway or before a residence, who has the obligation to

protect those who call for help or assistance, we must not make him responsible for what has happened. That would be absolutely unjust.[59]

Using his typically elevated language, Hassan II first criticizes the press for the way they covered the case. Although he admits that a small group of policemen will need to be dismissed, the king claims that Tabit's crimes—and, by extension, the press coverage of them—have created a situation in which the ordinary policeman is an innocent victim of the scandal. For Hassan II, Tabit's actions were individual, not systematic—as in the government's statement on the case—and the institution of the police should not suffer as a result. The fact that Hassan II intervened not about the press's calls for democracy but in its sensational coverage of the case and, in particular, to defend the police demonstrates that their public image was hitting desperate levels and that the state had lost control of public perception of the case.

It now appears, however, that Driss Basri and Hassan II's statements were not only a defensive response to the backlash surrounding Tabit. They were also a preventative measure for what was coming next. Soon after Tabit's trial was completed, journalists began seeking out new cases of police misconduct and cover-up as a way of humiliating the police and government further. As if Tabit had not done enough damage to the image of the police, journalists quickly found similar cases and continued wielding sensationalism as a political tool. Barely two weeks after the Tabit verdict, for example, in Azemmour, a small town on the Atlantic coast some fifty miles southwest of Casablanca, a thirty-two-year-old unmarried police officer named Bouchaïb Arbad was arrested for sexually assaulting boys and young men, taking Polaroid pictures of himself handcuffing and threatening them with his gun, and selling the photographs to foreigners. Like Tabit, Arbad reportedly videotaped some of his acts and kept notebooks with the personal information of his victims, which helped authorities later identify them. The case went public on April 1, after the parents of one of Arbad's victims finally pressed charges, reportedly emboldened after news of the Tabit Affair spread throughout the country.[60]

During the trial, which began almost immediately after Arbad's arrest and attracted enormous crowds, Arbad admitted that he had been committing his crimes for a decade. Twelve people—including a town advisor and a camera technician—were eventually charged in the case. As with the Tabit Affair, though not quite to the same degree, the national press played up the sensational and sexual nature of the case, graphically narrating how Arbad, whom they called "Little Tabit," would arrange orgies with his victims, who were almost all minors. Once again, the press used sensationalism to attract a massive audience to humiliate the police and call for reform. Headlines focused in particular on how he abused minors, took pornographic photographs, and abused his power to carry out his crimes and remain free for a decade.

Like Tabit, who was known to the outside world as a Hajj, Arbad was described as having a public persona that clashed with his hidden depraved real character. To the people who knew him, Arbad was a shy and modest young man who lived with his parents. "Correct, polite, courteous, and timid, he was respected by his colleagues," wrote one journalist. Neighbors described Arbad as normal and not having any problems.[61] One told the press that he was shocked to discover that Arbad was behind these crimes.[62] Even his parents had no idea about what he was doing. Arbad therefore displayed key elements of Tabit's shocking dual personality and provided a clear way for the press to link the two for the public. Tabit had a calm and dignified external demeanor while Arbad was polite and timid. Although Arbad never claimed to have a dual personality complex or to suffer from a sexual malady, he hid his crimes behind an air of respectability. The average person had no idea what lurked behind this outer demeanor, an element that the newspapers seized on in order to sensationalize the cases. For the media, outward propriety in the new era was suddenly no longer a reliable sign that you could trust someone. Rather, it became a ruse for covering up grave criminal acts.

Thanks to the sensational depictions of Arbad's crimes in the press, anger quickly boiled over in Azemmour, further emphasizing the crisis that the state was now facing. Newspapers printed reports that people in the city began throwing rocks at the police in outrage over the case, particularly since, like Tabit, Arbad exploited his position to carry out his crimes. After approaching victims on the street, he would tell them that he was a police officer and threaten to arrest them if they did not come with him. Once again, the entire institution of the police appeared to be on trial, especially since other cases of police sexual abuse, cover-up, and misconduct quickly hit the press, further inflaming public outrage.

Rumors about arrests within the ranks of the police for sexual scandals reached a frenzied pitch. Among the new accusations, two detectives in Casablanca were charged with sexually abusing a woman in her home after coming to arrest her husband, while police in Meknès were charged with videotaping themselves assaulting kidnapped women at an isolated farm. In a weekend special, the *Socialist Union* published a large map of Morocco showing where each of the new police crimes took place, together with details of the charges.[63] The accompanying article, entitled "Fall of Veils after Collapse of Tabit," not only suggested that Morocco had entered a new world after the trial of the century, but also that people were now free to register complaints about the police. This implied that such crimes had always been present but were covered up because of the widespread fear, silence, and press censorship of the Years of Lead. By mid-April 1993, a month after the Tabit verdict, it appeared as if more and more cases of police abuse would continue to emerge. After the brutal decades of the Years of Lead, the stunning downfall of Hajj Mustapha Tabit, and now reports of similar sexual abuses throughout the country, the image of the police could not get any worse.

Clearly, the state needed to find new ways to ensure social cohesion beyond fear and repression.

Morale within the ranks of the police sank so low that Hassan II's statement "We are proud of our Moroccan police" was printed on the cover of the spring 1993 issue of the internal police magazine, *Majallat al-Amn al-Watani* (Journal of National Security) in an attempt to rally the troops. The same issue included the speech the king gave on April 14, 1993, when he appointed a new national chief of police as part of the fallout from the Tabit Affair, just as Arbad was on trial for his crimes. Although he did not mention either scandal, Hassan II told the new chief, "Stand by the police once again since they deserve, as I have said, every sympathy and kindness. Restore their vigor, determination, and morale. Be for them the father who educates when education is necessary and rewards when reward is due."[64] From this perspective, the entire institution of the police came to resemble a troubled child who needed fatherly sternness, encouragement, and support. Even the palace was admitting that the police were now far from the feared and powerful establishment they represented only two months earlier. With the continuing wave of arrests and sensational reporting in the press, the appointment of a new chief, and patronizing public comments by the king, the image of the police was in need of a complete overhaul.

In its coverage of the appointment of the new police chief, the *Banner* published a front-page editorial about the change: "We believe that the mission of the new chief differs from that of his predecessors because he is devoted to rehabilitating the police. That can only happen with a new mentality and a new concept of authority."[65] The newspaper suggested that, after decades of maintaining social order through repression, the police were taking an interest in their image in society for the first time. Without a new police for the post–Years of Lead era, it would be impossible for the state to demonstrate to the public that it was responding to their demands in the aftermath of the Tabit Affair. Although a new image of the police and, consequently, state authority, was on the horizon, it would have to wait. The state's first step was simply to contain the immediate crisis of authority and stop the damage that the press was doing to the police.

Sensationalism Stifled

Although it seemed as if cases of police abuse and cover-up would keep erupting, by late spring 1993, once the new chief of police took over, the new sensationalism and series of police scandals suddenly began to disappear from the press. Gone were the bold headlines, shocking news of scandals, and sensational photographs that the new reading public clearly wanted. This was not because individual journalists misunderstood or failed to recognize the role of sensationalism as a means to attract a massive audience to the press. During the trial, for example, one journalist claimed that the Tabit Affair allowed journalists to wake up from their "long lethargy" and "to break out from silence and fully exercise their profession."[66] Another suggested that newspapers now needed to look for Tabit-like scandals in order to continue their record circulation figures because "the sensational fascinates the Moroccan terribly."[67] In an interview after the trial, Mohamed Berrada, the director of Sapress, the main newspaper distribution company in Morocco, stated that newspapers needed to adapt their content and focus "to conform to the demands of their readers."[68] What the Tabit Affair clearly taught the newspaper industry is that sensationalism sells.

Nonetheless, immediately after the fervor of the post-Tabit arrests, the daily press suddenly retreated back to its typical dry politicized language and lack of visual elements, abandoning the new audience that journalists had created with their coverage of the police scandals. No doubt, the Tabit Affair, with its direct connection to state power and authority, presented the palace with the perfect opportunity to begin the process of transitioning away from the repression and fear of the Years of Lead. This would explain why journalists were granted such unprecedented freedoms in covering the trial and attacking the police. From the perspective of the party press, the case represented an opportunity for political gain, especially for the opposition, the Socialist Union, and its political platform that called for reform. Nonetheless, once the scope of the public's anger became clear, the state faced a sudden crisis of authority and moved decisively to rein in the press and public discussion of the scandal. With the new chief of police on the scene, sensationalism was therefore restricted in order to avert a deepening crisis and to spare the police more embarrassment.

The Tabit Affair may have smashed taboos surrounding newspaper depictions of violent crime, lurid sexuality, and the police, but by the summer of 1993, it seemed as if sensationalism had left the Moroccan mass media for good. For the months following the Tabit Affair, the semiliterate audience that had participated in the daily press for the first time in the country's history had nowhere to go for the news they were craving. This new public eager for sensationalism and sordid details about scandal once again found itself shut out of the mass media. Even reports of Tabit's execution, which appeared on August 10, 1993, did not stir the press out of its sedate coverage. The *Banner*, for example, printed only a brief statement from the Ministry of Justice in a small box on the top of its front page that day, announcing that Tabit had been executed the day before. The *Socialist Union* printed its article on the story in a box on the bottom half of the front page, stating that Tabit had been shot to death only three days after his appeal had been denied.[69] Neither newspaper devoted headline space to the execution or added commentary on the case, an incredible turn of events considering the way that they had covered the Tabit Affair only months earlier.

And with that, it seemed as if Morocco's experiment with mass media sensationalism and freedom of expression was over, as if Tabit had never happened.

The lessons of the Tabit Affair, however, were not lost on the state. The frenzy surrounding the trial and its aftermath demonstrated that the state needed to pay attention to public opinion in the post-Tabit era and show that it could respond to its demands. Repression and coercion were no longer sufficient for sustaining the regime's hold on power now that the Years of Lead were ending. And while the state managed to rein in the press for the time being, it was unlikely that media censorship and intimidation would be adequate in the post-Tabit era now that journalists had tasted expanded freedom of expression. New forms of disciplining the public needed to be cultivated if the state was going to sustain itself and transform its brand of authoritarianism to correspond with public demands for change.

The sensationalism with which the press covered the Tabit Affair showed that the media could be used as a powerful tool to communicate with the broader public, regardless of the illiteracy rate in the country. While the party press retreated to its stoic reporting style, catering once again to its elite readership, a new media source would soon emerge that satisfied both the appetite of the new audience for sensationalism and the desire of the state to begin rehabilitating the image of the police for the new era. And unlike before, the state would participate in shaping the media's language, imagery, and message, establishing a radical new way to recast the police and their relationship with the broader public after the Tabit Affair.

2 "He Butchered His Wife Because of Witchcraft and Adultery"

Crime Tabloids, Moral Panic, and the Remaking of the Moroccan Cop

In September 1993, only months after the Tabit Affair, people walking down the city boulevards discovered a jarring new form of media awaiting them at the newsstands. Sitting next to the daily press and weekly magazines, which had returned to their stoic reporting style soon after Tabit's trial, were large color tabloids spread out on the sidewalks boasting covers with grisly crime-scene photographs and shocking bold headlines. The words "He Butchered His Wife Because of Witchcraft and Adultery," for example, were placed below a horrific color image of the female victim's bloodied and mutilated face. "He Stabbed His Friend to Death for Three Cents" appeared above a large color photograph of the killer pointing a knife toward a man, demonstrating for the police—and public—exactly how he committed the murder. The bold headline "Murder, American Style" introduced a large color image of the victim, a middle-aged man on his back after rigor mortis set in. "The Police Put Their Hands on Wide Prostitution Network" was printed next to a photograph of seven seemingly respectable women, all in traditional Moroccan clothes, under arrest. Never before had the Moroccan public seen real-world daily violence and moral degradation spread out on the cover of a newspaper, let alone with such dramatic color photographs and bold sensational headlines. For decades, crime was a topic hidden from the public eye. Now, all of a sudden, it was splashed on the front pages of these tabloids for anyone walking by the newsstands to see.

The shocking new tabloids announced to the public that the country was facing an immediate and terrifying crime wave in the most urgent terms possible. Building on the work of sociologists like Stuart Hall and Stephen Jenkins, this chapter will trace how the tabloids constructed the crisis through their photographs, headlines, and narrative reports.[1] This chapter will also examine how the tabloids presented this crime wave to their highly conservative readers as the result of a rapid decline in the country's traditional values, morality, and social bonds. The tabloids used the image of crime erupting uncontrollably and chaos spreading in society to alarm the public that the country's security and moral fiber were quickly unraveling. The tabloids constructed this crime wave and moral panic to show the pressing dangers of the post–Years of Lead era, with its apparent focus on transparency and personal freedoms.

The tabloids did not construct the crisis simply to terrify the public. They used these depictions of violence and moral disintegration to take the first steps in rehabilitating the image of the police in society after the Tabit Affair. At the same time as they disseminated shocking representations of crime and immorality, the tabloids presented the public with a new kind of police that was capable of combating the crisis and bringing it under control. The severity of the threat in the new era justified the tabloids' calling for a tough-on-crime response, celebrating a strong police that worked tirelessly to protect ordinary citizens from the new dangers. By presenting the police as the sole source of calm and solace in a world suddenly spiraling out of control, the tabloids worked to erase the old authoritarian image of the police and provide them with a new identity. The terrifying crime wave, which the tabloids constructed and disseminated throughout the country, therefore allowed the media to begin the process of transforming the image of the police as an institution that defended the elite and repressed ordinary citizens to an establishment that protected the non-elite ordinary public from the shocking new realities of crime. Fear became a vehicle to reestablish the legitimacy of the police in post–Years of Lead Morocco.

Although the state ignored the press during the Tabit Affair and left it free to define the case for the public, the state now became an active participant in the media construction of the crime wave and images of a strong police force capable of protecting society from the terrifying new dangers. They did this by collaborating directly with the tabloids. The state provided them with crime-scene and arrest photographs as well as police reports and sensitive case information.[2] This material allowed the tabloids to construct the crisis in an attempt to convince the public that the only response was a tough-on-crime policy, led by a newly invigorated police force. Through these tabloids and their sensational depictions of crime and punishment, the state played an active role in using the media as a vehicle for attempting to shape public perceptions of the police. Moreover, they did this not through the drab government newspapers that featured the usual stale propagandistic language of the Years of Lead, but through sensational and commercial crime tabloids that lacked the veneer of political allegiances and spoke to the public in an utterly new nonstate language. The birth and dissemination of the tabloids represents a fundamental shift in the relationship between the state, mass media, and public opinion. The tabloids prove that the state became deeply concerned with public attitudes after the Tabit Affair and show how sensationalism in general and images of crime and punishment in particular became the means by which they attempted to influence and shape the perceptions of the ordinary working-class public in order to ensure stability now that the Years of Lead had come to a close.

The construction of the crime wave and new police was not the result of a top-down decision made by a few powerful individuals. Instead, it represented the intersection of mutual interests. In the aftermath of the Tabit Affair, the state needed to begin the process of rehabilitating the image of the police, rein in the potential threat of the new non-elite public, and demonstrate that it could be responsive to public demands for change. Collaborating with the tabloids provided the state with a new outlet that could give a revived police visibility and credibility that could not be achieved through traditional state newspapers or old forms of propaganda. The tabloid publisher represented the growing commercialization of the media in the country and sought to capitalize on the expanding space for new readers and markets. Moreover, the publisher recognized that disseminating a positive image of the police would ensure that he would continue receiving his exclusive source material. And the ordinary public wanted to see not only a return of sensationalism to the press after the Tabit Affair but also the emergence of a new kind of media that took their concerns and worldview seriously. Evidence of this can be seen not only in the elements of the tabloids that catered in particular to working-class audiences but also in the enormous sales figures that the tabloids achieved in their initial years of publication. The net result of these aligned interests was a new, highly constructed image of crime and punishment that marked a major shift in the way the state attempted to form, manage, and direct public opinion in order to reestablish its legitimacy after the Tabit Affair.

Najib Skir and the Origins of the Moroccan Crime Tabloid

With their sensational color crime-scene photographs and shocking headlines, the tabloids seemed like a totally new form of media. During the Years of Lead, the party press only occasionally printed crime news. When crime did appear, the articles showed how the police quickly put an end to whatever danger was threatening a city or neighborhood. Although these articles would sometimes give details of a crime, they avoided sensational depictions of violence and moral degradation that would offend traditional sensibilities, focusing instead on the effectiveness of the police in apprehending suspects and bringing them to justice. The press as a whole during the Years of Lead presented society as having strong traditional values and morals. When the press printed crime news, these were individual and isolated events, typically motivated by anger or revenge, and had no larger implications for the safety and stability of particular cities or the country as a whole.

The new crime tabloids, with their large color photographs of murder victims, arrested criminals looking defiantly at the camera, and mounds of seized guns and drugs, brazenly depicted insecurity and violence. Headlines were set in brightly colored boxes and announced news that had never appeared on the front pages before, such as "Young Man Catches Mother Sleeping with Lover and Stabs Him to Death" or "She Killed Her Husband by Smashing His Genitals

Because He Became Impotent." Set next to the traditional party press with their sedate focus on political matters, the new tabloids clashed with other newspapers and magazines available in Morocco at the time. Besides the immediacy of the photographs, the tabloids, with their repeated images of widespread violence and moral degradation, suggested that society was no longer facing individual and isolated crimes of passion and revenge, as during the Years of Lead. Rather, the tabloid covers announced to the public that the country was now in the middle of a deep, widespread, and unprecedented crisis.

Despite the sudden emergence of these tabloids, there are important precursors that help explain their origins. Outside Morocco, crime journalism had thrived in Egypt for decades, beginning in the late nineteenth century. As Shaun T. Lopez has shown, crime reports in newspapers remained brief until the notorious 1920 Raya and Sakina case, which launched a number of other moral panics in the press during the following decades.[3] By the 1950s, the well-known Egyptian newspaper *Akhbar al-Yawm* (Today's News) published crime reports focusing on bizarre murders and boasting shocking headlines. The newspaper also specialized in sensational cases, such as the 1960 crime spree of Mahmoud Suleiman, which captivated the country and served as the basis for Naguib Mahfouz's novel *The Thief and the Dogs*.[4] In April 1992, *Today's News* began publishing a tabloid dedicated to crime, *Akhbar al-Hawadith* (Incident News), which boasted front-page photographs and shocking headlines.[5] Closer to Morocco, newspaper sensationalism emerged in Algeria during the political and media opening that took place after the October 1988 riots. The first Algerian crime tabloid, *al-Shuruq al-Usbu'i* (The Weekly Rise), which featured graphic front-page reports of rape and murder, appeared in 1993. Other crime tabloids quickly followed to capitalized on the trend.[6]

Within Morocco, Mustapha Alaoui began publishing the country's first independent weekly newspapers in the early 1960s. These weeklies had no party affiliation and specialized in sensational political rumors, not crime. Because the government was so opaque during the Years of Lead, Alaoui drew his audience from a public interested in rumors about political officials and various government offices. Since his newspapers touched on sensitive issues, the state frequently shut them down. This led Alaoui to launch a new title in place of the banned one, using the same style of reporting. Well-known for being fiercely independent, Alaoui developed a reputation as a reliable source for political news that was untainted by state authorities or political parties. Throughout his career, Alaoui has paid a heavy price for his independence and journalistic style. He has been tried for threatening public order, kidnapped and tortured by the Moroccan security services, and imprisoned multiple times for articles that he printed. One of his many newspapers, *al-Usbu' al-Siyasi* (Political Week), which first appeared in 1965, is still thriving today.[7]

In early 1992, a journalist named Mohamed Moumen printed a new weekly entitled *Liqa' al-Siyasi* (Meeting of the Political), which was modeled on the kind of newspapers that Mustapha Alaoui published. Like Alaoui, Moumen gave his weekly a politicized title and focused on rumors about the various parties and ministries. This subject matter and style suggested that Moumen too was independent from any outside influence. With headlines like "Rabat Buses Need to Be Retired," "Employment Office Out of Work," and "Hospital in Taza Has No Doctor," Moumen introduced his rumors with a hint of humor, clearly hoping to catch the eye of someone passing by the newsstand. By the summer of 1992, however, Moumen began diverging from the political rumor formula by including small headlines and stories about crime, together with occasional small black-and-white photographs of arrested criminals. Despite this significant innovation, his newspaper never approached the level of sensationalism that the crime tabloids would later reach. Rather, crime for Moumen was simply a new twist on the old social and political rumor formula.

Najib Skir, the director of the central prison in Kénitra during the 1980s, published his first weekly newspaper, *al-Maw'id al-Siyasi* (Political Appointment) in July 1992. Like Alaoui, Skir focused largely on political and socioeconomic rumors, but, like Moumen, he included occasional headlines about crime, positioned next to small arrest photographs. Issues would sometimes feature a short restrained article that outlined the events of a given crime, noting that the police made an arrest in the case, much like the occasional crime articles in the daily party press at the time. Although *Political Appointment* was largely devoted to political rumors, it targeted a less educated audience than that of the party newspapers. The cover of *Political Appointment*, for example, looked significantly different from other weeklies at the time since it included only headlines that were easy to understand and no additional text. Moreover, *Political Appointment* directly attacked the sophisticated style and political bent of newspapers like the *Socialist Union*. In one editorial from the time, Skir declares, "Readers have become bored with the demagogical and ideological discourses that party newspapers spew incessantly."[8] The independent press—like Skir's weekly, for example—"make it their goal to strike the emotional cord of the reader, to explore his desires, and to bring out journalistic material that entices him in both form and content." Before Skir, political rumor weeklies had targeted the same kind of audience as the party press. Skir, however, was the first to attempt to expand the genre to embrace a working-class audience that had little interest in politics. By incorporating elements of sensationalism, he set an important precedent for the crime tabloids that would soon appear on the newsstands. *Political Appointment* enjoyed high circulations and wide popularity, but Skir discontinued the newspaper in June 1993. Given the success of *Political Appointment*, it was not clear, at least at first, why Skir stopped printing the weekly.

Skir returned to the media scene only two months later when he published the country's first crime tabloid, *al-Yawm al-Siyasi* (Political Day), on September 13, 1993, the cover of which is featured in figure 3. He quickly followed this first tabloid with several more titles, including *al-Muwasil al-Siyasi* (Political Communicator) on October 23, 1993, *al-Mi'ad al-Siyasi* (Political Rendezvous) on December 14, 1993, and *Asda' al-Skhirat-Tamara* (Echoes of Skhirat and Tamara) on January 29, 1994. Skir issued a fifth crime tabloid, *Akhbar al-Hawadith* (Incident News) on June 6, 1995. Despite the different titles, Skir's tabloids strongly resembled each other in form and content. They featured similar front-page photographs, headlines, and layouts. Each issue, regardless of the tabloid title, commonly included an editorial written by Skir, local crime news from various regions and cities, and a narrative style that featured a mix of text taken directly from police reports and moralizing commentary.

The use of the word "political" in the titles of Skir's first three tabloids was no accident. Mustapha Alaoui built his reputation on having no direct ties to the political parties or state authorities and this bolstered the credibility of the information he printed in his weeklies. Moreover, the police targeted Alaoui and shut down his newspapers, events that underscored his independence from the state. When Skir issued his crime tabloids in the fall of 1993, he gave them titles that sounded like Mustapha Alaoui's weeklies in order to suggest that they too were free of state control, giving the tabloids at least the partial veneer of independence. The titles, with their surface links to the political rumor newspapers—in combination with the new sensational and commercial form and content of the crime tabloids—showed how Skir's weeklies provided the state with what appeared to be a nonstate media source in order to engage the public and attempt to manage public opinion.

Although accurate and precise circulation figures are impossible to obtain, Skir's new crime tabloids were a massive success. Thanks to the shock of the initial issues, the tabloids became so popular that they immediately spawned competition. The newsstands were soon flooded with imitations, though clearly of lower quality, by overnight publishers looking to turn a quick profit.[9] Weeklies that specialized in political rumors before Tabit were quickly turned into crime tabloids, in the hope of capitalizing on the phenomenon. This sudden fierce competition explains why Skir issued multiple titles, despite the strong similarity between them. Despite the competition, Skir was the clear winner. Mohamed Moumen's *Meeting of the Political*, for example, morphed into a full-scale crime tabloid but was unable to compete and disappeared from the newsstands within a year.

When I met him in 2006, Skir explained that he decided to move into journalism in the early 1990s after retiring from his position as director of the main prison in Kénitra. Skir said that he used his close connections and strong ties to the judicial system and police establishment to get access to official photographs and crime reports that were unavailable to other newspapers. He reveled in his exclusive material, fondly remembering particular cases and offering to show me his archive of crime-scene photographs from the most notorious crimes in Moroccan history. These images and police reports gave Skir his competitive edge, allowing him to dominate the market from the beginning. At the time of this writing, Skir's crime tabloids are the only ones still found on the newsstands in Morocco.

Skir's grisly photographs added an important new step in the transformation of the local mass media after the Years of Lead. Images of crime scenes or murder victims were considered highly sensitive material since they could only have originated from the police. Their appearance on the front-page of newspapers—regardless of the kind of newspaper—demonstrated in the most dramatic and concrete terms to anyone passing a newsstand that the country's mass media were taking bold new steps away from decades of strict press control. Just as the Tabit Affair smashed the taboo of criticizing the police in the media, Skir's tabloids brought the previously hidden world of crime and punishment to people across the country, opening the media up to yet another taboo. While these images contradicted the tabloids' veneer of independence from the state, they suggested to the public an unprecedented level of openness at the police stations since crime-scene photographs had never appeared in the press before.

Photographs were particularly important to the success of the tabloids. In Morocco, unlike the United States today, the newsstand and sidewalk display is still the dominant mode of newspaper sales.[10] With virtually no subscriptions and little advertising, the daily party press in the 1990s relied largely on street sales for revenues, but also had substantial supporting funds from the sponsoring political organization. The crime tabloids, however, had no explicit political associations and were presumably dependent on sales for the bottom line. The format of the tabloid covers—with their grisly photographs and shocking headlines—needed to demand the attention of the public as they passed the newsstands and sidewalk displays.[11] That marketing strategy worked perfectly since the Moroccan crime tabloids targeted a working-class and semiliterate readership in particular. As the Tabit Affair proved, the public wanted taboo-breaking photographs, shocking headlines, and simple prose that anyone with an elementary education could understand. And that is exactly what Najib Skir provided with his tabloids, thanks to their focus on photographic spectacle and de-emphasis on sophisticated written text.

Approximately one hundred thousand people bought one of Najib Skir's crime tabloids each week, but millions saw their covers and shocking headlines. The covers were so important for the success of the tabloids that Skir invested significant resources in them. The first Moroccan crime tabloid, published on September 13, 1993, and featured in figure 3, was the first newspaper of any kind in the country to use color, a technological advance that would not be matched by the mainstream press for almost another decade. The act of viewing the stunning covers on the streets led people to call them not tabloids but *jara'id al-rasif*, or "sidewalk newspapers," a term that is now synonymous in the country with sensational and lurid crime reporting. These covers, however, were only part of the strategy that Skir employed to target his tabloids at the massive semiliterate public in the country. Another was the way Skir focused on types of stories that had never appeared before in the local press, news that catered to the moral and social interests of the non-elite public.

News of the Weird, Dreams of the Poor

Before the Tabit Affair, the semiliterate public had never participated in the country's daily press because of its emphasis on elevated language, complex socioeconomic issues, political platforms, and cultural debates. The only photographs these newspapers typically printed were of the king, political meetings, or high-level party members. With their attention on elite cultural and political affairs—as well as high level of language and de-emphasis on visual elements and sensational topics with broad appeal—the country's newspapers had ignored the overwhelming majority of the public for decades.

Skir's tabloids broke with that tradition. Unlike the party press or the weeklies that appeared before Tabit, Skir's tabloids included no political news or elite cultural perspectives whatsoever. Instead, they focused on the kinds of news that people had never seen before in the press. They took news and information that were marginalized or completely shunned in other sources and presented them proudly on the front pages, typically with striking photographs and sensational headlines. Besides the shocking tales of crime and violence, Skir brought the world of the poor and neglected of society to the front pages of the press through a combination of news of the weird and bizarre as well as dreams of a better life. As a result, the tabloids proudly catered to the non-elite public, which had never seen a news source take its social outlook seriously. Moreover, Skir's weeklies displayed a strong moral compass and presented a highly conservative perspective that was intended to appeal to the non-elite public. Tabloids around the world use a strongly traditional morality to cater to a working-class audience, and the crime tabloids in Morocco were no exception.[12] These topics were meant to attract the new audience that followed the Tabit Affair, offering hundreds of thousands of Moroccans their first opportunity to buy a newspaper with information that they could not find anywhere else.[13]

What is considered weird and bizarre is, of course, a matter of local taste. In the world of the Moroccan tabloids, for example, animals feature prominently in these kinds of tales. In one article, the owner of a purebred dog gave it an abortion after he saw it mate with a wild dog. In another, the friends of a cart driver decided to play a joke on him by giving his horse ten uppers, which made it run frantically through the medina, gravely injuring a woman. From donkeys and mules eating hashish to the butcher who found psychotropic pills in the stomach of a ram, the tabloids repeatedly mix animals and drugs, seemingly to elicit the audience's laughter. In Skir's world, animals can also be dangerous—one article featured a photograph of a dog that bit off the face of its owner while another described how a cat ate a baby's intestines. The most common story involving animals, however, is that of the ambulant sausage seller who makes his product out of stray dogs, a tale that is so popular that it has now reached the status of urban legend in the country. Front-page articles announced how one sausage seller was on the run from the police for ten days before he was finally apprehended, while another slaughtered his neighbors' dogs for meat with the help of a butcher. Many of these stories focus on animals in the context of the impoverished medina area of the major cities, suggesting that Skir saw his readership as living in these sections and dealing with animals regularly in their daily lives. The crime tabloids marked the first time that members of the working class saw bizarre stories about their own neighborhoods and daily lives in the printed press, opening the country's press up to a new terrain for reporting.

Stories of the weird and bizarre in the Moroccan tabloids also focus on unusual and unexplained events, much like tabloids in the United States.[14] One front-page photograph, for example, shows the two-headed baby that a Moroccan woman gave birth to while another presents the ten pounds of snakes that reportedly came out of a child's intestines. In another story, a farmer found a turnip in the shape of a human hand, dripping with blood. A Moroccan tabloid favorite was the tale that emphasized a strange twist of fate. These include stories of an airline hostess who found her husband fleeing the country on her plane, a man who discovered his fiancée at a psychiatric ward, and a wealthy landowner who was inexplicably begging on the streets of a major city. The tabloids presented these kinds of news to grab the public's attention and to elicit their shock and surprise.[15]

Besides these bizarre reports, news of the weird in the tabloids emphasized moral and social degradation, featuring an outraged conservatism that is common in tabloids across the world but localized in the Moroccan context.[16] These include how handsome and respectable men steal shoes from mosques, an innocent-looking mother-and-son team lead a dangerous gang specializing in theft and gang rape, and a prostitute rents out her illegitimate child to homeless people to help in begging. Stories such as these emphasize how traditional morals are in decline in order to spark the public's outrage. One of the most striking stories of this variety combines the themes of sexual degradation, class conflict, and religion. The article explains how the imam of a mosque in Rabat was shocked when a man came and asked to consult with him about whether he had committed a sin.[17] The man tells the imam that he is the driver for a wealthy family and that when the husband was away on the Hajj, the wife called him into her bedroom. Wearing see-through clothes, she told him to sit down and ordered him to drink whiskey with her. He refused at first because of his good morals, but gave in when the woman slapped him across the face and threatened to fire him if he did not follow her orders. After they finished the bottle, the woman played the driver a pornographic video, ordering him to act out what he saw with her, slapping him again when he refused. The article explains that the driver finally gave in to the woman's demands, but solely out of fear of losing his job. Afterward, the woman gave him two hundred dirhams and told him to keep quiet about what happened. This article presents the kinds of sexual immorality that the party press celebrated during the Tabit Affair, but this time a woman was treating an innocent man like a prostitute. The article ends by quoting the imam's response to the man: "You've committed a grave sin. It was incumbent upon you to take the lesson from the story of our lord Yusuf, when Aziz's wife tempted him. As for now, rush to your Creator and repeatedly ask for forgiveness. God is forgiving and merciful." Told from the perspective of the poor driver who falls unwillingly into the clutches of the morally bankrupt wealthy woman, the article presents a tale of class conflict as sexual entertainment. Even though the imam condemns the driver for not resisting the woman—just as Joseph turned down the advances of Potiphar's wife—and tells him to repent, the lurid details of the article suggest that the audience would share a secret pleasure in the driver's adventures as well as a sense of moral outrage that a woman could abuse a man in such an immoral fashion, especially while her husband was performing the pilgrimage to Mecca.

Although news of the weird and bizarre were frequent in Moroccan crime tabloids, articles that manipulated and encouraged the dreams of the poor were even more common. One front-page story details how a garbage collector found twenty thousand dirhams inside a plastic bag buried in the trash, while another announces that a farmer struck it rich by winning the lottery. Both stories suggest that working long hours in manual labor can eventually make fantasies come true. Women also feature prominently in these kinds of stories—one front-page headline announces that a wealthy man gave his dancer girlfriend a drum of pure gold, hinting that one's boyfriend could always surprise with luxurious gifts. In addition to trash collectors, farmers, and penniless dancers, the tabloids targeted the country's unemployed youth in particular. Most issues of the tabloids, for example, include information about immigrating to Europe or the United States. From advertisements for student scholarships and employment to information about the educational system in France and the U.S. green card lottery process, the crime tabloids are full of promise for a better life outside of Morocco and provide their readership with concrete opportunities to escape. Blurbs congratulating Moroccan women for marrying Saudi men also appear, hinting to the audience that, one day, they too could marry well. A particularly poignant article of this type appeared in the September 15, 1995, issue of *Political Communicator*, detailing how a wealthy Belgian woman came to Marrakech for her wedding but fell hopelessly in love with a young Moroccan waiter she met at her hotel. The woman immediately broke off her engagement, married the lucky man, and took him back to Belgium with her. Another article presenting news of a better life abroad tells of a Moroccan Elvis impersonator entertaining audiences in Texas.

In direct contrast with these alluring possibilities of hitting the jackpot through immigration or marrying a wealthy foreigner are the frequent riches-to-rags stories. From the former professional soccer player who was now a homeless cigarette seller to the washed-up popular musician arrested for assault, theft, and rape, the crime tabloids aimed to please their readers by showing how far the wealthy can tumble. The moral universe of these articles, however, is not random. These people fell from grace not because of bad luck but because of their inner immoral nature or arrogance. One especially moving story of this type appeared in the June 8, 1994, issue of *Political Rendezvous*. The article describes how a man named Hajj Hamman worked his way up from total poverty to become one of the wealthiest businessmen in the south of the country. When he was in the process of building his career, he fell in love with a girl from a wealthy local family and asked her father for permission to marry her. The father insulted Hajj Hamman, telling him that he was not good enough to join their well-established family. Thirty years later, Hajj Hamman now had a large family and had amassed an enormous fortune, thanks to his persistence, hard work, and good morals. One day, Hajj Hamman began to look for a new maid and was shocked when the girl he proposed to thirty years earlier came to his house to apply for the job. The woman tells Hajj Hamman that her father married her to a business associate who divorced her after he went bankrupt. The woman's father also died in misery after going bankrupt, leaving her with nothing. Having no means to support herself or her children, the woman was forced to look for work as a maid. As with other riches-to-rags stories in the Moroccan tabloids, this article provides a clear reason for the woman's downfall. Her father's hubris and inability to recognize Hajj Hamman's hard work and strong morals brought ruin upon him and his daughter. Articles such as this one suggest that the wealthy and arrogant will one day get what they deserve and finish their days in poverty, a message that was intended to appeal to working-class readers.

The most innovative strategy intended to draw in the traditional segments of society, however, was repeated news and information about black magic and demon possession.[18] Witchcraft and fortune telling are extremely popular in Morocco—and among the working-class public in particular—and represent a method of treating illnesses that modern Western medicine cannot or does not recognize, such as possession, demons, and various kinds of spells.[19] These articles include terms that are widely known and used in Moroccan society, such as *mass* (possession), *sihr* (black magic), *tukal* (casting a spell on someone through their food), *hawatif* (screaming fits due to demons), and *thaqqaf* (being rendered impotent), but that had never appeared in the printed press before. Skir sent journalists to various cities to observe particularly popular magicians and report firsthand with interviews and photographs on their ability to treat people struck by these conditions. The tabloids catered to people who distrusted modern medicine, which, despite all of its scientific and technological advances, failed to cure the kinds of illnesses that struck the most traditional segments of society. As Skir wrote in an editorial, this explains why "spiritual treatment is a refuge for many people who have grown tired of numerous visits to medical clinics."[20] At the same time, Skir argued that it was the modern era and its dangers that have produced this situation: "As long as people in the twentieth century live in this age of anxiety and psychological problems, consulting the spirits will remain necessary." Articles about magic therefore gave legitimacy to those who sought solace for illnesses outside of modern medicine. As with the stories of the weird and the bizarre, Skir's weeklies were the first media sources in Morocco to take witchcraft seriously and provide the public with information about it.

The tabloids commonly featured large front-page photographs and full-page exposés on magicians who were particularly powerful, praising them and their *baraka*, or divine blessing, and urging readers to visit them at their shrines. One example is Hussein Obihi, who exorcised demons while chanting verses from the Quran and holding a copy of the Holy Book. Another is Sharifa Lubna, who specialized in "curing" men from cross-dressing. Her strong masculine features, fine blond wig, and heavy makeup, however, reveal all too clearly that Sharifa Lubna was herself a man posing as a woman. This points to the carnivalesque nature of popular culture, showing how it can be a site of contestation and resistance to traditional social categories. By featuring Sharifa Lubna, the tabloids, despite their highly conservative morality, included this element for readers.

The most popular magician in the tabloids, however, was a young man from Sidi Qasim named Sherif Redwan. In its first article on him, *Political Rendezvous* printed his address and phone number, urging readers to make an appointment. An anonymous journalist vouched that "we saw with our own eyes" how Sherif Redwan used his *baraka* to cure people from possession, paralysis, and other evils.[21] The journalist also adds, "Sherif Redwan doesn't have any intention of earning money from his *baraka*," but that he had earned enough money from his previous job that he was now able to devote himself full-time to what he called his "humanitarian work." A week after this first article, *Political Rendezvous* printed a follow-up, telling readers how massive crowds flocked from all over the country to Sherif Redwan in what was a "memorable day in the history of Sidi Qasim."[22] According to this journalist, people rushed to Sherif Redwan "to treat numerous illnesses that are incurable by modern medicine." The author interviewed several people treated at the scene, including a young woman possessed by a Jewish demon, which Sherif Redwan fought and exorcised in front of the crowds. In a move to identify with tabloid readers, the author of this article even confesses that Sherif Redwan used his *baraka* to cure them from a possession that they had suffered from for years.

Some issues included front-page photographs of Sherif Redwan in action, exorcising demons and evil spirits from flailing people. The January 11, 1995, issue of *Political Rendezvous* devoted most of the entire front page to photographs of Sherif Redwan treating people, as featured in figure 4. The article inside the issue proclaims the newspaper's "complete and total recognition" of Redwan's *baraka*. Some issues printed interviews with Sherif Redwan about how he feels when he heals people. One tabloid included an exchange with his mother, who claimed that she could feel Sherif Redwan's *baraka* as soon as she was pregnant with him. Others issues included interviews with people Sherif Redwan cured who had been suffering from demon possession for years or even decades and went to his shrine after reading news about him in the tabloids. One girl in particular claimed that she had been possessed by a French demon named François but that Sherif Redwan exorcised him and even converted him to Islam. Another article shows Sherif Redwan reading a copy of *Political Rendezvous,* declaring that he cured a young girl from paralysis in front of massive crowds of trilling and crying women, selflessly working until dawn for those in need. In that article, he tells the journalist that the Skir's newspaper group "has become his second family," further cementing the relationship between the two.[23]

In the United States tabloids regularly print stories that Elvis is alive, Jesus walks on earth, and aliens are among us. They provide millions of Americans with news and information that are not deemed respectable to the mainstream news establishment but that those readers take seriously. Najib Skir used the same strategy but adapted it for the Moroccan environment. When his tabloids appeared in the fall of 1993, the massive working-class and semiliterate public in Morocco had never seen a newspaper cater directly to their personal and moral interests. With this focus, Skir attempted to appeal to the audience of non-elites that had followed the Tabit Affair but were once again shut out of the media in its aftermath, attracting this enormous readership for his highly innovative message of crime and punishment. While Skir's personal goal may have been simply to sell newspapers, his tabloids performed another function besides catering to the interests of the semiliterate public and making money. They marked the beginning of the interface between state and media to construct and disseminate new representations of crime and punishment in an attempt to manufacture the public's consent to state authority after the Years of Lead. With their enormous non-elite audiences, the tabloids would begin the long process of transforming the image of the police in society for the post-Tabit era.

Murder, Moral Panic, and the Breakdown of the Family

With their grisly covers and sensational stories, the Moroccan crime tabloids presented their readers with the image that crime was suddenly out of control and society was in danger of collapsing, just as the country was emerging from the long decades of the Years of Lead. The most common category of crime in the tabloids was the breakdown of the family unit, the cornerstone of traditional Moroccan society. The tabloids repeatedly covered cases in which one member of a family killed another, usually in a spectacularly horrible way. These crimes typically took place within a working-class home and demonstrated that ordinary families across the country were now facing the threat of unimaginable violence. Reflecting an outraged conservatism, the tabloids presented these individual cases of murder within the family unit as evidence that the world of tradition and moral values was quickly unraveling because of a new immorality suddenly destroying the core of society.

A particularly striking example of these kinds of stories appeared on the front page of the June 19, 1994, issue of *Political Day* with the headline "Girl in Oujda Killed Mother with Fiancé's Brother to Hide Scandal of Her Pregnancy." Directly beneath the bold headline and next to the title of the newspaper appeared a photograph of the dead woman with blood covering her ear and neck, together with the caption "The Murdered Mother." Beneath that image was a picture of a young man and woman, squatting next to bloodstained clothes and the murder weapons, with the caption "The Killers—the Girl and Her Fiancé's Brother." The article begins by describing the case, stating that the "cause of the disgusting crime was immoral acts."[24] The author explains that a man who works in France proposed to a young woman named Bouchra. After she accepted the proposal, the man went back to France to work for two more years so that he could earn enough money to provide a home for Bouchra and left his fiancée in the care of her adoptive mother. The man's twin brother, Lahcen, began visiting Bouchra and they started having sex without the mother knowing. The article details how Lahcen would hide under the bed or in the bathroom in order to avoid being discovered. Bouchra soon became pregnant and tried to have an abortion, but to no avail. She and Lahcen then planned to murder her mother in order to prevent her from exposing them. On a Friday, Bouchra left the house and Lahcen attacked her adoptive mother in the bathroom with a large pestle, hitting her over the head twice. When she fought back, Lahcen grabbed a butcher knife and "stabbed her deeply in the neck, as if he were slaughtering a sheep for the Eid." Lahcen then cleaned himself, changed his clothes, wiped the murder weapons of blood and fingerprints, tossed them in a nearby desolate area, and then went out "as if nothing had happened!"

The article presents a strong condemnation of the couple and of Bouchra in particular. Adoption is far less common in Morocco than in the United States and adopted children have significantly fewer legal rights in Moroccan society. The article therefore implies that Bouchra overcame the odds when her mother adopted her and provided her with a good home. Moreover, despite the social disadvantages that come with being an adopted child in Morocco, Bouchra managed to find a fiancé who worked in France and could therefore offer her not only financial stability but also the possibility of immigrating to Europe, a dream for many. Despite having the odds stacked against her, Bouchra had gone from being an orphan to securing an ideal life for herself. And that explains her deep immorality. Bouchra threw everything away by beginning an affair with her fiancé's brother and plotting to kill her adoptive mother. On a Friday, a day of prayer in Islam, the lover attacked and killed Bouchra's adoptive mother, "this poor woman," Najib Skir explained in a later article that he wrote on the case, "whose only crime was adopting the person who would be the cause of her murder."[25]

Throwing away a dream life in France, having an affair with the brother of her fiancé, plotting to murder her adoptive mother who gave her everything, the article presents Bouchra as the epitome of immorality. Her lover may have carried out the killing and disposed of the evidence, but it is Bouchra who represents the new face of crime in the country and the breakdown of the family unit in the most brutal and horrific way possible. Skir, however, does not present this case as an isolated event. Rather, for him, it is an example of what was happening in Moroccan society as a whole—the breakdown of morality and the disintegration of the family, both of which, according to the tabloids, were suddenly spreading at an alarming rate in society. In an article entitled "Phenomenon of Crimes of Violence against Parents in Morocco Is Continuously Escalating!," Skir writes, "Religious inhibition has died inside today's youth, who don't understand the meaning of the Quranic edict 'paradise is under the feet of mothers.'"[26] He reminds his readers that according to the Quran, children must respect and worship their parents at all times. Even expressing displeasure toward one's parents, Skir emphasizes, is unacceptable to God.[27] The tabloids present Bouchra's case in the context of a wave of murders against parents, not as crimes with individual motives but as evidence of a widespread moral breakdown striking the country and its traditional values. According to Skir, the example of a girl arranging to have her mother killed is "a repulsiveness that proves without any doubt that people of this century have lost their mind."[28] For Skir, Bouchra's crime indicates a much larger sin—that the basic tenets of the Quran are under threat and that society as a whole will face the consequences. For the tabloids, this individual crime of matricide comes to symbolize the moral disintegration of society on the widest possible scale.

In the tabloids, murder within the family is not restricted only to matricide. Many crimes are tied to adultery and detail how two lovers plot to kill an innocent spouse. Since the tabloids aim for the most sensational cases possible, they typically focus on a woman who cheats on her husband and then arranges with her lover to kill him, crimes that are reminiscent of the most devious film noir tale. Sometimes, however, a married woman turns on her lover instead. *Political Appointment* published a particularly gruesome example of this type in its January 18, 1995, issue. In this case, the author explains that a married woman began having an affair with a man and that the two would meet in another city to have sex. One night, the man slapped the woman as they were getting drunk. She then calmly went into the kitchen, grabbed a knife, and stabbed him to death. The article provides little motive for the murder. Instead of revealing what drove the woman to kill, the tabloid article simply links the origins of the crime to the act of adultery, suggesting that cheating on one's spouse can quickly end in murder. The author explains, "The path of depravity leads the one who commits it to destruction and the unknown. When people renounce their principles and morals and live empty from the inside, they lose their dignity and are capable of anything. Everything before them seems the same, good and evil, strength and weakness, beauty and wretchedness."[29] In the tabloids, adultery is not simply a betrayal of one's spouse. Instead, it has far-reaching consequences for all of society. Adultery undermines the sanctity of marriage and prevents the person committing it from differentiating between what is right and wrong, an ability that is the foundation of any moral society. In the new Morocco, the tabloids suggest, adultery can destroy people's morality, making them snap and kill for something as simple as a slap.

Another example of the disintegration of the family as a pillar of society appears in the repeated reports of young men in the prime of life attempting suicide. These articles present a particularly powerful message to the traditional working-class audience of the tabloids since the Quran explicitly forbids suicide. The front page of the November 22, 1993, issue of *Political Day*, for example, features a large photograph of a teenager hanging from the top of an electrical pole, threatening to jump off and kill himself. The article on the incident ties this act to an epidemic of suicides among the youth that is suddenly on the verge of overwhelming the country, stating, "It seems as if feelings of frustration, despair, and loss of hope in life have reached their height in the souls of some youth in our society."[30] In this case, the police manage to save the young man, but others were not as lucky. In an editorial on the shocking rise in suicides entitled "The Necessity of Heeding This Dangerous Phenomenon," Najib Skir writes that the increase in suicides is connected to the socioeconomic challenges of the new era: "This phenomenon is considered a wake-up call to treat a cancer that has come to eat away at the being of our youth. They are the foundation of our future and a country with a frustrated youth is like a building without a foundation that is threatening to collapse at any moment."[31] For Skir, suicide is not simply the result of individual depression or desperation. It originates in the lack of opportunities for the country's youth and comes to symbolize the decaying state of society. This theme would have struck a chord for the working-class audience that was facing tremendous economic difficulties as the country began its experience of political opening during the 1990s. In the tabloids, the current generation is killing each other because of immorality and depravity while the next generation, symbolized by the young man threatening to jump off the top of a telephone pole, is killing itself because of the absence of economic opportunities. When these kinds of crimes strike the family unit all at once, the tabloids suggest, anarchy could overwhelm the country at any moment.

Tabloid coverage of the breakdown of the family also extended to marriage engagements. The cover of the November 16, 1997, issue of *Incident News,* for example, shows the color photograph of a handsome and respectable-looking man next to following headline: "Greedy for Money, He Killed His Fiancée's Mother and Tossed Her Body in Fez Woods." The article begins by stressing how the socioeconomic crisis in the country has produced shocking crimes in various cities.[32] Fez in particular, the article claims, has "experienced a sensational spread of criminal acts." Despite the fact that it is the country's spiritual capital, the article explains, "deviance and criminality have attacked Fez, like the other cities in the country that were considered safe until only recently." The article then describes how Abdellah, a thirty-year-old barber, was engaged to Halima, whom he helped find work in Saudi Arabia. Halima would send her family money transfers to help them financially, like thousands of other Moroccans living abroad. She would write checks to Abdellah, who was supposed to deliver the money to her mother. "The devil played with his mind," however, and Abdellah only gave the mother a small amount of the money, keeping the rest for himself. When the mother discovered how much money he stole, she immediately confronted her son-in-law. The two began insulting each other and started struggling until Abdellah threw her down a flight a stairs, killing her instantly. Abdellah then dumped her body in the woods and joined his fiancée, who had just returned to Morocco, at a party.

Abdellah seemed as if he were the ideal son-in-law—handsome and caring, he even found his fiancée work in Saudi Arabia so that she could send money back to her mother. Nonetheless, the current economic crisis—something that struck the target audiences of the tabloids directly—changed him from the ideal son-in-law into the epitome of immorality. The article emphasizes that Abdellah not only stole and committed murder but also met his fiancée at a party after the crime as if nothing had happened. For the tabloids, Abdellah represented a morality tale—the socioeconomic crisis facing the country can turn anyone into a sociopath, making them capable of the most horrendous crimes possible. In this context, the tabloids suggest that something as respectable as an engagement stands no chance in the face of the moral panic striking the country.

The new tabloids linked individual and isolated crimes of murder within the family and presented them to the public through color crime-scene photographs as urgent and pressing evidence that society was suddenly spiraling out of control. The tabloids, which emerged seemingly overnight with their shocking headlines and unprecedented photographs, articulated a moral panic, using these crimes to show that the working classes in particular were being targeted by these sudden changes. The family, however, was not the only site of this crisis. Crimes of violence that used to take place in secret—but were now revealed to the public eye in the new era—also gave the tabloids powerful evidence that traditional society could collapse at any moment.

Evil Lurks behind Closed Doors

Another common message of the crime tabloids was that in the new Morocco, people could no longer hide degraded inner realities behind respectable outer appearances. This theme first appeared during the Tabit Affair when the party press printed details of Tabit's defense. Tabit reportedly projected a respectable and religious outer demeanor to help him cover up the horrible crimes that he had been committing for years. This same depiction emerged in the newspaper coverage of Arbad's crimes in Azzemour. Although he seemed shy and dignified to his friends and neighbors, Arbad committed sexual assaults against young men behind closed doors for over ten years. The tabloids seized on and developed this theme, highlighting cases in which deceptive appearances provided a cover for murder. In the tabloids, opening up buried truths and exposing hidden secrets—a consequence of media transparency and freedom of speech—only revealed ghastly crimes and immorality. This allowed the tabloids to cast the new era in highly ambivalent terms, fronting the deeply disturbing contradictions embedded in making private lives public.

One of the most striking examples of this type of crime appeared in the September 15, 1995, issue of *Political Communicator* with the following headline: "He Butchered Old Man Violating Him for 19 Years Because He Asked Him to Continue Sexual Deviance between Them, Even Though He Renounced It." The cover of this issue is featured in figure 5. To the right of the headline was a small image of the killer and beneath it appeared a large color photograph of the bloody and mutilated body of the victim. The article on the case inside the newspaper lays out the details of "one of the most disgusting crimes of murder that has happened recently."[33] It took place in the small town of Sidi Slimane and caused a sensation among the residents. On August 22, 1995, a man was found at home stabbed to death with deep wounds all over his body. The article, based on information from the police report on the crime, provides the exact address of the house and states that the victim, Abdelkader, was seventy-three years old. It also explains that the murderer, a man named Noureddine, was forty-one years younger than the victim. According to police sources, Abdelkader and Noureddine were lovers and the two had been having sex since Noureddine was a teenager. The article explains,

> The methods of deviance in this perverted relationship developed to the point that the victim started asking the killer to have sex with him so that the actor became the acted upon and vice versa. The two began having sex with each other back and forth, but the criminal soon complained about this situation since he was used to having sex on the victim. He wasn't able to satiate the desire of the victim, who insisted on playing the role of the actor in the sexual act so that, with his turn, he could fully satisfy his deviant caprices.

When Noureddine eventually refused to let Abdelkader have sex with him, this led to a violent fight in which Noureddine brutally murdered Abdelkader, stabbing him in his chest, back, and hands. Abdelkader then "cut his throat, just as young sheep have their throats slit."

Every week, the tabloids featured incidents of murder and violent crime because of personal disputes. This case, which appeared prominently on the top of the front page of the tabloid, announced to the public that some of those disputes arise because of homosexual relationships, yet another topic that had been taboo during the Years of Lead. For the traditional working-class public, homosexuality was immoral and deviant, a sin in the eyes of God. Its appearance in such a public way was yet another indicator of the era's declining morality and traditional values. As with reports on matricide and suicide, the tabloid, in its coverage of the crime, assumed the outraged perspective of a highly conservative reader, giving voice to their attitudes in the press. The article condemns homosexuality, detailing how homosexual desires lead to murder and showing how Noureddine used "the most extreme limits" of violence in committing his crime, dehumanizing his victim to the point of slaughtering him like a sheep for the Eid.

The article does not stop with this graphic depiction of homosexual violence. It emphasizes that before the murder, no one had realized that Noureddine and Abdelkader were lovers. Instead, the article explains, everyone in the neighborhood—including their immediate neighbors, the people closest to the couple—thought that they were father and son. This suggested to the public that shocking immorality was not only taking place throughout the country but also, perhaps, right next door, hidden behind the most respectable appearances as Noureddine and Abdelkader were able to fool their neighbors for years about the nature of their relationship. This implied that in the new Morocco, the family unit, the pillar of a moral society, had become a ruse for hiding "deviant" sexual relationships that could lead to the most brutal of crimes. By printing these kinds of cases, the tabloids did not simply suggest that homosexuality was widespread and nearby, regardless of appearances. The tabloids also pointed to the contradictions inherent in the evolving press freedoms and political liberalization, highlighting the unpleasant consequences of opening up spaces that had been previously closed to the public eye.

The tabloids repeatedly stressed that, in the new era, trusting respectable demeanors can lead to murder. The entire cover of the December 31, 1995, issue of *Political Day* is devoted to a gruesome murder that took place in Salé, which lies just north of Rabat. It featured four large color photographs: one of the victim, a timid-looking teenage girl named Lubna; another of her killer, a man in his late twenties named Fattah; a third of the room where he committed the crime; and a fourth of the place where he dumped her body. At the top of the front page appeared the bold headline in red and white: "In Moment of Recklessness and Capriciousness, Mild-Mannered Young Man Turns into Killer."[34] The full-page article on the case inside the issue begins by describing the calm and security that the Hay al-Ramal neighborhood in Salé had lived in for years, but, only a week earlier, it became the scene of a "shocking and disgusting crime." Fattah was, according to the article, "an object of trust for everyone" in the neighborhood. One family in particular treated him like a son and two years earlier, Fattah proposed to their oldest daughter. The article explains,

> She accepted without hesitation, especially since he was blessed with such a good demeanor with her family, just as he won the respect and appreciation of everyone who lived in the neighborhood. He was trustworthy to the degree that anyone who needed help with something would go to him because of his uprightness and excellent morals. The criminal was a gentle man, kept to himself, and didn't smoke or use drugs or anything of that sort. Everyone would bear witness that he was a true man in every sense of the word.

Because of Fattah's seemingly good nature and trustworthiness, he appeared to be an excellent match for their daughter. A week before this article was published, however, Fattah's fiancée's younger sister, Lubna, disappeared when she came to visit Fattah's sister. Her anxious mother came to Fattah's house to ask about Lubna's whereabouts and Fattah went out with her to help look for Lubna. The article adds, "The strange thing about it was that the criminal who, by that time, had committed his disgusting crime, was searching with them with signs of grief and pain on his face." Even at this stage, the victim's family did not doubt him in any way. The family went to report Lubna missing and the police came to the neighborhood to investigate. "The criminal was the first person they questioned and he replied to them coldly that the victim came to visit his sick sister, gave her medicine, and left." The police combed the area and quickly found Lubna's body in the trash bins at the entrance to the old Jewish quarter of the Salé medina.

Thanks to an eyewitness, the police learned that on the day of the crime, Fattah tried to have sex with Lubna, who was shocked at his advances because of the long-standing bond between him and her family. She refused him and defended her honor "because of her good manners and praiseworthy morals." According to the article, Fattah then attacked her "in a moment of recklessness," hitting her over the head with a sharp instrument and strangling her with a necktie. Fattah waited to dispose of the body but someone saw him as he carried it to the trash bins. With the criminal under arrest, the article explains that the victim's family "never thought that one day, this person, who grew up among them and spent eight years in their embrace to the point that he became a member of their family and an object of trust for everyone, would be behind the murder of their daughter Lubna, who considered the killer like her uncle and an indivisible part of her family." This crime was so sensational that it made the front pages of numerous tabloids and even the *Banner*, a daily newspaper.[35]

As in the case about Noureddine and Abdelkader, neighbors believed that they knew Fattah well. While Noureddine and Abdelkader conducted their relationship behind closed doors and hid it from everyone, this article on Fattah emphasizes instead how until the moment of the murder, Fattah was an open and integral member of the community. His strong morals and friendly demeanor led the community to place their trust in him. Moreover, the family of Fattah's fiancée had known him for years and, because of his character, were delighted for him to become part of their family. In the tabloids, when murder takes place, it is typically because of what is presented as a hidden evil, such as homosexuality, adultery, or some form of moral deviance. With Fattah, there was simply no indication—either in public or private—that he would one day commit murder.

And this is what made the crime so shocking and terrifying. The tabloids presented the case without any kind of motive, pointing only to a sudden break from sanity. In the blink of an eye, Fattah, someone whom the entire community knew intimately for years, tried to have sex with his fiancée's sister and then murdered her. Moreover, he was so cold about the crime that he was able to accompany the victim's mother while searching for Lubna with tears in his eyes and coldly lie to the police about his involvement in the murder. The sudden break from sanity allowed the tabloids to link this individual crime of murder to the moral disintegration that was supposedly spreading through society. Fattah did not simply represent the schism between respectable outer appearances and degraded inner realities; he also demonstrated how anyone, even the most trusted and admired person in the community, a beloved member of the family, could snap suddenly without any motivation. In the new era, according to the tabloids, violence can arrive from the most unexpected sources. The message was clear—trust no one.

In addition to these kinds of crimes, the tabloids commonly presented the specter of horrible violence for the most trifling reasons. In one case, for example, a young man stabbed someone to death for a bottle of wine. In another, twin sisters attacked a girl and beat her to death simply because they were competing for the affections of the same boy. In the new Morocco, the tabloids stressed with each issue, murder can occur for something as trivial as spare change, a couple of cigarettes, or even a pot of mint tea. These kinds of stories appear in tabloids around the world but take on a particular meaning in the Moroccan environment. The tabloids used them to frame the message that crime and immorality had spread across society in such an alarming way that even walking down the street or having a simple dispute could lead to murder. Only months earlier, there was almost no crime reporting in the media. Now, the tabloids depicted crime as erupting seemingly overnight, sounding the alarm that anyone at any moment could become a victim.

An Epidemic Eating Away at the Heart of Society

Another kind of degradation that the tabloids presented as striking Morocco in the new era was organized crime. Just as the tabloids focused on terrifying acts of violence, degradation, and the schism between appearances and reality, they regularly printed shocking stories about the spread of gangs and drugs in society. Organized crime, however, has a particular symbolic value in Morocco. It indicates that illegal networks are thriving in the country, escaping the hand of justice. There may be little the state can do to prevent an individual crime of murder that takes place at home. But organized crime implies that groups of people are conducting illegal activities over an extended time period and that the state remains powerless to stop them. The presence of organized crime therefore suggests that gang members are strong because the state is weak. During the Years of Lead, the press rarely printed news about organized crime because of the negative image it would have given the police, indicating that they were unable to control security in the country. Now, all of a sudden, organized crime erupted in the press and came to symbolize the country's deeply ambivalent experience of globalization and economic opening during the 1990s.

Many cover photographs in the tabloids feature arrested members of a gang standing over smuggled drugs, stolen goods, or weapons that they used to commit crimes. These articles feature headlines like "Fall of Big Time Drug Dealer" or "End of Dangerous Gang Terrifying Casablanca." As in cases of murder, the tabloids presented the specter of new organized crime as a threat to the ethical and moral foundations of society. These included organized networks operating both inside and outside Morocco not only for drugs, but also weapons and stolen cars. Other gangs specialized in kidnapping young girls and smuggling them into Gulf countries for prostitution or selling fake European visas and residence papers. These cases, with Moroccans featured prominently in the arrest photographs on the tabloid front pages, showed that they too were taking advantage of the new era of globalization and open borders. For added shock value, the tabloids focused in particular on women involved in organized crime. For example, one tabloid story printed details that police arrested a gang specializing in stealing cars, led by a masked young woman. Many of the articles on the dismantling of prostitution networks had women in charge of them, not men. The tabloid covers typically printed arrest photographs of the women in traditional Moroccan clothes, looking ashamed of their crimes now that they had been caught.

One of the first issues of Skir's tabloids featured the headline "Arrest of Drug Emperor with Firearms," together with a large color photograph of a wall of hashish, bricks of cash, walkie-talkies, bullets, and a gun. The article explains, "The drug barons still consider themselves a state within a state and are going to extremes in their transgressions."[36] Guns are not only illegal in Morocco but are extremely difficult to smuggle into the country. They are therefore rich with symbolic value. When a drug dealer is caught with a gun and bullets, it shows that they were able to flout the state and bring weapons into the country from abroad. Moreover, it indicates that drug dealers have weapons that could threaten public safety. For the tabloids, drug dealers are therefore operating cut off from state control, spreading an evil in society that is causing many of the crimes of violence that appear on the front pages. Dealers are a threat to the country's youth but also to its stability.

Organized crime was not only connected to drugs and weapons. It was also tied to illegal immigration, which represented an unexpected danger in the new era of globalization and opening borders. The cover of the December 31, 1994, issue of *Political Day* featured the following headline: "Tangier Police Stop Illegal Immigration Boat of Death Holding 15 Moroccans." Underneath this headline appeared a photograph of the group of immigrants—all young men and women—together with the arrest photographs of the two men responsible for the network. In the tabloids, illegal immigration represented a new form of degradation that was tied directly to the era of globalization and imposition of visas on Moroccans in the early 1990s. By the mid-1990s, tens of thousands of Moroccans were risking their lives to cross the Strait of Gibraltar in small fishing boats that were locally called the "boats of death" because of the number of drownings that resulted from failed attempts. The phenomenon of illegal immigration therefore represented a striking condemnation of the state and society, showing that thousands were willing to risk death in order to escape the misery of their daily lives in the country. The tabloids seized on this phenomenon and put it on the front pages as a way of condemning the new era in general and globalization in particular.[37]

Drugs were a particularly important issue for the tabloids, not simply because of organized crime and the threat they posed for the country's moral character. The tabloids described drugs and alcohol as the backbone of the new economy, linking the country's economic development in the era of globalization and open borders to the consumption of these addictive and destructive substances that produce escalating violence and destruction. Drugs were presented as a virus spreading through society and attacking the working-class public, destroying it from the inside because of addiction among the youth. Moreover, drugs represented the dangers of international smuggling, as the tabloids depicted Europe as trading hard currency for widespread crime and social disintegration in Morocco. The drug dealers were exploiting the recent opening of the local economy for their own personal gain while ordinary Moroccans—the intended readers of the tabloids—presumably pay the price by facing the moral collapse of society.

Week in and week out, the tabloids constructed the crime wave that threatened to turn people across the social spectrum into criminals and addicts. The tabloids opened up society for all to see, exposing the dark side of crime and degradation that had been hidden from public scrutiny during the Years of Lead. These shocking images—made immediate and pressing through front-page color photographs—demonstrated to the public, readers of the tabloids, and anyone seeing them on the country's newsstands, that the end of the Years of Lead also meant the spread of crime and violence. This image of social insecurity and instability positioned the tabloids to urge the public to demand that something be done to protect the country from what appeared to be rapid disintegration. Not surprisingly, the tabloids had the perfect solution to the crisis.

We Say Bravo to the Police!

The tabloids linked the spectacle of crime spiraling out of control to a new image of the police as hardworking and law-bound in arresting criminals and returning law and order to the community. Tabloid articles repeatedly depicted the police as a source of calm and solace, praising them for their effectiveness and presenting them as the public's only protection in the new era of crime and moral panic. By doing so, they sought to reconcile their massive working-class audience with the police of the post-Tabit era, attempting to provide the police with a new identity that was tied directly to the media depiction of crime, violence, and degradation.

The tabloids did not work alone to achieve this. The state provided them with the necessary materials not only to construct the crime wave and moral panic but also to encourage the public to demand a strong police force in a time of threat and crisis, encouraging a tough-on-crime response. Thanks to their depiction in the tabloids, the police took on entirely new characteristics that had little connection to the authoritarianism and brutality of the Years of Lead. They became the response for what had to be done to secure society in the new era. By collaborating with the tabloids, the state intersected with the commercial media for the first time, attempting to manipulate sensational depictions of crime and punishment in order to manufacture public opinion and remake the image police after the crisis of the Tabit Affair.

For example, in the case about Bouchra, who killed her adoptive mother, the effectiveness of the police in solving the murder counterbalances the shocking degradation of morals that the article presents. After Lahcen casually leaves the murder scene, the article states, "the vigilance of the Criminal Police prevented him from getting away with his crime."[38] The article explains how the police, while examining the evidence, astutely noticed that Bouchra was acting strangely. They then decided to question the friend who was with Bouchra when the murder took place and learned that Bouchra told her about the crime. They arrested Bouchra and moved to arrest Lahcen too: "With a very intelligent plan, one of the inspectors went to the killer's house and told one of his family members that he was their neighbor and wanted Lahcen to help him fix his electricity." Lahcen quickly emerged from the house for the chance to make some money and was immediately arrested. The two then confessed to their crime and told the police where the murder weapons and bloody clothes were located. The article explains that "this evidence, together with the killer and his accomplice, were presented to justice on June 13, 1994," only three days after the murder took place.

While this article paints a stark picture of the new degradation and brutality of crime in Morocco, it also presents a model for the new police. Hardworking, cautious, and alert, the police in this case quickly noticed that Bouchra was nervous, which led them to question her friend, who helped them quickly crack the case. Instead of simply raiding Lahcen's house, as they would have done during the Years of Lead, the police in this article present a ruse in order to encourage him to come out on his own free will. Once he does, however, it does not take them long to recover all of the evidence in the case and skillfully get a confession. The article therefore presents the police in a new light—a police that is vigilant, observant, and bound by the law. Moreover, the article emphasizes that the police cracked the case in only three days, showing how they act quickly to solve crimes that take place among not only the wealthy but also the working class. The photographs of Bouchra's case on the tabloid cover therefore emphasize two separate but related elements of post-Tabit Morocco—brutal and immoral crime is a terrifying new danger to society, but the new police are able to arrest the perpetrators and keep the shocking chaos at bay. Just as the tabloids constructed a new kind of criminality, they presented their audience with a new police to protect society.

As for the case of Noureddine, who killed his older lover, Abdelkader, the article emphasizes that the police overcame the odds in solving the murder: "Noureddine tried to hide all the traces that would guide the police, a fact that compounded the difficulty of the mission facing the team of investigators. Despite these challenges, they were able to arrest the criminal in a masterful way and in a short amount of time."[39] The blood that they found on Noureddine's clothes helped the police "clear up the mystery that surrounded the case at first." Noureddine initially denied any role in the crime but, the article explains, "he was in front of the intelligence of Mr. Mu'addib, the chief of the Criminal Police in Kénitra, and Mr. Rahmani, the head of the first unit of the Criminal Police, who both pressed the accused with hard questions and evidence. Before the cleverness and experience of the aforementioned officials, the criminal didn't have any other option but to confess to what he did." The article then states, "A meticulous police report, corroborated by photographs, was prepared so that the criminal could be presented to the criminal court in Kénitra." Emphasizing the intelligence, efficiency, and experience of the police, this article shows that despite the efforts of the criminal to cover up his crime, he was still brought to justice. Articles like this, which present real case information to the public, demonstrate that the police base their investigations on material collected at the crime scene and rely on hard evidence to solve cases instead of brute force.

In many cases, articles simply state that the police made an arrest after a criminal tried to escape. Even if a given article presents no detail about the investigation, the tabloids still find ways to depict the police in a positive light. Most articles end with a statement like the following: "In the end, the only thing left for us to do is to praise the earnest and responsible work of the members of the first criminal brigade, under the leadership of Detective Shiri, Inspectors Madih, Darbiki, and Abdelkafifi, and all the members of the police who work together to prevent crime from running wild in the city."[40] As in the previous example, naming individual officers in the media gives them a level of importance. It also encourages continuing cooperation between the police and the tabloids, giving individual cops a personal stake in the tabloids by seeing their names in print. These cops—and others like them—would certainly read about the coverage of their success in the tabloids and continue to collaborate with the tabloids in order to see similar reports in the future. Moreover, naming police officers not only singles them out for praise, but also encourages readers to see them as individuals, not faceless representatives of the system, and the public to see them in a sympathetic light. It is these individuals that solved a horrible crime but also continue to protect the city and its residents from future acts of violence.

After providing the gruesome and shocking details of a given case, the tabloids regularly praise the work of the police in fighting crime and soothing the fears of citizens. Articles typically describe the "intensified efforts" of the police as they work "day and night" to solve a case. They commonly end with a description of the police arresting dangerous criminals, saving a given city from their nefarious activities. Articles frequently add comments like, "We say bravo to the police!" or "We hope that the police continue their efforts without interruption to root out the evil of criminality and deviance."[41] An article about the arrest of a criminal gang in Meknès ends with, "And so the criminal activities of this gang were stopped thanks to the cleverness and vigilance of the team of young men who don't sleep for the sake of the comfort and safety of innocent citizens."[42] In another case about the arrest of a violent gang in Casablanca, the article concludes, "It only remains for us to point out that local public opinion has applauded this accomplishment, which the members of the first criminal brigade have achieved. For our part, we congratulate this team and its great vigilance in protecting the safety and security of citizens."[43] Another article that detailed how a young man killed his friend explains, "The vigilance of the police and their extreme prudence allowed them to arrest the criminal."[44] This article details in particular how an inspector received a phone call at one thirty in the morning from a resident of the city where the crime took place, tipping him off that the criminal was heading to the train station. Thanks to the participation of the public, the police were able to arrest the criminal after a "marathon" chase that lasted until five o'clock in the morning. The police here are so effective and admirable that the public is calling them at home in the middle of the night in order to ensure that criminals are brought to justice. The image of the police that used violence and repression to maintain public order for the elite during the Years of Lead is nowhere to be found in the tabloids. Instead, the tabloids present the new police as being completely at the service of ordinary people.

Tabloid photographs further emphasize this message. The front pages frequently state that the police arrested a "ghoul" or "the most dangerous criminal of the year" that had terrified the residents of a given city, commonly after a "Hollywood-esque" chase. Many of the accompanying photographs show menacing criminals with terrible scars. Others display arrested criminals in tears, holding up a plaque for the camera with all of the details of their arrest, emphasizing for the public that crime does not pay. Virtually all of these photographs are mug shots, taken by the police after arresting a criminal and bringing them to justice, showing how the tabloids fused official sources with mass-media sensationalism. These large color photographs of criminals, originating directly from the police stations and given to the tabloids, emphasized the effectiveness of the police, providing the audience with a powerful sense that the police were in control of crime, despite the shocking images and stories filling the tabloids. Seeing these mug shots on the covers of the tabloids as they walked by the newsstands, the public could confirm that order had been restored thanks to police vigilance.

The tabloids also encouraged sympathy with law enforcement by printing articles about dangerous criminals attacking and even murdering police officers. During the Years of Lead, such articles never appeared in the press because they would have indicated that the police were weak and vulnerable, pointing to an attack on state authority. But in the post-Tabit tabloids, depicting the police—and not just ordinary citizens—as under attack from the sudden new violence in society made them appear sympathetic, tying them more closely to the public, since they too were facing the dangers of the new era. One story of this type appeared on the front page with a large photograph of a dignified man in a police uniform next to the following caption: "The Victim Detective."[45] The article focuses on the extreme violence of how the criminal decapitated and cut up the detective's body, put it in plastic bags, and threw it down a well. It describes how the victim's wife and four children became anxious when he did not return home one night. Once notified, the police quickly cracked the case and discovered that the detective went to sell his Mercedes to a stranger, who attacked and killed him for the car and then disposed of his body. The article emphasizes that doing something as simple as selling your car could have horrific and fatal consequences in the new era, even for the police. The article ends as follows: "From this platform of ours, we fully condemn this disgusting crime that was committed against a policeman well known for his integrity, uprightness, and service to the general good, especially since he left behind a number of children. We present to his small family and to the family of the police our most sincere condolences." This article focuses on the police victim's good morals and strong family life. Unlike the articles about the police in the party press, here they become working-class individuals, with a wife and children. They are not only part of the social fabric—not cut apart from it, as during the Years of Lead—but they too have families to protect. This shows the public that the police are just like anyone else and face the same dangers spreading through the country. The police in today's Morocco can fall victim to the same kinds of crime as the working-class public, such as brutal murder for doing something as simple as selling a car.

Thanks to collaboration with the state, which provided Najib Skir with crime-scene photographs, mug shots, arrest reports, and other sensitive case information, the tabloids were able to construct a powerful image of violent crime and immorality spreading rapidly through society, especially when compared with the image of safety and security in the mass media during the Years of Lead. The tabloids emphasized that the new era of globalization and freedom of speech in the mass media was not one of progress and development but of anxiety, distrust, depravity, and fear. At the same time, Skir used the material that the state provided him to present the public with a blueprint for the new police who were needed for this terrifying age—intelligent, tireless, law-bound police who fight for the safety of working-class citizens in the face of this shocking decline in security and morals.

The Party Press Strikes Back

Predictably, the party press considered the crime tabloids tasteless and immoral, repeatedly attacking them as lacking journalistic standards. In particular, the political left, represented by the Socialist Union and its newspaper, saw Skir and his tabloids as a threat to the development of democracy in Morocco. To the left, Skir used his tabloids as a tool to spread fear in society and to present and reinforce the idea that the answer to crime was not political transparency but a stronger security force with less restraint. Skir, in their view, was calling for a return to the police state of the Years of Lead and a new tough-on-crime policy as the answer to what appeared to be shocking new crimes in society, an image that he was largely responsible for constructing in his tabloids.

The first attack in the *Social Union* appeared only about two weeks after Skir began publishing his crime tabloids. In it, the author decries the lack of censorship and oversight for these new weeklies, asking, "How, I wonder, could those charged with supervising the press permit the distribution of these kinds of disasters in an Islamic society? Is their goal more dissolution and the shattering of morals and family and human ties?"[46] The author argues that the tabloids should be shut down and fined, in accordance with Moroccan laws concerning obscenity in the press. At the very least, he argues, they should not be sold to anyone younger than sixteen years old and that it should be forbidden to display the tabloids on the streets and sidewalks, where anyone can see their covers. Finally, the author asks how the tabloids are permitted to appear on the newsstands without any kind of penalty, while the Ministry of the Interior monitors the newspapers of the political left closely and occasionally shuts them down for reporting on issues such as governmental fraud or corruption.

In the next article, which appeared six weeks later, Hadin Saghir, the well-known court reporter for the *Social Union*, makes explicit what the first author only hinted at. For Saghir, it was the Ministry of the Interior that was flooding the newspaper market with the tabloids in a direct attempt to contaminate the legitimacy of the country's press.[47] He argues that the appearance in the tabloids of arrest photographs and sections of official police reports—together with sensational labels like "dangerous criminal" and "blood-letter"—violates the rights of those charged with crimes, since these documents are published before suspects can defend themselves in court. According to Saghir, the final verdict is therefore issued on these suspects before they receive a trial. Saghir also viewed the tabloids as a direct threat to the country's mass media, charging them with lowering standards and lacking any kind of professionalism. Skir's high circulations were no doubt a serious threat to the party newspapers, but journalists like Saghir took aim at him first and foremost as presenting shocking crimes directly from police establishment sources as a way to call for the return of the police state. For Saghir, the tabloids were direct state propaganda published in a new and dangerously effective media form.

In addition, the party press saw Skir as particularly dangerous because of his audience of working-class readers, whom the left felt that they needed to win over in order to call for more political and democratic reform. For journalists like Hadin Saghir, Skir encouraged cultural and political regression back to the Years of Lead, not progress in freedom of expression or democracy. Moreover, for the party press, Skir, with his focus on sensationalism and sales, dangerously degraded the level of journalistic standards in the country by using simple language, unchecked sources, and amateur journalists who lacked basic training in the profession. In a three-page weekend section in the *Socialist Union* on June 17, 1995, entitled "The Sidewalk Press: Profiteering, Dissolution, and Derangement," various journalists attacked the tabloids for fabricating the news, spreading slander, and printing articles without standard sources.[48] This section also includes a comical anonymous confession of a former employee of an unnamed Moroccan tabloid who describes the editor of his newspaper as an illiterate profiteer who uses a network of café waiters and ambulant shoe-shiners as his "correspondents" and regularly pays for news or simply makes it up. The anonymous former employee warns readers to avoid this "media cancer that is getting out of control in the honest, clean, and committed media corps."

In the face of these charges, Skir defended himself vigorously. Days after the party press began attacking his newspapers, Skir issued a response in an editorial entitled "Every Freedom Has Limits."[49] In it, Skir ironically joined the *Socialist Union* in attacking the tabloid press, claiming that the country was witnessing an explosion of different newspaper titles, a state of affairs that represented the country's growing commitment toward political and media pluralism. At the same time, he argued, the new space of the mass media was discovering "a lack of restraint and regulation." According to Skir,

> We become sad when every Tom, Dick, and Harry issues vulgar newspapers without bothering even to look for editors with professional standards, since it's enough for them to pirate news from somewhere else and repackage it. For that reason, we say yes to freedom of expression, but only with imposing conditions on those who want to translate it to reality.

Skir therefore joined Hadin Saghir in calling for guarantees in the professional standards of the press. To Skir, his newspapers are not the ones that the left is criticizing. Instead, he takes aim at the fly-by-night tabloids that were springing up and competing with his weeklies.

When I met him in 2006, Najib Skir told me that the tabloid press supported democracy rather than hindered it. He said that crime reporting was a necessary component of freedom of expression in democratic countries and performed a great service to the public by providing an accurate image of what takes place in society. This stand was echoed in a long piece he published in the March 13, 1996, issue of *Incident News*. There, Skir argued,

> There's no doubt that the media, whether it be print or audiovisual, plays an important role in the process of enlightening individuals in society. These media, therefore, in our current era, have taken their place next to the home and the school to cultivate and educate individuals, both young and old. . . . Of course, these media convey everything that happens within society, whether positive or negative. . . . But some people, when they read the columns

of newspapers that feature photographs of tragic events, rush to pass judgment, describing them as presenting dangers that negatively influence society. They forget that these media don't make anything up, but that all these news, events, and photographs are from the heart of reality, a reality in which different kinds of events—and negative ones in particular—dominate since crimes such as theft, violence, rape, and murder, are on the rise.[50]

For Skir, newspapers like the tabloids uncover social reality and unabashedly lay it bare for the public. He casts the tabloid press as having a didactic role for the public, a function that should not be curtailed simply because most of the news is tragic. He therefore defends the tabloid image of society as being in rapid decline, arguing that his newspapers simply present real-world crimes that are an unfortunate but realistic part of society. Also in this article, Skir argues that his tabloids do nothing different from the press of democratic countries such as England, the United States, and France, whose newspapers present crime through a variety of narrative forms.

Nonetheless, it is easy to see why journalists like Hadin Saghir believed that the state backed the tabloids. The arrest photographs clearly came from police sources, as did the gruesome crime-scene images, proving that the state provided the tabloids with the raw material for the construction of both the terrifying crime wave and the new image of the police for the public. Moreover, many tabloid articles explicitly state that police reports were consulted in preparation of the news. Some articles quote directly from a police report, providing seemingly sensitive information such as the address, birthdate, and identity card number of the criminal or victim. Also, as the party press claimed, the tabloids repeatedly printed graphic stories about immorality but the state never shut them down. The tabloids praise the police for their efforts at bringing a criminal to justice in nearly every article. They single out particular inspectors and detectives for their hard work and self-sacrifice in the name of justice, presenting them in a highly positive light during a time in which the image of the police was at its nadir because of the Tabit Affair and the ensuing police scandals. As is well known, police reports published in the press present the agenda of the police to the public.[51] This would form another reason why the political left was so disturbed by the success of the tabloids during this period of supposed liberalization.

At the same time, the goal of this collaboration between the state and the tabloids was not necessarily an attack on the party press or civil rights, as Hadin Saghir claimed. Instead, it demonstrates how the state in general and the police in particular were adapting to a new media environment in which public opinion mattered. People across the country of all socioeconomic backgrounds followed the Tabit Affair, and the case demonstrated to the state that public attitudes were important. During the Tabit Affair, public opinion, voiced through the newly emboldened press, represented a threat to the state and the status of the police in society. Starting with the tabloids, however, mass media sensationalism became a resource for embracing that public once again. In particular, the state-tabloid collaboration sought to transform how the public saw the role of the police in society and the nature of state authority. During the Years of Lead, the police inspired fear among the public. The tabloids worked to shift fear from fear of the police to fear of crime, pushing the non-elite public to demand protection against the sudden and shocking new threat. The answer to this manufactured crime wave was the new police, a police that respected the law and was worthy of praise. Fear became a vehicle for building a new relationship between the police and citizen, a relationship that had continued to serve as the direct link between state authority and public consent in Moroccan society.

Compared with the United States, the strategy of using fear to bolster public support for law enforcement was nothing new. Throughout the twentieth century, fear has been used as a political tool to influence crime policy and manage public perception of the police. A well-known example of the fusion between popular culture and a crime wave occurred during the 1930s when J. Edgar Hoover was at the head of the FBI. This was the era of the "public enemy," the gangster, which stirred up widespread panic and fear among the American public. Hoover seized on this figure and presented the public with a new crime-fighter, the G-man, or FBI agent, as the only force that could rein in the new terror. According to Richard Gid Powers, Hoover believed firmly that "law enforcement . . . was dependent on public attitudes" and he collaborated with a variety of popular culture industries to present the public with images of G-men fighting crime in sources as diverse as cinema, radio, magazines, novels, and comic books.[52]

A more recent example of this phenomenon is the apparent crack crisis that spread through the United States during the 1980s. As Jimmie L. Reed and Richard Campbell have argued, the success of Reagan's war on drugs during that period was dependent on the mass media presenting the public with highly biased and terrifying reports on the effects of crack cocaine, leading to a moral panic in the country.[53] Moreover, during the 1990s—the same time period as when the crime tabloids flourished in Morocco—the mass media in the United States began relying on fear more and more for ratings and sales. As David L. Altheide has shown, fear not only increases audiences for the mass media but also helps justify expenditures for the police.[54]

Instead of working with the party press, which had always been hostile to it, the Moroccan state collaborated with an entirely new form of media that was based on the same principles as the Tabit Affair coverage. The Tabit Affair showed the state that sensationalism was a powerful tool for reaching the larger public. The tabloids put this lesson to work, targeting the massive working-class public with their double message of moral panic and urgent need for police protection. Nonetheless, the tabloids used a new sensational language and nonstate media format that was full of ambiguities and contradictions. These ambiguities helped produce a space for image production that did not appear, at least immediately, to be a direct product of the state. By using this new form of media to attempt to manufacture and direct public opinion, the state showed that it was moving away from violence, repression, and force for social cohesion. It was now participating in creating, managing, and directing public opinion, inaugurating a new form and function for authoritarianism in the country.

In Morocco, the formula of the state collaborating with the sensational and commercial media in an attempt to direct public opinion and remake the image of the police for the new era was innovative. Yet this was far from the end of the story. By October 1998, the country's first independent daily, the Arabic-language *Moroccan Events,* appeared on the newsstands and represented a significant step forward in freedom of the press. This newspaper quickly became the highest-circulation daily in the country, demolishing the sales figures of the party press. Its success was based on the combination of tabloid sensibilities with nonpartisan news reporting. In particular, it invented a new kind of narration, one that I call Moroccan True Crime, in order to blur the lines between police fact and fiction. Instead of focusing on fear, *Moroccan Events* turned real-world police investigations into entertaining narratives of crime and punishment that demonstrated to the public that the country was entering a new era of respect for human rights and the rule of law. Into the place of the tabloid cop that protected the working-class public from the sudden crime wave would step the law-bound, self-sacrificing, and, above all, sympathetic cop who defended all of society.

3 Crime-Page Fiction
Moroccan True Crime and the New Independent Press

The mid- to late 1990s was a particularly charged time in Morocco as the country continued moving away from the repressive authoritarianism of the Years of Lead. Not only did the media open up to new audiences and forms of representation but the state also initiated political, social, and legal reforms. Recognizing the need for more inclusive government, in 1993 King Hassan II launched the process of *al-Tanawwub*, known in French as *Alternance*, with the stated aim of bringing the political opposition into the government. Although they refused to enter the government that year, the political opposition, under the leadership of the Socialist Union, eventually accepted the king's offer after the 1997 parliamentary elections. Abderrahman Youssoufi, head of the USFP and former political prisoner, was named prime minister in February 1998. After over four years of public discussion, the inclusion of the opposition and nomination of Youssoufi marked a significant transformation in the political sphere and launched a period of widespread optimism about the pace of reform. The concept of *Alternance* was based on the idea that the country was entering a new era of power sharing and democratic transition, including respect for the rule of law, freedom of expression, and human rights.

Social movements and NGOs took advantage of this atmosphere of increasing change during the 1990s. Women's groups vehemently protested the Tabit Affair and continued their activities throughout the 1990s by opposing the highly conservative *Mudawwana,* or family legal code, which curtailed women's rights to divorce, education, and inheritance. Although the family code would not be reformed until 2003, women's groups became more organized and active throughout the decade, demanding improvements in gender equality through protests, newspaper articles, and other forms of public participation. The spread of social movements such as women's groups during this period demonstrated that the state was willing to permit more public dissent and freedom of expression in the new era.

Moroccan human rights NGOs also became significantly more active and emboldened during the 1990s. The beginning of this process can be tied to the appearance of Giles Perrault's book *Notre ami le roi* in 1990.[1] Although it was published in France and confiscated in Morocco, the book, despite its inaccuracies, brought a number of human rights violations and secret prisons to the attention of the international community. Partly due to significant international pressure at the time, many political prisoners were soon released and Tazmamart, the most notorious secret detention center, was shut down. Nonetheless, the survivors of these ordeals were treated as pariahs and the subject of political prisoners remained a taboo in Moroccan society until the mid-1990s when human rights NGOs became more prominent.

When King Hassan II appointed Abderrahman Youssoufi as prime minister in early 1998, the symbolism was powerful. Former political prisoners seized the opportunity and began publishing narratives of their experience behind bars in a variety of literary forms. While several prison narratives had been published in the 1970s and 1980s, they were immediately confiscated and banned. Starting in 1998 with the publication of *al-'Aris* (The Bridegroom) by Salah El Ouadie, dozens of works began appearing, marking not only a break with the Years of Lead but also a significant expansion of public expression and freedom of speech.[2]

Although the transformation in political participation, women's rights, and human rights has been well documented, the birth and rise of the independent daily press has yet to receive any scholarly attention. The first of these newspapers, the Arabic-language *Moroccan Events,* which first appeared on newsstands on October 22, 1998, the same year as the new *Alternance* government, marked the launch of a radical new form of media in the country. *Moroccan Events* not only signified a significant expansion of public discourse and freedom of speech—a tangible change in the new era of *Alternance*—but also shifted the country's daily press toward commercialism and sensationalism. Within only several years, the independent press would far surpass the party press in circulation and has remained at the forefront of the country's newspaper industry ever since.

Moroccan Events built its success by appropriating and transforming strategies of the tabloids in the daily press. Among other elements, the newspaper invented a new form of cultural production, one that I call Moroccan True Crime. In these articles, journalists used a fictional style to narrate real-world crime and police investigations. The inspiration for this new kind of writing did not come from the tabloids, however. The Arabic police novel, which first appeared in Morocco in 1997, provided the local precedent for narrating police investigation as entertainment and heavily influenced the newspaper's journalists. Although police narratives represented an innovative form of writing within modern Arabic literature, they would take on an entirely different cultural life in the pages of *Moroccan Events.*

The primary goal of *Moroccan Events* in printing sensational new narratives of crime and punishment was to increase sales and expand its audience. At the same time, the state helped bolster the newspaper's success by providing its journalists with real-world police reports on which to base their true-crime articles. The articles therefore served not only the commercialism of the newspaper but also the interest of the state in continuing to use the police as a vehicle in the media to recast the relationship between the wider public and state authority. Moroccan True Crime offered the state another nonstate language—one that was significantly different from the tabloids—for transforming the image of the real-world police among the broader public. The new form of writing blurred the lines between actual police investigation and fictional narrative, presenting the real-world police in the guise of a fictional hero who embodied the democratic values of *Alternance*. In the process, the state sought to push the public to see crime through the eyes of the police in an attempt to establish an unprecedented model of trust and cooperation between them.

Through the new independent press, the state continued fostering sensational depictions of crime and punishment in an attempt to maintain legitimacy in the new era and manage public opinion. By helping to create entertaining narratives of real-world police investigation in the daily press—and not only the tabloids—the state deepened its involvement with the sensational media. Since *Moroccan Events* was independent from the explicit political bias and control of the typical party or government newspapers, Moroccan True Crime, despite the ambiguities and contradictions inherent in its narrative style, served as a vehicle to disseminate a new nonpartisan image of the police in society and to show the public that the changes of *Alternance* had reached all the way to the heart of the police station. In the process, the police would continue to serve as the direct symbol of state authority. Instead of the repression and violence of the Years of Lead, Moroccan True Crime presented the police to the public as signifying a new era in which state authority implied respect for the rule of law and human rights.

Moroccan Events and the Tabloidization of the Daily Press

When the first issue of *Moroccan Events* appeared on the newsstands on October 22, 1998, an independent daily was a totally new concept, even though independent weeklies had been a regular part of the media scene in the country since the 1960s. Muhammad al-Barini, who was the editor-in-chief of the *Socialist Union* from its beginnings in May 1984 until 1995, served as the editor-in-chief of *Moroccan Events*. He published a large editorial on the middle of the front page of the first issue, introducing the newspaper and explaining its goals and purpose. Al-Barini began the editorial by focusing on the challenges and opportunities of *Moroccan Events*:

> Publishing an independent daily newspaper in the Morocco of today, at a time when the portents of the media revolution have begun to invade the cultural

and social sphere of the Moroccan citizen, ... is a difficult test, a large wager, and a heavy responsibility.... What we offer and are committed to fulfilling is the desire to make this media project serve the highest interests of our country and our people and to join in the fight to widen freedoms and achieve the right of information and knowledge, to create public life and political practice, to form a space for dialogue and application, and to participate in the movement to change and modernize the Moroccan media scene....

The independence of *Moroccan Events* is a real independence from political authority, governmental or nongovernmental, and from other general powers, central, regional, or local. The newspaper does not speak in the name of any political or unionist group, any organization or any financial or economic power, and is subject in its editorial line and stances only to what serving the general good and highest interests of the country impose on it.[3]

For al-Barini, the newspaper represented part of the widespread reforms that were taking place in the country during the late 1990s as part of *Alternance*. At the same time, according to al-Barini, the newspaper not only benefitted from these changes but also actively participated in them, expanding freedom of speech in the media. He emphasizes the newspaper's independence from political parties and other interest groups, indicating that it will address multiple points of view on a particular issue, not simply those that support the newspaper's editorial line, as the daily party press had done in the decades after independence.

Al-Barini instead stresses that the newspaper is responsible only to the "general good" and the greater public. Although this may sound like political rhetoric, al-Barini quickly clarifies why he places such emphasis on his readers:

In order that the independence of the newspaper hold up before various political and financial pressures, among others, it has to be directed, protected, and strengthened. *Moroccan Events,* which has no political or financial powers behind it to ensure its continuity, relies in maintaining its independence only on the support and backing of its readers....

Suffice it to say that *Moroccan Events* considers that its responsibility toward its audience is to win them over, to exceed all their expectations. In other words, this is the obligation of respecting the reader, not treating them with condescension or paternalism . . . and by respecting their personal life and right to respond to the news that concerns them or that they find lacking credibility.

Although he does not explicitly cite the party press, al-Barini takes aim at them. By setting *Moroccan Events* in opposition to other newspapers—and inviting readers to participate in the life of the newspaper—he criticizes the party press for belittling their readers. Al-Barini's strategy of creating a newspaper that elevated the status of readers was not simply based on political pluralism or expanding press freedoms. It was highly practical. Unlike the other daily newspapers in the country at the time, *Moroccan Events* was entirely dependent on sales and circulation. Al-Barini needed the widest possible audience for the newspaper's survival. Focusing on any particular political or interest group would only exclude others. Given the fact that advertising revenue in the Arabic press is meager and subscriptions are almost nonexistent, the staff of *Moroccan Events* faced a significant challenge. Although the strategy of "respecting the reader" marked a new phase in the daily press—a press that would not simply dictate political platforms to its readers—al-Barini and his journalists needed concrete strategies that would attract an audience large enough to sustain the newspaper and make it profitable.

Not having the financial backing that all other dailies enjoyed created precarious conditions for the newspaper, but it also presented opportunities. The party press in Morocco at the time could not duplicate the sensational elements of the tabloid press because they were responsible first and foremost for disseminating the political, cultural, and socioeconomic views and politics of the party that they represented. Since *Moroccan Events* was not bound by any such policies, it had the freedom to mix its political and socioeconomic coverage with proven journalistic strategies to increase sales, such as a sensational, personalized, and dramatic approach to news and information. Just as the sensationalism of the Tabit Affair served as a model for the tabloid press, the tabloid press in turn would provide considerable inspiration for the country's first independent daily newspaper. In particular, *Moroccan Events* appropriated the tabloid press's lurid and sensational focus on sex and crime to build and expand its audience.[4]

The weekly tabloids commonly incorporated taboo details about sex, but these were invariably presented as a kind of deviance threatening the moral core of Moroccan society. In the tabloids, sex was typically depicted as incest or adultery, disgraceful acts that were presented to their highly conservative audience as opening the door to even worse crimes, such as murder. The sex act was usually presented as illegal, especially when the tabloids covered pedophilia, prostitution, or homosexuality, which is still considered a crime in Morocco. Although the tabloids would front the salaciousness of sex, the topic typically served as a way to expand the lurid nature of a given crime and deepen the depiction of the country for the tabloid audience as facing dangerous moral and religious degradation.

Moroccan Events also used sex to shock its audience, but did so in a highly distinctive and innovate way: the newspaper presented sex as something identifiable to its readers, a topic that they could relate to in their daily lives. Sex appeared not as part of a horrific crime or further evidence of the country's moral disintegration, but as a topic that was present everywhere in private in Moroccan society but typically covered up and treated as taboo in public. With regular articles about the bedroom habits of ordinary Moroccans and the daily realities of prostitution as seen from the eyes of sex workers, *Moroccan Events* broke through important barriers in the media. Although the newspaper printed special weekend reports on sex, *Moroccan Events* concentrated its reporting on the subject in its semiweekly section entitled *Min al-qalb ila al-qalb* ("From Heart to Heart"), which featured readers' letters describing relationship and sexual problems and then asking for advice. It described in graphic terms not only sexual issues such as impotency and sexual dissatisfaction but also the pain of unrequited love and the disastrous personal aftermath of adulterous affairs. The newspaper typically published about two dozen of these letters on Tuesdays and then printed responses from readers on Thursdays. Considering the importance of modesty and privacy in sexual and emotional matters in the country, "From Heart to Heart" shocked the public and helped fuel the newspaper's commercial success.

The section's highly public, graphic, and sensational approach to sex and private relationship issues was not the only reason for its success. "From Heart to Heart" was the first section in a daily newspaper in which Moroccans from a wide spectrum of social classes could read open and realistic depictions of relationship problems. A less daring advice column had appeared in the Francophone daily *L'Opinion* during the 1980s, but this catered to a wealthy and well-educated audience. *Moroccan Events* was the first newspaper to do so in Arabic—a language read and understood by a much larger percentage of the population than French, the language of the former colonial powers—and had a much larger circulation. By inviting readers to submit their problems and also to respond to appeals for advice, the newspaper was able to attract a new audience that was thrilled to see the press treating subjects that most people faced in their personal lives but had previously remained silent about. The independent press broke a powerful taboo about discussing intimate personal matters in public, an element that served as another signpost for the sociopolitical transformations taking place in the country during the 1990s.

Sex was not the only shocking and sensational strategy that the newspaper employed to expand sales and engage readers. The other was crime. *Moroccan Events* followed the tabloids in focusing on sensational depictions of violence in order to build its readership. Starting with its second issue, which appeared on October 23, 1998, the newspaper printed crime stories every week in its Friday "Justice" section and by January 2002, they appeared every day. Like the tabloids, *Moroccan Events* focused on horrifying and graphic crimes, such as rape, patricide, and necrophilia. *Moroccan Events* also mimicked the tabloids' eye-catching headlines for its crime articles, both at the top of the front page and in the articles inside each issue. Examples of typical headlines include, "He Killed His Wife and Sat near Her Body Drinking Wine," "Female Students in the Prime of Life . . . Victims in the School Bathroom!," and "He Strangles His Lover to Prevent Her from Telling His Wife!" In addition, *Moroccan Events* printed articles about the same kinds of crimes that appeared in the tabloids. These most commonly included murder for the most trifling of reasons, such as for a single cigarette, a soccer ball, or spare change. In one article, a wife runs over her husband with her car after they had a fight over the furniture. In another, a man kills his sister when she refuses to do the laundry. Some articles detail matricide—a subject that was a tabloid favorite because of its religious and moral symbolism—while others narrate youth in the prime of life committing suicide. Additional story types that *Moroccan Events* appropriated from the tabloids include the butcher who sells sausage made from dogs that he stole from the neighbors, the witch doctor who swindles patients out of enormous sums of money, and the ironic twist, such as a man who goes to a doctor for knee pain and winds up losing his sight.

Even though *Moroccan Events* co-opted many elements from the tabloid press, there were fundamental differences between the two. First and foremost was the intended audience. With their large photographs and short, simple prose, the crime tabloids targeted a semiliterate readership that had been neglected by the traditional party newspapers for decades. Moreover, the moral outrage of the tabloids also appealed to the religious and cultural conservatism of their audience. The Tabit Affair uncovered this semiliterate audience in the country but it also proved that the educated public, which followed the press coverage of the shocking trial with as much enthusiasm, wanted sensationalism mixed in their daily news too. Before *Moroccan Events*, the daily press continued to ignore this audience of educated Moroccans who were likely repelled by the form and content of the tabloids. As a result, by late 1998 the traditional audience for the daily press had no "respectable" source for scandal, sensationalism, and crime.

Moroccan Events targeted this audience while, at the same time, working to differentiate itself from the tabloids. Focusing on political and socioeconomic issues and including daily national news from a nonpartisan perspective was not enough to distinguish *Moroccan Events* from the tabloids. It also had to dispense with the tabloids' trademark photographs of crime scenes and murder victims, on both the cover and inside pages. Doing away with the images and prioritizing text emphasized to the audience that the newspaper was intended for the educated public, even if it included the kinds of stories similar to those that appeared in the tabloids. Moreover, daily newspapers in Morocco had to have at least the veneer of respectability and *Moroccan Events* rejected the crime-scene photographs in order to avoid resembling the tabloids to people passing by the newsstands, even if the paper still incorporated eye-catching tabloid-style headlines.

Another way *Moroccan Events* differentiated itself from the tabloids was that it presented crime without the outraged editorializing that society was experiencing moral disintegration or the explicit praise of the police. Although many of the crimes that the newspaper covered suggest a decline of safety and security in the country, detailing, for example, how an abduction or murder took place in broad daylight, none of the articles include explicit commentary on a moral panic or breakdown of traditional values. By not assuming the outraged conservatism of the tabloids, the newspaper avoided catering to the social values of the traditional working-class public, leaving the social meanings behind each crime open to the interpretation of readers.

The most important step in distancing the paper from the tabloids—while still appropriating their story matter and sensational elements—was to expand the length of the crime articles and to infuse them with a style that was totally distinct from the dry tabloid prose. The text of tabloid articles, which was of secondary importance for the audience, was taken largely—if not entirely—from police reports. It was the images and headlines that sold the tabloids. *Moroccan Events,* on the other hand, focused on narrative style, expanding the length and sophistication of the prose of the crime articles. By doing so, the newspaper shifted the audience's attention from photographic images to narrative text. In the process, the newspaper invented a new kind of narrative form, Moroccan True Crime. Although the tabloids inspired the newspaper's emphasis on sensational and shocking depictions of crime and violence, the origins of Moroccan True Crime lie in an entirely different source—the new Arabic police novel, which first appeared in Morocco only a year earlier.

The Birth of the Arabic Police Novel

While the origins of the police novel, or police procedural as the genre is also known, lie in the United States in the mid-1940s with the publication of Lawrence Treat's *V as in Victim,* it was popularized in the 1950s, thanks to the television series *Dragnet* and novelists such as Hillary Waugh, John Creasey, and Ed McBain.[5] Unlike previous crime writing, the author of the police procedural places a cop in the center of the narrative, depicting how he employs actual police techniques to solve a believable real-world crime. Instead of using a masterful intelligence like Sherlock Holmes of the classic detective novel, the hero of the police procedural employs tools familiar from cop investigations, such as interrogation, forensic evidence, phone taps, twenty-four-hour surveillance, and informants.[6] While the hard-boiled Raymond Chandler–Dashiell Hammett detective typically works alone without regard for the law, the police procedural hero operates in teams, relies on his partners, and is bound by legal methods. Perhaps most importantly, the hero of the police procedural has a real-world counterpart—the recognizable cop who works in an understaffed department, defending society not only because it is his job but also because he and his family are part of the social and moral fabric that is threatened with each crime. The depiction of the police hero's family life was employed not simply to ground him in society. It personalized and humanized him, giving him a solidly middle-class way of life with which readers could identify. In turn, this allowed the genre to reposition readers, making them active rather than passive, transforming them into "secret accomplices" in the process of solving crime.[7] As Christopher P. Wilson argues, the human face of the police helped them "both 'stand for' public authority and 'stand in' for citizens themselves . . . to make the simulation between policing and citizenship reversible."[8] This strong link between readers and cop hero is one of the defining characteristics of the genre.

As the name of the genre suggests, these kinds of novels emphasized police procedure from the beginning. The genre fronts collaboration in investigating and solving crime, highlighting the role of professionalism, technique, and detached analysis, downplaying emotions, intuition, and individual perception. The emphasis on procedure in the genre during the 1940 and 1950s, according to Christopher P. Wilson, was "part of a broader reforming of political consent to police power."[9] The genre encoded public perceptions of crime and punishment, using them to rewrite the link between police and public. Moreover, the spread of the genre in the United States after World War II appears to have been tied to transformations in social expectations of morality and work ethic. According to Leroy Panek, "The morally ambiguous private detective did not well suit the middle class mores of post-war America, and the amateur dilettante [of Agatha Christie] had been growing more and more irrelevant even in the 1930s. . . . The moral, hardworking, middle-class man held more attraction for the audiences of the period."[10]

From the 1960s on, the police procedural became increasingly widespread in the United States. While television cop shows certainly helped popularize the genre, the police procedural evolved greatly thanks to significant changes in both the nature of crime and police work and their representations in the mass media. New and shockingly violent forms of criminality—as exemplified by the Boston Strangler, Charles Manson, and John Wayne Gacy—erupted into public view and repositioned the real-world police and their counterpart in fictional narratives. Thanks to this dialogic relationship between real-world policing and the police procedural, the genre, with each fictional case neatly solved, offered a way of soothing the public's escalating anxieties about crime.[11] Since the early 1990s, the police procedural has become extremely popular around the world as authors from countries as diverse as Cuba, Sweden, Angola, and Israel have adapted the genre to their political and cultural environments.[12]

The first modern Arabic police novel did not appear until 1997 in Morocco.[13] There are many reasons for this delay, such as the highly negative public perception of the police in the Middle East and North Africa, the status of the novel as an elite form of literary expression, and the lack of genre fiction in Arabic. An important factor for why the police procedural developed in Morocco during the late 1990s was the issue of political and cultural environment. At the time, the country was experiencing the sudden spread of widely read crime journalism, coinciding with what appeared to be a sharp increase in terrifying forms of urban violence. Moreover, the rapid political liberalization and expanding freedom of expression in the era of *Alternance* emboldened authors to begin experimenting with a variety of literary genres, such as novels focusing on the experience of political imprisonment and illegal immigration. The Arabic police novel appeared in the context of these changes and dialogued in particular with the new crime press and political opening that was taking place in the country.

The first police procedural, *al-Hut al-aʿma* (The Blind Whale), cowritten by Miloudi Hamdouchi and Abdelilah Hamdouchi, was published in mid-1997.[14] In the introduction to *The Blind Whale*, the authors describe the inspector, explaining,

> He's simply an instrument for logical interpretation, a person others can understand, with whom the reader can self-identify and create a friendship, wanting always to accompany on a new journey into a mysterious crime.... The intelligent cop becomes a loved cop, quickly turning into a people's cop, and this is what the spread of the police novel demands."[15]

For the authors, the cop is not simply a hero for the people. Readers must be able to identify with him to the point of being able to participate along with the police in the investigation. The model proposed here by the authors is something radically new in Morocco—while the tabloids encouraged the public to view crime through images of murder victims and the arrested criminal, the authors of the police novel attempted to shift the audience's perspective instead to the police and their investigation. The cop here is therefore not simply someone whom readers can see themselves in. The genre does not simply invite readers to participate in the process of solving a crime. Rather, the spread of the police novel, according to the authors, necessitates a widespread symbiosis between the character of the cop hero, the act of criminal investigation, and readers. There needs to be a shift among the public from simply seeing crime to seeing crime through the eyes of the police.

After reminding readers that the police novel emerged in neighboring Spain only in 1974 with the fall of Franco, the authors explain their ambition and objective:

> We, then, are setting the first brick in the project of a Moroccan police novel because we believe that this literary type is able to dissect social truth, especially since Morocco is experiencing great changes on the legal level and the rights of the individual. The goal of a Moroccan police novel is to accompany the movement of society and to create a kind of legal education for the reader.[16]

Drawing a parallel between Spain in 1974 and Morocco in 1997 is both daring and highly optimistic. It implies that Morocco is emerging out of decades of brutal authoritarianism and beginning a process of widespread economic, political, and social reform similar to that of post-Franco Spain. The authors see the police procedural as reflecting large-scale social change taking place in the country. At the same time, the authors claim that the novel serves a didactic purpose for readers. By participating with the cop in the investigation, readers become more aware not only of the law and the steps in a criminal investigation but also of civil and human rights.

Explaining the character of the novel's cop hero, Detective Yaqdhan, the authors explain, "He is, quite simply, a citizen who is wholeheartedly devoted to his work. . . . Accomplishment for him is not an issue of intuition or personal insight as much as working hard, analyzing facts, constructing theories, and applying the law."[17] Yaqdhan is not only diligent and incorruptible. He also operates according to facts and the law, selflessly following the evidence wherever it might lead, regardless of the consequences. The image of the sleuth, subjectively working on intuition and hunches, has no place in the new Morocco. Rather, the authors emphasize, Yaqdhan is simply a vehicle for evidence-based analysis, consistent application of the law, and rational formulation of leads. This is the new cop for the new era, the representative of a force that bears no connection to the repressive and brutal police of the Years of Lead. Instead, Yaqdhan is the embodiment of not only the public but also the new era's democratic ideals.

Set in modern-day Casablanca, *The Blind Whale* begins as Detective Yaqdhan is interrupted on a day off to respond to the shooting death of a young Moroccan woman. Although murders have been on the rise, the police in the novel are shocked at the sheer audaciousness of the crime since there is strong gun control in Morocco. The police identify the victim, discover that she had an Italian boyfriend, and soon locate him but find that he too has been shot to death. Under heavy pressure because of sensational newspaper reports on the case and the murder of a foreigner, Detective Yaqdhan must solve the killings quickly. Yaqdhan soon reveals that the victims had a connection with a Spanish man who directs a large import-export company that operates out of the Casablanca port. The police know that they are on the right track when two men brazenly try to shoot Yaqdhan soon after he questions the Spanish man. The police then place the Spaniard under surveillance and record a puzzling phrase after tapping his phone: "The blind whale in the water, same song."[18] Thinking it might be related to drug trafficking, Yaqdhan goes to talk with a reformed drug lord, who helps him crack the puzzle of the phrase: it means "hashish, night, at the port, same way."[19]

The detective and his partners rush to the port to intercept the Spaniard's cargo boat and find large amounts of hashish stuffed in olive cans. The Spanish exporter is arrested but denies any involvement in the murders or the attack on Yaqdhan. The police believe, however, that the Italian victim was killed for trying to blackmail the Spaniard after he found out about the smuggling operation.

The police also think that the Moroccan woman, the first victim discovered, was murdered simply because she could have provided the police with information about the blackmail. The novel ends as Yaqdhan is called to the house of the reformed drug lord who revealed the meaning of the puzzle—he too has been found shot to death. Although the Moroccan police solved the local case of drug smuggling through the Casablanca port, the novel's ending shows that they are powerless to stop the international mafia that controls the country's drug networks and can order professional killings at will.

The Blind Whale takes a number of key elements from the police procedural as a genre and localizes them in the Moroccan environment. One of the most prominent of these is the depiction of the cop hero as a middle-class family man. For the first time in the history of Arabic fiction, a policeman is portrayed at home with his wife and kids, a depiction that humanizes his character. Emphasizing this aspect, the novel opens in the detective's apartment. When the text introduces Detective Yaqdhan in the novel's second paragraph, he not only has a name, but also a full physical description:

> He was in the bathroom, shaving in front of the mirror. He was a large, tall man, about six foot one. He had a thin mustache that was short on both sides. His hair was graying without any trace of going bald. . . . Even though he was only about fifty years old, his face preserved the features of the shy child that he was in his youth. He took a long time shaving while singing songs off the cuff.[20]

Unlike the nameless and terrifying cops of Moroccan prison narratives, Yaqdhan resembles a timid boy singing while shaving in the bathroom. The text then explains that Yaqdhan and his family live in a middle-class neighborhood of Casablanca. The initial pages also describe the rest of his family. Jamal is Yaqdhan's fifteen-year-old athletic son who goes to a Thai boxing club and harasses his sister, Samira, who is thirteen. Yaqdhan's wife, Halima, is thirty-eight years old and attractive. She works in the same bank where the family took out their mortgage. In addition to physical descriptions and basic character information, this opening scene introduces readers to Yaqdhan's family problems, which are common in any home—Halima, for example, complains about Jamal's aggressiveness and asks Yaqdhan to discipline him. With this first chapter, the text demonstrates how the police in the country have a home life like any other middle-class family, a move that humanizes the cop hero and makes him sympathetic, linking him to readers from the beginning of the novel.

When the phone rings and the police call Yaqdhan down to the first murder scene, the repeated conflict between the cop's work and home life emerges, another common element of the genre. As the detective selflessly leaves to join his colleagues, Halima is furious that their planned Sunday lunch now has to be postponed for the fourth week in a row because of Yaqdhan's work. She is also angry that he comes home late at night and neglects his children because of his job. At the same time, she tells him throughout the novel how she is appalled and terrified by the rising levels of crime and declining morality in the country, much like the audience of the crime tabloids. The conflict between work and home life points to the intersection between the detective's family and society. Yaqdhan is a cop defending not only the streets against shocking violence but also his family. Yaqdhan and his family do not live cut apart from society and above the law, as the police did during the Years of Lead. They are grounded in society and have a personal stake in the country's security. The cop, through the depiction of his home life, becomes part of the social fabric that the police protect every day on the city streets.

Yaqdhan's family and home life are not the only elements that differentiate him from the cops of the Years of Lead. As soon as he arrives at the first crime scene, other important aspects emerge. He examines the area closely with his partner for clues that others might have missed while the forensic team processes the crime scene and carefully collects material in plastic bags in order not to contaminate any evidence. Teamwork—another important connection with the police procedural genre outside Morocco—is a theme that runs through the novel as Yaqdhan's partner, Inspector Omar, accompanies him at each stage of the investigation and plays an important role in uncovering pivotal case evidence. Much of the narrative is taken up by their legwork in conducting the investigation: they question the Moroccan victim's mother and coworkers, the employees at the port companies, concierges, and other suspects. In order not to compromise their investigation, the pair not only know the law but also respect it when they confirm suspect identities, bring the appropriate number of witnesses when they conduct searches, and perform surveillance. Moreover, when the commissioner wants to arrest the Spaniard after the police discover the second body, Yaqdhan is careful to wait since they do not yet have sufficient evidence to secure a conviction.

At the same time, the case is not left solely to Yaqdhan and his partner. The entire police station works together to solve the crime. The ballistics office analyzes the bullet casings and trajectories, the records department helps identify the victims, and the medical examiner walks Yaqdhan through the autopsy in order to uncover clues to the slayings. The novel depicts a police force that collaborates in investigations but also uses forensics, science, and proper legal procedure to secure fast results working under tremendous pressure. Although the novel encourages the audience to participate in the case through the central figure of Yaqdhan, police work is very much a team endeavor. The novel presents this as a paradigm shift in Morocco—cases are now solved through the collaboration and oversight of multiple people and offices, showing that trumped-up charges and fabrication of evidence by corrupt cops is no longer possible. Teamwork therefore becomes a way to emphasize the rule of law and transformation of the police in the new era of *Alternance*.

Another important element of Yaqdhan's character is his self-sacrifice, establishing a new model for the police of the post-Tabit era. Much like the detectives of police procedurals in other countries, Yaqdhan stays at work late and gets up early in the morning to return to the investigation, regardless of how exhausted he is. While there is no clear boundary between his work and home life, his profession always takes precedence. After they initially question the Spaniard about the investigation, for example, Yaqdhan gets a call by someone claiming to have information about the case. He leaves his family during dinner to go to the Hyatt in central Casablanca to meet the caller but two men on a motorcycle shoot at him in the hotel parking lot. The attack is an audacious challenge to the authority of the police. It shows how the detective too is at risk—like the public—in this new era of crime, a strategy that the tabloids employed to make the police more sympathetic to readers. The bullets, however, only graze Yaqdhan and after being treated at the hospital, he is quickly back on the case. Emphasizing his self-sacrifice and how he is simply a vehicle for the application of the law, Yaqdhan tells his partner, "Even if they kill me, the investigation will continue."[21]

As for the first victim, a young Moroccan woman named Hind who came from a poor family, the police investigate her murder with great care, showing that they treat all cases the same, regardless of the socioeconomic background of the people involved. The police serve not only the wealthy but also those without any money or connections, emphasizing how the law is now applied in a democratic way in the new era. At the same time, Hind's character displays an important element seen in the tabloid press. She initially appears to be a conservative young woman forced to work at a bakery to support her family after her father died. Nonetheless, the police reveal that she was leading a double life. Despite her modest appearance, she was secretly dating an Italian man who would take her to upscale restaurants and nightclubs, buy her expensive clothes, and bring her back to his apartment for sexual encounters. Hind lived at home but her mother had no idea about her relationship with the Italian or even about her expensive clothes. During the Tabit Affair, the press revealed the double life of the police to the public eye. In *The Blind Whale*, however, it is the police who reveal the double lives of others, turning the tables on who has the power and authority to make private lives public. In the tabloids, the schism between respectable appearances and degraded inner realities typically provides a cover for someone to commit murder. Hind, however, becomes the unwitting victim of her double life as she is killed because of her secret relationship with her Italian boyfriend.

Hind is not the only person in the novel manipulating appearances to mislead others. The Spanish suspect is described as having great wealth and elite status in Morocco. The police investigate him with extreme care for fear of attracting unwanted attention from the embassies and international human rights organizations. Nonetheless, the police in the novel soon reveal that despite appearances, the Spaniard is operating an import-export business as a cover to smuggle hashish out of Morocco. As in the tabloids, this points to Morocco's anxious encounter with globalization in the new era of opening borders. Europeans have come to the country ostensibly to participate in opportunities resulting from economic liberalization during the 1990s. The Spaniard, however, exploits this new terrain—and his privileged status with the police—to run a drug-smuggling operation and deflect attention from his activities. Just as with Hind, the novel depicts the Spaniard's double life as symptomatic of the new era, highlighting the role of the police in grappling with its contradictions and uncertainties.

An important connection between *The Blind Whale* and the global police procedural is the novel's ending. Many recent police procedurals from diverse national literatures do not end with clear resolution. From Henning Mankell's *Faceless Killers* to Luiz Alfredo Garcia-Roza's *A Window in Copacabana* and Miyuki Miyabe's *All She Was Worth,* police procedurals since the early 1990s have repeatedly refused to present readers with a neat solution to the case at the center of the novel, favoring ambiguity instead.[22] *The Blind Whale* also fits this paradigm, but adds a new perspective. While Yaqdhan cracks the case of the hashish smuggling, none of the murders are solved at the end of *The Blind Whale*. In fact, the final scene, in which Yaqdhan stands at the edge of the swimming pool staring at the reformed drug lord's floating body, indicates a form of chaos that is barely kept at bay. Guns are the instruments of new terrifying crime in the novel and criminals are startlingly experienced and professional. The killer fired on both Hind and her Italian boyfriend at close range and without any resistance. Both victims were shot several times, while the reformed drug lord was shot six times. They were not simply murdered, the novel suggests. All three were victims of overkill. Ballistics prove that the same gunman killed the first two victims, but that is all the evidence the police have in the case. Since the police at the end of *The Blind Whale* have no other leads on the shockingly violent and professional killer, the novel ends not with a fully solved crime but with an image of the country's detectives, embodied by Yaqdhan, as steps behind the killer, powerless to stop the next murder.

This certainly suggests a form of weakness on the part of the police. Nonetheless, within the Moroccan context, it points to a highly positive image for the police, an image that had never appeared before in the country. The police have no evidence to make an arrest, so the crime remains unsolved. During the Years of Lead, news of unsolved police investigations—let alone a triple homicide committed with a gun—never appeared in the media. In *The Blind Whale*, the press follows the case and prints sensational news about the ongoing investigation but the police do not solve the murders. Rather than condemning the police as weak, it suggests that they fail to make an arrest because they do not yet have sufficient evidence in the case. This new police, symbolized by Yaqdhan and his partner, are bound by the law and willing to appear weak if that means that the law is respected. The police do not need to produce arrests in order to establish their legitimacy for the public. Instead, they gain legitimacy by obeying the rule of law. Despite the sensational and terrifying nature of the crimes, the police cannot make an arrest if they do not have evidence. The authors of *The Blind Whale* incorporate the unsolved ending, commonly found in other global police procedurals, in order to show that the rule of law and proper procedure of the new era now trump the old image of the police from the Years of Lead.

The Blind Whale marked a new beginning in fictional representations of the police in Morocco. Between 1999 and 2003, both Miloudi Hamdouchi and Abdelilah Hamdouchi published some fifteen police novels that continued to develop the image of crime and police work that they established in *The Blind Whale*.[23] Despite the highly innovative step of localizing the police procedural in the Moroccan context and creating a new image of the police that matched the democratic aspirations of *Alternance,* their work had a highly restricted audience. The readership for novels is extremely limited throughout the Arab world, and Morocco is no exception. Selling only a few thousand copies of a novel in Morocco makes it a bestseller. Moreover, the two Hamdouchis did not inspire imitation, as they remain the only authors of Arabic police novels in Morocco. Nonetheless, the new image of the Moroccan cop as sympathetic, self-sacrificing, and law-bound would soon be disseminated across the country to the wider public in other forms of media, including newspaper articles and television movies. The first step in this process was the way the Arabic police novel influenced the new independent press. The image of the police and the narrative style of the Arabic police novel would form the basis for the new true-crime narratives in *Moroccan Events*. In turn, this form of cultural production would mediate a new kind of relationship between the state, police, and citizen for the new era.

Moroccanizing True Crime

True crime is the most popular form of nonfiction writing in the United States. According to Anita Biressi, the Anglophone version of the genre is comprised of "non-fiction narratives based on actual events, packaged and promoted for entertainment as 'leisure reading.' They may be of any length from a feature article to a book study but, unlike reportage, the event does not have to be contemporaneous or currently newsworthy."[24] True crime is therefore quite distinct from police fiction. While both may share similar narrative properties and serve as entertainment for readers, true crime is intimately linked to an act that actually took place. As Biressi explains, "It is true crime's anchorage to real events, people and experiences that defines its very form and substance."[25] This allowed true crime to focus on not only real-world violence but also the police that investigate each case. As Christopher P. Wilson argues, true crime encouraged "a generalized law enforcement ethos," providing the police with a "startling new visibility in American mass culture."[26]

At the same time, the fictional element of the genre should not be ignored. According to Mark Seltzer, "True crime is crime fact that looks like crime fiction."[27] The first modern example of the genre is widely seen as Truman Capote's *In Cold Blood*, which set the standard for future writers. Jane Murley argues that the novel's innovations "include the shaping of real people into literary characters and the introduction of fiction-writing techniques into non-fiction writing."[28] True crime therefore shares many of the narrative properties of crime fiction, such as dialogue, suspense, and other forms of dramatic techniques. In fact, Mark Seltzer argues for a direct link between the genre and the novel: "True crime... knowingly takes the crime novel as its prototype and tries it out on real life."[29] Seltzer suggests a kind of experimentation on the author's part, a genre that is always in flux but remains bound by fictional narrative applied to real-world crime.

There are important differences between Anglophone and Moroccan True Crime. First and foremost, the genre exists only in newspapers in Morocco. There are no true-crime books written in Arabic or French detailing the career of a particular criminal and how the police brought them to justice. Moreover, just as the police novel has no direct literary precursors in Arabic, true crime is an entirely new form of writing in Morocco. In the United States, on the other hand, true-crime narratives can be traced to nineteenth-century execution sermons.[30] When the genre emerged in *Moroccan Events* in the fall of 1998, nothing like it had appeared before in the press. The style therefore clashed with typical crime reporting, which was a dry narrative based on the facts of a police report. Finally, while certain journalists, such as Abdelmajid Hachadi, became particularly skilled at writing true-crime narratives in Arabic, no single author has become synonymous with the genre. There is no Moroccan William Roughead, Ann Rule, or Truman Capote. Instead, there are dozens of journalists who write the genre.

Moroccan True Crime, like the genre in English, is a fictional narrative of crime and punishment that is based on actual events. It features common fictional conventions, such as character description, dialogue, flashback, and plot development. While it looks like fiction, the genre only appears in the press. Much like the Anglophone genre, Moroccan True Crime is produced for commercial purposes, especially since it helped fuel the success of the country's first independent newspaper that was entirely dependent on sales for its survival. Journalists get case information directly from the police report on a real-world crime but instead of simply quoting the report, they turn it into a fictionalized narrative that is intended for popular entertainment. Its mode of production, the newspaper article, directly restricted and shaped the narrative possibilities of the genre. As the newspaper became more and more successful, however, it eventually expanded its true-crime articles to match the length of the novels, allowing journalists to mature the representational properties of the genre and blur the lines between depictions of real acts of crime and fictional narrative in increasingly sophisticated ways.

Unlike the tabloids, Moroccan True Crime does not attempt to explain the ontology of crime. In the tabloids, crime occurs because of widespread moral disintegration, a construction that exploited fear in order to mobilize the public to demand a strong police to protect society. In Moroccan True Crime, crime occurs for purely individual reasons without any larger moral implications behind each incident. At the same time, the genre in Morocco has a didactic function—it produces knowledge not only about crime but, most importantly, about the police, the legal system, and the rule of law in the new era, especially since the genre, while designed for entertainment, explicitly depicts real-life events.

Since the police cooperated with journalists and provided them with the police reports on which they based the articles, Moroccan True Crime also reflects an indirect attempt on the part of the police to control their image in the mass media, just as they did with the crime tabloids. The genre therefore also represents a new nonstate language and mode of representation for using entertainment to present the public with a radically new image of the real-world police. In the process, the genre works to encourage readers to see crime through the eyes of the police by employing a mystery-puzzle format and suspense-filled prose. It situates the police as the double of the reader—fusing the two—as they investigate a case and bring the perpetrators to justice.

In 2006, when I first met Abdelmajid Hachadi, the main true-crime journalist for *Moroccan Events*, he told me that he was an avid reader of the Arabic police novels and set out to imitate their style in his crime articles in an effort to increase readership for the newspaper. As Mark Seltzer claimed about the Anglophone genre, Moroccan True Crime is therefore an attempt to apply the Arabic police novel to real-world crime. In the process, journalists like Hachadi present the public with a real-world cop with the characteristics of Detective Yaqdhan in *The Blind Whale*, a policeman who embodies the democratic ideals of the new era of *Alternance*. Thanks to this new fictionalized image of the real-world police—and their direct connection to state authoritarianism—the genre disseminated a new paradigm for state power, one that had left behind the repression of the Years of Lead and moved into an era of respect for the rule of law and human rights. The genre therefore allowed the state to use fiction as an engine to improve on the image of the real-world police for the larger public, shifting popular attention away from crime to policing, presenting the public with a new kind of police that served as a signpost for their evolving relationship with the state.

Moroccan True Crime took some time to develop. During the first few months of publication, journalists experimented with a variety of narrative strategies in their crime articles. They structured most of these articles in the form of a confession, a legitimizing gesture that ties up any loose ends in a police investigation. The narratives typically begin by quoting the criminal as they detail the events that led up to the incident, providing them with nuanced character development and taking their perspective in the narration. Instead of simply condemning the criminal, as was common in the tabloids, journalists give them a somewhat sympathetic depiction, seeking to explain the individual circumstances that led up to the crime. Nonetheless, the newspaper was careful not to appear overly sympathetic with the criminal. These articles typically narrate murder in gruesome detail and, despite possible mitigating circumstances, show how the criminal is found guilty of murder before the law. These early articles therefore present the killer paradoxically as both a sympathetic victim of events beyond their control and a brutal criminal deserving of punishment.

Unlike the tabloids, the police are almost nowhere to be found in these early articles. The narratives typically begin after the criminal has already turned himself in to the authorities and sits confessing his crimes without any kind of police investigation. Unlike the tabloids, which typically explain that the police caught a suspect and praise them for their vigilance, *Moroccan Events* sidelined the police entirely at this stage. Although the police are almost absent from these first narratives, they still connect the position of the police with that of the reader. Both serve as the audience for the criminal's confession.

The initial true-crime articles form a transitional period since the newspaper could not—at least at first—appear overly sympathetic with the police. Doing so would have jeopardized the newspaper's claims on political independence and disengagement from the government or palace. Presenting the police in a positive light, especially when only the tabloids, with their ambiguous political allegiances, praised them, would have suggested that the state was meddling in the new independent press. And that would have compromised the newspaper's appeal and threatened its livelihood from the beginning since the public was turning to the newspaper partly because of its independence from political and state power. Starting in early 1999, however, journalists began lengthening their depictions of police work until the true-crime articles reached their final form and presented the public with highly stylized narratives that featured all of the hallmarks of police fiction, positioning the reader as the partner—even the double—of the police as they investigate real-world crime.

Seeing Crime through Police Eyes

In early 1999, some two months after *Moroccan Events* first appeared on the newsstands and began building its readership with sensational depictions of crime and sex—in addition to nonpartisan political and editorial coverage—journalists began the move toward focusing their crime articles on police investigations rather than criminal confessions. This started when journalists added a simple explanatory narrative in the final paragraph or two of an article to detail how the police solved the case. It soon expanded to match the narrative form of the police procedural. Many of the strategies for presenting the police as sympathetic were adapted directly from the Arabic police novel, such as depicting the detective's home life, self-sacrifice, and respect for the rule of law. By co-opting and disseminating the strategies of the Arabic police novel in journalistic depictions of real-world crime, *Moroccan Events* brought the style of police fiction to hundreds of thousands—if not millions—who would never have encountered it. In the process, they also took the first step in the mass media to spreading new images of the real-world police along the lines of a hard-working, law-bound, and, above all, sympathetic fictional cop. Thanks to *Moroccan Events,* fictionalized narratives of police investigations took their first step out of the confines of the neglected novel and into contact with the real world, presenting the public with a cop who embodied the values of state authority in the era of *Alternance*—the rule of law, democratic reform, and human rights.

One of the first articles to focus on the police was "Who Killed the Teacher?!," which was published on March 12, 1999.[31] This article, which appears in the bottom half of figure 6, begins as Allal's wife is extremely nervous because her husband did not come home the day before. She then receives a phone call that the police found a human head near the school where her husband worked. Devastated by the news, she does not believe that it could be her husband since, she claims, he does not have any enemies. Nonetheless, Allal's wife goes to the morgue and identifies the remains, which the killer cut up with great skill and precision. At this point, the article begins narrating the police investigation into the case as they question potential suspects and discover that Allal had a number of secret affairs with married and unmarried women. With the entire city talking about the murder and rumors swirling that the killer was a "professional," the police come up empty in their investigation of the victim's affairs with women. They then identify a possible suspect but the article ends as follows: "The suspect continues to deny any connection with the crime, maintaining his previous statements even in the face of witness statements. He still claims his innocence almost a year after the crime was committed." Despite the intensive police investigation, the article concludes without any resolution. The murder remains a mystery.

In this article, one of the first that focused on a police investigation, the journalist employs several key features of the police procedural. The first of these is to narrate a criminal investigation as it unfolds instead of simply reviewing a case after it has been completed. In "Who Killed the Teacher?!" the narrative begins not with the basic details of the murder—as in the tabloid articles—but by describing in present time the morning after the crime has taken place. "Unlike usual, [the victim's wife] got up early to prepare breakfast for her kids. She hadn't slept a wink all night but stayed up thinking about her husband who left the day before and hadn't come home yet." The author reveals that the victim's remains were discovered at the same time as the wife learns the news. More and more detail is presented about the victim and the police investigation, but only as the article shows each stage in the aftermath of the murder.

This new perspective radically transformed the style of crime reporting in the country. In the party press and the tabloids, crime was narrated in a dry matter-of-fact style with text taken directly from a police report after the incident was tried in court. The articles in *Moroccan Events*, however, turned crime journalism into a present-time fictionalized narrative about crime and punishment. Narrating the investigations of the crime—not the events of the crime itself, as in the confession articles—further emphasizes the puzzle element. The police do not know how the crime was committed or who the culprit is, and that gives the journalist the opportunity to start the article from the perspective of an audience of police fiction, one that is expecting a mysterious crime followed by an intriguing investigation. This puzzle element increases the suspense of the narrative style and serves as an invitation for readers to follow along with the police as they use all of their resources to crack the difficult crime. In turn, this situates readers to see the crime through the eyes of the police—to identify with them—as they attempt to bring the criminal to justice. It encourages readers not simply to self-identify with the police but also to occupy their position in the narrative, repositioning the public and tightening the connection between the two.

The victim is also familiar from *The Blind Whale*. To all who knew him, including his wife, Allal appeared to have been an upstanding man. Nonetheless, the police reveal that he has led a secret life, which may or may not have been related to his murder. Like Hind in *The Blind Whale*, who managed to deceive her mother about her double life, Allal's wife had no idea about his affairs or that anyone would want to hurt her husband. In the tabloids, crime commonly occurred because of hidden deviance. "Who Killed the Teacher?!" indicates how police investigations in the new era are significantly more complicated because victims—not only criminals—are not who they appear to be. This adds a strong level of ambiguity to police work, infusing the cases with a further level of uncertainty and confusion. The parallel between Hind and Allal also marks real crime with a fictional element of intrigue and deceit.

Another important similarity between "Who Killed the Teacher?!" and *The Blind Whale* is the depiction of the killer. The narrative explains, "Some thought that a single person could not commit a crime of this type because of how it was carried out. Others thought that the criminal was a trained killer. . . . How could the crime have been committed without its perpetrator or perpetrators leaving behind a single piece of evidence?" As in *The Blind Whale*, the murderer is depicted as a professional, someone who is steps ahead of the police thanks to their skill and cunning. *Moroccan Events* brought to the press a new kind of criminal, one taken from the pages of police fiction. In previous crime reporting, the criminal was frequently someone easy to identify—a scorned spouse, an angry son, or a greedy friend. "Who Killed the Teacher?!" shows readers that real-world killers—and not just those of police novels—are becoming not only more difficult to arrest but also more skilled at committing their crimes, representing a significant new challenge for the police of the new era.

Perhaps the most striking element of this article—and the depiction of the killer—is that the case remains unsolved at the end, just as in *The Blind Whale*. The police work to arrest the culprit using every possible means but come up empty. This strategy is familiar from the Arabic police novels as a way of making the police more sympathetic to the audience. A sensational and horrible crime has occurred that terrified the community but the police fail to make an arrest after a long investigation. This indicates that the police of the new era are bound by proper procedure and the law. Without proof, they cannot charge someone for the crime. The criminal may still be at large, but the police's inability to arrest them does not reflect their ineffectiveness. Rather, it emphasizes their reliance on material evidence—not trumped-up charges, manufactured evidence, forced confessions, or torture—to solve crime. This article therefore breaks a powerful taboo in the Moroccan media. It depicts a police investigation into a crime that went unsolved. In the process, it recasts real-world crime in the guise of fiction to emphasize that the rhetoric of democracy and the rule of law in the new era have now penetrated the police stations, the heart of the old authoritarianism system and site of human rights abuses during the Years of Lead.

During 1999, *Moroccan Events* focused its crime articles more and more on the perspective of the police and their investigations, solidifying the link between the police and readers. Although articles in which the case remained open at the end were common, most depicted the police solving a particular crime. At the same time, journalists adopted the properties of Arabic police fiction more and more in their writing, such as describing in present time the discovery of a body, the step-by-step police investigation into a crime, the interrogation of a criminal, and the arrest. By early 2000, despite the short space of a newspaper article, *Moroccan Events* began developing a focus on individual detectives, personalizing them—as in other sensational media texts—and emphasizing their self-sacrifice and dedication in tracking down criminals, mirroring the depiction of Yaqdhan in *The Blind Whale*.

One of these articles, "A Smart Killer Who Fell in the Evil of His Deeds!," which appeared on February 11, 2000, begins as the detective sits in his office, rereading the police and eyewitness reports on a murder. The author explains that the police received a call that a wealthy man had been murdered at home. They immediately go to the man's villa and conduct the crime-scene investigation. After several visits to question the victim's family, police suspicions fall on a classmate of the victim's son. The police soon learn that the classmate had prior arrests for swindling and theft. The detective brings the suspicious classmate in for questioning, eventually producing a confession. The classmate killed the father in hopes of stealing his wealth from the son after he inherited it.

Like most true-crime articles in *Moroccan Events,* this one is written in a puzzle format, starting with a crime and encouraging readers to follow along with the detective in the process of investigating the case. An important innovation at this stage, however, is the author's focus on the individual detective. The article begins by taking the perspective of the cop: "The detective reread the inspection reports and witness statements and paused for a long time at the details and tangible ideas in the lines without hitting on the key to the puzzle of the crime."[32] The article emphasizes how the detective usually develops leads soon after reading a case file because of his many years of experience, but this crime is different. The case is depicted as exceptionally difficult in order to present it as a challenge to the diligent detective.

As in the Arabic police novel, the boundary between work and home for the detective has been elided. After rereading the case file,

> the detective noticed the time, realized that he was late, and pulled himself together. He left dragging his feet since he wasn't used to not solving a case quickly. He reached out to the file that was sitting on his desk and took it with him. He headed for his car, threw himself inside, and tossed the file on the front seat. He then turned on the engine and took off racing toward his house.

The cop of the new era is so dedicated to his investigations that he not only loses track of time at the station and forgets about dinner but also takes his work home with him. He reluctantly leaves the station and once he arrives at home, he is unable to leave work at the door, blurring the lines between the police officer's professional and personal life, as in *The Blind Whale*. Even though there is little space in a half-page newspaper crime article, the author depicts the cop's home life as he gets in bed after dinner:

> The detective got in bed feeling overwhelmed by exhaustion. Despite that, he couldn't fall asleep because of how much he was preoccupied with the case. As he closed his eyes, a glimmer of hope appeared to him when he remembered a marginal point that he had heard during the interrogation of the son and the maid. He didn't pay any attention to it at the time but now he hoped it might be the key that could lead to the killer. He got up from bed and decided to visit the crime scene once again.

This focus on the individual detective—the blurred line between his work and home life, and his perspective—gives the central figure of the article an identity beyond the face of state authority. It humanizes him, positioning him as a double for the reader, inviting the reader to follow along in the process of investigating the crime. This scene also shows the detective's hard work, dedication, and personal effort in investigating crime, demonstrating that he too has a stake in cracking the case. Although he could simply leave his work at the police station, today's detective cannot sleep until a criminal is brought to justice. The cop of the new era is so invested in his profession—and protecting the public—that he can never rest while there is a criminal at large.

Despite the uncommon intelligence of the criminal, the article emphasizes that the detective cannot be fooled. In "Who Killed the Teacher?!," the police are up against a particularly shrewd killer and are unable to make an arrest because they do not have enough material evidence. In this article, however, the case is presented as a puzzle that the detective is able to solve. The detective's intelligence plays a key role in cracking the case but the article stresses his dedication, self-sacrifice, and diligence. This detective, thanks to his hard work and vast experience, is no longer steps behind the criminal. He represents the new face of the police, one that is not only hard-working and sympathetic but also effective. The detective of this article also represents the public and the desire for law and order. This dynamic allows the article to cast the detective in a new model through which the public can situate themselves in relation to the police and state authority. As Christopher P. Wilson noted, "Ultimately we need to read the police procedural not merely as a mystery subgenre, but for the way it drafts a new police-citizen relationship."[33]

From early 2000, the crime articles in *Moroccan Events* became formulaic, taking on a clear didactic function, producing and disseminating knowledge about the police through entertaining narratives of crime and punishment. They treated crime like a mystery that the police must solve, emphasizing the unusual difficulty of the case and employing an exciting, suspense-filled narrative style. They typically begin with the police hard at work at the station when they receive a phone call informing them that a body has been discovered. The police rush to the scene and conduct a thorough investigation, collecting all available evidence, and transfer the body to the morgue for examination. The police then interview witnesses and identify the victim. A meticulous examination of the crime-scene evidence—or the crime lab report—usually gives the police a new lead, which helps them track down a new suspect, eventually producing an arrest and confession thanks to teamwork and cooperation between various departments. Emphasis on crime-solving techniques like precise forensic analyses and autopsy reports, as well as elements such as cell-phone records, computer forensics, and clever use of evidence recovered from the crime scene suggest that technological modernity—with its emphasis on hard fact and not subjective interpretation—has now entered the previously opaque and closed world of the Moroccan police.

By early 2002, *Moroccan Events* had become the highest-circulation newspaper in the country and had increased its crime reporting from weekly to daily articles. From this time, the newspaper began including more and more front-page news about murder, further solidifying the position of crime in the mainstream daily press. Crime became such a sales draw that *Moroccan Events* began labeling its true-crime articles with the phrase "The Case of the Issue," implying that readers could expect to have a crime with each day's newspaper. By 2005, the connection between true crime and fiction became further solidified in the newspaper when the articles received a new rubric: *qissat jarima*, or "Crime Story." The use of the word *qissa* or "story" emphasized the entertaining narrative element of the articles, explicitly drawing attention to the fictional nature of retelling real-world crime. By publishing true crime every day, the newspaper significantly expanded its reach, providing the reading public with daily contact with the genre, further disseminating this new image of the police throughout society. Moreover, the repetition and daily nature of these articles became an essential element of their character. They standardized crime journalism in the mainstream press, making the fact/fiction fusion part of the identity of the Moroccan police in print media and establishing an intimate relationship between reader and police in the new era.

Despite the largely formulaic and repetitive nature of Moroccan True Crime, there were important developments in the genre once it became a daily phenomenon. Besides an increasing focus on suspense and entertainment through unusual crimes, exciting chases, and particularly dangerous criminals, an important depiction of the police in Moroccan True Crime is that they investigate all cases, regardless of the social standing of the victim. "He Kept Abusing Them with His Deviance So They Proceeded to Kill Him by Fire!," which appeared on December 5, 2003, narrates how the police work to solve the case of a murdered street child.[34] It begins like many articles from this period by focusing readers on the cop at the center of the investigation:

> The detective could barely get a grip on himself. . . . Weariness had crept into the detective's body and he was forced to throw himself on his desk chair in an attempt to catch his breath. About ten hours had passed and the crime had only become more confusing. He stayed there for a while with his mind wandering. From time to time, he exhaled smoke from his cigarette. Maybe between one puff and another he would discover some lead that would produce an arrest.

The author then reviews the case information: the police received an anonymous phone call about a charred body and quickly went to the scene, where they found the corpse of a teenager without any identification. The police soon discover that the victim was doused in gasoline and set on fire. The detective soon suspects a seventeen-year-old homeless boy, who eventually confesses that he and four other homeless teens committed the crime. The victim, Hassan, was one of their companions but, the boy explains, they killed him in revenge for their honor. Hassan was much bigger than the others and raped them numerous times over many months. After a long period of suffering and terror, the boys decided to put an end to the abuse. They poured gasoline on Hassan while he slept and set him ablaze.

This article emphasizes that the police work with the same efficiency and care in all of their cases, regardless of the socioeconomic background of the victim. Street children are perhaps the most marginalized group in the country. Although they are highly visible in major cities like Casablanca and Tangier, they live largely set apart from civil society. The article opens with a focus on the detective, who is so anxious and weary from the investigation that he must sit down to catch his breath. This anxiety, however, is over a victim who is a street child. This symbolizes that the police today are as involved in solving crimes related to the most marginalized in society as they are for the elite. For the police of the new era, all are equal and deserve the same level of attention and resources. Moreover, despite the social standing of the victim, the police are under pressure to crack the case quickly, just as they would be if a wealthy Moroccan or foreigner had been killed. Even though the victim was homeless, the detective in charge of the case is feeling the pressure only ten hours after the discovery of the body. The status of the victim—coupled with the perspective of the detective—therefore serves as a vehicle to demonstrate that democratic principles have now entered not only the parliament with the *Alternance* government but also the police station.

Hassan is able to rule the group with an iron fist and sexually abuse the others because there is no one to intervene. The fact that the children take justice into their own hands emphasizes that they are marginalized from not only civil society but also law and order, without access to the police. Nonetheless, once a crime is committed, the police investigate fully. Even though the victim was homeless and sexually abused other boys, the article demonstrates that he too deserves justice. The article therefore presents a police who are at the service of all citizens in the country, regardless of socioeconomic standing. In addition to cases involving street children, *Moroccan Events* commonly published true-crime articles in which the police investigate the murder of housemaids, who are typically uneducated adolescent or teenage girls from the countryside with little protection against abusive employers. In these cases, the police are not at fault that society has produced such marginalized people. It is their responsibility, however, to treat everyone equally with the same rights, as in any other democratic society. Articles focusing on street children or housemaids show the public that in today's Morocco, the rule of law has finally triumphed.

While daily true-crime articles in *Moroccan Events* disseminated knowledge about the police and the judicial system in an entertaining format that encouraged the public to adopt the perspective of the lead detective, giving them the opportunity to practice state authority, journalists were restricted in their ability to flesh out the character of the cop or fully develop their fictional narrative style because of the length of the articles. It is difficult to depict a detective's home life, include dialogue, or provide additional details of police investigations within the confines of a short piece in a daily newspaper. By 2000, however, *Moroccan Events* began printing true-crime serials, which, when taken together, formed the length of a novel. These serials, which appeared during the summer and Ramadan, gave the newspaper the opportunity to develop true-crime narratives in a form even closer to that of the Arabic police novel, further solidifying the connection between the real-world police and fiction in the daily press.

Newspaper Police Novels

Newspaper circulations typically increase two times of the year in Morocco: Ramadan and the summer, when people have more free time and seek out entertainment from both the press and television. Newspaper serials during these periods existed in Morocco during the 1990s, but the phenomenon changed radically in 2000, when both the party press and *Moroccan Events* began publishing serials that focused on the police and criminal investigations. These serials are particularly important for the spread of police fiction through the press because they provided journalists with the opportunity to extend their depictions of crime and punishment beyond the confines of a single article. The length and format of the serials allowed the press to develop the personal characteristics of the detective as well as various aspects of police investigations, such as analyzing crime scenes, questioning suspects, tracking down false leads, and chasing culprits. As a result, the serials reframed Moroccan True Crime from short daily articles to extended texts, creating an intertextual link between the two and further solidifying the fictional depiction of the real-world police.

The first of these appeared during Ramadan 2000, when *Moroccan Events* published a thirty-part serial entitled "Cases under the Microscope." Although all of the articles were unified under this rubric and had a similar theme of displaying the role of science in police investigations, each part was self-contained and varied in time and location, even though a single journalist, Abdelmajid Hachadi, wrote all of the articles. Narrated in present time, the articles typically depict how the police recover a body, process evidence, and rely on the reports of the crime lab and medical examiner to crack the case. Several articles show that the medical examiner is the key who confirms whether a crime has even taken place. For example, one case demonstrates how a young boy, who was discovered deep inside a well with a ball, did not die by accident but was in fact murdered. With its focus on procedure and forensics, this series served a highly didactic purpose for the public. In the new era, the police use science—objective fact—

in order to crack cases. Science eliminates subjectivity—and the possibility of corruption—from police investigations. Moreover, a focus on procedure centers readers on the function and legitimacy of state authority. As Richard V. Ericson, Patricia M. Baranek, and Janet B. L. Chan have shown, the press and the police work together to produce media texts that emphasize procedure in order to establish the legitimacy of state justice.[35]

A particularly striking depiction of the new police appears in part six of "Cases under the Microscope," entitled "Minister of Justice Buries the File but Justice Convicts Those Involved."[36] The article begins by narrating how Mohamed arrived at the Tangier port in October 1996 from Holland. Mohamed was shocked that the police commissioner at the port ordered his men to search his car for drugs. Mohamed was soon arrested and taken to the police station, where he died four hours later. During the Years of Lead and into the 1990s, deaths in police custody were not uncommon. The police typically recorded these highly suspicious incidents as "suicide" in death certificates, even though human rights groups repeatedly argued that the victims died because of torture and abuse. The case of Mohamed was particularly suspect—a young man in excellent health had just arrived in Morocco with a car full of gifts for family members whom he had not seen in years. It made no sense that he would commit suicide only four hours later. The police, however, claimed that he died from an overdose of ecstasy, which he supposedly took while in custody.

Hachadi, the author of the series, immediately takes a critical stand on the death:

> After the naïve justification that police officials offered about Mohamed's death, they continued burying the truth and ignoring the facts about the case. When the public prosecutor examined the body, he simply confirmed in his inspection report—and without awaiting the results of medical tests—that there were no signs of violence on the victim.

Based on this report, three doctors, whom Hachadi emphasizes were not pathologists, also examined the body. "Naturally," he writes, "the report of the doctors continued to cover up the facts as they too determined that the death was not the result of violence." Even the minister of justice at the time supported the position of the police and validated the reports.

After a year of repeated protests, Mohamed's father finally convinced the public prosecutor to order an autopsy on the body. Saeed Louahlia, the director of the Institute for Forensic Science in Casablanca at the time, conducted the examination and found bruises on the right cheek and lower lip as well as on the genitals. These wounds confirmed that Mohamed died as the result of torture and not suicide. The case was reexamined and a report was finally issued in July 1999 that charged the detective, inspector, commissioner, and station chief with murder. The detective and inspector were found guilty of the crime without intent and sentenced to ten years in jail, while the commissioner and station chief were given eight years.

This article presents a striking new depiction of the justice system. It shows that only four years earlier, the police still falsified death certificates and their superiors in positions as high as the minister of justice backed them in doing so. This article demonstrates that in the new era, however, science—an objective measure of verifying evidence—now takes precedence over corruption and suppression of facts. The medical examiner Louahlia plays a heroic role in revealing the truth behind the case. Deaths in police custody served as a reminder of previous police abuses but Hachadi draws a clear line between the previous period, which lasted until as recently as 1996, and the new era. Hachadi mocks the police and the judicial system for trying to cover up the murder. This article shows that in the new era, no one is above the law and that science, material evidence, proper procedure, and an open desire for justice have now solved one of the most pressing and long-standing human rights problems in the country. The message of the article is clear—accountability has reached all the way from the basements of the police station to the desk of the minister of justice. This, the article suggests, will finally put an end to deaths in police custody.

In less than a year, *Moroccan Events* expanded its true-crime serials even further. Between August 1 and September 10, 2001, the newspaper printed a new police serial entitled "From the Files of the Criminal Police." Composed of forty-one total parts, the serial featured several smaller multipart continuous series, most of which were developed into longer narratives from single crime articles that the newspaper had printed previously. Even though each subseries is based on real-world crime, "From the Files of the Criminal Police" features all the hallmarks of the Arabic police novel. Unlike the daily crime articles, the lead detective in each subseries is named and given a full physical description. Not only are the articles narrated in present time, leading readers through the case, but each subseries also quotes dialogue as in a short story or novel, such as when police officials discuss a case and interrogate a suspect, discussions that a journalist could not possibly know firsthand. Moreover, the subseries feature framing techniques such as lengthy descriptions of locations—including city streets and the port—that have little to do with the case. Each subseries also boasts sensational elements, such as exciting manhunts and police chases, suspense-filled surveillance of suspects, and puzzle-cracking interrogation scenes. Almost all of the cases in the series are based on shocking and sensational crimes, better suited to police fiction than real-world crime reporting. These include murder-for-hire cases, adulterous affairs leading to intricate murder plots, and a dead body found in a car registered to the palace. Most parts in each subseries end with a cliff-hanger, leaving readers in suspense until the next day's installment, such as when the detective discovers a new lead in a case or another body is discovered.

One subseries entitled "The Phantoms" describes how a police team in Casablanca hunts down a group of criminals. After an exciting chase through the Casa Port train station, the main suspect tries to stab the lead detective, illustrating that the real-world police are under threat in today's Morocco, much like the cops of the tabloids or Yaqdhan in *The Blind Whale*. Despite the fact that the criminal attacks the detective, the police arrest him using proper procedure. This shows that by respecting the rights of the criminal, the police in today's Morocco respect the rights of all citizens, regardless of circumstances. After the police make the arrest, "The Phantoms" ends by quoting the real police report on the case, with all of its legalistic language, singling out the lead detective, Detective Abdu, for praise. The inclusion of such documentation serves to remind readers that despite the highly fictionalized narrative form, the series depicts real-world crime. The Phantoms were a well-known criminal gang who attacked a variety of people in the economic capital. Detective Abdu, despite the fictional narrative, is a real cop who risked his life to crack the case. In addition to the police report, other elements point to the fact that the cases in the series are based on real-world crime, such as license plate numbers, street addresses, birthdates of suspects, and dates of events. By late 2001, when "From the Files of the Criminal Police" appeared, *Moroccan Events* had solidified the connection between newspaper reporting on real-world crime and fictional narratives of police investigations, pointing also to the ambiguities and contradictions involved in fusing the two together in the daily press. The newspaper had also cemented its depiction of real-world cops in the trappings of police fiction, blurring the lines between fact and fiction for readers.

Now that the newspaper had extended the single true-crime article into a short multipart series, it was only a matter of time before much longer series appeared, mimicking the police novel even more closely in form and content. By summer 2002, *Moroccan Events* published its first continuous thirty-part true-crime series, which, in total, equaled the length of a novel. It was also around this time that new Arabic police novels stopped appearing in the bookstores.[37] This suggests that the crime journalists of *Moroccan Events*—such as Abdelmajid Hachadi—replaced the two Hamdouchis as the most influential writers of police fiction in the country. Few in Morocco read novels, but the newspaper brought police fiction narratives to its massive reading audience. By co-opting the police novels and disseminating the fictional form through the daily press, the newspaper brought a new kind of police fiction—a highly stylized retelling of real-world crime and police investigation—into contact with a much larger readership than the authors of the police novels could ever have hoped for. Thanks to its daily crime stories and seasonal series, Moroccan True Crime made the police novels redundant, replacing them as the dominant form of police narrative in the country. Instead of buying expensive novels, the public simply got their police fiction with each day's newspaper.

The first of the novel-length serials in *Moroccan Events* appeared during summer 2002. For the next several years, the newspaper published at least one novel-length serial each summer and Ramadan. These serials covered a number of sensational cases, such as Weld Arisha, who killed several people in the early 1980s; the killer of Bin Slimane, who murdered a police office and several others; and the notorious serial killer of Casablanca, whose case will be covered in chapter 5. These works feature important characteristics of the police novels, such as following a lead detective as they investigate a sensational crime, providing detailed information about teamwork among the various officers and departments to crack a case, depicting a particularly intelligent and challenging criminal, and, most importantly, constructing an image of the police that emphasizes their transformation in the new era. Unlike the police novels, however, these serials present real-world crime—journalists used fictional narrative structure to depict actual events based on crime reports that the police provided them.

In Ramadan 2002, *Moroccan Events* published a thirty-part serial entitled "Magician from Meknès: Journey from Swindling to Murder!"[38] It focused on a sensational crime from the 1980s that received almost no press coverage at the time: the case of a magician who killed four people. While this serial features many of the standard elements of Moroccan True Crime, it adds the final and perhaps most important element of police fiction: an extended personalization of the detective and his family. It begins as Detective Azzedine reads a report about four bodies discovered in a car found at the bottom of a cistern in Meknès. After identifying the victims, Detective Azzedine uncovers their involvement with a local magician who swindled two of them out of enormous sums of money over the span of several years. The police investigate the magician and soon arrest him, eventually forcing him to confess to the crime.

While all of the extended crime serials depict the lead detective's relationship with his family, this one emphasizes in particular the tension between the detective's work and his home life. The series begins as Detective Azzedine sits in his office exhausted, struggling to stay awake. At first, this seems like an unexpected way to begin a true-crime serial since the police are supposed to be alert and vigilant. Nonetheless, the text explains why the detective can barely keep his eyes open:

> Azzedine was transferred to Meknès only about a week before beginning this case. Despite his youth, his merit and hard work enabled him to advance quickly through the ranks. He worked in more than one location before coming to Meknès. As much as the latest promotion made him happy, it forced him to leave his wife and young daughter behind since he had to go without being able to set up a home for them in the new city. Until he could do that, he had to travel to visit them every weekend before arriving at dawn every Monday on the night bus. That morning, Azzedine went straight to his desk after the long trip during which he didn't sleep a wink.[39]

While many true-crime articles depict the detective as forgoing dinner to stay late at the station, this series shows how Azzedine's sense of sacrifice for his profession has led him to move to a number of cities. Moreover, his latest post has forced him to leave his family behind. Nonetheless, he travels long distances to see them every weekend, staying up all night on the return trip before arriving at work. His exhaustion at the beginning of the serial therefore symbolizes his self-sacrifice and commitment to the police and to his family—he is willing to travel all night in order to bridge to gap between the two.

Azzedine immerses himself in the investigation but the line between his work and home life remains permeable. This is particularly clear as Azzedine and his partners rush to intercept the magician at his house. On the way, Azzedine cannot escape his feelings for his family:

> As the detective started thinking about the questions surrounding the case, the image of his daughter, who he wouldn't see this week because of work, appeared to him. The case prevented him from going home as he usually did every weekend. He remembered how his wife yelled at him on the telephone when he called to apologize for not coming. She blamed him for being cold and distant during the week, and that was before he said he wasn't coming home. Her harsh words were still ringing in his ears, as was the crying of his daughter who yelled out as if to make him feel guilty on purpose. He felt an unusual desire for his family and decided to take advantage of the first opportunity he could to bring them to Meknès. That's the only way he'll have enough time with them since his job didn't always give him days off. Crime doesn't stop during the weekend.[40]

In this scene, just as Azzedine rushes to arrest the prime suspect in a quadruple murder, thoughts of his wife and daughter take over. This passage shows how Azzedine has internalized the conflict between work and home life that has arisen because of the nature of his profession. The role of the family in this serial grounds the real-world detective in his family life, connecting him even closer to his police fiction counterpart. Just as Yaqdhan in *The Blind Whale* struggles to reconcile cop work with his family life, serials such as this one show that the real-world cop of today faces the same challenges. This makes him more sympathetic and identifiable to readers, breaking down barriers between the public and the police, and also further links him to his fictional counterpart, eliding the line between fictional cop and real-world detective. By incorporating strategies to encourage readers to view the real-world police in the guise of fictional cops, these works sought to reposition the public in their relationship with the state, attempting to use the police as a vehicle for improving public opinion of power and authority in the new era.

With the Ramadan and summer serials, the genre reached its maturity. These narratives, in the form of both daily articles and seasonal serials, allowed *Moroccan Events*, with its fusion of fact and fiction, to give the police a new identity that matched and reflected state aspirations for democratic reform in the country. In turn, the new image of the police suggested that state authority was also transforming to meet the needs of the new era. The new fictionalized police in the highest-circulation newspaper in the country showed readers that the state was no longer using force and coercion to maintain safety, security, and stability. Rather, the new police—thanks to their character and methods—embodied a new respect for the rule of law and democratic principles. This transformed identity for the police produced an innovative channel through which the public could resituate their relationship with state authority in the new era.

While the tabloids presented a striking new depiction of the police to the working-class public, by mid-1998 the daily press had yet to engage in rehabilitating the image of the police after the Tabit Affair. The audience of educated Moroccans who read the press was also important for the state's message of police reform and rule of law in the new era of *Alternance*. The journalists of the daily party newspapers, in the aftermath of the Tabit Affair, had proven themselves hostile to the police thanks to their continued coverage of police scandals. The state therefore needed a new kind of ally for disseminating the new image of the police for the era of democratic transition in the daily press. The country's first independent newspaper, *Moroccan Events*—with its commercial focus and sensational techniques—proved to be an ideal partner. Thanks to its Arabic-language readership, high circulation, and lack of apparent partisanship, it brought the new fictionalized image of the police to a much more diverse and non-elite audience than the elite party press. Moroccan True Crime, with its ambiguities and contradictions that pointed at the same time to sensational entertainment and state manipulation of the media, worked to encourage the public's continued acceptance of state authority as the country moved away from the coercion and violence of the Years of Lead.

In interfacing with the new independent press, the state was doing nothing new. In fact, the police in countries around the world commonly provide the raw source material for media depictions of crime. As Regina G. Lawrence notes, "Commercialism can dovetail nicely with official efforts to manage the news, such as in the case of most crime reporting: As news organizations have discovered, crime sells, and much crime news is premised on police-supplied images of police and crime fighting."[41] Moreover, during the 1980s and 1990s, police departments in Canada, the United States, and elsewhere became significantly more media savvy, attempting to direct the press's depiction of their activities in order to establish and maintain legitimacy. As Richard V. Ericson, Patricia M. Baranek, and Janet B. L. Chan have shown, "publicity is an integral component of the policing mandate and activity."[42] By collaborating with *Moroccan Events*, the state was simply joining in this well-established game, attempting to direct the image of the police in the highest-circulation newspaper in order to maintain public acceptance of its authority in a rapidly evolving political, social, and cultural environment.

This does not mean that there was a conspiracy between *Moroccan Events* and the state to improve the image of the police. Rather, the invention of a new form of media narrative, Moroccan True Crime, simply suited the interests of multiple parties. It was a distinctive way for the newspaper to boost sales and build its audience while distancing itself from the tabloids. It catered to educated readers who were seeking a nonpartisan daily newspaper that featured sensational elements. *Moroccan Events* also happened to employ journalists who were well aware of the new Arabic police novel and the ability of fictional depictions of crime to attract readers. Moreover, these journalists were clearly not averse to working directly with the police, even though they certainly did not intend to produce state propaganda. Hadin Saghir, the court reporter for the *Socialist Union*, told me that he was opposed to using any source that came from the police for fear of bias. Abdelmajid Hachadi and crime journalists like him at *Moroccan Events*, on the other hand, not only welcomed police reports but also needed them as raw material for their true-crime articles and series. No doubt, this influenced their depiction of the police and encouraged them to produce the desired image of the rule of law in the country. Positive portrayals meant that the police would continue working with them and provide them with the police reports necessary for creating their narratives. As a result, Moroccan True Crime served as a nexus for multiple interests, the net result of which was a striking new police image that was widely disseminated in the country.

Fictional narratives of police work were essential to the growing success of the independent press and, subsequently, the transformation of the country's print media in the new era. *Moroccan Events,* however, was not the only media source to blur the lines between fiction and reality in order to replace the old images of the police from the Years of Lead with something radically new. Television, a considerably more popular media format in Morocco than the press, would embark on a similar process. Just as with the independent press, police fiction would function to expand audience as the two television channels turned to police television movies, or téléfilms, as the cornerstone of their programming in the new era. Like *Moroccan Events,* the television channels would use these narratives to cast the real-world police in the role of a fictional hero and position the public to see crime through their eyes. This, in turn, would encourage viewers not only to identify with the police but also to continue reevaluating their relationship with state authority. And with programs in Moroccan colloquial Arabic, television was not bound by issues of literacy or education. It could reach a much larger audience than the press, disseminating new fictional images of the police to elite and non-elite alike.

Figure 1. The *Socialist Union,* March 16, 1993. The headline reads, "Photo-report from Final Moments of Trial of Tabit and Those with Him." Tabit can be seen in the top two and bottom left photographs. The other photographs are of codefendants, judges, lawyers, and journalists. These are the first contemporaneous images of the trial that appeared in the press after journalists were allowed back into court.

Figure 2. The *Banner*, March 16, 1993. The top headline announces the verdict in the case: "Death for Main Defendant Mohamed Mustafa Tabit." Tabit can be seen in the center of the left photograph. Slouched in shame between the two guards, Tabit here symbolizes the disgrace of the entire police establishment as the trial came to a close.

Figure 3. *Political Day*, September 13, 1993. This was the first crime tabloid issued in Morocco. It was also the first newspaper in the country's history to feature color images. The headline under the top left photograph reads, "He Butchered His Wife Because of Witchcraft and Adultery." The headline for the bottom right photograph reads, "Fall of Dangerous Pancho Gang." Other headlines include "Trash Collector Finds 20,000 Dirhams inside Garbage Bag" and "Brother of Former Minister Implicated in Grave 'Tabit-like Acts.'"

Figure 4. *Political Appointment,* January 11, 1995. The cover of this issue features Sherif Redwan performing exorcisms. The top headline reads, "Sensational Details of Method with Which Sherif Redwan Heals His Sick in Sidi Qasim." The black boxes with white letters describe how he fights demons, orders a demon to leave the body of a man, and pleads to God to help him treat people. Exposés such as this were intended to attract the attention of the country's working-class and semiliterate public, which had never seen news of black magic in the media before.

Figure 5. *Political Communicator,* September 15, 1995. The top left portion of this tabloid cover features the photograph of seventy-three-year-old Abdelkader, murdered by his much younger lover Noureddine, whose photograph is presented on the top right. The top headline reads, "He Butchered Old Man Violating Him for 19 Years Because He Asked Him to Continue Sexual Deviance between Them, Even Though He Renounced It." Neighbors were shocked by the murder because they thought Abdelkader was Noureddine's father.

Figure 6. *Moroccan Events*, March 12, 1999, "Justice" section. The true-crime article "Who Killed the Teacher?!" appears on the bottom half of the page along with the subheadline "The Crime, the Puzzle!" This is one of the first articles to narrate a criminal investigation entirely from the perspective of the police.

Figure 7. A still from Hassan Rhanja's police téléfilm *The Blind Whale*. This shot takes the perspective of the viewer standing outside the central police station in Casablanca, behind the locked gate of the police. The shield of the police can be seen in the center of the building. *The Blind Whale* was the first television movie to bring the public inside real-world police stations. This particular police station, the most recognizable in the country, would serve as the shooting location for the majority of the police téléfilms.

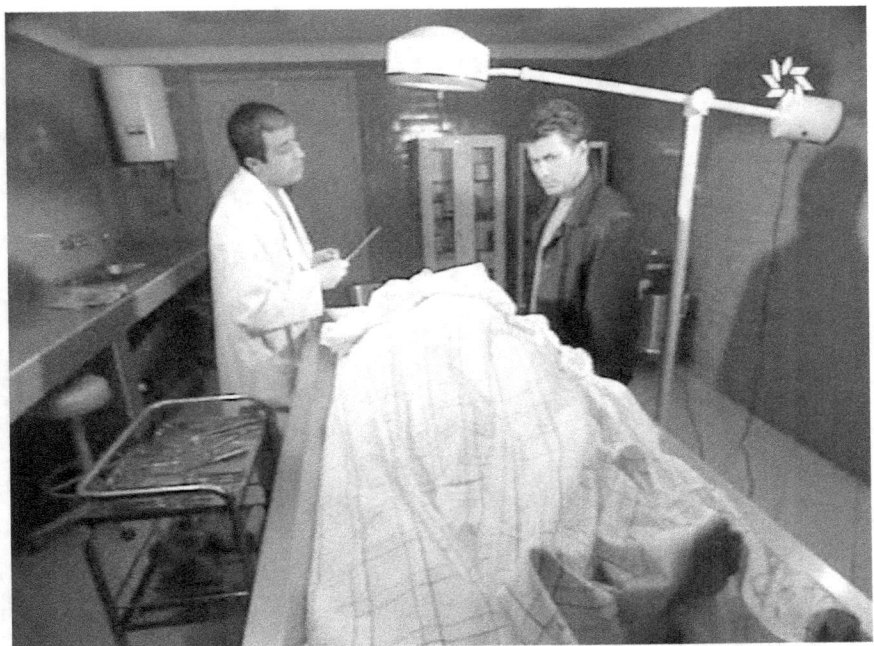

Figure 8. A still from Hassan Rhanja's police téléfilm *The Blind Whale*. Detective Yaqdhan (right) and the medical examiner (left) inspect the body of the first victim, Hind. This scene was shot on location at the real medical examiner's office and laboratory in Casablanca and shows many real implements, such as autopsy instruments and the examination lamp.

Figure 9. A still from Hassan El Ouahidi's police téléfilm *Sofia's Restaurant*. Detective Allal (center) and his partner, Inspector Omar (left), question the main suspect, Othman (right). The confident Allal is meant to symbolize an experienced police force that is at the height of its skills in the new era.

Figure 10. A still from Jamal Belmajdoub's police téléfilm *White Nights*. In this scene, Ahlam, with her gun displayed under her left arm, aggressively interrogates an older man about his role in the drug distribution network. Despite Ahlam's empowered depiction in the film, female criminal detectives did not exist in Morocco at the time.

4 Prime-Time Cops

Blurring Police Fact and Fiction on Moroccan Television

WITH THE EMERGENCE of *Moroccan Events* in 1998, the independent daily press became responsive to a mass audience and established a new prominence in the Moroccan media that has lasted to this day.[1] Following on the coattails of *Moroccan Events*, other independent newspapers emerged and imitated many of its features, such as a sensational depiction of sex and true-crime narratives. These newspapers presented the public with a new identity for the police, one that recast them in the guise of fictional heroes, attempting to erase their brutal past and place them in a new relationship with the public that reflected a transformed concept of state authority based on respect for the rule of law and human rights in the era of *Alternance*.

The relationship between the independent press and the state in creating and disseminating these new images of the police points to a paradox of agency. The state sought to foster sensational depictions of crime and punishment in the tabloids in an attempt to manage and direct public opinion after the Tabit Affair. A similar relationship can be seen in the emergence of true crime in *Moroccan Events*. These new media sources produced forms of representation that aimed to transform how the public saw the police and, by extension, state authority. While the state had a clear stake in this process, it was involved only indirectly by providing journalists with source material on which to base their articles. It was the media that performed the task, creating a new nonstate language in a radical new format—crime tabloid and independent daily press—a medium that only served to bolster the credibility of the source and distance it from explicit propaganda. The state benefited from this paradox as the print media, through these new ambiguous forms, worked to influence public perceptions on its behalf.

It was only a matter of time before a similar focus on sensationalism and audience-building would reach the television industry. Television in Morocco was a considerably more conservative and restricted medium than the press, partly because of its potential for reaching a much larger audience. Nonetheless, a new television station named 2M, or "Deuxième," since it was the country's second station after RTM, began broadcasting on March 4, 1989, under the administrative guidance of Omnium Nord-African, the country's main investment company, which is principally owned by the royal family. The station aired for more hours per day than RTM and featured a more progressive lineup in general that focused overall on French-language programming. From its beginning until early 1997, the station broadcast in encrypted form and the public needed to buy a decoder box to watch it. Although these boxes sold well—and many figured out how to pirate the broadcast—2M was viewed by a restricted audience and lost money throughout the 1990s. It therefore had a much smaller budget than RTM and was unable to produce its own television movies or sitcoms during its first decade. In 1997, after 2M continuously lost money, the state took over 2M's operations.[2]

Starting in the late 1990s—with the arrival of the *Alternance* government and the new king, Mohamed VI—both RTM and 2M began undergoing significant changes. The television stations would start demonstrating to the public that they were opening up to the new era and moving away from the tight state restrictions of the past. Both stations employed sensationalism and sought to build their audience by, among other strategies, producing cop television films—or téléfilms—that presented the public with an image of the police that paralleled that of the true-crime articles in the press. Like *Moroccan Events,* the two television stations would blur the line between fact and fiction in their police narratives. Due to the sensitive nature of the project, however, the state, which controlled and funded both stations, would become significantly more involved in producing these new televised images of the police. The state arranged for film directors to use well-known police stations and morgues as shooting locations and outfitted movie stars with actual cop cars and implements in order to present the public with an image of the real-world police in the guise of a fictional cop. In the process, these films transformed the taboo space of the police station from a site of torture and repression to the location for exciting cop movies, blurring the lines between real-world police and televised cop in the process. There were moments of contestation and slippage of control in producing the desired image of the police in these films. Nonetheless, these films sought to indoctrinate the public in the inner workings of real-world police stations and the practice of state authority, further solidifying the link between police and public in the new era.

Starting with the police téléfilms, the state would become more and more involved in producing mass-mediated images of the police in society. This demonstrates an active attempt on the part of the state in eliding the line separating the fictional cop from his real-world counterpart. In turn, this shows that the state sought to expand the use of the mass media from the press to television in order to continue reforming its brand of authoritarianism by attempting to manage public opinion on an increasingly wider scale. In the process, it moved to foster new kinds of entertainment that encouraged the wider public to view the police of today—like their counterparts on television—as having opened up to reform, with all of the implications for the rule of law, civil liberties, human rights, and state authority.

Television not only allowed for greater involvement of the state in constructing the new image of the police but also brought that image to millions of people across the country, elite and non-elite alike. Since few go to the cinema and people spend long hours at home with their families watching television together, these films, which were produced in Moroccan Arabic rather than French, reached a much larger audience than any media representations of the police before. The television stations would use these highly positive depictions of the police in the téléfilms to demonstrate to people across the social spectrum that the state and real-world police were enthusiastically supporting the changes of the new era. Once a closed and highly conservative medium for blatant propaganda, television would become a vehicle for using sensational and entertaining depictions of crime and punishment to disseminate innovative new images of police and state authority. As a result, television would expand the reach of the state in attempting to redefine the relationship of the citizen to the police under Mohamed VI.

2M and the Beginnings of the Police Téléfilm

Abdelilah Hamdouchi had written the screenplays for several téléfilms and sitcoms for RTM in the 1980s and 1990s and was therefore no stranger to the world of Moroccan television when he published the first Arabic police procedural, *The Blind Whale*. Even though there were few opportunities for local television productions in Morocco, Hamdouchi saw the possibilities for bringing police fiction to the small screen even before he published his book. Evidence of this can be seen on the novel's cover, which features the well-known Moroccan actor Mohamed Miftah dressed in a suit and tie, wearing a trench coat, and matching the physical description of Yaqdhan on the first page of the novel. As Hamdouchi explained to me about the cover, he was hoping to draw media attention to the novel and cast Miftah in the role of Yaqdhan.

The Blind Whale did not escape the attention of television executives. Soon after the novel's publication, 2M invited Hamdouchi to speak live about the novel on the main weekend news broadcast, which attracts the largest audience of the week. Hamdouchi spoke about the strong connection between the police novel and democratic development, a daring subject for television at the time, especially considering that it had yet to undergo significant reform. Among those who saw the interview was Hassan Rhanja, who had recently stopped directing episodes of a local crime documentary series for 2M named *Waqa'i* (Events) and was looking for a new project.[3] After discussions with the director of production at 2M, Rhanja approached Hamdouchi and proposed that he write a police series of thirteen episodes, each forty-five minutes long. This would be 2M's first local fictional production of any kind.

Hamdouchi quickly got to work and wrote nine episodes during 1998. The project, however, was delayed for administrative reasons and when nothing was produced by mid-1999, Hamdouchi decided to take a faster route to bringing police fiction to the small screen: he wrote the screenplay for *The Blind Whale*, which 2M accepted and put on schedule for production. The arrival of a new director of 2M, Noureddine Sail, in April 2000, however, stopped all projects. Sail and his new director of production, Mohamed Abderrahmane Tazi, began the process of modernizing 2M in general by launching productions that would appeal to the widest possible Moroccan audience with the goal of the station becoming responsible for its own finances.[4] In this, 2M shared a similar situation as *Moroccan Events*—both were dependent on audience for their survival. In recognition of this, Sail and his team believed that the station had to increase its national television production dramatically. The cornerstone of this reform, however, was the decision to begin making local téléfilms, which the station had still never produced. Moreover, the films would be shot in the Moroccan dialect, which both the educated and the uneducated could understand. With the aim of increasing the station's overall viewership, Sail launched a plan to screen one téléfilm a month, although it would take two years to reach that level. By late 2003, the station announced the goal of increasing production to two téléfilms a month, which it would surpass by 2006.[5] The first project Sail and his team turned to in order to launch the new era at 2M was the screenplay for *The Blind Whale*. With it, Abdelilah Hamdouchi created not only the first police television film in Morocco, but also the first téléfilm in 2M's history.

The Public Enters the Police Station: *The Blind Whale* on Television

Shot in early 2001 and aired on April 19, 2001, the téléfilm *al-Hut al-aʿma* (The Blind Whale) was a sensation.[6] Among several articles that appeared on the film in the press before and after its release, one called it a "pure Moroccan téléfilm in all of its measures . . . smooth, tightly woven, and bold in form and content."[7] From the perspective of plot, the film closely follows the novel, detailed in chapter 3. Nonetheless, the audiovisual medium of television gives the work new possibilities for presenting a sympathetic image of the Moroccan police to an audience of millions, blurring the boundaries between real-world policing on the streets and the representation of cops on television.

The film begins as a Mercedes drives on the highway. The initial shots show a man wearing a trench coat and black leather gloves driving the car as a young woman in the passenger seat playfully flirts with him, asking where they are going. The car stops and the two walk through some woods as the woman laughs. The man suddenly pulls out a gun and shoots the woman in the head. The killer's face never appears but there is a close-up of the woman on the ground with the gunshot wound clearly visible and her eyes staring blankly. Another bullet is then heard, showing that the killer fired on the woman again even though she was already dead, suggesting overkill in the crime. Just like the tabloid press and police novels, the introduction of the film emphasizes the shocking danger of crime in the new era. A brutal and professional killer just shot a young woman to death, even though guns are illegal in the country. The crime was committed in broad daylight, not far from the highway, and the woman clearly had no idea of the impending danger. This opening sequence, which the novel lacks, establishes from the beginning the kind of danger that police are facing in the film and ties it to the crime press that had been circulating in the country since after the Tabit Affair. The killers of the new era are shockingly bold and professional and can strike at will.

After the credits, the film moves to the detective's home as he and his family get ready for their Sunday brunch date. Younès Migri, a well-known singer and actor, plays the role of Detective Yaqdhan. With his handsome looks, soft voice, and expressive eyes, he represents a clear foil for the brutal killers depicted in the opening sequence and throughout the movie. In the foreground of one shot, Yaqdhan's wife brushes her hair, looking at herself in the bedroom mirror, as Yaqdhan stands behind her. Yaqdhan's wife then gets up and spins around for him, showing off her new dress as he tells her how beautiful she is. These sequences depict a strong intimacy between the couple, humanizing them for the audience and making them seem like any middle-class couple at home. The bedroom in Morocco is considered a private space but the camera presents the two there in order to create a sense of closeness between them and viewers. The public begins the film in an intimate relationship with the couple because of their access to the bedroom. At this point, there is no indication that Yaqdhan is a cop. He, his wife, and kids could be any middle-class Casablanca family getting ready to head out for Sunday brunch.

Nonetheless, police work quickly intervenes and positions Yaqdhan as a cop. The phone rings just as the four are about to leave the apartment and Yaqdhan is called to the crime scene. As in the novel, he was supposed to have the day off but a woman shot to death takes precedence. Yaqdhan's wife immediately realizes that their brunch date has been canceled and she and the kids are devastated. The sequence is the first of many in which the line between private and public life for the detective breaks down, with police work taking priority. The site of these scenes is invariably the detective's home. For example, the film later shows Yaqdhan's wife in bed yelling at him for coming home late; the couple in their pajamas, sitting in the kitchen, talking about the Moroccan woman's vicious murder; and Yaqdhan getting dressed slowly, putting on his gun holster in the bedroom, talking with his wife. Perhaps the most powerful scene that breaks down the boundary between work and home life is when Yaqdhan is resting in bed alone after he is attacked. He gets up, opens the door to his children's bedroom, and stares at the empty bed. Using a low-angle slow zoom shot, the film shows Yaqdhan in his pajamas with a band-aid on his forehead, staring off in thought, accompanied by dramatic music. The film then cuts to a flashback of when the two men on the motorcycle shoot at him and he falls to the ground. It then returns to Yaqdhan, as he walks out of the bedroom, clearly worried about the fate of his children if he does not survive the investigation into the murders. Being a detective today has little connection to the Years of Lead. It threatens not only the detective but also his children.

Hassan Rhanja skillfully employs a variety of camera shots and angles to encourage viewers to identify with Yaqdhan. For example, when Yaqdhan takes the call about the first murder, there is a long shot of him standing with the phone in his hand, looking anxiously at his family. With this shot, the film presents him through the eyes of his family, a perspective that places viewers not only at home with Yaqdhan but also in the position of having to understand that police work allows no division between home and professional life. When Yaqdhan arrives at the first crime scene, the camera follows him from behind, as if viewers are walking along with Yaqdhan as he takes the lead to examine Hind's body. The handheld camera shakes as he and his partner Othman walk through the woods, an element that reinforces the realistic nature of the sequence. In the scenes when he is talking about the case with Othman, Yaqdhan is foregrounded in the shot to emphasize that he is the lead detective in the case. In other scenes, the film shows a close-up eye-level shot of his face and shoulders, a strategy that emphasizes parity and sympathy between viewers and the detective.

The close-up shots of Yaqdhan's face also serve another purpose: as the film progresses and he comes under attack, a hint of worry and fear can be seen in his eyes. Although this could be read as giving the cop a weak character, Younès Migri plays the role perfectly—like the public, he too is worried about the increasingly ruthless and professional criminals and the place of his family in the new Morocco. Close-up shots of his eyes throughout the film further emphasize the connection between the lead detective and viewers. Yaqdhan's fragility, however, is reinforced when gunmen on a motorcycle attack him in Aïn Diab, an affluent district on the Atlantic coast. This scene is followed by a sequence in which Yaqdhan lies in bed at the hospital, being treated by doctors. He is clearly wounded, exhausted, and scared. In the final moments of the movie, Yaqdhan fights a guard on the Spaniard's boat and even though he knocks the guard out, Yaqdhan grasps his shoulder and winces in pain. Throughout the film, Yaqdhan's frailty is emphasized to present him as human, identifiable, and sympathetic to the audience. No longer are the police terrifying strongmen operating above the law.

Yaqdhan's home life establishes him as a sympathetic, middle-class family man. The main police station in Casablanca, which is the principal shooting location for the film, solidifies him as a cop. The use of this location, which appears in figure 7, was highly daring. Despite the improvements in human rights and the circulation of police narratives in novels and the press, police stations in early 2001, when *The Blind Whale* was first aired on television, were still a terrifying and secretive world. They represented the heart of the security establishment, a world closed off to the public. Setting scenes of a novel in a Moroccan police station may be innovative, but using the main station in Casablanca—a building immediately recognizable to the public—as a location for a television movie was shocking because of its connections with abuses during the Years of Lead.

The film is careful to bring the public into the forbidding world of the police gradually. The building initially appears through slow panning shots from the outside. The first of these, which appears only five and a half minutes into the film, shows the main entrance of the building from the street. As seen in figure 7, the low-angle shot centers on the massive glass front of the station with a Moroccan flag over the shield of the police. It then pans out, showing the locked gate before the sidewalk. This shot suggests—even admits—the closed world of the police station, presenting the intimidating massive building and the shut gate before the public. It places the audience on the sidewalk, standing at the locked gate far from the main entrance, a position symbolic of the public's distant relationship with the police since independence.

The second of these panning shots, which lasts a full thirteen seconds and appears after Yaqdhan has begun investigating the first murder, is also a low-angle shot of the imposing building. This time, however, it pans in from the locked gate past the massive shield and flag, slowly zooming in on a pair of office windows. In the final seconds of the shot, Yaqdhan is heard talking with the commissioner about the case, indicating that the office with these windows, which the camera zooms in on, is where the discussion is taking place. This second zoom shot brings the audience, which the first panning shot established as first being on the street behind the locked gate, into the police station, along with Yaqdhan for the investigation. With the handsome and sympathetic Yaqdhan as their guide, the audience has moved from the initial sequences in the intimacy of his bedroom and family home to processing the crime scene of the first murder victim and, finally, inside the most imposing police station in the country.

Now that the film has brought the audience into the commissioner's office, it does not repeat the long pans of the building. As Yaqdhan discusses the case with the commissioner in the real locations where the city's police work, the film opens up the secretive world of the police, blurring the lines between fact and fiction. Sequences show bookcases full of actual case files, Moroccan flags neatly arranged, pictures of the king on the walls, and modern computers on the desks. Others depict men wearing real Moroccan police uniforms standing at the commissioner's office door, saluting him and the detective as they enter to discuss the case. A number of scenes are set in the station, showing cops in real uniforms working on computers and Yaqdhan sitting at a large desk with case files spread out on it.

The offices at the main police station in Casablanca are not the only real-world locations or props used for the film. In the opening minutes, when Yaqdhan arrives at the shooting scene to examine the woman's body, he parks next to a real police van and ambulance. When he examines the body, it is blocked off by police tape to protect the crime scene from tampering and surrounded by several police officers in uniforms while a forensic photographer takes pictures of the area. When the police process the crime scene where the second body was discovered, the film presents the same attention to realism and procedure. Although the crime scenes and actors are fictional, the film uses real police props, vans, and uniforms in an attempt to produce as realistic an image of crime-scene examinations as possible.

This image presents viewers with several striking elements. First, the previously closed-off world of the real police is opening up to television cameras, showing the public that the police have nothing to hide in the new era. This demonstrates a new transparency at the core of the police, suggesting to the public that democratic values are now entering the country's police stations, the heart of the regime's authoritarian power during the Years of Lead. Next, it proves to the public that the television is stepping into previously taboo subjects, a strategy that indicates that restrictions on the audiovisual mass media—and not only the press—are finally loosening. Finally, it makes the films more realistic, blurring the lines between police fact and fiction, as in Moroccan True Crime. As a result, the boundary between the real-world police and a popular actor like Migri becomes significantly more porous. This pushes the public to see a sympathetic actor like Migri playing Yaqdhan in the space of the most recognizable police station in the country, encouraging them to view Migri in the role of a real-world cop.

In addition to the central police station, the film brings the audience into another real-world location previously closed off to the public: the morgue at the Ibn Rochd Hospital in Casablanca. With its true-crime articles and series like "Cases under the Microscope," *Moroccan Events* disseminated knowledge about the role of forensics in police investigations. Building on this precedent, 2M takes the public into the real morgue. After discussing the Moroccan woman's murder with the commissioner at the police station, Yaqdhan goes to the medical examiner to look at the body. As he arrives, the medical examiner waits outside the building, wearing scrubs and a white lab coat. Just as the medical examiner welcomes Yaqdhan into the morgue, the audience follows too. After they enter the building, the medical examiner leads Yaqdhan into the autopsy room, which is lined in blue tile. As seen in figure 8, a sheet covers the body, which is in the foreground. The wide-angle shot presents the room, showing all the necessary professional implements: a large examination lamp posed over the corpse, two metal side tables with dozens of autopsy implements, several large medical cabinets with vials, and a sink with its own hot-water heater. There is a close-up shot of the medical examiner's hand as he takes a metal pointer from among the implements on the side table. As the medical examiner and Yaqdhan talk, the film mixes close-up and reverse shots of the two discussing the victim, together with the wide-angle shots of the corpse and the room. The medical examiner presents the body to Yaqdhan as if educating him about pathology. Much like the true-crime articles of *Moroccan Events*, these didactic scenes serve a purpose for viewers as well, demonstrating the connection between forensic science and criminal investigations in the actual location where autopsies are conducted in Casablanca.

Although the medical examiner does not appear again in the film, forensic science plays a key role in the investigation. For example, when Yaqdhan questions the Moroccan woman's mother, she tells him that her daughter worked at a bakery. As the camera zooms in on Yaqdhan's face, the medical examiner's voice is heard when he explained to the detective in the earlier scene that he found almond and walnut cookies in the victim's stomach. Later in the film, Yaqdhan discusses the medical examiner's report on the second victim in which it was determined that they were both killed by the same gun. Although newspaper accounts of police investigations in *Moroccan Events* show how the medical examiner was pivotal in solving cases, these articles report on the police investigation only after the crime has been solved and the criminal brought to justice. *The Blind Whale* téléfilm, however, demonstrates how the medical examiner and forensic science help the police during the process of investigating a crime, an element of police work that had not appeared in the press before since newspapers had almost never reported on ongoing police investigations. The film's detailed depiction of the medical examiner, his laboratory, autopsy room, and participation with the police in a criminal investigation would soon provide a powerful model for how the police would present real-world ongoing investigations to the public. Forensics became particularly important for the new image of the police because it tied their investigations to objective science as opposed to subjective interpretation, which permitted corruption and violation of civil and human rights. Forensics and the medical examiner served as a vehicle in the mass media for showing that the police are becoming as modern and law-bound as the state in the era of *Alternance*.

The police station and medical examiner's office were not the only real locations used in the film. Casablanca is by far the most common city where television films are set and *The Blind Whale* takes full advantage of the city's recognizable neighborhoods to ground the film. Yaqdhan and his partner, for example, frequently discuss the progress of the case as they drive through the main areas in the city. Yaqdhan is attacked at night outside a well-known hotel on the Aïn

Diab coast. The film also presents the central Casablanca port with wide-angle pan shots as the police arrive to search the Spaniard's boat for hashish. The world of the police station and morgue that Yaqdhan and his partner navigate may have been closed off to outsiders, but the streets and neighborhoods situate the film in the city in a way that is widely recognizable to the public. Mixing the two makes the depiction of the police work and the shooting locations in the film more realistic, bringing them closer to the public and further blurring the lines between fact and fiction in the film.

At the same time, these elements of realism are contrasted throughout the film with old-fashioned Hollywood excitement. In one scene, Yaqdhan waves his gun as he enters an empty apartment, even though real-life Moroccan police are only permitted to handle guns if they are under attack. In another sequence, Yaqdhan and his partner keep the Spaniard under surveillance and tail him through the city accompanied by exciting music. After he questions the Spaniard in his office, Yaqdhan becomes furious at the Spaniard's acting as if he is above the law. On his way out, Yaqdhan turns around, points his finger at him from across the office and dramatically declares, "We'll meet again one day!" In the novel, however, Yaqdhan simply walks out of the office without any kind of confrontation. The difference in these scenes is indicative of the form and media in which they appear: on the extremely conservative medium of television, it is essential that Yaqdhan not appear too weak in the face of corrupt and degraded foreigners. Moreover, an exaggerated foe helps the police appear more sympathetic. These scenes present the police as exciting, mimicking the image of the police in American movies and television series. While the locations in the film may be real, these various scenes add a strong element of entertainment to police work, allowing the film to tap into the meta-text of the American television cop show.

With *The Blind Whale*, the cop of the new era made his debut on Moroccan television. As in the novel and true-crime articles of *Moroccan Events*, the police in the film face an intelligent and terrifying foe. At the same time, *The Blind Whale* téléfilm pushes the audience to self-identify with the detective and see the police investigation through his eyes, much more so than in the true-crime articles. Thanks to powerful scenes in the detective's apartment, the breakdown of boundaries between his home and work life, and skillful camera shots, Hassan Rhanja uses the medium of television to encourage the public to sympathize and self-identify with the fictional police. Moreover, the various chase scenes provide the film with a strong entertainment quality that points to an American television cop movie. At the same time, the use of the main police station, morgue, and well-known city landmarks as shooting locations add a strong element of realism to the work, allowing the film to blur the lines between police fact and fiction, pushing viewers to see the real-world police in the guise of fictional hero, with all of his characteristics. The combination of these elements gives *The Blind Whale* its innovative quality and would set a precedent for the dozens of Moroccan police movies that have appeared since 2001. In turn, these films would disseminate this new image of the police that represents a new concept of state authority for the entire public across the country.

The Cop on State Television: Adapting *The Final Bet* for RTM

Although not nearly as wide-scale as 2M, RTM was beginning its own process of modernization. Unlike 2M, however, RTM had been producing local television films and series for years, though at a modest rate of about two each year. The station's modernization would therefore not be tied directly to the production of téléfilms. Rather, it would be measured by the channel's ability to turn its back on its extremely conservative semiofficial programming. By early 2001, during a time when 2M was moving full speed ahead in its reforms, RTM was still seen as stagnant. One journalist at the time, comparing the two stations after discussing the tremendous changes at 2M, wrote that RTM "is still as it was, immersing the spectator in official ceremonies, coverage of inaugurations, visits of the ministers to regions, and marathon statements by the heads of parliamentary committees."[8] Moreover, the station was criticized for repeatedly reairing old series and films, mostly from the Arab Middle East, and as being so overwhelmed by bureaucracy that change could only come at the slowest of paces.

Abdelilah Hamdouchi understood at the time that change was beginning to sweep through even RTM. He saw that police téléfilms represented a valuable opportunity for television executives to demonstrate that the country's audiovisual mass media were beginning the process of moving away from tight state restrictions. This would include not only the Western-leaning 2M, but also the highly conservative semiofficial RTM. Soon after writing the screenplay for *The Blind Whale*, Hamdouchi wrote a second police téléfilm, *Mat'am Sufiya* (Sofia's Restaurant), and submitted it to RTM in 2000.[9] Taking the audience into the previously closed world of the police showed the public not only that the television station was opening up to long-standing taboos—much like the press did when it finally printed articles about the police—but also that the police themselves were adapting to the new era. These cop films, however, needed to cater to the demands and culture of each station.

It was a delicate process to create cop téléfilms in a country in which the police had a long history of grave human rights abuses.[10] In *The Blind Whale* téléfilm, for example, Hamdouchi and Hassan Rhanja walked a fine line between presenting Yaqdhan as a sympathetic middle-class everyman and a cop hot on the trail of an organized crime network. Because of the more liberal environment at 2M, it was possible to portray the cop not only in Hollywood-esque images with his gun drawn, but also as weak and scared in the face of new forms of crime that appeared to be spiraling out of control. Because of his experience writing screenplays for RTM during the 1980s and 1990s, Hamdouchi understood well that these images were not possible at the conservative and tightly controlled RTM, despite the desire at the station to transform itself and match the aspirations of the new era under Mohamed VI.

Sofia's Restaurant was tailored specifically for the station's conservatism. The movie was filmed in early 2001 and screened on December 14, 2001. Hamdouchi wrote the screenplay at the same time as he wrote his fourth police novel, *The Final Bet*.[11] The two are based on the same story but the differences between them are profound and clearly demonstrate the limits of criticism on Moroccan television as compared to the Arabic novel. *The Final Bet*, which first appeared in Arabic in 2001, tells the story of a thirty-two-year-old Moroccan man, Othman, who is married to a French woman forty years his senior, Sofia. They live together in the most exclusive neighborhood in Casablanca, Anfa, and Othman runs Sofia's upscale restaurant on the Aïn Diab coast. Othman married Sofia not for love but because of his desperate financial situation at the time, crushing unemployment, and lack of any future prospects. For her part, Sofia is depicted as having a deviant sexual desire for young men and was attracted to Othman for his good looks and virility.

Miserable in his marriage, Othman begins an affair with the beautiful Naeema. One night, after meeting Naeema in a park near his house, Othman comes home to find Sofia stabbed to death in their bedroom. The police begin investigating the case and quickly zero in on Othman as the prime suspect because much of the evidence appears to point to him. First and foremost, Othman's fingerprints were found on the murder weapon. The police then discover that he had a motive to kill Sofia since she had willed her entire estate to him. Moreover, he was having an affair at the time of the murder. Finally, Othman fled when the police came to arrest him. Before they capture him, however, Othman manages to visit a lawyer, who undertakes his own investigation into the case. The lawyer ultimately reveals in Perry Mason style that it was Sofia's son who committed the murder. At the end of the novel, Othman is freed and cleared of all charges, but without the help of his lawyer, the novel stresses, he would have spent the rest of his life unjustly behind bars.

The Final Bet is a scathing condemnation of a police force that needs radical reform. Unlike the energetic, handsome, and self-sacrificing Yaqdhan of *The Blind Whale*, the main detective in the novel is old, frail, and on the verge of retirement. He represents the Moroccan police of the 1970s and 1980s that used torture and false confessions to solve cases. The novel shows the detective struggling to adapt to the new age of respect for human rights and the rule of law in the country. Without being able to resort to torture anymore, he looks for evidence that will lead to an easy conviction and stops investigating other leads as soon as he has a prime suspect. In particular, the novel criticizes the practice of *al-i'tiqal al-ihtiyati*, or *garde à vue*, in which a lawyer is barred from meeting with his client for the first forty-eight to seventy-two hours after arrest.[12] The evidence against Othman may appear convincing at first—especially the fingerprints on the knife—but a lawyer would have been able to refute it.[13] The novel suggests that for Morocco to respect human rights and not simply pay them lip service, lawyers must be able to enter the police station, consult with their clients from the moment of arrest, and defend them against an overzealous police. If not, countless men like Othman will be convicted for crimes they did not commit.[14] The title of the novel therefore refers to the all-in bet that the country must now make on democracy and human rights in order to navigate its political transition successfully.

Sofia's Restaurant, the téléfilm adaptation of *The Final Bet*, differs radically in its images of the cop, the police investigation, and political transition. When Hamdouchi wrote the screenplay for *Sofia's Restaurant*, he did so with the constraints of RTM firmly in mind. He knew that it would be impossible to depict a failed police force and aging detective who were struggling to adapt to the demands of a post–Years of Lead Morocco. He also realized that he could not depict a lawyer investigating a case and arriving at the real killer because the police were unable or unwilling to do so themselves. Moreover, he certainly understood that he could not suggest—as he did in the novel's title—that the country needed to place all of its chips on a bet for democracy. Hamdouchi was well aware that the image of the police and society in the téléfilm had to conform to the interests of the establishment while, at the same time, reflect the kind of openness and reform that RTM wanted to present by producing a police movie. From this perspective, the screenplay displays the kind of self-censorship that an author must master for the establishment television station to accept and produce their work.

For the first fifteen minutes, *Sofia's Restaurant* closely follows the narrative of the first chapter of *The Final Bet*. The changes begin, however, when the narrative shifts to the police after the murder. In the novel, the detective is named Alwaar—meaning "rough guy," symbolizing his connection to the Years of Lead—while in the téléfilm, he has the bland name of Allal. Aziz Mawhoub, a well-known Moroccan actor in his sixties, plays the role of the detective. As in *The Blind Whale* téléfilm, the detective first appears in his bedroom. But unlike the scenes in *The Blind Whale*, the cop hero is alone. In stark contrast with *The Final Bet*, which introduces the detective as he dreams of losing a bet on his favorite horse—a symbol of his misplaced allegiance to the old system—the detective in the film sits upright in bed with the light on reading aloud from a large copy of the Quran. The phone rings and Allal's partner Omar, who in the novel is named Bukrisha—meaning "pot-bellied," an image that was intended to clash with the youthful and handsome police of the new era—informs him about the crime. Hanging up the phone, the confident Allal springs out of bed and gets dressed in the fine cream-colored suit that he wears throughout the film.

In the novel, Detective Alwaar is a relic from the past. He wheezes from years of chain smoking and needs to pause to catch his breath after climbing only a few stairs. He has bags under his eyes from exhaustion and puffy weak features. He wears an old worn suit and tie and remains disillusioned after years of working without a promotion. He struggles to adjust to the new era in Morocco, with its focus on human rights:

> This difficult transitional period made Alwaar feel out of place. His work became confusing; it was hard for him to get confessions without slapping or kicking a suspect or sending them down to the torture room in the basement of the police station before interrogation. Alwaar didn't know how to do his job without brutality. He just couldn't get used to sitting in front of a suspect without being aggressive or insulting, talking to them like they were in some smoke-filled café. He had to crack the whip.[15]

A remnant of the old order, Alwaar is a detective out of place in the new era. His retirement therefore symbolizes the end of the police from the Years of Lead that he represents. He is addicted to gambling and is all too happy to arrest Othman without fully examining the case evidence, caring more about putting the case behind him than achieving justice. In short, he is the complete opposite of the new image of the police that the novels and true-crime articles present to the public.

In the téléfilm, this image of the relic from the Years of Lead has been completely replaced by the morally upright, energetic, and professional Detective Allal. Aziz Mawhoub may be in his sixties, but he looks alert, fit, and healthy. Instead of the faded outfit that Alwaar wears in the novel, Allal, as seen in figure 9, boasts a cream-colored suit and dark shirt that give him a youthful appearance. Rather than call on a young detective who symbolizes the new police, the police rely on the older, more experienced and confident Allal to investigate the murder of a foreigner. Allal tells his wife before leaving for the crime scene, "When they have some big problem, they don't know what to do and come to me." In the film, detectives like Allal represent the calm and stability of the police establishment in the face of shocking crime.

The film then moves to Sofia's house, where the police process the crime scene. Police vans, an ambulance, and uniformed officers stand outside the villa. Inside Sofia's bedroom, a man takes photographs of the victim and the crime scene with a large camera, while another wearing latex gloves processes the room for fingerprints. Detective Allal arrives, strolls through the house into the bedroom, examines the crime scene, and then questions Othman slowly, as seen in figure 9. This is the first of many scenes in the novel in which Allal questions people involved in the case, but they all have a similar quality—Allal stands with firm posture, methodically and slowly asking questions, confidently taking notes, holding his hands together or placing them in his pockets, looking people directly in the eye. It is as if he is imitating Peter Falk in *Columbo,* which was a highly popular series in Morocco during the 1970s and 1980s.[16]

Allal may be on the verge of retirement, but unlike Alwaar in the novel, he is at the height of his police skills, a cop in his prime. The film reinforces this image not only through Aziz Mawhoub's acting but also through camera work. In *The Blind Whale* téléfilm, Hassan Rhanja uses a number of close-up shots to show Yaqdhan's eyes and his anxiety and fear while investigating the case. In *Sofia's Restaurant,* director Hassan El Ouahidi typically shoots the detective from a distance, placing him either level with the frame or at the top, looking confidently into the camera. He never uses a close-up shot of Allal's eyes or face to emphasize his emotions in the case. Moreover, unlike Yaqdhan in *The Blind Whale,* Allal operates unencumbered by the pressures of the police, free to investigate the case as he pleases. He works unemotionally at his own pace, operating without the threat of others meddling in his investigation, even though the case centers on a foreigner, which would normally attract an enormous amount of attention from both the police administration and the press. Yaqdhan is attacked as he investigates the case, but Allal in *Sofia's Restaurant* is never threatened. At no point in the film is his confidence undermined or shaken.

This televised image of the confident Moroccan police is reinforced by the locations and props used in the movie. As in *The Blind Whale* téléfilm, *Sofia's Restaurant* uses a real police station as its shooting location. Instead of the main police station in Casablanca, however, the film uses the smaller and lesser-known Salé police station. It is a striking new building that appeared in a number of police téléfilms that RTM produced between 2001 and 2003, and which was clearly meant to celebrate the police stations of the new Morocco. The film shows the outside of the building in several scenes, each with low-angle shots of the large police crest in the foreground. Once again, the téléfilm takes the audience inside the station, shooting the commissioner and the detective's office as well as the main stairwell. At the same time, the scenes of Othman in the station prison cell after his arrest show a space that is clean and empty, with four neatly positioned beds on the ground. This is an image that sharply contrasts with the widespread public perception during the Years of Lead that Moroccan prison cells were filthy and overcrowded bare cement spaces overrun with cockroaches and vermin. The film—and several others that used the same shooting location—conflicted sharply with the image of police stations that were circulating at the time in the dozens of narratives of former political prisoners that were published after 1998.

As in *The Blind Whale* téléfilm, *Sofia's Restaurant* includes sequences with the medical examiner and emphasizes his cooperation with the police. When Jacques goes to see his mother's body, for example, the film shows the inside of the real morgue in Rabat and the room where corpses are kept. As Jacques walks outside the building grief-stricken, Detective Allal discusses the case with the medical examiner, who is wearing a white robe with the crest of the hospital on the front pocket. Before the two part with a warm handshake, the medical examiner establishes the time of death and promises to send his forensic report as soon as possible. The medical examiner's findings later confirm that Othman's fingerprints were found on the knife handle, the final element that pushes the police to arrest Othman and charge him with the crime.

The stark differences between the novel and the film, however, are not limited simply to Aziz Mawhoub's portrayal of the cop hero or the sanitized depiction of police work. Even more importantly, in *Sofia's Restaurant* it is the police—and not the lawyer—who solve the case and reveal the killer. In fact, the lawyer is entirely missing from the téléfilm. As soon as the police receive the forensic report about the fingerprints on the knife, they arrest Othman without the dramatic chase depicted in the novel. Nonetheless, Detective Allal still has his doubts. In sequences that are absent from the novel, Allal returns to Sofia's villa to examine the crime scene once more and discovers a watch pin on the bedroom floor. The next day, he goes back to the villa with Jacques, Michel, the accountant, and the commissioner. When they arrive at the gate, Allal notices that Jacques has his own set of keys to the villa. He could have therefore entered the house on his own to murder his mother. Once inside, Allal asks Jacques what time it is and notices that the pin is missing from Jacques's watch. He then establishes that the pin he found on the floor the day before came from Jacques's watch. Becoming increasingly suspicious, Allal asks the accountant who would inherit Sofia's estate after Othman's arrest and is surprised to hear that Jacques is now the legal heir. Finally, on their way out, Allal asks Michel is if he spoke with Jacques in Paris on the night of the murder, and Michel confirms that he only talked with him the next morning.

Detective Allal gets in his car with his partner and tells him, "The evidence leads to the arrest of the suspect, but not always to the truth!" The two police officers then have the same conversation as the two lawyers in the novel about Selwa's possible role in the crime and decide to trail her. They follow her from the accountant's office to an upscale hotel and Inspector Omar discovers from the receptionist—without having to use a bribe, as in the novel—that Selwa was visiting Jacques. In the next scene, Jacques goes to the airport to leave the country and when he gives his passport to the border guard—played in a cameo by the writer Abdelilah Hamdouchi—the police are waiting in a backroom to examine it. They discover that he was actually in Morocco the night of the crime and arrest him on the spot. In the next scene, shot at the detective's office in the police station, Jacques confesses in detail to the murder. Unlike in the novel, his motives are purely financial. He explains to the police that he discovered that his mother had cancer and was afraid that her estate would soon go to Othman. He never mentions his anger and shame that his mother married a much younger man or that

Othman was having an affair, as he does in the novel. This allows the television to downplay the moral aspect of the crime, emphasizing instead that the main motive was money.

The final scenes in *Sofia's Restaurant* confirm the image of the Moroccan police as strong, confident, intelligent, and triumphant. The fact that all of the evidence points to Othman is a heavy condemnation of the police in *The Final Bet*, whereas in *Sofia's Restaurant* it appears as a innovative way of praising them. In the téléfilm, the police chase down all leads and when that evidence leads them to an innocent man, they are intelligent and professional enough to correct their error and find the real criminal. In the novel, it is the lawyer, not the police, who reveals the truth, even when it clashes with the evidence. The film therefore shows that the police are in total control of safety and security in Morocco. This image is further highlighted by the crime in the film: a French man kills his mother for money. In total contrast to the tabloids, crime in *Sofia's Restaurant* comes from abroad and not from within Moroccan society. In turn, this provides viewers with a comforting depiction of deviance in the country, one that parallels the image of crime in the press during the Years of Lead as well as the conservatism of RTM. Unlike *The Blind Whale*, which depicts a country facing a terrifying assault by professional killers and international drug smugglers, the crime in *Sofia's Restaurant* is simple and contained, involving only foreigners with little negative implications for the country and its future.

Moreover, a Moroccan man is wrongly accused of the crime but the police make every effort to uncover the truth and exonerate him. The film shows that when crime does take place, the Moroccan police are intelligent enough to solve it, regardless of how complicated and difficult the case is. In *Sofia's Restaurant*, therefore, the lawyer is not necessary. The police naturally arrested Othman because it is their job to apply the law wherever the evidence leads them. In the rare instance when the evidence is misleading, they will correct the error before it is too late and bring the real criminal to justice. In *Sofia's Restaurant*, there is absolutely no need for a lawyer to be present during garde à vue. The threat that a lawyer could pose to state authority is therefore eliminated.

The screenplay for *Sofia's Restaurant*, carefully adapted for RTM, provided the highly conservative television station with a timely and effective opportunity to take the first steps toward modernizing its local productions while avoiding the daring image of crime and police work of *The Blind Whale*. Abdelilah Hamdouchi provided them with a model of a cop who fit the television station's requirements. Allal, on the verge of retirement but still confident and intelligent, served as a parallel for RTM as an institution and gave the station the cultural structure it needed to present the model cop. Even though the image of the cop and police work were highly conservative, the act of making a police téléfilm—and taking the cameras into the police stations—was a major step forward for RTM and demonstrated a massive shift in its programming agenda. RTM and

2M filmed their first police téléfilms at the same time and even though they each presented significantly different images of the police, both films demonstrate a radical transformation within the television establishment.[17] *The Blind Whale* and *Sofia's Restaurant* opened up the police station for all to see and allowed viewers to accompany the films' detectives as they investigated crime in the new Morocco, establishing a new democratic concept of state authority for the wider public in the process.

No One Is Above the Law: Censoring Adil Fadili's *The Witness*

The success of both *The Blind Whale* and *Sofia's Restaurant* on television encouraged immediate imitation. Between 2001 and 2003, a total of fourteen police téléfilms were produced and screened. One of the most important police téléfilm directors from this period, Adil Fadili, would move the genre in a new direction thanks to his highly contentious depiction of the Moroccan police and their investigations. Fadili's films combine exciting police chases with images and mise-en-scène that consciously imitate those of American television and cinema. His work from this period develops the increasingly fantastic—even Hollywoodized—nature of Moroccan police téléfilms. Fadili's use of close-ups, bright colors, dramatic music taken from American films, and sensational plot elements far from any Moroccan reality would bring the image of the police on television away from Hamdouchi's law-bound middle-class detective to a Moroccan cop who resembled a character in a Hollywood movie. The increasing turn toward Westernized and fabricated depictions of the Moroccan cops in the mass media worked to recast the real-world police into a role that embodied American and European concepts of the rule of law, equal rights, and technological modernity.

One of Fadili's films from this period, *al-Shahida* (The Witness), produced by 2M and aired on September 23, 2003, marked a new stage in the development and control of the image of the police on Moroccan television.[18] While Abdelilah Hamdouchi would be careful to tailor his screenplays for the culture of each channel, Fadili's film was so daring in its image of the police that the executives of 2M would censor it and radically transform its message without the director's knowledge or approval. The uncut film represents an audacious challenge and contestation to the reforms taking place in Moroccan society. By unilaterally censoring the film, executives at 2M demonstrated how deeply they were invested in disseminating the desired image of the police and, consequently, state authority on television. *The Witness* points to the widening network of actors involved in producing the new images of the police in society. It also shows the mechanisms by which acts of contestation and dissent were suppressed in the new era.

The film begins as a young man, Redwan, sits at a nightclub with his girlfriend, listening to pounding techno music. Redwan goes to the bathroom, snorts two lines of cocaine—a drug that is restricted only to the country's wealthy—and takes his girlfriend roughly by the arm and pulls her out of the club. They then speed along the Casablanca seacoast in his convertible BMW—another symbol of his wealth—as Redwan becomes increasingly agitated under the effect of the drug. The film then cuts back and forth between a nurse who is caring for a sick woman in her home and the couple in the car, who stop on the street outside and begin fighting, set to traditional drum and pipe music. The nurse looks out of the window and watches as Redwan attacks his girlfriend and kills her on the sidewalk. After Redwan leaves, the nurse comes down to the street, looks at the body, and finds a wallet, which Redwan accidentally left behind before fleeing.

The film then cuts to the main police station in Casablanca. The camera takes a wide-angle waist-high shot from the side of the building as two uniformed officers walk through the main entrance. The camera then moves up while maintaining a wide-angle shot until it centers on the large shield of the police at the center of the building. Much like the long panning shots in *The Blind Whale*, Fadili uses this sequence to confirm the location for the audience, emphasizing the connection between the real-world police and the fictional film. The scene then shifts to a pair of inspectors, Aziz and Khalid, as they sit in the commissioner's office discussing rising crime in Casablanca. Aziz has a striking goatee and is dressed entirely in black, including a black leather jacket. Khalid, on the other hand, wears stylish glasses, a light shirt, and a suit jacket. The pair look young and modern, plainclothes detectives ready to act.

The commissioner puts the two on the case of the murdered woman found on the sidewalk. As the two inspectors leave the commissioner's office and walk through the police station, the film begins the conflict between them that lies at the core of the narrative. Visibly angry and disgruntled about having to work the case, Aziz begins talking first:

> Aziz: Whenever there's a bitter deal, they stick us on it.
>
> Khalid: Why you telling me this? Go tell the commissioner. You're the alarm bell, you tell him.
>
> Aziz: Why don't you go tell him?
>
> Khalid: Because for me, cases are all the same. And the one we're on now, somebody got murdered.
>
> Aziz: Murdered? C'mon, man! Is this first time someone got murdered? I want to know, where do you live, where? Mars? I'm talking with you and you're laughing, man. We need a case we can bite into like brothers.
>
> Khalid: We need a case? Go on in, brother, and tell him. No one's stopping you. See you later.

As Khalid walks off, Aziz steps in his direction menacingly with a disgusted look on his face. This quick exchange draws a clear division between the two cops. Aziz represents the corrupt police from the previous generation, always looking for ways to make money on the side, not serving society and applying justice. He uses the phrase "bitter deal" to tell his partner that there is no way for them to profit from a murder case. The word for "deal" in Moroccan Arabic—*hamza*—signifies a way to make a lot of money quickly with little effort. For Aziz, that would mean arresting someone for frequenting a prostitute, for example, with the sole intention of taking a bribe to let them go. Telling Khalid that they repeatedly get "bitter deals" is another way of complaining that they do not get put on cases in which they have the chance to make quick money. He is annoyed that they are stuck investigating a murder victim from an impoverished family with no possibility of kickbacks.

As far as Khalid is concerned, he works all of their cases in exactly the same way. According to him, this latest case involves murder, the most egregious of crimes, and the victim deserves justice. Aziz mocks Khalid for this, however, by asking if he is from Mars. He says that they need a case in which they can work together "like brothers" to make money but Khalid pats him on the back and dismisses him before walking off. The two have this exchange in the heart of the police station, right outside of the commissioner's office, without trying to lower their voices, indicating the deeply rooted nature of corruption among the police establishment. Several uniformed officers even walk by as they have this loud exchange, showing that Aziz has little concern about hiding his corrupt ways. Khalid, on the other hand, represents the presumed enthusiasm among the police for the new era of the rule of law, *Alternance,* and respect for human rights. Through these characters, conservative Moroccan television has openly and daringly presented a corrupt cop to the public for the first time. The film uses the relationship between Aziz and Khalid not simply to demonstrate how television is opening up to taboos but also to explore the conflict and contention at the heart of the police establishment between the cops of the older generation—the Years of Lead—and those of *Alternance* over the future of the rule of law in the country.

This conflict deepens once they investigate the victim's background. They learn about Redwan and discover that his father, Mr. Hamdani, is a former minister. Predictably, Aziz is unable to hide his excitement that they will investigate someone with vast connections and wealth. He tells Khalid that they have to "come to an understanding" so that they can profit from the case, but Khalid refuses and chastises him. As the conflict continues to simmer between the two cops, they go to Mr. Hamdani's house to serve him a summons for his son. The charged scene deepens the conflict in the film over the rule of law and corruption by linking it to the wealthy former minister, a figure who symbolizes state authority and privilege:

> AZIZ: Your son must come with us to the police station so we can question him.
>
> MR. HAMDANI (INCREDULOUSLY): My son is going to go stand at the police station with you? My son is going to be questioned? Incredible!

Aziz: There's nothing incredible at all, Mr. Hamdani. Your son is a suspect in a murder and he has to, he has to—

Khalid (cutting off Aziz):—be treated like everyone else. The law is clear. Unless you think, sir, that you're above the law.

Mr. Hamdani (firmly): What's this idiocy, son? Keep it to yourself. Don't you know who you're talking to?

Aziz: Mr. Hamdani, these are just normal measures.

Khalid: Normal for us, Aziz. But for you, Mr. Hamdani, I think you still haven't heard the news that the country has changed and the times have changed. We're the children of the new day.

Mr. Hamdani (mockingly): Spare me the speech, son, and keep it to yourself. My boy isn't going with you to the police station. And you're not going to investigate him. Do whatever you want. Go ahead, apply your law.

Aziz: Mr. Hamdani, we've only come so we can find some way to arrive at a—

Khalid (cutting him off): What way, Aziz? What way? He told you to apply the law. I'm going to apply the law and do my work and that's it.

Mr. Hamdani (angrily): What's that mean, son? Are you trying to scare me? Are you challenging me? Are you saying that with this job of yours, you can challenge me?

Khalid: I'm not challenging you, Mr. Hamdani. I'm just here to do my job. And my job right now is your son! (He points rudely at Mr. Hamdani.)

Aziz: Hey, Khalid!

Khalid (raising his hand): And I'll add something else. Your son is up to his ears. Goodbye.

Khalid hands the former minister the summons at the beginning of the scene so that Mr. Hamdani knows that the situation is serious and requires a significant bribe in order to get his son out of it. When Mr. Hamdani mocks them for thinking that his son would go to the police station, Aziz tries to tell him that it is just a standard measure and nothing to be worried about, leaving the door open for them to "come to an understanding." Once Mr. Hamdani becomes angry at Khalid, Aziz steps in and tells him that they have come to see him only so they can find a solution to the problem, showing that he is ready to do business. Before he can even utter the word, however, Khalid cuts him off. Khalid accusingly tells Mr. Hamdani that he is not above the law and mocks him for acting as if the times have not changed in Morocco, taking this bold stance out of firm conviction that the country has made a fundamental break with the past.

Even though Mr. Hamdani knows that his son killed the woman, the film stresses that he does not live in the same Morocco as the rest of the country. Mr. Hamdani and his son represent the "important people"—known in Moroccan Arabic as *lkibar*—who live above the law and at the expense of poor, symbolized by the murder victim at the beginning of the film. In a tone underscoring the class conflict of the situation—a wealthy former minister is dealing with two low-level inspectors—Mr. Hamdani mocks Aziz and Khalid for thinking that his son will come to the police station for questioning. For Mr. Hamdani, the law in Morocco is for others, not him and his family. His sense of privilege and immunity leads him to tell the inspectors in a mocking tone "to apply their law," as if it does not concern him. Mr. Hamdani—and his cocaine-addicted murderous son, Redwan—represent the class of arrogant and elite Moroccans who live set apart from the rest of society, doing whatever they want, whenever they want. They are the people whom the police served during the Years of Lead and who still act as if nothing has changed in "the new day."

Despite Khalid's confidence, the commissioner soon gets a phone call from his superiors—presumably the chief of police—ordering him to stop investigating the case. Khalid is furious and confronts the commissioner, but can do nothing to restart the investigation. At this point, the film toys with the audience, suggesting that the times have not changed in Morocco and that the rich and powerful can do as they please, as they have since independence. Someone higher than the commissioner intervened to stop the investigation, suggesting that despite the slogans of the state and enthusiasm of inspectors like Khalid, the institution of the police is the same as in the past. The police work simply to protect the wealthy, not to guarantee the rule of law.

In a heroic move, the nurse who witnessed the murder at the beginning of the film arrives at the police station and tells the inspectors what she saw. Clearly agitated by the new development, Aziz tries to meet with her alone—implying that he will suppress her complaint if given the opportunity—but she insists on seeing both detectives. Khalid exuberantly brings her statement to the commissioner, who becomes furious. Shocked at the development, he yells out, "Her blabbering is going to bring us big problems!" The commissioner, therefore, worries only about offending his superiors and keeping his job, not necessarily about following justice or applying the rule of law. Despite his original orders, however, the investigation must now go forward. The police cannot bury the case if there is a witness who insists on testifying. Nonetheless, it soon becomes clear that Aziz has been meeting secretly with Mr. Hamdani, giving him information about the case in exchange for bribes. By doing so, Aziz puts the witness's life in danger as Mr. Hamdani's henchmen soon threaten her and her son.

Next, Mr. Hamdani visits the commissioner at the station to see where things stand. He is more direct with the commissioner than he was earlier with the inspectors:

> I came to see you personally to find out if you're with me or like the others. Are you too going to tell me "the law is above everyone" and "the times have changed"? You're the ones who've changed! And that woman, that woman

you're giving all this attention. She said (Mr. Hamdani adopts a mocking tone), "I'm an eyewitness." So what? If she has something to say, don't listen to her! Don't pay attention her! Even if you do what she wants, bury the police report. Hide the evidence. Is that so hard for you?

The commissioner explains that unless he receives orders otherwise, Mr. Hamdani should hire a lawyer for his son. Suddenly, the commissioner receives a phone call from his boss, who tells Mr. Hamdani that the case is taken care of and that he has nothing to worry about. Mr. Hamdani then stares furiously at the commissioner and mocks Khalid as he walks out of the police station. This sequence begins by showing Mr. Hamdani's shock that the police appear to have changed in the new era because they are taking the testimony of a nurse seriously. It ends, however, by showing that in a case of witness statements, the rich and powerful remain above the law.

In the next scene, however, the witness finds Redwan's wallet, which she had forgotten about, in her closet. Clearly having faith in the rule of law in the new Morocco, the witness decides that she must bring it to the police and testify. She arrives at the station and runs into Aziz first, who tries to take the wallet from her, but Khalid comes and brings the witness into their office. With the wallet found at the murder scene now in police evidence, Redwan will be charged with the crime. Mr. Hamdani then quickly arranges for a Canadian visa for Redwan and tells him to pack his bags. They all go to the Casablanca airport and the film ends as Khalid and Aziz take Redwan away under arrest on the tarmac with Mr. Hamdani and his wife watching from the gate. Mr. Hamdani has a pained and defeated look on his face. The film's credits then roll across the screen and the message is clear—the times have truly changed in Morocco and even though there may still be corrupt cops on the force like Aziz and arrogant former ministers like Mr. Hamdani, they cannot influence the course of justice. Moreover, Aziz participated in the arrest, right in front of the powerful ex-minister's eyes, showing that he has now been forced into the new era despite taking bribes. No one is above the law and police corruption will eventually be overcome. The days of important officials and their families acting with impunity are over. Khalid now symbolizes today's police, who treat all cases and suspects the same. They will seek justice in all investigations, regardless of the obstacles put in their way, even if those obstacles come from a corrupt partner or a commissioner who puts the orders of his superiors before justice. The film therefore presents the public with a striking condemnation of the privileges of yesterday, the old excesses of the police, and the previous lack of rule of law in Morocco. The times have indeed changed.

There is only one problem with this analysis. The ending of *The Witness* that 2M screened and the Moroccan public saw was not the ending that Adil Fadili filmed or that he and his fellow screenwriters wrote. In fact, when Fadili watched the movie when it aired, he was shocked to see that 2M had censored his film—

and changed its entire meaning—without informing him. In the original ending, which was described in an article published in *Moroccan Events* on September 29, 2003, the film continues after Redwan is arrested at the airport.[19] The film shows him in jail and then, at the day of his trial, the witness appears walking hesitatingly toward court. Before she gets inside the building, however, two hired killers approach and stab her to death. The film then shows Mr. Hamdani get a call on his cell phone inside the courtroom telling him, "The witness has been silenced forever." Mr. Hamdani smiles and when a mistrial is announced, Mr. Hamdani and Redwan leave the court. The film ends after the two talk with the press outside the building and walk away free.

The film's uncut ending gives it an entirely different—and audacious—meaning. It shows that the wealthy and powerful in Morocco are in fact above the law and that enthusiastic inspectors like Khalid are powerless to change that. In the end, Mr. Hamdani's power and prestige allow his son to get away with murder, thanks to the help of corrupt cops like Aziz and the commissioner's boss. With this original ending, all talk of the times changing in Morocco is simply an illusion. In the uncut version, Khalid looks naïve and foolish for believing that the country is truly changing. The rich and powerful will always act with impunity and do as they please, regardless of what propaganda is being disseminated in society. In the original ending, the "new Morocco" is simply a fabrication, nothing more than empty talk to cover up the fact that only slogans have changed, making the film a shocking act of contestation against state authority.

Fadili was furious that 2M cut his film and *Moroccan Events* mocked the station for doing so. The journalist who wrote the article explained derisively, "In Morocco, there are no corrupt judges, no murderers, no children of the rich and powerful who pass easily through the biggest problems. No, in Morocco 'everything's great.' There's no need to give it something like Fadili's image, and most of all, not on television." The article refers to the closely monitored mass media of the Years of Lead, media that fabricated and projected an image of Morocco as being a land of safety and security as well as the rule of law. It also suggests that despite the recent apparent changes at RTM and 2M, television has remained the highly restricted and controlled medium it has always been. The article states that 2M did, in fact, inform Fadili about the change and when he refused, they went ahead with it anyway. Fadili insisted to me, however, that he first learned of the change to his film as he watched it on television. By making this cut, the author of the *Moroccan Events* article explained, 2M changed *The Witness* into a false witness on reality.

The issue goes well beyond what the article in *Moroccan Events* discusses. In its censored form, *The Witness* presents a powerful depiction of the new Morocco that matches the carefully crafted image of police and state authority disseminated by the true-crime articles and other téléfilms. The message of the censored film is clear: someone as influential as an ex-minister can no longer skirt justice.

Khalid, the cop of the new era, triumphs, and no one, not even someone who is considered one of *lkibar*, is above the law. In direct contrast to the original version, the censored film depicts the Moroccan judicial system as making a fundamental break with its corrupt past. The act of censorship therefore transformed the film from a daring act of contestation into a work that celebrates the state's message of respect for the rule of law and civil liberties in the new era. As such, Fadili inadvertently used his depiction of the conflict between the two inspectors and the former minister to disseminate exactly the opposite message from what he intended. Moreover, by filming in the main police station in Casablanca while using real-world police cars, props, and uniforms, Fadili fuses police fact and fiction to give credibility not to his act of dissent but to the depiction of the new Morocco circulating elsewhere in the mass media.

The censored version of *The Witness* demonstrates the lengths to which 2M went to control the image of the police on television. 2M executives not only arranged for *The Witness*—like other cop téléfilms—to be shot with real props in the main police station in Casablanca but also moved to edit the film unilaterally to ensure that it presented a highly positive image of the police and justice system, one that matched the aspirations of the state in the new era. This shows how sensitive the image of the police and state authority was on television, which reached an audience of millions. It also demonstrates what happened when someone challenged the image of state authority that had been circulating in the various media. As will become clear in the following chapters, *The Witness* represents an important precedent for the increasing involvement of the state in the mass media in order to construct and carefully manage the image of the police for the broader public.

Fabricating the Police in Jamal Belmajdoub's *White Nights*

More téléfilms appeared after *The Witness* that continued to disseminate the image of the Moroccan police as representing a fundamental break with the country's authoritarian past. The most striking of these works was Jamal Belmajdoub's *Layali bayda'* (White Nights), produced by 2M in 2004 and aired on November 11, 2005.[20] *White Nights* is Belmajdoub's only police téléfilm, but in it he created a new, highly fabricated image of crime and cop work in order to expand the construction of the police as representing key democratic values, such as the rule of law and gender equality. He also revised the cop television film to target a different kind of audience with the message of the new police and their relationship with state authority in the era of *Alternance*—Morocco's youth.

In *White Nights*, Casablanca is in the middle of a massive drug epidemic. The police are extremely anxious because teenagers are dying seemingly every day from cocaine overdoses. In the opening of the film, a drug middleman named Rojo kills his dealer for betraying him. When the dealer turns up dead the next day on the city shore, the police begin investigating his background and find that he was selling drugs to a number of students at a high school in the city center. The police question the students and then search the dealer's house. There, they recover a notebook, which has the name of the supplier, Rojo. After a long investigation, the police track down Rojo, but find him dead. It appears that he hanged himself, but the police are suspicious that he may have been murdered. While processing the scene, Nabil, the lead detective, finds a piece of a key chain that eventually leads to the film's shocking ending. The detective discovers that the chain belongs to his own brother, who turns out to be the mastermind of the drug network that the police have been investigating throughout the film. Faced with the choice of bringing his brother to justice or preserving his family, the lead detective demonstrates that no one is above the law in Morocco. The film ends as the police arrive at the detective's home, where the brother also lives, to make the arrest.

The most prominent aspect of the film is the clash between realism in shooting locations and fabrication of Hollywood elements in a Moroccan environment. As in other police téléfilms, much of the film is shot on location at the main police station in central Casablanca. Long pan shots of the main entrance with its massive shield precede nearly every scene that takes place in the station. The film also shows the criminal and forensic police working crime scenes meticulously, wearing latex gloves, taking pictures of victims, and transferring bodies for autopsy. Real ambulances and crime-scene equipment appear in these scenes. Like other Moroccan police téléfilms, *White Nights* emphasizes the role of the medical examiner, whose reports the police discuss at length and rely on for leads in the case. Like *The Blind Whale*, the film takes the audience inside the Institute for Forensic Science at the Ibn Rochd Hospital in Casablanca as Rojo's widow arrives to identify his body. The film also depicts realistic mundane elements of cop work in great detail, such as the way the police separate suspects into interrogation rooms for questioning, spend the night in unmarked cars conducting surveillance, search the home of a suspect, and work under tremendous pressure to solve the case quickly.

In addition to the depiction of the central police station and cop work, Belmajdoub goes to great lengths in *White Nights* to set scenes in the city in realistic locations. As the film's title suggests, much of the action takes place at night. Belmajdoub shoots the dark Casablanca streets in the city center from a variety of angles. In addition to shots from above the city looking down on the buildings and traffic, scenes are shot in seedy alleyways, dingy drug dens, and dark bars full of drunken men. The film includes many panning shots of recognizable city streets, as well as a large high school in the center of town, grounding the narrative in a credible depiction of modern-day Casablanca.

In stark contract to these shots, the film boasts a number of highly fabricated elements that both point to and draw from American television and cinema. The first of these is the depiction of drugs. At the time the film was shot, the press was reporting on what appeared to be skyrocketing drug and alcohol abuse among the country's youth and the way these addictions led to violent crime. Drugs common among Morocco's youth are either hashish or a kind of local speed named *qarqubi*. The film, however, depicts young Moroccans at a large public school addicted to cocaine. Cocaine may be the drug of choice among Hollywood elite but at the time of filming, it was extremely rare in Morocco. Since distribution routes do not typically pass through the country, the drug is so expensive that few can afford it, especially when compared to the massive local trade in inexpensive drugs such as cannabis-based products. To this day, cocaine remains the drug of the wealthy and elite, of a character like Redwan in Adil Fadili's *The Witness*, not ordinary high school students. The rampant use of cocaine in the film suggests an imitation of drug abuse among the youth of American cinema and television, not the streets of Morocco.

Belmajdoub does not stop there. He also depicts cocaine drug deals in a way that clashes with Moroccan reality. For example, Rojo, the middleman, meets another dealer in a dingy location to buy a large quantity of cocaine. Rojo hands the man a briefcase packed with cash while the other man gives him a briefcase full of cocaine. Rojo dips his finger in the cocaine, and then rubs it in his mouth—audibly—to check the quality of the drug. In another scene shot in a run-down abandoned warehouse, Rojo's men—wearing cloths over their mouths and noses—use spoons to measure out amounts of cocaine from carefully wrapped bricks into dime bags on a rusty metal scale, which squeaks loudly as the men check the weight of each bag. The grimy locations suggest that Rojo is dealing cheap drugs such as *qarqubi*, not a product that costs thousands of dollars. Just as the image of a cocaine epidemic among the Casablanca youth starkly contrasts with Moroccan reality, the depiction in the film of dealers buying briefcases full of the drug and dividing it up from bricks into small bags strongly alludes to the representation of cocaine deals on American television as opposed to anything credible on the Moroccan terrain.

Belmajdoub alludes to the American cop show throughout the film for a purpose. The depiction of cocaine use and drug deals in the film is used as a tool to transform the local terrain of Casablanca and the Moroccan police for the audience. Instead of facing a case of ordinary local drugs, the police in the film are investigating an entirely new challenge. This sudden drug epidemic is rich with Hollywood symbolism, not only for crime but also the police in the film. Depicting Casablanca flooded with cocaine may be a fabrication, but it provides the opportunity for the film to present the Moroccan public with their local police investigating a case familiar from an American environment. This allows the film to tap into the meta-text of programs like *Miami Vice*, elevating the kinds of crime taking place on the streets of Casablanca and recasting the role of the Moroccan police to resemble their American counterparts, with all of the implications for transforming their image into that of exciting and cool cops.

This highly fabricated depiction of Moroccan drug culture is reinforced by the strikingly modernist style and imagery that frame the film. For example, *White Nights* opens at night as a drug addict walks through central Casablanca. The scene's colors are warped red and the film uses a combination of slow motion, blurry tracked images, and distorted sounds to give the audience the sensation of seeing through the addict's eyes. Throughout the film, sequence transitions jump quickly with sharp electric shock sounds. Scenes are shot with deep, rich colors and are spliced together to give the film a feel of an MTV production, something radically different from the conservative camerawork of *The Blind Whale* or *Sofia's Restaurant*. *White Nights* also uses music much more extensively than other police téléfilms from the period. As the film's cops jump into their cars, arrest suspects, or raid houses, they are accompanied by the same exciting electronic music that comes across like theme music celebrating the police. In contrast, scenes with drug dealers are accompanied by droning dramatic electronic music, suggesting to the audience that they are particularly nefarious.

In addition to the depiction of drugs and the modernist audiovisual techniques, the film focuses in particular on high school students. In one scene, a group of male and female students leave school with their arms around each other and head toward a Mercedes, which is full of their friends listening to pounding techno music. After they get into the car, one takes a compact disc and begins to snort a line of cocaine from its surface. The snorting sound is emphasized as the music cuts off sharply, followed by rapid electronic scraping as the student shakes his head and holds his nose. With the music, cocaine, and imagery, scenes like this establish the film as one of the first television programs directly catering to youth culture in the country. Just as the tabloids targeted the semiliterate and working class public and *Moroccan Events* tailored its crime reporting to an educated reading audience that rejected the party press, *White Nights* represents the beginning of a focus on Moroccan youth culture in the mass media, which has exploded in the country since the film was made. In the process, Belmajdoub brought the new image of the police and state authority to this previously neglected audience, adapting the police téléfilm to their expectations for sensationalism in the audiovisual mass media. This points to a multiplicity of not only forms but also audiences of the police procedural in Morocco after the late 1990s.

The film's modernist images, colors, music, and focus on youth culture, however, form the background for the striking opposition between realistic and fabricated images of the Moroccan police. The film features three main cops, each with well-developed characters. Ahlam is an overeager Francophile female detective who works well with her partners and appears as a source of calm throughout the movie. Saeed is rough, temperamental, and athletic. Played by Driss Roukhe, who played the main Moroccan cop in the Oscar-winning film *Babel*, Saeed intimidates suspects, interrogates them harshly, and wants quick results. Finally, Nabil is the leader of the team. Played by the police téléfilm veteran Rachid El Ouali, he is sensitive, handsome, well dressed, and thoroughly obsessed by his work. All three wear leather jackets and shoulder holsters with semi-automatic guns, as if in an American television movie. In addition to this team of main detectives, the cops in the movie include a number of uniformed officers as well as a terse police commissioner who wears a stylish Burberry scarf and meets with the team for updates, pressuring them to solve the case quickly.

Belmajdoub's inclusion of Ahlam, the female detective on the team, is perhaps the most fabricated element in the film's depiction of the Moroccan police. Ahlam participates along with the other two male cops in all of their activities. For example, she interrogates the suspects arrested near the school along with her male counterparts. In one sequence, as seen in figure 10, she wears a shoulder holster with her gun visible and leans over an old man, trying to intimidate him into cooperating by questioning him about how he manages to support his two wives and four children. At first, it seems like the tables in Moroccan gender relationships have been turned as a young female cop browbeats an old Moroccan man. The problem, however, is that in 2004, when the film was shot, female criminal detectives did not exist in Morocco. Even if Jamal Belmajdoub was not aware of this, the police overseeing the filming at the main police station in Casablanca certainly would have known.

The fabricated nature of Ahlam's character is further emphasized in the scenes in which the team raids the dealer's house and Rojo's villa. In both, Ahlam holds her gun above her head and yells out "Police!" as the three rush in. Not only did Moroccan female detectives not exist at the time of filming, but the Moroccan police are only permitted to use their guns as a last resort, only when they are under attack. Any other use of a firearm can lead to the officer's dismissal and arrest. The image of the team—together with a female detective—raiding a house with their guns drawn high is therefore a direct imitation of Hollywood films with no basis in Moroccan reality. At the same time, this blatant fabrication—set in opposition to the real locations and props—allows the film to stress that the Moroccan police now embodied equality of the sexes, another signpost on the march toward democratic reform in the country. Even though there were no female criminal detectives in the country at the time, this did not stop Belmajdoub from improving on reality in order to present the public with evidence that the police in the new era promote gender equality.

Another element that gives the police a highly fantastic—and Hollywoodized—image is the way Nabil analyzes the case. He photocopies the drawings from the dealer's notebook and tapes them onto a dry erase board, drawing a series of arrows and the name "Rojo" with a black marker. This kind of analysis gives the Moroccan police station a similar image as that commonly seen in American cop television shows. In a scene that appears particularly absurd from the Moroccan perspective, Nabil brings in a doctor to give a psychological analysis of the victim's drawings. The doctor stands at the dry erase board, explaining to the lead detective how each drawing reflects the dealer's internal struggles. Although the use of a psychological profiler has become common in American crime shows, it appears in the Moroccan police téléfilm as pure style with no substance. Psychology has little standing in Moroccan society. Nonetheless, the television cop uses the same tools as his American counterpart, even if there is no basis in fact. The film therefore attempts to improve on reality, suggesting to the audience that the Moroccan police now act like American cops and bring in a specialist to analyze the psychological state of a drug dealer through his notebook drawings.

Although there are important differences between the sociocultural and economic environment that Baudrillard discusses in his work and that of contemporary Morocco, Baudrillard's concept of the hyperreal and simulacrum is valuable for understanding the importance of this image. According to Baudrillard, modernity is marked by the replacement of the real by simulations.[21] In turn, the real becomes a fabrication and counterfeit of something that does not exist. For Baudrillard, we understand the world through these simulacra, which are signs without a signified tied to reality. From this perspective, Belmajdoub can be seen as extending the work of police fiction in the Moroccan mass media. Sources such as the independent press and téléfilms sought to present the real-world police in the guise of fiction. In *White Nights,* Belmajdoub takes this process and extends it, fabricating Moroccan cops with little basis in reality but setting them in real-world locations, such as the central police station in Casablanca. In the process, Belmajdoub seeks to disseminate an image of the police that fosters gender equality, depicting the Moroccan police operating like American cops in order to reinforce the democratic values of the real-world police and their embodiment of the new era, even if it is patently false. The simulacrum becomes a tool for Belmajdoub to present viewers with an image of police that improves on the fictional images circulating in other police texts in society at the time.

In addition to the clash between realistic and Hollywoodized imagery, *White Nights* marks a significant development in the depiction of the lead cop and the rule of law in the country. The film spends considerable time developing the character of Nabil, the lead detective on the case, and his relationship with his fiancée, brother, and mother. The film introduces viewers to Nabil not at the police station but at his engagement party. Nabil appears well dressed in a sharp suit and his fiancée is wearing an ornate Moroccan dress. The rest of Nabil's family is present, including his mother and his brother Omar. Just as *The Blind Whale* introduces the audience to the main detective in the intimacy of his home, *White Nights* presents Nabil for the first time not in the police station but in an intimate private family gathering celebrating his engagement.

More so than any other police téléfilm, *White Nights* explores the intimacy of the lead detective's home life. In one early scene, after he is assigned to the cocaine investigation, Nabil brings the case files home and spends the day drinking coffee and reading the material on the living room couch. Nabil's mother tenderly tells him to stop drinking coffee and Omar playfully tries to distract him from his work. Their father passed away years earlier, but they live in a large, modern, and comfortable apartment in Casablanca thanks to Omar's supposed business deals. In another scene at home, Omar rests his head on his mother's lap as Nabil tells the two about his day's work trying to crack the case. In several scenes, Nabil's fiancée begs him to stop talking about his work when they are together. In other scenes, Omar makes fun of Nabil for not being able to separate his work and home life. By emphasizing Nabil's family life, *White Nights* taps into the work-home conflict at the heart of other police procedural narratives circulating in Morocco since the late 1990s.

The film develops the relationship between Nabil and Omar at length for the payoff in the final minutes. After Nabil recovers part of the key chain at the scene of Rojo's hanging, he comes home late at night. Nabil notices Omar's keys and after looking at them closely, he realizes that the part of the key chain that he discovered near Rojo's body came from his brother's key chain. Devastated but wanting to confirm his suspicions, Nabil leaves with Omar's keys and uses them to search Omar's office, where he finds proof that his brother is in charge of the cocaine network that he has been investigating throughout the film. Devastated that the comfortable house that he and his family have been living in for years was funded by Omar's drug operations, Nabil wanders the streets sobbing. As he collapses on the city steps, images of him crying are overlaid with shots of Saeed and uniformed police officers taking Omar away in handcuffs as their mother screams hysterically. Nabil is not there, but she yells out his name repeatedly, clearly blaming him for the destruction of their family, just as the film comes to a close.

The climax to the conflict in the film is played out not on the city streets but in the detective's home. Nabil finds the key to the case sitting on his living room table and it leads directly to his brother. *White Nights* shows the deep bonds of the Moroccan family and develops the home life of the cop more than any other Moroccan police téléfilm. But when Nabil discovers that his brother is the criminal that he has been tracking throughout the film, he makes the arrest without hesitation, despite his grief and understanding of what it will do to his family. In *White Nights*, it is never an option for Nabil's allegiance to his family to rise above his respect for the law. The film emphasizes to the public that the police of today embody stronger bonds than even the tightest family. In the film, the police in the new Morocco resemble their American counterparts in not only style but also substance—for them, the rule of law trumps all else.

With *White Nights*, the mass-mediated image of the Moroccan police entered a new phase. The film developed techniques that Adil Fadili began in his work, including striking modernist visual and aural strategies as well as a highly fabricated—even Hollywoodized—image of the police, set in direct opposition to the realism of the shooting locations. In the process, the film improved on reality, urging the public to see the real-world police through this fabrication. The televised Moroccan cop could embody and symbolize the new concept of state authority—with its democratic values—better than the real-world cop on the street. In this, *White Nights* stands as a direct attempt to simulate the Moroccan police for its youth audience, to replace the real-world police with fabricated cops like Ahlam and Nabil.

In 2001, 2M and RTM turned to police thrillers to begin the transition from the conservative television of the Years of Lead to a modernized television that reflected the aspirations of the new era of Mohamed VI and appealed to a mass audience. In this, Moroccan television was simply following a trend that was happening elsewhere as fictional police and crime television programming exploded in popularity in the United States after 2000.[22] Even though 2M and RTM have lost audience share to satellite channels in recent years, they still enjoyed wide viewership up to 2005, when *White Night* was aired. These téléfilms, with scripts in Moroccan Arabic, not French, were therefore a significantly more far-reaching and influential medium than the press for spreading the new image of the police to viewers across the country. Moreover, the sheer number of police téléfilms—several dozen—during this short period demonstrates a clear priority on the part of the two television channels to use the genre to mark a break with the past. It also shows how the stations made the image of the police on television something commonplace and banal, just as with the true-crime articles and serials in newspapers like *Moroccan Events*. With the newspapers and téléfilms—and the intertextual relationship between them—the blurring of fact and fiction in representations of the police spread through society, establishing a new way for the public to view not only the police but also themselves in their relationship with state authority.

In addition, the police cooperated with all the productions, examining scripts in preproduction, bringing film crews into central police stations, overseeing shoots, and outfitting the best-known actors in the country with uniforms, holsters, forensic equipment, cars, and vans. In the 1990s, such transparency and cooperation was impossible. By 2001, it not only became commonplace but also a sign that the real police stations in the country were open for all to see. The téléfilms therefore indoctrinated the public in the real police stations in an attempt to heighten public identification and familiarity with the real-world police through fictional narratives, erasing their long-standing image as sites of torture and human rights violations during the Years of Lead.

As was the case with the press, the fusion of fact and fiction on television was not the result of some crude high-level plot. Instead, the positive image of the police in the films was something beneficial for all involved. Directors, screenwriters, and actors wanted to make the best possible product and please television executives so that their next project would be funded. This was particularly important since there were only two television stations in the country that produced small-screen films. With limited budgets, all involved in a film's production know that competition will be fierce for the next round of accepted projects and are eager to gain whatever edge they can. As for the state, there was clearly a desire to open up the police stations to the public as part of the process of trumpeting the reforms taking place under the new king, using the police as a vehicle to show the public that there was a fundamental shift away from repression in state authority and into an era of transparency. The blurring of fact and fiction in these films also allowed them to produce and disseminate throughout society an image of the police that improved upon the flesh-and-blood cop on the streets.

The police establishment certainly sought positive publicity, and welcoming television crews into the police stations for supervised shooting—rather than letting them film elsewhere—would ensure that. Moreover, when the finished product did not produce the desired outcome, as happened with Adil Fadili's *The Witness*, the television station was prepared to intervene to ensure that the appropriate message was conveyed: the country has changed and the police have changed with it. This shows that the television administration wanted to please the police as well, especially since the state owned and oversaw the two stations.

Just as the depiction of the police in the novel *The Blind Whale* would have a profound influence on the way the independent press presented crime and punishment, the move in films like *White Nights* toward an increasing blurring between realism in location and fabrication in depiction of the police would prove particularly powerful in the next phase in the development of the image of the police in the new Morocco. The state would become increasingly more involved in the production and dissemination of these images. And it would employ a combination of realism and simulated representations anchored in Western imagery as a tool to redefine the police for the public and attempt to establish a new kind of citizen for the new era.

5 The Moroccan "Serial Killer" and CSI: Casablanca

Between the mid-1990s and the mid-2000s, fictional narratives of the police spread through Moroccan society. They first appeared in the form of a novel, *The Blind Whale*, and then moved to the country's first independent newspaper, *Moroccan Events*, which appropriated the novel's narrative strategies to invent true-crime reporting in the press. This new form of cultural production not only bolstered the newspaper's circulation but also disseminated a groundbreaking depiction of the police through the law-bound detective who represented a complete break from the Years of Lead. The main innovation of Moroccan True Crime, however, was the fusion of fact and fiction in presenting the public with a new image of the real-world police in a highly credible nonstate media source. This new format gave the real-world police an image that corresponded to the state's aspirations for a new era characterized by democratic principles, the rule of law, civil liberties, and human rights, encouraging the public to resituate their relationship with state authority.

The process of fusing fact and fiction continued to escalate when RTM and 2M began producing police television films in early 2001. Just as true-crime narratives served as an important vehicle for transforming the press, police téléfilms launched the local television industry on a process of radical change. These films brought the new image of crime and punishment from the novels and newspaper narratives to the small screen, demonstrating to the public that television was finally becoming responsive to a mass audience. At the same time, the films took the innovation of fusing fact and fiction to new levels: directors used well-known police stations and morgues as movie sets and actual cop cars, uniforms, and tools as props. Thanks to this combination of the real world of the police with fictional scripts and well-known actors, television disseminated the new image of the police that was established in the true crime articles on a scale much wider than the press. For the first time in the country's history, the real world of the police was opened up for the public, gaining widespread visibility throughout the country. In the process, the films sought to indoctrinate the public in well-known police stations, transforming them from locations of abuse and torture during the Years of Lead to sets for exciting television movies celebrating the new era. They also fabricated new kinds of detectives—like Ahlam in *White Nights*—who allowed the films to improve on reality in presenting the public with images of the real-world police, suggesting that the flesh-and-blood cop on the street matched the simulated police on the small screen.

New transformations in crime after 2002 challenged state officials and forced them to reevaluate their strategies for manufacturing the image of the police. The first of these was the emergence of a Moroccan "serial killer." The second, which the next chapter will discuss, was the terrorist attacks in Casablanca on May 16, 2003. Both events presented the state with completely unexpected new crime challenges for which the police suddenly appeared to the public as utterly unprepared. Both disrupted the carefully constructed image of the police in the mass media and necessitated that the police change once again in order to demonstrate that they were able to face the terrifying new reality of crime in the country. As part of their response to these unforeseen threats, the state became significantly more proactive in constructing and disseminating the image of the police for the public.

This chapter, which, like chapter 2, is deeply indebted to the work of social construction theorists like Stuart Hall and Stephen Jenkins, traces the emergence of the Moroccan "serial killer" and the way this new type of criminality both terrified the public and represented a deep crisis for state authority. Starting in May 2002, mutilated bodies began turning up on the streets of Casablanca. The sensational press—both independent and party newspapers alike—quickly linked the victims to a single murderer, proclaiming that Morocco now lived in the age of the serial killer, a type of criminality that was presumed to exist only in the United States and Europe. The emergence of this new criminal demonstrated to the public that embodying democratic values—the rule of law, individual rights, and freedom of expression—also meant embodying its deviance.

The press used the body count and gruesome methods of what appeared to be a single killer to contest the authority of the police for the first time since the Tabit Affair, quickly igniting fear and panic among the city's population. Put on the defensive, the police at first vehemently denied that there was a serial killer behind the murder spree. But when more bodies turned up over a ten-month period and the public remained in the grip of terror because of the inability of authorities to crack the case, the police began a new media campaign to address the threat and soothe fears. This chapter will trace how the emergence of this seemingly new form of criminality led to a new fabricated image of the police among the public. Before the serial killer, the public image of police was that of the hard-working, law-bound, and sympathetic detectives of the true-crime articles and police téléfilms. Now, apparently with a real-life serial killer on their hands, the state collaborated with the media once again to produce and disseminate a new image of the police that was needed to control the threat—one grounded in forensics, science, and rationality based on technology, an image widely known in the United States today thanks to television programs like the *CSI* franchise.

As before, the state turned to its familiar custom of cooperating with the media to disseminate this message by blurring fiction and reality. This time, however, it brought journalists—and not simply television actors and film directors—into the police stations and crime labs in order to present the new image to the public. This demonstrated a growing level of awareness and concern that the police had for public relations and for taking direct control of constructing their public image for the new era. By the time the police were finished with their media blitz, newspapers and television created a radical new identity for the Moroccan police in the country's economic capital—CSI: Casablanca. In turn, this transformed the identity of the police—and, consequently, state authority—by bringing them into the age of science, forensics, DNA, and modern crime labs, making their image as Western as the kind of criminality the country was suddenly facing.

Defining the Serial Killer

As has been discussed at length elsewhere, the FBI invented the term "serial killer" during the late 1970s and the American media popularized it during the 1980s.[1] The media in the United States set the stage in its sensational coverage of multiple murderers like John Wayne Gacy, Ted Bundy, and David Berkowitz during the 1970s. The FBI became interested in the phenomenon of serial killing thanks to the work of two of their agents, Robert Ressler and John Douglas, who began interviewing convicts who had killed multiple people in an attempt to understand the motives for their crimes. The pair soon conducted a systematic study of some thirty-six killers, including Gacy, Bundy, and Berkowitz, and used their data to create a new form of crime-fighting called "profiling." According to Ressler, criminal profiling "is a way of deducing a description of an unknown criminal based on evaluating minute details of the crime scene, the victim, and other evidentiary factors."[2] Profilers such as Ressler and Douglas created a list of common characteristics of the killers, such as suffering an abusive childhood, exhibiting cruelty to animals, excessive bed-wetting, and starting fires at a young age.

According to their study, serial killers have a compulsive obsession with acting out perverse fantasies. Establishing control and domination over their victims was another key element, as was a marked escalation in the nature of violence with each new crime. Ressler and Douglas classified serial killers as either "organized" or "disorganized," but they were typically sociopaths, sexually dysfunctional, loners, and intelligent, though they were not successful at school and typically could not hold down a job. They kept mementos from their victims, followed press coverage of the police investigations into their crimes, and typically returned to the scene of the crime or otherwise involved themselves in the police investigation. They also commonly suffered from a split personality disorder. Almost all serial killing was sexual in nature, commonly homosexual. Perhaps most importantly for the FBI, serial killers were described as targeting strangers, operating without a clear logical motive, and crossing state lines to commit their crimes. These final characteristics demonstrated why the FBI believed local authorities were incapable of fighting serial killers. Local law enforcement would not be able to connect the dots between seemingly random and motiveless crimes committed in different states by a single offender.[3] The FBI alone therefore had the experience and data to face the serial killer threat head on.

The FBI's interest in the serial killer came at a time in which the director of the Bureau "had been given a mandate to take the FBI in a new direction."[4] As Richard Gid Powers has shown, the FBI has a long history of exaggerating criminal threats in order to gain public support for increased funding and expanded jurisdictional powers.[5] Starting in the 1930s, for example, the FBI worked with popular culture industries and the mass media to sensationalize the threat of the gangster and publicize the FBI's "G-men" as the only answer to this new form of criminality. During the 1970s, however, the prestige and status of the FBI were heavily damaged once the public learned about the way the Bureau illegally spied on American citizens in previous decades. By the late 1970s, the FBI needed a new identity, and the creation of the serial killer and criminal profiler was part of a long-standing public relations strategy. As David Schmid has argued, "The FBI's approach to serial murder was just the latest example of the Bureau's habit of creating a variety of public enemies and then defining itself as the only effective way to deal with those enemies."[6] Moreover, the serial killer was presented to the public during a time in which the Reagan administration's tough-on-crime ideology dominated public discourse on safety. This atmosphere—together with trumped-up statistics—allowed the FBI to demand increased funding to meet the new danger.

From its earliest days, the FBI paid close attention to its public image and collaborated with popular culture industries such as Hollywood, television, and radio, as well as the press, in an attempt to direct the way the public then viewed them. Robert Ressler, acknowledging sociologist Philip Jenkins's claims that there was a panic during the mid-1980s, admits that the FBI worked directly with the media to publicize the serial killer:[7]

> We at the FBI . . . did add to the general impression that there was a big problem and that something needed to be done about it. We didn't exactly go out seeking publicity, but when a reporter called, and we had a choice whether or not to cooperate on a story about violent crime, we gave the reporter good copy. In feeding the frenzy, we were using an old tactic in Washington, playing up the problem as a way of getting Congress and the higher-ups in the executive branch to pay attention to it.[8]

The FBI, of course, did not simply cooperate with journalists about serial killers. They collaborated with writers and filmmakers to disseminate and celebrate the image of the criminal profiler and the serial killer. The best-known examples of this include the novels of Thomas Harris, who received raw material for his work directly from Ressler and Douglas, as well as the Oscar-winning film *The Silence of the Lambs,* which was filmed on location at the Behavioral Sciences Unit at FBI headquarters in Quantico, Virginia, in a way that served as a precedent for the use of Moroccan police stations as sets for cop téléfilms. As with the Moroccan police movies, *The Silence of the Lambs* presented a highly fabricated and uncritically positive image of the FBI for the public. Moreover, the box office success of *The Silence of the Lambs* launched enthusiastic coverage of serial killing in cinema, television, and print media in the United States throughout the 1990s.[9]

In the United States, the serial killer represents a form of cultural knowledge that exists at the intersection between real-world murder, sensational news coverage, and the bureaucratic interests of the FBI. It is also connected to the emergence of new concepts of policing, the rise of dominant conservative political ideology, and the mass media's lust for ratings and audience share. A string of murders based on a particular pattern of activity over a period of time does not create a serial killer. The collaboration of the mass media, real-world policing interests, and entertainment industries—together with the murderer's crimes and habits—do. Without this nexus of industries and interests, the concept of the "serial killer" does not exist, as was the case before the late 1970s.

An Illness That Only Exists in the West

There are many infamous criminals who killed multiple people over a period of time but were not called "serial killers" while they were active, such as the Boston Strangler, John Wayne Gacy, and Ted Bundy, because the cultural conditions for the emergence of the serial killer did not exist at the time. American media and law enforcement have since grandfathered them into the club—ignoring the fact that the term "serial killer" has the particular cultural and historical meaning outlined above—because it has proven useful for the mass media and FBI in the United State to have precedents on which to base the concept.

As in the United States, there were criminals in Morocco who murdered multiple people with characteristics that resemble the FBI's definition of a "serial killer." Nonetheless, these criminals were never labeled as such. One example is Mustapha Moutachawik, who was arrested in 1978 for killing seven people during the 1970s. There was little crime coverage in the Moroccan press in the 1970s and 1980s, and Moutachawik's crimes did not appear in newspapers at the time when they occurred.[10] His arrest, however, made front-page news in January 1978. Moutachawik's trial, which took place the following month and lasted for only a day and a half, also appeared in the press. Nonetheless, his case emerged during a time in which there was little sensationalism in the Moroccan media and the police had little interest or need to manage their image for the public. Although the term "serial killer" had already been invented, it had not yet been widely used in the United States. Unlike with Gacy and Bundy, however, there was never an attempt in Morocco during the 1990s to reexamine Moutachawik's case and label him a serial killer. One of most famous television broadcasts in Moroccan history, the first episode of the hit show *Waqaʻi* (Events), which aired on 2M in December 1993, featured an in-depth investigation into the Moutachawik case. Although news of American serial killers had appeared in the Moroccan media at the time, *Events* never attempted to label Moutachawik as a serial killer in retrospect.

The case of Mohamed Belharash, better known as the "Killer of El Jadida," was considerably more recent. His name erupted in the Moroccan press in June 2001 when the police arrested him after he stabbed a woman, who later died of her wounds. During his interrogation, Belharash casually mentioned to the police that this murder was not the only one that he had committed.[11] He explained that he had killed four other women during the 1990s. His first murder took place in June 1993, when he killed a prostitute. According to his statement to the police, he carefully watched and studied her for months to figure out her schedule and confirm when he would find her at home alone.[12] He then went to her house, had sex with her, and stabbed her to death in bed just as he was climaxing, "without the least feeling of fear or disgust."[13] Before leaving the apartment, he stole five thousand dirhams. Two innocent men were quickly arrested for the crime and found guilty of the murder.

With the first murder apparently solved, Belharash was free to hunt again and, in 1995, he repeated the same plan with another prostitute who lived alone, also stealing cash from her before leaving. He soon attacked a third woman, but she survived and did not report the crime to the police because she was married and did not want to attract a scandal. Two years later, in 1997, Belharash killed again. This time, he targeted and murdered a woman, who also worked as a prostitute, and her mother. With the police filing these cases as unsolved, Belharash acted again. In June 2001, he attacked and stabbed his final victim, but she cried for help and neighbors came to her aid, leading to his arrest.

By the criteria of the FBI, Belharash was no doubt a serial killer. The initial press coverage of his case explained that the police charged Belharash "with committing numerous murders" at various dates, and that there was "great similarity in the way in which the killer targeted the five women."[14] The press detailed how he stalked the women in a fashion similar to what the FBI call an "organized" serial killer, determining their schedules and obsessively planning his crimes so that the police would not catch him. He would also gain control over his victims through sex and then murder them when they were most vulnerable. Although he did not take mementos from his victims, Belharash did involve himself in the case. As was reported in the press, he attended the trial of the two men who were wrongly accused of his first murder and would regularly greet the wife of one of the men on the street, telling her that he hoped her husband would be released from jail.[15]

Belharash's personality also eerily fit the characteristics that the FBI laid out. The press emphasized how he was intelligent but unemployed. He was a loner who lived with his parents and was socially awkward and introverted. The main journalist covering the case for the independent daily *Morning* interviewed neighbors about Belharash's childhood and was told that he was "spoiled" as an adolescent and violent as a teenager.[16] Although journalists did not dwell on his childhood, unlike the media coverage of serial killers in the United States, they did emphasize his sociopathic personality. One journalist wrote that Belharash's behavior "indicated that he was a gentle person, but that appearance hid a terrifying killer who tirelessly chose his victims from women, desiring to sate his sexual instincts."[17] The wife of one of the wrongly accused men told the press, "The killer gave the impression that he was one of the best-natured people. No one knew what he was hiding inside."[18] The press also reported repeatedly that he committed his crimes "in cold blood" and that he invited friends for a "celebration" and night of drinking at the local bar after he killed each victim.[19]

Finally, all of his crimes were highly sexual in nature. The sensational media reported how Belharash had sex with his victims right before killing them but focused at first on the apparent motive of theft. Just before his trial got underway in October 2001, however, the press published Belharash's statements to the investigative judge that theft had nothing to do with the murders. Instead, he confessed that he killed the women when he was unable to achieve an erection with them. He claimed that he became infuriated when he failed to have intercourse and, blaming the women for his impotence, took his anger out on them.[20] Belharash's trial only lasted for two days and he was found guilty and sentenced to death on October 16, 2001.

Despite the clear indicators, no one in Morocco at the time claimed that Belharash was a serial killer. This was not because Morocco lacked the key elements necessary for the emergence of this kind of criminality. There was clearly a killer who murdered multiple people according to a set pattern over a period of time. There was also a sensational press that was free to cover crime, even from the time of Belharash's first victim in 1993. Moreover, there was a police that was seeking to shape public perceptions of its work. Nonetheless, the police and the press did not connect the dots during the 1990s when Belharash was active because the form of criminality known as "serial murder" simply did not exist in the country at the time. Rather, as the next section will explain, serial murder was widely considered an illness that existed only in the West and did not affect countries like Morocco.

When Belharash committed his murders, the police, media, and public could only have viewed them as individual incidents. Moreover, they were unsolved cases, which the press shunned before the true-crime articles of *Moroccan Events* that began appearing in the late 1990s. The police only discovered that there was a single person behind the multiple murders once they arrested Belharash and he was no longer a threat to public safety. There was therefore no widespread fear or panic that the police needed to calm. In turn, there was no need for the police to trumpet a new kind of criminal—as the FBI had done in the 1980s—since Belharash was arrested before he was ever viewed as a threat to public safety. Another opportunity for the police to transform their image in the face of a new kind of criminality, however, was right around the corner.

Mohamed Zouita and the Invention of the Moroccan Serial Killer

The story of Morocco's first encounter with a serial killer began with a brief article that appeared on the front page of the May 28, 2002, edition of *Moroccan Events*. It read as follows:

> Discovery of Man's Mutilated Body in Casablanca!
> Yesterday morning, Monday, the lower half of the body of a man about twenty-five years old was discovered on Judge Iliyas Street in the Maârif section of Casablanca, on one of the corners of an abandoned villa, near the Ibn Tufayl High School.
> Members of the Anfa Criminal Police went to the scene, where the remains were transferred to the morgue, and they opened an investigation into the identity of the victim and the perpetrators.[21]

Morning also picked up the story and printed a front-page article about the discovery on the following day, stating that police and medical sources confirmed that the victim had been mutilated. Moreover, authorities stated that they did not believe that the victim had been homeless because his feet were clean.[22] This last piece of information suggested that the victim knew his attacker. If the victim had been homeless, this could have indicated that it had been a crime between two strangers, something that was seen as rarely happening in the country.

These two articles appeared during a time in which the daily press was undergoing significant changes in the way it reported on crime. In early 2002, the true-crime articles of *Moroccan Events* began appearing every day instead of once a week in the "Justice" section. The style of these true-crime articles also influenced other newspapers, which began printing their own crime articles in a similar form. By 2002, independent newspapers like *Moroccan Events* and *Morning* began printing longer true-crime articles within each issue as well as straight news on the front pages about cases under investigation, signaling that they were competing for readers. When the story of the half-body turned up on the front page of both newspapers, it was part of a wide-scale trend that was taking place in the press. And like most crime stories at the time, this one soon faded into the background. Neither *Moroccan Events* nor *Morning* published another report on the torso in the following weeks since there was no arrest in the case.

Two and a half months later, on August 15, 2002, another body was found on the streets of Casablanca, this time in the Ben Msik section of the city. While the press only devoted a brief article to the first murder, this one commanded significantly more attention and challenged the police on how to respond. Instead of a news brief on the side of the front page, the case appeared as the lead story in *Morning* with the following bold headline: "Discovery of Young Woman's Body Cut Up and Packed into Bags in Casablanca."[23] The remains of a seventeen-year-old female high school student were found dismembered in five black plastic bags. The police suggested that the motive was revenge because of the great level of violence committed against her, indicating to the public that the killer knew the victim. Nonetheless, the crime clearly troubled the police from the outset since they immediately began cooperating with the press on the investigation. This initial article, for example, quoted a "well-placed security official" as its source and cited the medical examiner's report as well.

At first, journalists—in cooperation with the state—relied on their well-honed methods of presenting the public with a skillful criminal who was difficult to capture, a strategy commonly seen in Moroccan True Crime. This can be seen in the headline of the August 19, 2002, article in *Moroccan Events*: "Autopsy Shows Killers Are Professionals."[24] According to this article, the medical examiner's report indicated that "the killer was a professional or had knowledge of butchery because of the high degree of precision with which the dismemberment was conducted." The medical examiner's report offered plenty of detail about the crime and also stated it was likely that—because of the complexity of the crime and the sheer brutality with which it was committed—there was more than one person behind the murder. Thanks to the forensic detail, the terrifyingly violent and skillful killer served as foil for the hardworking and law-bound police. While the police had yet to catch the perpetrator, the forensic information at this stage was intended to demonstrate to the public that the authorities had the case under control.

The press employed another familiar strategy for interpreting the crime in the *Morning* article on August 19, 2002.[25] This article reported that the victim's family had told police that a girl knocked on their door in the evening and that the victim went out with her and never came back. Nonetheless, the victim's father said that his daughter did not have any enemies and "lived a normal life." In the same article, neighbors told the press about the victim's "uprightness and good manners," saying that she would never have left the house in the evening without a good reason. The article therefore suggests that the victim led a double life, appearing virtuous to her family but having relations with someone who killed her out of revenge for some unknown reason. The press therefore packaged the case into a form that was familiar to the public as early as the Tabit Affair and reappeared frequently in the tabloids, police novels, and true-crime articles.

The strategy of suggesting a professional killer and a victim with a double life is effective in calming public fears if the police solve the case quickly. Both elements represent obstacles to the police but add to their triumph once the killer is under arrest. After a few days, however, it started to become clear that the police would not crack the case as quickly as they had thought. Sensing that the crime could set off a wave of panic among the city's residents, the police continued communicating directly with the press in an attempt to shape public perceptions of the crime. For its part, the press was all too happy to support the police, printing front-page headlines about the "intensive investigations" into the case.[26] In its August 22 article on the case, *Moroccan Events* relied on its typical true-crime language, stating that the police were trying "to crack the puzzle of the murder."

The police continued relying on their old methods of crime publicity by juxtaposing their incredible efforts with the extreme complexity of the case. On August 27, *Moroccan Events* published another front-page article on the case, this time with a photograph of the victim. A shift in how the police attempted to manage the case can be seen in how a police source told the newspaper, "The perpetrator committed the crime after studying and observing the victim many times before killing her." The same source also admitted that "police could not exclude that the case has some connection with previous crimes and . . . that the investigation is proceeding with regard to one of the crimes that took place recently and whose perpetrator has not been arrested yet." By stating that the criminal studied the victim and that the most recent crime might be connected to the past cases, the police admit that they might have a serial killer on their hands.

Why would the police do this? Now that almost two weeks had passed since the body was discovered, the police needed to present the increasingly terrified public with a convincing reason for why they had been unable to crack the case. For the first time in the country's history, the press was following along as the police conducted an ongoing investigation into a murder, adding significantly to the pressure on authorities to crack the case quickly. Even when *Moroccan Events* presented a true-crime story about an unsolved crime, it was well after the murder had been committed and there were few suggestions that the killer could strike again. Now, the press was following along in real time, creating a new kind of true-crime serial from a real-life murder spree, and the police needed to manage their message to the public in order to combat rumors and calm fears. At first, they relied on their usual playbook, emphasizing that the killer was a professional, someone who knew how to avoid leaving evidence behind. Nonetheless, the police also suggested that the most recent murder might be linked to previous crimes. The police presented no evidence for this claim but they seemed to be pointing back to the case of Mohamed Belharash, the Killer of El Jadida, which had been cracked a year earlier, or even the murder from May, which remained unsolved. These suggestions, however, indicate that the police did not have a coordinated strategy for presenting the case to the public and were losing control of the message to the press. The new information provided the police with a reason for why they had been unable to crack the case, despite their hard work and forensic analysis. At the same time, it further inflamed the public's fear about the murders.

It was in this charged context that a third body turned up. On the morning of September 10, 2002, two trash collectors discovered the lower half of a female torso in two black plastic bags on the sidewalks of the La Gironde section of Casablanca. Thanks to the obvious similarities, the press immediately tied this new crime with the previous one. The front-page headline of *Moroccan Events* on September 11 read, "After Last Month's Crime in Casablanca, Discovery of Young Woman's Body Cut up into Three Parts with No Head!"[27] The article focused on the brutality of the crime—in addition to dismembering the body, the killer mutilated the victim with a razor in order to remove any identifying traits. The article also stated that the police hoped to identify the victim after transporting the remains to the medical examiner for autopsy and looking into missing-person records and recovering any latent fingerprints. It then concluded by highlighting the previous month's murder, which had not been solved yet.

It was at this point that *Morning*, in its front-page article on September 11, pointed back to the body discovered in May and suggested that all three murders might be connected.[28] Now that a third victim had been discovered, the public and press followed the case so closely that even party newspapers like the *Banner* and the *Socialist Union*, which had largely avoided crime reporting up to this point, began publishing front-page news about the murders. These included bold headlines and photographs of the location where the latest victim was discovered. The enthusiastic participation of the party press demonstrates how sensational the crimes had become. Even these stoic newspapers could no longer ignore the puzzling series of murders.

In the following days, the press detailed how the police, under tremendous and unprecedented pressure, furiously investigated the case, attempting to identify the latest victim and recover the missing head. Nonetheless, *Moroccan Events* began tying the case to the city's security, challenging the police to make an arrest. Its September 13 article linked the crime with the August murder and concluded, "Some people believe that Casablanca's security is before a test to prove itself by dealing with two crimes of an unusual sort."[29] This would be the first of many instances in which the press presented the murders as a way of discrediting the police and questioning their ability to crack the case. In the process, the press only added to the pressure on the police to respond effectively and soothe public fears.

In its issue on September 14, *Morning* shifted press coverage in the direction of serial murder, putting the police further on the defensive. The newspaper introduced the lead story with the following headline on the top of the front page: "Murder Series and Mutilation of Bodies Is Terrifying Young Women in Casablanca." The accompanying article explicitly links the three murders, citing widespread fear in the city among women because of the inability of the police to solve the crimes. The newspaper took the additional step of printing a full-page special on the murders, featuring five articles on the case, including highly graphic photographs of dead bodies reminiscent of the tabloids. The articles reviewed the details of the three murders, emphasizing the similarities among them: all the victims were mutilated to hide their identity, dismembered, stuffed into black plastic bags, and left on the streets of Casablanca. The main article provided updates on the investigations, emphasizing how the police had no additional clues, and criticized the lack of security in the city and the inability of the police to solve the murders. Moreover, the articles highlighted the rising level of terror in the city and interviewed women who explained that they were not straying far from their houses because of "the killer of Casablanca." One woman told the newspaper, "These crimes are strong indicators to the chief of police in Casablanca that he has not and will not be able to achieve security in the city."[30] With the crimes, press coverage, and public fears, the police were now being challenged from all directions.

While the perception that a serial killer was stalking the city grew, not all accepted this idea. The primary reason was that the public believed that serial murder was a form of criminality that only appeared in countries like the United States or France. The *Morning* special addressed this explicitly:

> It's very possible that the killer is a single person and that they are psychologically ill. No young woman that we interviewed, however, accepted this. Most of them confirmed, "These kinds of illnesses that we hear about in American movies don't exist in our society. These sicknesses only exist in Western societies." But what makes this possibility unlikely for these young women and also for investigators who have followed a number of murders in Casablanca is that, according to a security official, there has never been a crime committed in this country with a psychological motive.

The article admits that the concept of a psychopathic serial killer is foreign to Morocco. According to the women interviewed for the article, it seemed more appropriate for a Hollywood movie than for the streets of Casablanca. As for the police source, the serial killer is someone motivated by psychological disturbances. Psychology, however, is largely denigrated and neglected in Morocco as a science. As a result, it seemed impossible to admit that someone could commit a murder for psychological reasons and not something as simple as revenge or anger.

Despite the strong insinuations of the special in *Morning*, it was the well-known Moroccan Francophone magazine *Tel Quel* that spelled out for the first time what was becoming obvious to many people. In an article entitled "Serial killer in Casablanca?," the magazine wrote, "A serial killer is on the prowl in Casablanca. Is it necessary to believe it? At any rate, in the space of three months, and in similar circumstances, three bodies without a head, mutilated, dismembered, and placed in plastic bags have turned up."[31] As in *Morning*, the *Tel Quel* article mentions that many people do not believe that a serial killer could be on the loose and instead suggests that most are blaming Islamic radicals for the crimes. The article ends, however, by mocking the police for not recovering the victims' heads: "Our Islamists can remain calm. The heads are still missing for our 'profilers' to make the connection." By calling the police "profilers" at this point, the magazine ridicules the police for not acting like their American counterparts and triumphantly cracking the case. The elite Francophone press was now doing its part to discredit the police in their efforts to solve the crimes.

Widespread fear, public pressure, and criticism created a crisis for the police and pushed them to change the way they managed their message to the press. First and foremost, the police began vehemently denying the possibility of a serial killer. As seen in the front-page headline of *Moroccan Events* on September 16, the police claimed, "There was no way to link the [crimes]."[32] The unnamed police official quoted in this article also emphasized that contrary to what was being reported in the press, the police had a number of leads that they were investigating, stating that solving the case was simply "a matter of time." The newspaper reported more details about the latest crime in an attempt to calm the public, including that the police recovered traces of semen from the latest victim.

The most important shift in police strategy was the way they publicized information about forensics and science. This started in the September 17 issue of *Morning*, which included a full page of articles about the murder cases. Even though the police had no new leads, they disseminated more details, suggesting that forensic science would help them identify the victims and the killer. Newspapers began publishing interviews with medical examiners, who used the opportunity to communicate with the public about their work and its connection with police investigations. Previously, the medical examiner had only appeared in true-crime articles, police téléfilms, and the police novels. Now, the real medical examiner of Aïn Chok in Casablanca, Farida Bouchta, explained to *Morning* how she examined the latest victim for external evidence that could help solve the case, such as marks on the skin, damage to the sexual organs, and the state of the feet and hands.[33] She also detailed how she sent material recovered from the victim for crime lab analysis, such as blood, stomach contents, and any semen. The medical examiner now emerged from police fiction and appeared in the press not simply as a didactic vehicle for educating the public about forensics but as a new public relations strategy to calm escalating fears over the crime spree.

Bouchta's appearance in the press was no isolated incident. *Moroccan Events* printed an interview with medical examiner Saeed Louahlia, the director of the Institute for Forensic Science in Casablanca who had been involved in previous cases such as the apparent suicide of Mohamed at the Tangier port police station, discussed in chapter 3. With a long bold front-page lead, the newspaper introduced the interview by quoting Louahlia on the case: "Multiple people committed these crimes . . . and here are their descriptions!"[34] In the full-page interview, Louahlia emphasizes the basic role of forensic analysis and autopsy in any criminal investigation today. Louahlia then discusses the current case, commenting on the kinds of evidence that can be gleaned from the three recovered bodies. At the same time, he emphasizes that he does not think that the murders are related: "The killer in serial crimes always selects his victims from a single type because his idea is to kill a victim whose image obsesses him. They may be light-skinned with green eyes, for example. So if we had a group of victims who share the same characteristics, I could say that we are facing serial murder or a single killer." This coordinated appearance of the medical examiners suggests that the police recognized the escalating fears among the public that there was a serial killer hunting women on the streets of Casablanca. The front-page denials of Louahlia—the main authority in the country on forensic science—shows that the police sought to redirect the media's depiction of the case, demonstrating how the stigma of a homegrown serial killer was so strong that the police pushed hard for the theory of multiple killers instead.

Nonetheless, the police could not control the press so easily anymore. Just as newspapers printed the denials of the police and the medical examiners, they continued publishing information about mental illness and its connection to crime, further solidifying the construction of the concept of serial murder for the public and contesting the state. One article appeared in this period, for example, that explained that most serial murderers faced violence in their youth and that they have troubled relationships with women.[35] In turn, this helped underscore the possible psychological dimensions of the case, even if they seemed far-fetched to part of the public at the time.

Despite the incredible pressure on the police, they were unable to find the killer before another body turned up. On December 2, 2002, a thirty-year-old woman was found cut up into three pieces and placed in a bag in the Hay Hassani neighborhood of Casablanca. According to the press, the police immediately sent the remains to the medical examiner for autopsy. In its article on December 4, *Moroccan Events* emphasized the serial nature of the crime with the following headline: "New Part in Series of Murdering Young Women and Cutting Up Their Bodies in Casablanca."[36] This article begins by highlighting the police's inability to crack the cases: "After the police in Casablanca mobilized their best members to uncover the secrets of the two murders whose victims were young women cut up into a number of parts, they find themselves before a third crime committed in the same way." The article uses highly sensational language to describe the victim's remains, stressing the similarities between this latest crime and the earlier murders.

The next day, the press continued its oscillation between publishing sensational news of a serial killer and highlighting police attempts to calm fears. *Moroccan Events* printed another front-page article on the crimes, stressing the hard work and coordination of "the best elements of the police" across the city in investigating the case and that they were trying to identify the latest victim as quickly as possible.[37] Moreover, the article stresses how the Scientific Police, the Institute of Forensic Science, and the Department of Criminal Autopsy were working in coordination on the case. With the headline "Medical Examiner's Report in Advanced Stages to Identify Victim," *Moroccan Events* detailed how the medical examiner went with the police to search the crime scene for more evidence and reported that they were not losing their optimism despite the extreme difficulty of the case.[38] Nonetheless, the newspaper explained, "it is possible with the techniques used in the scientific investigation to collect some formations on the skin that might help identify the victim." With these articles, the press continued to publicize and celebrate the role of science in police efforts to catch the killer, throwing the spotlight onto forensics instead of simple detective legwork.

In a new effort to calm the public about the unsolved murder spree, especially considering that three of the four victims were still unidentified, the director of security in Casablanca at the time, Bouchaïb Rmaïl, took the unprecedented step of giving an interview directly to the press. He spoke with Abdelmajid Hachadi, the true-crime journalist who wrote for *Moroccan Events,* which published the interview on January 4, 2003.[39] Rmaïl first claimed that Casablanca's security was much better than comparable capitals and then quickly commented on the murder spree: "I want to confirm that the three murders [of the women] have absolutely no connection and that all talk about serial murder is wrong." He then outlined the cooperation among the police across the city and stressed that the medical examiner was working closely with them.

Despite the denials of the chief of police, this interview appeared above a long article about psychological motives for crime and opposite a full-page article about the series of murders.[40] This latter article begins,

> Is Casablanca living under the effect of a killer roaming its streets, lying in wait for the opportunity to murder its young women and dismember their bodies? . . . Does the intelligence of the killer and the way he cuts up his victims' bodies reveal a psychosis? . . . Has the level of criminality in Casablanca developed to the point of mutilating bodies, something that usually happens in Western capitals? Is it now possible for us to talk about what is known in these capitals as serial crimes?

The article discusses the various characteristics of serial killers in the West and stresses the fear hanging over the city, linking the recent murders and repeatedly asking why the police have been unable to solve the case or identify most of the victims. It emphasizes how the latest murder had turned the public toward the theory of a serial killer and that the threat of this new criminality had overwhelmed the economic capital.

The next victim, who turned up on January 25, 2003, would demonstrate the power of the sensational media to shape public perceptions. The body of a man dismembered and put into eight plastic bags was discovered in the Médiouna trash dump in Casablanca. With the headline "How Long Will Series of Cut Up Bodies in Casa Continue?," *Moroccan Events* published details of the crime on the top of the front page of its January 27 issue.[41] Within a day, however, the police were able to identify the victim, who was thirty-five years old. The press reported that the crime took place in the victim's home and that four people were being held for questioning. Optimism quickly spread that the police had finally cracked the series of murders in the city.

It immediately became clear, however, that this was a false lead in the real-life hunt for the Casablanca serial killer, showing how the case was like something out of a police novel. *Moroccan Events* reported the next day that the police had solved the most recent crime: the victim's girlfriend killed him and mutilated his body with the help of a friend and two hired men.[42] The woman explained to the police that they decided to murder her boyfriend in the same style as the "Killer of Casablanca" in an attempt to cover up their crime. On the one hand, this copycat murder gave credence to the police's claim that the crimes were all isolated murders, each committed because of revenge or anger. Moreover, the arrest gave the police the opportunity to present a victory to the public for the first time since the spree began. On the other hand, the latest killing showed that the case had become so prominent that someone committing a murder believed that the police would see the crime as yet another victim in the crime spree. It also indicated that not only did the girlfriend think that there was a single serial killer in the city but also that she believed the police would quickly include the crime as part of the string of murders. With this act, the media had attracted attention to the case to the point of influencing real-world murder.

The victory would be short lived. On the morning of February 11, 2003, the day before Eid al-Adha, a man was seen getting out of a taxi on Ibrahim Roudani Street in the Maârif district of Casablanca near the police station and placing two cardboard boxes on the sidewalk. The police were called to the scene, found the body of a man in the boxes, and transported the remains to the medical examiner for autopsy. The victim was a man in his late twenties, but he was not immediately identified because his facial features were mutilated and his fingers were cut off. His penis was also severed. The fact that the killer dropped the boxes off so close to the police station led *Moroccan Events* to call the crime "a new challenge to the Casablanca police" in its front-page headline on the murder and linked all six bodies together.[43] The same day, the *Socialist Union* published a front-page article about the crime, with a large color photograph of the location where the first box was found and another photograph of the eyewitness.[44] Stating that "once again Casablanca awakes to the rhythm of a new part in the series of murders and mutilations," the article describes the latest body as an affront to the police, calling it a "message" to the director of national security, who had visited the city the previous week to hold a meeting about the murder spree and visit the crime scenes.

Fear gripped the city after the latest victim, as both the party and independent press reported on the terror people felt on the streets. The similarities among the crimes made it impossible to believe that they were isolated events and the press began to criticize the police severely for being unable to arrest the killer. Newspapers stressed "the new type of crimes" that were taking place in the city.[45] The latest murder confirmed for the public that the new era produced not only expanded freedom of speech and a new concept of authority but also a terrifying new form of criminality that the police appeared incapable of matching.

Facing extreme pressure and loss of faith, the police vehemently denied that there was a serial killer in the city and continued presenting forensic information to the public. In an interview with *Morning* published on February 15, 2003, Farida Bouchta, the medical examiner of Aïn Chok working the case with the police, explained that the killer did not suffer from mental illness but that he cut up his victims in order to cover up his crimes.[46] She also reiterated that revenge was the likely motive for the murders. In this way, she denied two of the basic elements of serial murder—that the killer suffered from mental illness and was targeting strangers. The same day, the sensational news broke that police had discovered a handwritten letter, with a woman's signature, inside one of the cardboard boxes in which the latest victim was found. In the letter, the killer explained that she murdered the man and mutilated his penis in revenge for him raping her. Although the police believed that it was simply an attempt to throw them off the case, they announced that they would study the letter with their forensic resources. The letter seemed to support police claims that the killer was not targeting strangers and that the murder was a crime of passion. At the same time, few believed that a woman could have committed such a heinous act.

The press saw the letter not only as a sensational element, but also as another sign that the city faced a serial killer. In its February 15, 2003, front-page article, *Moroccan Events* described the killer as playing cat and mouse with the police, as in a Hollywood movie: "In famous international crimes, the killer—who is an unsound person—resorts to these kinds of styles as a means of provoking the police."[47] This was not simply because the police were unable to crack the case but also because it appeared as if the killer was challenging the police by committing yet another murder and leaving the latest body almost on the doorstep of the police. For the press, it seemed as if the real-world Moroccan police were dealing with a killer straight out of a Hollywood movie.

With the unprecedented crime spree reaching a fever pitch and the police facing a crisis of authority unlike at any time since the Tabit Affair, the public tuned into the evening news on the night of March 2, 2003, to discover that authorities had finally cracked the case. 2M had reported on the crime spree on the evening news seven weeks earlier after the Médiouna victim, presumably to present a police victory to the public. Otherwise, the television news had remained silent about the case. The clip on March 2 began by showing a tall, newly constructed building and then a group of about fifteen men standing together in what looked like an empty studio apartment. Next, the camera showed a dead man lying on his back inside a bathroom with an orange towel covering his face. There followed a long shot of the body with two bottles of drain cleaner sitting beside it. The clip then showed two men wearing latex gloves shifting the body while others, also wearing latex gloves, were seen handling evidence at the scene, collecting material using a briefcase full of scientific equipment. The narrator explained that the dead man, whose name was Mohamed Zouita, was the main suspect in the most recent murder and had apparently committed suicide by ingesting the drain cleaner. The report also explained that Zouita was the guard of the building and that the latest victim was found in a cardboard box that had been used in the construction of Zouita's building. The report ended by explaining, "Investigators did not rule out that the suspect in the Maârif murder who committed suicide might have been behind the other murders as well." Here, the clip demonstrates how the police quickly began shifting their tone now that they had a suspect, suggesting that there might have been a single killer in the crime spree after all.

This news report was a highly significant step for the police. For the first time, investigators brought television camera crews with them into the location where they discovered a dead body. In the process, they imported the crime-scene images of the tabloids onto the nightly news. This report also presented live images of their triumph over what appeared to be the notorious serial killer, who had been terrorizing the public for months. Moreover, the television crew filmed the sequences before the body was removed from the bathroom, bringing the entire public onto the crime scene. This report appeared on the evening news in both French and Arabic and the inspectors spoke to the television in Moroccan colloquial. In the process, the entire public, elite and non-elite alike, saw how the police finally put an end to the crime spree that had lasted for nine months.

The next morning, all of the daily newspapers in the country printed large front-page stories on Zouita, including the image of him lying on his back that appeared on the evening news. The press provided much more information on the victory, explaining that the police located him after tracking the origins of the two cardboard boxes in which the most recent victim was found. Serial numbers on the boxes led police to a recently completed office building on Mohamed V Street. There, they found Zouita, the thirty-five-year-old building guard, who told them that he gave the boxes to a friend. When the police returned the next day, Zouita was gone. Becoming increasingly suspicious, the authorities decided to enter Zouita's apartment, which was located in the building, and found blood marks on the walls, latex gloves, and a notebook that forensic handwriting experts at the Scientific Police were convinced had been the source of the letter found with the last victim. The building immediately became a crime scene and members of the Scientific Police came to collect forensic evidence. The police issued a countrywide search memo for Zouita and when he did not turn up, they began searching the entire building. When they arrived on the ninth floor, they discovered Zouita's cold body in a bathroom.

Continuing their search of the building, the police recovered more evidence, such as the knife and cleaver he used to cut up the bodies as well as victims' clothes. The press reported that everything found at the scene was transferred to the labs of the Scientific Police for analysis. In several storage spaces in the basement, the police found the remains of the last victim's face, including his jaw and nose, which were sent to the biological department of the Scientific Police in an attempt to construct an image of the victim. The police also arrested two prostitutes who knew Zouita. They told investigators that he had an extremely violent temperament and that he had had a fight with the September victim, discovered in the La Gironde district of the city, just before she disappeared. The two—together with the victim's sister—identified the victim, thanks to photographs of her thigh and ornately polished fingernails.

Now that Zouita had been found dead, the ambivalence over his identity as a serial killer ended. An article in *Moroccan Events* the same day quoted police sources claiming that Zouita mutilated his last victim's genitals out of revenge "because of a sexual relationship."[48] This suggested to the public that there was a sexual motive behind the crimes, linking the Moroccan serial killer to the criteria previously printed in the press and trumpeted in American depictions of serial murder. The next day, *L'Opinion* announced on its front page, "Guard Who Committed Suicide Was Probably a Serial Killer."[49] The article explains, "Inspectors seemed to move toward the idea of a bloodthirsty psychopath serial killer who acted alone." Much like the FBI's description of the serial killer, the article describes how Zouita lived a solitary life and that his family had not heard from him in several years. These comments came in the context of the police announcing that Zouita had had a connection with the first victim, whose remains were found in May 2002. Police sources told *Moroccan Events* that Zouita cut up his victims with "artistry . . . as if he were savoring it," something which led the police to suggest that he was an "unhealthy person."[50] In addition to his sexual motivations for committing the crimes, this indicated that Zouita was psychologically ill, another essential characteristic on the Ressler-Douglas checklist for serial killers.

Now focusing on the criminal's behavior, *Moroccan Events* printed a front-page story on March 7 with the headline, "Criminal Was Struck by Sexual Madness and His Actions Were Not Always Natural."[51] The police investigation revealed that Zouita was "confused sexually," as one prostitute provided details of her encounters with him. The investigation also discovered that "his nature and behavior could change quickly" and that he had "incomprehensible actions as well as unnatural and terrifying stares." This type of description would be repeated in the press in the following days, showing the broader public that the killer was both sexually deviant and unstable. Another article, which suggested that Zouita was the "Jack the Ripper of Morocco," explained that the way Zouita disposed of his victims was "intelligent of him, in addition to his skill in eliminating everything that could identify his victims."[52] Zouita was therefore not only sexually disturbed and psychologically unstable but also intelligent and went to great lengths to conceal his crimes. More and more the media presented him to the public in the categories popularized by Ressler and Douglas.

As they tied up the loose ends in the case, the police turned to perhaps the most important element in the Western construction of the serial killer. The March 15 front-page article in *Moroccan Events* included the following subheadline: "Security Officials Think Theory of Moral and Emotional Disputes between Maârif Victim and Building Guard Who Committed Suicide Likely."[53] The police now suggested that the motive for the crime was not simply sexual but homosexual. The move linking homosexuality to extreme violence had already been made in tabloid articles such as Noureddine's murder of his older lover, discussed in chapter 2. It had reappeared in many *Moroccan Events* true-crime articles as well. Now the press followed the tradition of the Western media in linking serial murder and homosexuality.[54] This article explained that the police considered the letter, which they found with the victim's remains and which Zouita wrote in a "feminine script," was "the true key to the motives for the crime." While it was reported at first that the letter was simply a way of throwing off investigators, *Moroccan Events* now explained that Zouita wrote in the letter "sometimes as a male and others as a female, something that expressed his psychological state between his desire to distort the truth and to express his real motives."[55] The police used the letter to prove that the extreme violence with which Zouita dismembered his last victim—and mutilated his genitals—demonstrated that he was indeed a serial killer. Paralleling the American model of killers like John Wayne Gacy and Jeffrey Dahmer, the police cast Zouita as a violent homosexual who could not stop himself from acting out his violent fantasies.[56]

With the construction of Zouita as a serial killer circulating widely among the public, the police set it in opposition to the role of science and forensics in the investigation. Now that they had established through the media that there was an entirely new form of criminality present on the Moroccan scene, the police needed a new image for themselves that would show the wider public that they were able to control the serial killer threat. It was in this context that the media began disseminating more and more information about the Scientific Police and their forensic work. For example, the press published news that the Scientific Police had used DNA analysis to prove that the first Maârif victim from May 2002 was Zouita's nephew. At the same time, Saeed Louahlia told the press that DNA analysis confirmed that a strand of Zouita's hair was found among the remains of the second Maârif victim from February 2003. He also explained that DNA proved that the victim's blood was found on a cardboard box in Zouita's storage area. The press detailed how the crime lab was working hard to identify the second Maârif victim, using the remains of his face and blood recovered from Zouita's storage areas. Moreover, the police used scientific evidence to disperse rumors that Zouita had not actually killed himself, including the autopsy report and analysis of his stomach contents.

By March 15, the Moroccan press demonstrated the forensic skill of the police to the entire public when they published the color computer reconstruction of the second Maârif victim's face. This image can be seen in figure 11. The victim was a building guard who was from Zouita's village. His mother and sister were able to identify him from the computer image Saeed Louahlia created from the remains. Louahlia told the press, "The techniques that were used in this operation were extremely precise and were able to achieve important results that helped speed up the investigation."[57] Louahlia explained that he created the image after more than forty-eight hours of continuous work, which included an operation to reconstruct the victim's face from the discovered remains using plastic surgery. With saliva and hair samples from family members, the police also conducted DNA tests to confirm the victim's identity.

The police did not limit their collaboration with the media to the press and evening news to publicize their new scientific acumen in the face of serial murder. A special edition of the 2M documentary program *Grand Angle* was produced on the case. This groundbreaking episode represented a new attempt on the part of the police to manage the mass media and is remarkable for the way it uses the documentary form to celebrate the Scientific Police for controlling the serial killer threat. The episode begins as the host explains that they had asked for months to follow the police in their investigation of the crime spree. He says that the police finally accepted their request just as they began to crack the case. The crew spent eight days with the police, the first time in the country's history that the police allowed a television crew to tape them as they worked.

The footage begins in the building where the police found Zouita's body and then shifts to the medical examiner as he begins to conduct an autopsy on Zouita's body. As seen in figure 12, the medical examiner, Hicham Benyaich, and his two partners wear full scrubs, masks, and latex gloves. As is clear from comparing figure 8 with figure 12, the scene was shot in the same room that Hassan Rhanja used to film the autopsy sequence in *The Blind Whale*. This demonstrates yet another aspect of the connection between police fact and fiction on Moroccan television. The Casablanca morgue first appeared on television as the shooting location for police téléfilms but now became the site of the real autopsy on the country's first serial killer. Rhanja used the location as a way of bringing sympathetic actors into the previously taboo inner world of the police, seeking to shape the public's perception of the police along the lines of the téléfilms. Now, *Grand Angle* brought the public back into the same room but with a decidedly different effect. Instead of seeing the autopsy through the eyes of Detective Yaqdhan, who now symbolized a police force incapable of capturing the serial killer, the sequence focuses the audience instead on accompanying the medical examiner and conducting scientific analysis of evidence. The scene transfers the autopsy room from criminal detectives like Yaqdhan to the real-world Scientific Police while still pointing to its first appearance as the set of a television film and establishing an intertextual relationship between the two.

The camera crew tapes one of the men coming out of the autopsy room carrying a tray of blood, urine, and gastric samples from Zouita and the man explains that they will send the samples for toxicological testing. Scenes at the headquarters of the Scientific Police appear next, showing the samples at the laboratory in vials labeled "Mohamed Zouita." A scientist explains that they will attempt to match up the drain cleaner that Zouita supposedly drank with what they found in his stomach. The shot pans from the scientist wearing a white jacket to a large white machine and computer conducting the tests. There are then a number of shots of men working in lab coats next to a variety of advanced equipment. These sequences demonstrate to the public the level of technological modernity with which the police now investigate and control crime.

Technicians show the crew the bloodied cartons in which the second Maârif body was discovered and the director of the laboratory presents the notebook on which Zouita wrote the letter that was found with his last victim. The director holds up the bloodstained letter and shows where it was taken from the notebook and the impressions that were left on the remaining notebook pages from writing it. The crew then walks through the lab and shoots other evidence in the case: an axe, razor, clothes, and gloves. Another lab technician shows the bloody fingerprints left on the cardboard box and compares them to Zouita's fingerprints. The camera crew then reenters the morgue and tapes as the medical examiner, wearing scrubs, latex gloves, and a mask, holds the skull of the Maârif victim after the flesh recovered from Zouita's building has been placed on it.

Next, there is a shot of the main police station in Casablanca and of the investigation team inside. As a group, they sit together around the television waiting for the evening news on 2M. The camera rolls as the news begins. The men clap and laugh once the news of the discovery is announced. In these scenes, the documentary elides the line between police and public as both become the audience for the news about the serial killer. Afterward, the television crew enters a triumphant meeting at the main police station between the lead inspectors, the chief of Casablanca police, Bouchaïb Rmaïl, and Saeed Louahlia. As the episode ends, this image of the team demonstrates how the police are in control once again of the city's security thanks to men like Rmaïl and Louahlia and the acumen of the Scientific Police.

This episode of *Grand Angle* set a powerful precedent on Moroccan television. In the United States and Europe, programs like *Cops*, which have been commonplace since the late 1980s, demonstrate an acute awareness on the part of the police of the use of the media as an arm of public relations.[58] In Morocco, the Zouita case provided the police with the first opportunity to bring a camera crew along with them as they investigated the series of murders and cracked the case. The case cut across the mass media, from independent press and crime tabloids—which also followed the murder spree—to television programming, reaching the broader public. In addition, the episode demonstrates a growing initiative on the part of the police to use public relations to control their image among the wider public. At the same time, the episode represents a significant transformation in the way the state blurred fact and fiction to present the public with images of the police. The episode brought the real-world police onto the locations that had been established as the sets of the police téléfilms, replacing actors like Younès Migri with real-world cops. Moreover, the police used the episode of *Grand Angle* as well as the press to construct and disseminate the new image of the Scientific Police and to demonstrate to the public that they were now able to match the threat of a Moroccan serial killer. The state used the new Scientific Police to encourage the public to see their law enforcement as modern and effective as that of countries like the United States and France.

Nonetheless, a close look at the investigation reveals that neither forensics nor the Scientific Police had much of a role in cracking the case. Instead, it was simple legwork—tracking down leads on the cardboard boxes—that brought the police to the killer. The celebration of science and forensics during and, especially, in the aftermath of the case demonstrates how the state used the media to construct a new image for the police in order to address the public failures of the Zouita investigation. The value of forensics was not in catching the killer. Instead, it was in establishing a new identity for the police and to regain their credibility and legitimacy in the public eye for the new era.

Despite the coordinated attempt to cast Zouita as a serial killer, it is clear that he did not fit the part. Of the six murders committed during the crime spree, he was responsible for three. He knew each of his victims extremely well—unlike the "stranger crimes" of serial murder—and killed them after personal disputes of some sort. Of the three remaining murders, one was a copycat crime and the final two, the Ben Msik murder of August 15, 2002, and the Hay Hassani murder of December 2, 2002, remain unsolved. Nonetheless, the media, during the crime spree, and the police afterward created the impression for the public that there was a single killer behind all of the murders. Zouita as serial killer was a fabrication, a sensational invention by the media and state that provided an opportunity to present the public with a new scientific and highly rational image of the police for the age of technological modernity. What started as an utterly new form of criminality and a direct challenge to the authority and legitimacy of the police allowed the media to recast the police into an entirely new role that matched state ambitions for modernity in the new era. With the celebration of DNA testing, complex technical equipment, and men in white lab coats, the media and state constructed the serial killer and Scientific Police in an attempt to convince the public that the Moroccan police were now as technologically savvy as their counterparts in the West and just as capable of controlling perhaps the most dangerous form of Western criminality—the serial killer.

The Serial Killer of Taroudant: The Scientific Police Make Bones Speak

The police learned their lesson from the slow and disorganized reaction to the Casablanca crime spree and were ready to act the next time a serial killer emerged. They would not have to wait long. On the morning of August 20, 2004, the skeletons of eight boys between the ages of ten and fifteen were discovered in a ravine outside the city of Taroudant.[59] With large front-page headlines, the press reported that members of the Scientific Police went to the scene to examine the remains and transfer them to the medical examiner's office in Casablanca. While it took months for the press to celebrate the role of science and forensics in the Casablanca murders, only two days passed before newspapers printed more front-page articles with bold headlines on the case and, as seen in figure 13, photographs of the chief medical examiner, Saeed Louahlia, and his assistant wearing scrubs, gloves, goggles, and masks examining the recovered skulls. These images, which appeared in all of the daily newspapers, demonstrated from the outset that the Scientific Police were on the case. The press also reported that families of missing children from the area were undergoing DNA testing in an attempt to identify the bones. Louahlia provided the exact measurements of the bones to the press and explained that his team was examining the victims' teeth for more evidence. Thanks to dirt stuck to the skeletons, investigators could see that the bones had been buried previously but were dug up and put on the side of the road. As a result of the immediate flood of scientific information on the case, the press presented a police who were in full control of their investigation, lacking the disorder with which they approached the Zouita case.

Just as the press depicted the confidence of the Scientific Police, they began situating the crimes as the work of a serial killer from the outset. Investigators told the press that the case was "complicated and bizarre" and lacked a "logical motive."[60] The press released news that some of the bones displayed signs that the victims' hands had been tied together and that the killer had cut up the bodies. Louahlia quickly issued a statement that one of the victims had been dead for at least three months while the others were murdered between six months and three years earlier. Also, the press reported that a piece of paper had been stuffed into an empty sardine can was found near the bodies and that the Scientific Police were analyzing it for fingerprints. The letter was a page torn out of a datebook and, according to the press, included the phrase, "I swear to God I'll get revenge." One article explicitly tied the letter to the one recovered from Zouita's last victim, explaining that it revealed the mental state of the criminal and was left beside the bodies "in the style of the Killer of Casablanca."[61] Rumors soon began swirling that more victims would turn up. On August 26, for example, *Moroccan Events* printed the following bold headline on the top of its front page: "Sources Find It Likely That Number of Butchered Child Victims in Taroudant Is Much Higher Than Reported Cases."[62]

Even at this early stage, the press began speculating about the sexual nature of the crimes. One journalist wondered, "Is it possible that the criminal or criminals who committed this massacre have a sexual perversion toward minors?"[63] The same article compared the killer of Taroudant to Zouita, suggesting, despite the paucity of information, that they are "close in terms of acts and psychology." The article also quoted sociologist Ayad Ablal, who explained that the killer is "sick psychologically and a sadist." *Moroccan Events* pursued this line as well, printing the following headline on the top of its September 1 edition: "Investigating a Number of People with Sadistic Sexual Predilections."[64]

In an effort to calm escalating public fears, the press counterbalanced these depictions with the resolve of the Scientific Police. Together with a new color photograph of medical examiners working with the remains, *Morning* published the following headline on August 26: "Forensic Medicine Makes Bones of Taroudant Bodies Speak."[65] The next day, *Moroccan Events* printed the following bold headline on the top of its front page: "Over Ninety Investigators from Different Security Branches Tracking Killer of Taroudant."[66] The press also reported that the police were combing houses and abandoned areas in an attempt to catch the killer. More documentary evidence appeared in the press, such as photographs of the location where the bones were found.

Pressure mounted on the police to solve the case. Not only did the crimes terrify the public, but the families of missing children also gave interviews to the press suggesting that the police did not act quickly enough to investigate their complaints because they were all from marginal and disadvantaged backgrounds. In order to stave off this potential crisis, the police continued disseminating information about the scientific aspects of their investigation. *Moroccan Events,* on the top of its August 31 issue, printed a subheadline explaining, "Appointment of Team Members Who Underwent Training at FBI."[67] Thanks to this association with American law enforcement, the new team further legitimized the group of Moroccan investigators urgently hunting the killer.

Media coverage of police efforts continued to ramp up with each passing day, indicating much more efficient press management by the police than during the Zouita case. On September 2, *Moroccan Events* printed several front-page headlines about the investigation, such as "Police Get Report on Results of Medical Test Conducted on Victims and Families of the Missing." According to the main article on the case in *Moroccan Events* that day, "investigators have raised the degree of their activities to the furthest level possible. They are conducting searches, investigations, and suspect interrogations twenty-four hours a day."[68] The same article reported that Saeed Louahlia would head to Taroudant to present the police personally with the results of his DNA analysis, signifying the importance of the case to the public.[69] The press repeatedly emphasized that the DNA results would help lead investigators to the perpetrator. As a result, the press presented science to the public as the secret weapon in the hunt for the killer.

This confident image of the police during the investigation would be matched by the speed with which they cracked the case. After only two and a half weeks—compared to over nine months during the Zouita investigation—the police arrested the killer on the afternoon of September 7. The next day, *Moroccan Events* printed huge front-page headlines, together with photographs of several victims, announcing the arrest of a man who worked as a porter and snack seller at the Taroudant train station. The headlines praised the police in a variety of ways: "Revelation of Secrets of Child Massacre after Three Weeks of Intensive Investigations" and "Arriving at Suspect Based on Analysis of Letter Found with Remains." The newspaper reported that the killer met his victims at the station and would lure them back to the shack where he lived. The killer told authorities that he would murder his victims, have sex with their bodies, and then bury them under his shack. Sometimes, he explained, he would kill his victims as he was having sex with them. He dug up the remains recently and moved them because he feared that the land where he lived had been sold for a building project. According to the article, the police captured the killer based on the page he left behind at the ravine where he dumped the bodies, which included the name "Hadi," a well-known family in the area. The police tracked down all the people in the city with that last name and also focused on the train station, where many of the missing children reportedly spent time. The police then found the forty-two-year-old Abdelali Hadi and searched his shack, recovering corroborating evidence such as the datebook from which the page found near the corpses originated.

The case was a massive public relations success for the police. To cap it off, huge crowds of local residents and the press followed the killer as he calmly and methodically reconstructed his crimes for the police and television cameras. These images spread across the country on the evening news and the front pages of the press. They showed Hadi led out of a police van in handcuffs, stand beside his makeshift shack, and point out the place where he originally buried the bodies. He demonstrated for the cameras how he dug the graves, carried the large sack full of bones, and then tossed the bones in the ravine where they were later found. The police also recruited a child to act out the role of a victim and the press printed images of Hadi pretending to suffocate and strangle him. While narrating the reenactment, journalists emphasized the calm and confidence with which Hadi committed his crimes. Hadi apparently lured his victims back to his shack by giving them candy and biscuits but would snap as soon as they entered his shack, pulling out a knife and binding them. The images of the police parading Hadi in front of the public—images that appeared in all of the daily newspapers and on the evening television news—were clearly intended to calm their fears and demonstrate the power and effectiveness of the police in making the arrest.

Once again, now that the danger was under control, the press moved quickly to confirm the image of Hadi as a serial killer. First, journalists described in gruesome terms how he would sexually assault and kill his victims. One article on the case in *Morning* suggested Hadi's intelligence in committing the murders: "The crimes revealed the professionalism of the criminal who escaped arrest and punishment ever since the first crime."[70] On September 9, *Moroccan Events* printed a photograph of the killer on the top of its front page with the headline, "The Accused Confessed to Murdering Children Calmly As If He Had Killed Flies." The same article explained how another sandwich seller at the train station knew Hadi well and described him as

> the solitary type who didn't have friends and kept away from people. For a long time, he'd show up suddenly and then disappear without attracting any attention. No one suspected him at all, no one at the train station thought for a second that he was lying in wait for his victims, setting traps for them.[71]

To people who knew him, Hadi was a loner who managed to divert people's attention. Suggesting that he was a disturbed sociopath, a police source told the journalist, "The calm [with which he committed the murders] hid behind it some psychological complex." The press used this depiction to update the schism between respectable appearances and degraded inner reality that had appeared as early as the Tabit Affair and continued in the tabloids, police novels, and true-crime articles. This schism now appeared as one of the basic characteristics of the Moroccan serial killer.

Hadi was brought before the investigative judge the next day and confessed in cold and precise detail to his crimes, which he committed between 2000 and 2004. He killed a total of nine children during this period. Soon after the arrest, the press began to focus on Hadi's childhood, searching for answers to why he committed such horrible crimes:

> According to sources, it was revealed during the investigation that the suspect was sexually assaulted during his childhood by a group of people when he visited his father in the town of Inezgane. This explains, according to other sources close to the investigation, why he went to such extremes in sexually assaulting and killing his victims.[72]

While the role of Zouita's childhood was never discussed, this was the first time that the Moroccan press focused so closely on traumatic experiences in a killer's youth to explain his crimes. This element was one of the most important characteristics of the serial killer that Robert Ressler and John Douglas developed in their work.

Now that the police had arrested Hadi and the media disseminated images of him reconstructing his crimes for the public, the press began examining the serial killer as a phenomenon attacking the country. On September 15, *Morning* printed a two-page special with the bold headline "Sexual Crimes Strike Moroccan Society" together with photographs of Hadi, Zouita, and Belharash, the "Killer of El Jadida."[73] This article began by connecting the three killers through the brutal and sexual nature of their crimes, stating that many consider the phenomenon of the sexual killer as something entirely new in Moroccan society, a kind of criminality that used to exist only in the West. The journalist interviewed a specialist in sexual and psychological illnesses, Abubakr Harakat, who, following the work of Ressler and Douglas, claimed that these killers suffered some kind of traumatic event in their youth that provided a shock and impetus for their pathological criminality: "In most cases, there is a latency period for their illness. The person lives for many years without anything arising from it. But there is no doubt that they will explode one day." Further emphasizing the FBI's definition of a serial killer, Harakat explained that people like Zouita and Hadi were loners:

> They're both introverts, naturally because they were living in deadly isolation.... They don't ever talk about themselves, they keep silent about everything having to do with them, and they live in their thoughts and imagination. That's because their pathological personality feeds off the thoughts that circulate in their mind.

Harakat also demonstrated how Hadi, for example, was highly organized in the way he would lure his victims back to his shack and then take control of them, calling him a "psychopath." Moreover, these kinds of killers seem like anyone else: "There are a lot of cases in which those who rape children seen outwardly simple, kind, charming, and nice but, at the same time, they carry a latency of the illness that boils over sooner or later." While this image of suddenly snapping appeared as early as the tabloid depiction of Fattah's murder of his fiancée's sister, as seen in chapter 2, it now reemerged as an explanation of how the Moroccan serial killer was able to avoid suspicions.

A second article in the section explained in detail how Hadi was a "serial killer" because of the way he murdered his victims at different times over a long period. The article also pointed to the way Hadi savored detaining and abusing his victims before killing them, emphasizing his sadism. Moreover, the author highlighted Hadi's victims, who were all of similar ethnicity, age, and sex, and that Hadi suffered from a split personality disorder as seen in the way he hid his sexual urges from the public and then acted upon them in private. The author of this article also suggested that Hadi enjoyed followed the media coverage of his crimes and savored the way he terrified the public.[74]

Since Zouita committed suicide, the media never had the chance to let him speak for himself about his crimes. In the United States, the media not only covered the trials of serial killers for the fascinated public but also presented interviews with them. Killers such as John Wayne Gacy and Ted Bundy enjoyed talking about their crimes with the media, putting the public in the role of Ressler and Douglas, who originated the concept of interviewing the serial killer. This gave the American public direct access to the monstrosity that the FBI was attempting to control.

In the case of Hadi, the police finally had their serial killer in custody. As Hadi was awaiting trial, *Morning* took the highly unusual step of publishing parts of his confessions in a five-part series. In the killer's own words, the public learned how Hadi lured each child back to his shack and then assaulted and killed them. Hadi demonstrated his monstrosity to the public by stating, "I'd savor strangling my victims, especially after I climaxed."[75] Moreover, he confirmed that "if the police hadn't arrested me, I'd have continued committing my crimes." The new police, with their scientific and skill and ability to arrest Hadi quickly, were presented to the public as the only answer for containing this horrific new form of criminality.

Unsurprisingly, the press sensationalized Hadi's trial, which lasted only two days. When the judge questioned him, Hadi confirmed his image as a monstrous sociopath when he explained that he "felt elation and joy" as he killed his victims.[76] He also explained that he felt nothing when he buried his victims. He confirmed for the judge the story that a group of boys raped him when he was fifteen years old. This event, the press repeatedly emphasized, damaged him so severely that it motivated him to commit his crimes decades later. On December 2, 2004, after deliberating for six hours, the court found Hadi guilty of murdering nine children and sentenced him to death.

Only three months after the trial, the police themselves published an interview with Hadi, the "serial killer," in the first issue of *Majallat al-Shurta* (Police Magazine).[77] The cover of this issue can be seen in figure 15. In this way, the police began the process of interviewing captured serial killers and disseminating that information to the public, much like FBI agents Ressler and Douglas had done in the United States some three decades earlier. As in the Ressler and Douglas interviews, Hadi is depicted as enjoying talking about himself and his crimes. He explained that he would study his victims before selecting them, and then described his crimes in graphic language. Through this interview—as well as his published confessions and television reports on his crimes—the public encountered Hadi directly. It was this extreme form of monstrosity—something that the media brought to the public directly—that made the new police, with their forensics and science, necessary.

Despite the triumphant depiction of the Scientific Police and the role of forensics in the investigation, these elements once again had no role in how the police arrested the serial killer. The police caught Hadi because of simple door-to-door legwork while questioning people about the name that appeared in the letter left by the victims' remains. Much like the Zouita case, this aspect of the investigation was strongly downplayed in favor of celebrating the new image of the police as Western as the type of criminality the country was now facing. Even though science and forensics played no role in the arrests, they took center stage in the media's depiction of the investigation and resolution of the case. Science and forensics were necessary for producing an image of the police that matched the expectations of the public for controlling crime in the new era. Science served as a new way to legitimize the police after the failures of the Zouita investigation and recast the image of the police for a new era of technological modernity.

CSI: Casablanca—Mediating a New Police

Thanks to the emergence of the local serial killer, Morocco had entered the age of the crime lab and Scientific Police. After Hadi, this new kind of law enforcement began appearing in the press with more regularity, thanks to a variety of sensational cases. For example, the Scientific Police prominently helped identify the explosives used in the May 16, 2003, Casablanca bombings. They returned to the public eye when the headquarters of *Moroccan Events* received a mail bomb in January 2004. This event came as a total shock since the offices of the newspaper that relied on crime journalism for its success had become a crime scene. The Scientific Police stepped in and were quickly able to identify the material used in the package, partially calming the fears of both the public and the press. The Scientific Police also provided key evidence in a number of sensational murder cases, including the infamous Hay Hassani triple homicide in Casablanca and the shocking Histou killings in Meknès, among others.[78]

As during the Zouita and Hadi cases, the Scientific Police opened their doors to the press, which printed a number of exposés celebrating their work. The first of these, which appears in figure 14, is entitled "Day at National Center for Scientific Police: Experts Armed with Technique for Uncovering Puzzles of Crimes" and describes the experience of approaching the headquarters of the Scientific Police in Casablanca as if the journalist were leading the public in his footsteps.[79] This narrative is juxtaposed with a large photograph of the outside of the building reminiscent of the police television films, which typically included a long panning shot of the front of the police station in order to encourage the audience to enter along with the cop hero. Next to the photograph is a headline describing the location of the building in the city—identifying it for the public—and explaining that while the mission of the Scientific Police is completely different from other security units, their work is integral to the overall success of crime-fighting in the country.

The detailed full-page article narrates the experience of walking through the six-floor building and visiting the various departments, providing the public with a clear image with which to picture themselves following along with the journalist. The article describes the specialties of the different departments, such as arson, explosives, ballistics, bio-evidence, DNA, fingerprints, counterfeiting, poisons, chemicals, and drug analysis. The article personalizes various members in a way reminiscent of how the Arabic police novel, Moroccan True Crime, and téléfilms humanized the police. This image is reinforced by four photographs of the officers, both men and women, standing in front of chemical analysis tables, working on computers, and examining samples under microscopes and using other impressive technical equipment.

A second headline at the top of the exposé explains that the "experts" of the Scientific Police wear white and are "armed with modern technology." The use of the word "experts" here was no coincidence. In French, the well-known *CSI* television series is known as "Les Experts." Moroccan television aired the series during this period and the public came to know the show by its French name. *Moroccan Events* and *Le Journal*, among others, printed more exposés on the Scientific Police, each with photographs of various officers, presenting them as if they were part of the cast for *CSI: Casablanca*.[80] In the process, the media sought to shape reality along the lines of a fictional genre, encouraging the public to view the local Scientific Police through the lens of the mediated image of their Western counterparts.

One of the most prominent advertisements for the Scientific Police came, not surprisingly, from television. Just as the two television stations created police téléfilms that celebrated the Criminal Police and detectives like Yaqdhan and Khalid, 2M produced a new series of feature-length films starting in 2006 named *al-Qadiya* (The Case), directed by Noureddine Lakhmari, which performed the same service for the Scientific Police.[81] Each film in the series debuted during Ramadan—when television has the largest viewership—and has been reaired numerous times since. The films are remarkable for their excellent camerawork, rich colors, quick transitions, and highly Westernized feel in a Moroccan context. Most importantly, they continued the process of using television to blur the boundaries between fact and fiction in representations of the police. Like the téléfilm *White Nights,* they disseminated a highly fabricated image of the police that served as a model for recasting the real-world police into a fictionalized role.

The first film begins as two hunters discover the body of a girl in the woods. After the initial credits, there is an extended sequence in which the cop hero of the first four films, Zeineb, stands in scrubs and goggles conducting an autopsy. Advanced scientific equipment on the counters surrounding the room complements the scene as Zeineb performs her work alone. There is a close-up shot of her examining samples under a high-powered microscope. She then turns back to the corpse with a satisfied look on her face after determining that the cause of death was homicide. An officer wearing a white lab coat with the shield of the Scientific Police enters the room and interrupts her, explaining that the commissioner wants to see her. She then slowly walks through the halls of the headquarters of the Scientific Police, establishing the location and the team of officers for the audience.

The Blind Whale introduced the detective to the audience in the intimacy of his home and then brought the audience along with him as he examined a crime scene and entered the police station. In the opening minutes of the film, it was Yaqdhan's personal life that made him identifiable, sympathetic, and human to the audience. *The Case,* however, bypasses the cop's home and takes the audience directly into the headquarters of the Scientific Police, introducing the various officers in the initial sequences as they perform forensic analysis without any of the slow panning shots. Thanks to the prominence of the Scientific Police in Moroccan society since the Zouita case, the film assumes that viewers already have a sympathetic image of their CSI: Casablanca. Displaying the officers' forensic acumen at the beginning of *The Case* simply reinforces their sympathetic depiction to the audience. The cold and scientific cop of the crime lab has replaced the humanized criminal detective at the heart of the police téléfilm.

After Zeineb is assigned to the murder of the girl in the woods, she continues walking in the corridors of the headquarters and sees a serial killer responsible for seven murders being led away in chains. The remainder of the film takes place in a village in the Middle Atlas Mountains as Zeineb investigates the murder of the young woman. She solves the murder, but—as in the cases of Zouita and Hadi—without any recourse to forensics and science. Other films in the series also take the audience into the real-world labs of the Scientific Police in Casablanca and show them analyzing crime scene evidence and various forms of case material. In the background of the series is the escape of the serial killer, depicted in chains in the first film. This element further solidifies the relationship between the serial killer and the Scientific Police. The serial killer continues his murder spree, taunting Zeineb and Meriem, the lead detective in the fifth and sixth films. Although six films have been made in the series, there remain three that have yet to be produced, and presumably they will focus on the way the Scientific Police hunt the serial killer and eventually bring him to justice.

While *The Case* series is striking for its camerawork and depiction of CSI: Casablanca, it follows in the footsteps of the previous police téléfilms in one important aspect. The films use fiction to improve upon reality. In particular, the Scientific Police in Morocco do not conduct criminal investigations on their own. Instead, they simply aid the Criminal Police in analyzing crime scenes and processing evidence. The films therefore mimic the way *White Nights* presented the public with a cop as a simulacrum, one that has no model in Moroccan reality. Just as there were no female criminal detectives in Morocco at the time *White Nights* celebrated Ahlam breaking down doors with her gun raised high, *The Case* presents the public with an agent of the Scientific Police who leads a murder investigation. Depicting an agent of the Scientific Police investigating a murder allowed Lakhmari to celebrate a new kind of supercop, even if that figure did not exist in the country. In this respect, the films present an image of the Scientific Police that is not simply lacking credibility, but seeks to mislead the public on the role of the Scientific Police in criminal investigations. As a result, the films parallel and extend the way the state trumpeted the role of the Scientific Police in the serial killer investigations. Even though traditional police legwork cracked the cases, the media, with their heavy emphasis on forensics, suggested to the public that it was the Scientific Police and their forensic acumen that brought the criminals to justice. *The Case* improved upon the image of the Scientific Police already circulating in society in order to establish and disseminate the image of a supercop who soothed public fears because of their ability to face and overcome the dangers of the new era.

Both the Scientific Police and the serial killer emerged in Morocco after 2002 once several key cultural and political conditions were in place. The first was the ability of the press to follow a crime spree in real time as the police investigated the case. Almost all crime reporting before Zouita focused on cases that were either cracked or declared unsolved. The press reported on the cases of Zouita and Hadi as they were unfolding, presenting the public with updates on the investigations and reports of new victims, spreading fear and discrediting the police in the process. Second, the increasing move toward competition in the daily independent press created circumstances in which the media were inclined to trump up a string of murders, using sensational categories such as "serial killer" in order to boost sales and compete for readers. This increasingly commercial environment—and the attention that the independent press received at the time—greatly contributed to the fear and panic that hit the streets. Third, rapidly escalating public fear in the face of what appeared to be a new form of criminality put tremendous pressure on the police and created a crisis to which they had to respond in an utterly new way. Even though *Moroccan Events* had printed true-crime articles about forensics and the work of the medical examiner in supporting police investigations, the emergence of the "serial killer" gave the state the opportunity to trumpet a new kind of police, one that could respond to the new forms of crime that the country was apparently facing. The serial killer was therefore an invention that permitted the state to present the public with an entirely new kind of police who based their authority on scientific and technological fact. In turn, CSI: Casablanca represented an attempt to mold the Moroccan police along the lines of televised American and European law enforcement, with their technological savvy and scientific know-how, cloaking the Moroccan police with the same kind of image—and legitimacy—as their Western counterparts.[82]

The Moroccan serial killer represented both a deep threat to and unique opportunity for the police. An entirely new crime challenge, however, soon erupted that provided the police with the opportunity—and necessity—to transform their image once again for the public. The May 16 Casablanca bombings would discredit the police, generating a new crisis of authority for the state and raising questions about their ability to protect the public against crime in the new era. The event, which was widely considered Morocco's 9/11, would have profound ramifications for the country and fundamentally challenge the police to prevent another attack. The police once again needed to recast their image to demonstrate to the public that they were able to match the new kind of criminality that the country was suddenly facing. Their response, however, would be by far the most radical yet in their attempts to use the mass media to transform the image of the police and manage public opinion.

Figure 11. *Morning,* March 15, 2003. The center color image shows the computer reconstruction of the face of Zouita's final victim by the Scientific Police. The top headline reads, "Discovery of Second Maârif Victim's Identity." This image demonstrated to the public the technological savvy of the Scientific Police as they helped complete the investigation into the country's first serial killer.

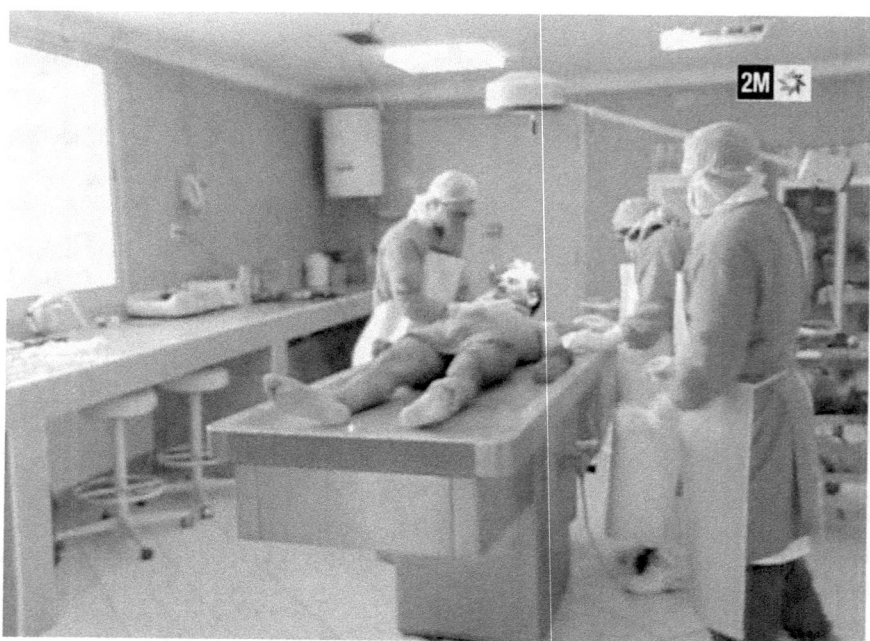

Figure 12. A still from the episode of *Grand Angle* on the serial killer of Casablanca. This image shows a team of medical examiners inspecting Mohamed Zouita's corpse. It was shot in the same location used for the autopsy scene in *The Blind Whale* téléfilm, as seen in figure 8. In this way, the program alluded to the sets of the téléfilms but substituted the real-world Scientific Police for fictional cops.

Figure 13. *Moroccan Events*, August 24, 2003. The center image shows medical examiner Saeed Louahlia inspecting the remains of the Taroudant victims. Images of the Scientific Police and medical examiner appeared prominently in the press coverage of the investigation and helped recast the image of the real-world police along the lines of CSI: Casablanca.

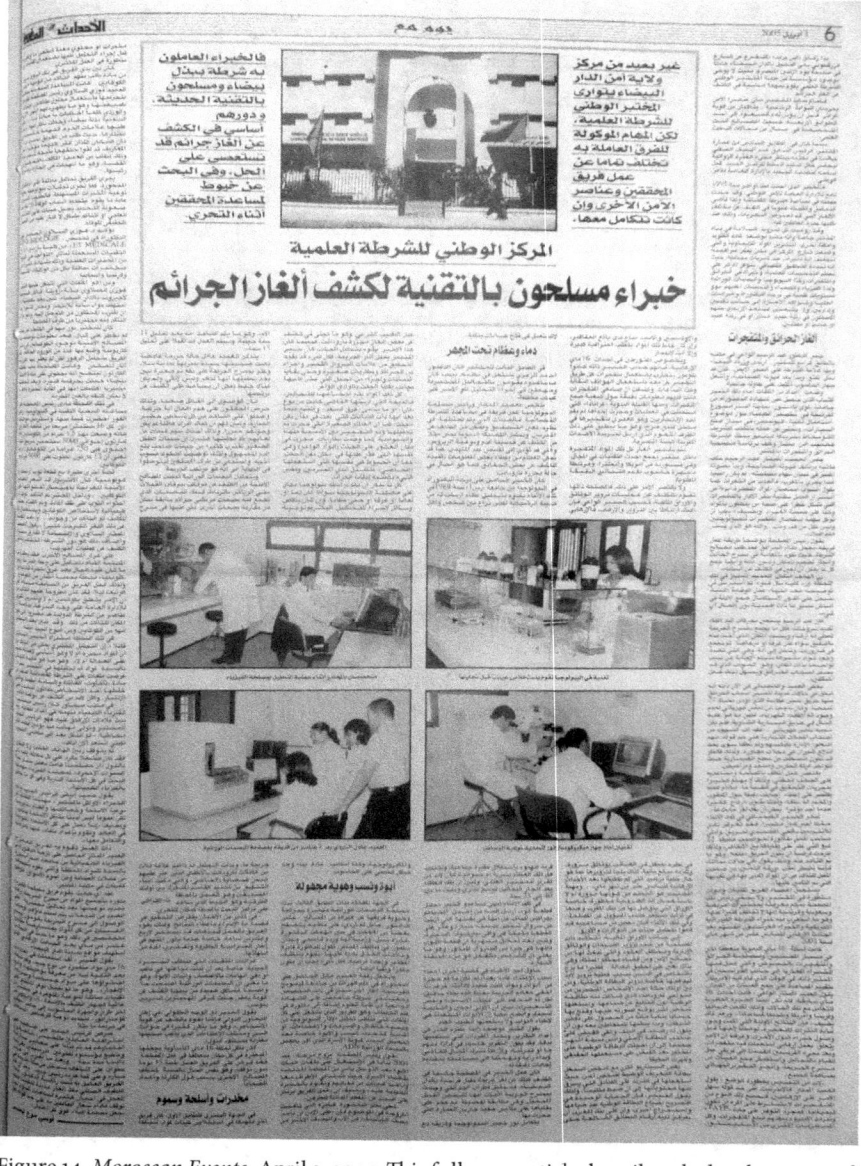

Figure 14. *Moroccan Events*, April 3, 2005. This full-page article describes the headquarters of the Scientific Police in Casablanca, personalizing its members and narrating the experience of walking through the building's halls. The headline "Day at National Center for Scientific Police: Experts Armed with Technique for Uncovering Puzzles of Crimes" points to the depiction of the Scientific Police as the local manifestation of CSI.

Figure 15. *Police Magazine*, February 2005. This is the first issue of the new *Police Magazine*. This cover features the headline "These Men We Fear" juxtaposed with the image of a young and athletic GUS officer. The bottom left image is of Abdelali Hadi with the headline, "The Serial Killer of Taroudant Talks to Us about His Crimes." This and other media interviews with Hadi brought the public into direct contact with the monstrosity of the Moroccan serial killer.

Figure 16. The "Photo of the Month" from the February 2005 issue of *Police Magazine*. This two-page image, which was taken from the television advertisement celebrating the GUS, shows a scene of safety and security in which the handsome officer helps school kids with their homework.

Figure 17. *Police Magazine*, March 2005. The main headline reads, "Women in the Police Establishment." This issue emphasizes how the police now embody democratic values and gender rights by incorporating women into their ranks.

Figure 18. *Police Magazine*, September 2005. This image, taken outside the Hassan II Mosque in Casablanca, appeared in a variety of contexts, from independent magazines to television advertisements and billboards.

Figure 19. A still from the final seconds of Boomerang's GUS television advertisement. The police formation seen in figure 18 fades behind the shield of the police and the phrase "The National Security: The Police Are Close to You for Your Security."

Figure 20. The *Casablancan*, October 24, 2005. The headline "Laânigri's Pharaohs" appears above the glamour shot of the GUS officer. The magazine used this cover photograph to mock the image of the GUS as supercops cast for American television.

6 From Morocco's 9/11 to Community Policing

State Advertising and the New Citizen

From the tabloids to Moroccan True Crime, the state had only indirect input on the construction of police images in the new mass media. Starting in early 2001, the state became more proactive, welcoming television camera crews, directors, and actors into the formerly closed world of the police stations in order to make new and daring cop movies that blurred the lines between police fact and fiction in order to improve the image of the real-world police in society. When a serial killer seemed to emerge in 2002, the police faced severe criticism over their inability to combat this apparently new form of criminality. This crisis forced the police to engage the media directly in order to control their image for a terrified public. For the first time in the country's history, the police gave interviews to the press, invited journalists into the police stations and morgues, and brought film crews along with them as they cracked a real-world criminal case. In the process, the state managed the nonstate media in order to disseminate a new image of the police—CSI: Casablanca—that was just as modern and Western as the criminality that they were now facing.

When a group of suicide bombers struck Casablanca on May 16, 2003, the police once again faced an entirely new form of criminality for which they appeared utterly unprepared. There was a deep and long-standing belief among the public that the country was immune to international terrorism. Thanks to the War on Terror in the aftermath of the September 11 attacks, terrorism was widely seen as something that struck the West, not Morocco. It therefore appeared in Morocco as a new form of Western criminality, much like the serial killer. The Casablanca attacks came as a total shock and served as Morocco's equivalent of 9/11. The government quickly passed new antiterrorism laws, expanding the power of the security services to arrest and detain suspects. Perhaps the most influential response was when the king appointed a new chief of police, Hamidou Laânigri, who arrived with radical new ideas about the role and function of policing in society.

The Casablanca bombings created a new crisis of authority for the state. Once again, the state needed to prove to the public that the police were capable of facing and overcoming the new threat. Both the true-crime and téléfilm detective hot on the trail of a professional criminal and the scientist in the lab coat hunting the serial killer were suddenly no match for the reality of international terrorism. The state needed a new cop who was able to protect the public against this shocking new danger and successfully defend its legitimacy in controlling the country. Recognizing the severity of the situation, Laânigri moved to reinvent the institution of the police from the ground up in order to meet the challenges of the new era and mobilize public opinion against radical Islam. As the centerpiece of this transformation, Laânigri created a community policing program—one mimicking French, British, and American models—that would be based on closeness and mutual sympathy between his officers on the street and the wider public.

This project was simply too important to both Laânigri and the state to cede the construction of the new image of the police to the commercial media, as had happened before. Like J. Edgar Hoover, the former director of the FBI, and much more so than any other Moroccan official before him, Laânigri believed strongly in the role of the mass media and public relations in effective policing. In order for his community policing project to succeed, he recognized that the state needed to produce a new kind of citizen, one who would sympathize with the police to the point that they would voluntarily participate in the policing process and communicate with them about crime. Considering the long and contentious history of the Moroccan police and their relationship with the public, that would be no easy feat. After years of increasingly blurred lines between fiction and reality in representations of the police in the mass media—as well as a model of police-public collaboration in solving crime in the true-crime articles and téléfilms—the cultural and material conditions were now in place for the state to take a much more proactive role in constructing mass media images of the new community police and, consequently, a new citizen who would participate with them in crime fighting. With the help of an international advertising firm, Laânigri created a public relations campaign unlike any seen before in the region. The widespread campaign appropriated and employed the strategies of police fiction in the mass media and applied them to the real-world community policing force in an attempt to produce a new kind of cop and citizen for the age of international terrorism.

Despite the highly sophisticated public relations campaign and tight management of the media during this period, the new community policing force would eventually be revealed to be just as brutal, violent, and lawless as the police of the Years of Lead. Disruptions and contestations—from both the media and the public—would challenge the state, condemn the community policing project to failure, and, after only two years, lead to its cancellation. Despite the highly public brutality of the new police, there was another reason for the failure of community policing in the country. Earlier depictions of the police in the mass media did not demand a direct response from the public. By seeking to interpellate a new citizen, along the lines of Althusser's theory of ideology, the state now pushed the public to look too closely at the police, a process that revealed all too clearly that new police were a simulacrum, a fabrication without basis in Moroccan reality, leading to the public's rejection. This shows how the public—once the state took over producing and circulating police images in the mass media—refused the command to participate in real-world policing, demonstrating how they could not be easily prodded into acting on a new relationship with the police and state authority.

May 16 and the End of Moroccan "Exceptionalism"

Unlike the United States and Western Europe, Morocco had never been the target of international terrorism.[1] By early 2003, despite the attacks on September 11, 2001, the concept of "Moroccan exceptionalism"—the idea that the country was immune from a destabilizing terrorist attack—was still dominant. In the eyes of most Moroccans at the time, terrorism was something that happened mostly in Western capitals, not in their country. In June 2002, the Moroccan secret services reported that they had foiled a plot in which a tanker was set to blow up as it went through the Strait of Gibraltar. The sense of exceptionalism was so strong that it was widely suggested in the press at the time that the state had contrived the plan to please the United States in its War on Terror. Morocco might have religious extremism and be home to hundreds of men who fought in Afghanistan during the 1980s and the first Gulf War. There might have been widespread resentment at the country's participation in the War on Terror. And there may have also been large belts of shantytowns full of misery and poverty in the Moroccan cities. But the overwhelming consensus in the country—from politicians down to ordinary people on the street—was that terrorism was something that struck other countries, not Morocco.

That all changed on May 16, 2003. At approximately ten o'clock that Friday evening, a group of thirteen suicide bombers attacked five separate locations in the city, causing a total of forty-four deaths. Two bombers struck Hotel Farah in the city center, blowing up the reception area and the entrance to the hotel. Four targeted the Jewish Alliance Club, destroying the entrance and much of the right side of the building. Three others blew themselves up outside the Positano Restaurant, just opposite the Belgian Consulate. A lone bomber set off his explosive in the old city of Casablanca, near Bab Jdid and a Jewish cemetery. Finally, three others cut the throat of a security guard at the Casa de España Club, walked into the building, and blew themselves up, causing by far the largest number of casualties. No victims were claimed at the Jewish Alliance Club, as the attackers apparently did not know that it would be empty because of the Sabbath.

The Moroccan police managed to arrest two of the bombers alive, as well as another man who ran off before the others reached their targets. The first,

Mohamed Omari, was with the group that attacked Hotel Farah. The explosions caused by the first two bombers blew him back and made him drop the explosive that he was carrying in his backpack. He tried to flee, but the Moroccan police apprehended him nearby. The second bomber, Rachid Jalil, was with the group that attacked the Jewish Alliance Club. After seeing the first two men detonate their explosives, Jalil decided to drop his bomb and flee the scene. He was later arrested on May 18, the same day that the police arrested the final member of the group, Hassan Taoussi, who slipped away from the others before they took taxis to the center of Casablanca for the attacks. All three would be tried and sentenced to death on August 19, 2003.

The arrested terrorists, who were apparently members of the Moroccan extremist group *Salafiyya Jihadiyya*, were reported in the press to have provided the police with valuable information. Omari, who was in charge of executing the attacks, was particularly useful. He not only helped identify the eleven bombers who blew themselves up, but also apparently revealed an entire network of terrorists who were planning to follow the Casablanca attacks with bombings in other cities, including Marrakech, Agadir, Essaouira, Fez, and Tangier. He also gave the police the name of Abdelhaq Bentassir, known as the "Shoe Seller," who was apparently the main coordinator behind the attacks. After Bentassir was arrested on May 26, he died in police custody from what authorities claimed was a heart attack.

In the days and weeks following the bombings, the press printed many details about the bombers, including photographs of their parents and homes. They all came from the Sidi Moumen shantytown in Casablanca and were between twenty-two and thirty-two years old. Omari and Jalil were among the founding members of the cell, and helped lure others into the attacks over a span of two years. According to the press, another Moroccan extremist group, *Sirat al-Mustaqim,* was also involved in the attacks. Moreover, the press reported that the group met at Omari's house the night before the attacks and left together with their watches synchronized so that the bombs would go off at exactly the same time.[2]

As in the response to the 9/11 attacks in the United States, the May 16 bombings launched wide-ranging legal and security changes in Morocco. New counterterrorism laws were quickly enacted to provide the police with more legal authority to conduct searches and detain suspected terrorists for longer periods of time. The police used the incident to dismantle extremist organizations in various cities and arrest suspected radicals. The press covered the front pages with news of arrests and raids on cells throughout the major cities. The names and photographs of suspected terrorists appeared, as did details of particular arrests and the discovery of training grounds.

Within one year of the bombings, the Moroccan police admitted to arresting over two thousand suspects, although Human Rights Watch put the number as high as five thousand. Moreover, it is suspected that many confessions in the case were extracted under torture. It is clear that human rights in Morocco—despite the far-reaching improvements with the end of the Years of Lead and the buildup to the country's Equity and Reconciliation Commission—took a major step backward in the arrests after the attacks. The secret services were accused of abducting suspected Islamic radicals and torturing them in their secret detention center in Témara, just south of Rabat. Human Rights Watch issued a damning report in 2004 about the post–May 16 crackdown, suggesting that the Moroccan authorities were repeating the tactics of the Years of Lead, but this time were targeting religious extremists instead of the radical left.[3]

What was clear was that the May 16 bombings had a deep impact on both the security forces and the public. For both, international terrorism symbolized the new face of crime in the country. During the 1990s, Najib Skir printed news of drug-smuggling networks on his tabloid covers, demonstrating to the public that the country was entering the world of globalized crime at the time. After 9/11, that image of global crime shifted to international terrorism, with its transnational networks of funding, recruitment, and training. Just as the United States faced this new type of criminality after 9/11, Morocco entered this new era as well after the Casablanca bombings. In the 1990s, images of drug smugglers, organized crime, and gun violence symbolized a threat to Morocco's stability. Now, international terrorism became a significantly more terrifying danger that could destabilize the country. As in the case of the serial killer, the country faced an entirely new form of criminality that demanded a fundamentally new kind of police to protect the public. With the stability of the country apparently at stake, a new police—a force that was able to control the kind of global crime the country was facing—was considerably more urgent.

Hamidou Laânigri and the Modernization of the Moroccan Police

Despite the widespread sense of "Moroccan exceptionalism" in the face of international terrorism, there was one person who had been sounding the alarm even before September 11, 2001. The head of the Moroccan Secret Police, also known as the Department of Territorial Security, or *al-Idara al-'Amma li-Muraqabat al-Turab al-Watani/Départment de sécurité territoriale* (DST), Hamidou Laânigri, had been warning the king about the possibility of a terrorist attack on Moroccan soil since at least 1999. When Mohamed VI became king during the summer of 1999, he began to change his father's long-standing security apparatus. Driss Basri, widely considered the architect of the Years of Lead, had been in charge of the DST since January 1973. In a move intended to show Moroccans that the country had entered a new age of respect for the rule of law and human rights, Mohamed VI deposed Basri and put Laânigri at the head of the DST on September 30, 1999. At the time, little was known about Laânigri except that he was a lifelong military man and that he spent the 1980s in the United Arab Emirates directing the Moroccan security team protecting Sheikh Zayed. Since 1989, Laânigri had served as the vice-director of the General Direction of Studies and Documentation, or *al-Idara al-'Amma li-l-Dirasat wa-al-Tawthiq/Direction générale des études et de la documentation* (DGED). He was known for his passion for technology and his utter contempt for Islamists.

From the time of his appointment at the head of the DST, Laânigri quickly became known as the strongman of the new regime.[4] His name was synonymous with human rights abuses in the new Morocco under Mohamed VI in general and for directing the secret detention center in Témara in particular. Paradoxically, Laânigri was also responsible for modernizing the DST and bringing a new level of transparency to it. He sought closer links with the FBI and brought in new technological equipment, such as computers and radios. Moreover, he encouraged his men to communicate with the press. One journalist met with Laânigri soon after his appointment in 1999 and was shocked by the difference between him and Driss Basri: "Friendly and smiling, Laânigri asked me questions about the liberalization of the audiovisual media, the liberty of the press, and the philosophy of mass media plurality. He even explained to me that he needed journalists to install an administrative office at the DST and to create magazines."[5] Laânigri's interest in the mass media as a means of achieving transparency for the DST was striking, especially compared to the opaque methods of his predecessor. It would serve as an important precedent for how he would later bring reform to the police establishment.

While at the head of the DST, Laânigri repeatedly warned the palace and the government about the possibility of a terrorist attack on Morocco. In addition, he encouraged the palace to strengthen security ties with the West after September 11 and to do everything possible to fight terrorism. It was Laânigri who released news that the DST had foiled a terrorist plot to blow up a gas tanker as it went through the Strait of Gibraltar in June 2002. He used it as proof that the terrorism threat to Morocco was real and imminent but had not been taken seriously. When May 16 struck, Laânigri was suddenly thrust to the center. For years, he had been arguing to insiders for a total restructuring of the police in order to confront the new realities of terrorism and the lack of security in the major cities. Laânigri had played a large role in the initial investigation into May 16 and the mass arrests of suspected terrorists immediately afterward. He was so forceful in his arguments about the need to restructure the police for the new Morocco that the king eventually decided to put him personally in charge of the project.

On July 25, 2003, the king named Hamidou Laânigri as the new head of the General Direction of National Security, or *al-Idara al-'Amma li-l-Amn al-Watani/Direction générale de la sécurité nationale* (DGSN), the administrative name for the police, replacing Hafid Benhachem, who had served in the position since 1999. Once again, Laânigri brought his love for technology and communication to an outmoded and massive bureaucratic security apparatus. Unlike his impact on the DST, however, Laânigri's influence on the DGSN would have profound changes on the culture of the police in Morocco. He would soon take his focus on the mass media to unprecedented levels.

In the face of escalating crime and the suddenly emerging threat of terrorism, Laânigri began the wide-reaching project of modernizing the police soon after his appointment at the head of the DGSN. In October 2003, Laânigri lobbied parliament for an increased police budget and, at this early stage, undertook a study on ways to improve the image of the police among the Moroccan public. He sent one hundred policemen to the United States for training with the FBI in March 2004 and issued a memo that summer forbidding female police officers from wearing the hijab and male officers from growing beards, ensuring that the public face of the police had nothing in common with the public's image of terrorism. In June 2004, he created a team of twenty-two air marshals for the Royal Air Maroc flights between Casablanca and New York/Montreal in order to defend against any incident involving the country's transatlantic air route. In addition, he launched a large center of technology within the DGSN, began to implement a new "biometric" national identification card, and modernized the traffic police, providing them with radars and cameras.

Laânigri soon became convinced that the answer to the country's new security challenges was to create a form of community policing in the large cities. This was particularly important because the police had limited coverage of the shantytowns and other urban areas that were seen as the breeding grounds for criminality and terrorism. The shantytowns posed a particular problem because they were the result of decades of rural migration to Casablanca, combined with the spread of misery, poverty, and extremist religious ideology. Laânigri believed that the best way to improve security in the major cities—and ward off another terrorist attack—was to involve the public in the policing process and for them to hold the police accountable for their efficiency and effectiveness.

Laânigri called this radical new program *Shurtat al-Qurb*, or Police of Proximity, and argued that it was the cornerstone of a total restructuring of the Moroccan police in the era of Mohamed VI. Borrowing this idea from community policing programs in France, England, and the United States, Laânigri wanted to create a police that he saw as compatible with the new Morocco, with its "notions of openness, respect for human rights, liberty of expression, and the new concept of authority."[6] First introduced by King Mohamed VI in a speech in October 1999, the phrase "new concept of authority" referred to the openness, freedoms, and rights that were intended to characterize the new era as compared to the reign of King Hassan II. Laânigri used his new police to show that the days of the old corrupt and brutal police were gone. The police who were seen as protecting the regime and the elite against the people were now a thing of the past. Instead, they would be completely updated for the new era. The police, according to Laânigri, would finally match the slogan seen at the entrances of police stations across the country and work "at the service of the people."

Laânigri based his community policing program on three fundamental concepts—visibility, communication, and closeness to the citizen. He wanted the new police to be as conspicuous as possible in the city streets in the hope that their presence would deter criminals and potential terrorists. Visibility meant seeing the police as much as possible in the city streets so that the public would come to view them as a natural part of the urban landscape and their fears would be allayed. It was also strongly tied to Laânigri's concept of communication. For decades, the police had remained an opaque establishment shrouded in secrecy. During the previous decade, however, the police increasingly opened up to the public thanks to growing collaboration with the mass media. This can be seen in the way the police provided the tabloids with crime-scene photographs, the independent press with crime reports, and movie directors with access to police stations, cars, and props. By the time the serial killer panic hit Casablanca, the police began cooperating much more closely and directly with the mass media, giving interviews to the press and nightly news. In the style of *Cops*, the police also took television crews with them as they cracked the case of Casablanca's notorious serial killer. This closer collaboration demonstrates the growing concern of the state for public relations and the importance of managing the image of the police in the country in an attempt to manufacture public acceptance of state authority in the era of *Alternance*. The evolution of the police in the new era was intended to reflect the larger reforms taking place in the country.

For Laânigri, this level of cooperation was not enough. He insisted that the police ramp up their direct communication with the public through the media. He pushed police commissioners to give press conferences and encouraged the police to host journalists at the police stations. Laânigri ushered in a new era of increased collaboration with the press, driven by the belief that media played a fundamental role not only in building and disseminating the police's image in society but also in the process of policing itself. In this way, Laânigri resembled a new J. Edgar Hoover, who, decades earlier, created deep connections with the American media and Hollywood, in the belief that popular culture industries—and the public's perception of the police—were an essential component in the fight against crime.[7]

Finally, Laânigri believed that in order for the police to confront the new era of rising urban crime and, most importantly, international terrorism, the Moroccan public needed to feel close to their police. For Laânigri, communication through the media was not simply to demonstrate openness, transparency, and reform to the public. Instead, he had a much more radical view. Laânigri wanted the media to work to convince the public to communicate directly with the police. He sought to use the media to create a new police-citizen relationship in which the public voluntarily participated in policing by providing information about potential threats in their neighborhoods and possible leads in order to prevent another May 16. Laânigri therefore saw the media as a means by which the police could create a bond with ordinary citizens in order to protect the nation. This new citizen-police relationship would be based on mutual sympathy, respect, and closeness, or "proximity."

Laânigri saw his new concept of policing—and media involvement—as a revolution within the ranks of the security services. While the image of the police had changed radically in society since the early 1990s, Laânigri's move to uproot the old police and initiate a new level of involvement with the mass media indicates that the state believed that the real-world police still had a public relations problem. Laânigri recognized that there was difference between the way the public viewed the fictional cop of the novels, true-crime narratives, and police téléfilms, on the one hand, and the real world cop on the streets, on the other. Nonetheless, the collaboration between the state and commercial media during the previous decade had created the cultural conditions necessary for Laânigri to begin implementing a community policing project in the country. Laânigri would soon turn to the strategies and mechanisms of this earlier collaboration in order to cast a new police-citizen relationship for the era of international terrorism.

The Birth of the GUS and the Challenge of Community Policing

The cornerstone of Laânigri's reforms was the new community police force, the Urban Security Units, or *al-Majmuʿat al-Hadariyya li-l-Amn/Groupes urbaines de sécurité* (GUS). Trained for three to six months, the GUS first appeared on the streets on October 17, 2004. Not surprisingly, the GUS was announced at a press conference, which was held two days later. The chief of general security, Bouchaïb Rmaïl, the former chief of police in Casablanca who received a promotion after his handling of the Zouita case, told the press that crime had developed tremendously in recent years. He continued, "That explains the concern of the nation with security and its strong feelings for the danger that it is facing. Today, it has new aspirations for achieving security and has come to desire the presence of a police that is closer to them, more present and effective, able to avert all the different forms of criminality and daily transgression with character."[8] Rmaïl provided the press with an outline of the new units and how they were organized. A total of four thousand men appeared in Casablanca, Rabat, and Marrakech and soon spread to other cities. The stated mission of the GUS was to intervene rapidly in order to maintain public order and safety, including in acts of rioting, severe car accidents, crime incidents, and especially terrorism. Each brigade consisted of four units of forty-eight men, each of which was divided into patrol groups consisting of seven or eight members. They were a mobile force, outfitted with striking new Toyota SUVs, police vans, cars, and motorcycles as well as the most modern technological equipment, such as handheld radios, computers, and pistols. GUS training was as advanced as their equipment, as they were all well-schooled in martial arts and spoke English as well as French.

The GUS were stationed at what were called Police of Proximity Posts, or *Marakiz Shurtat al-Qurb/Postes de police de proximité* (PPP), which were small buildings constructed in strategic positions in various neighborhoods in the major cities where the community policing program would be based. At the time of the GUS's launch, one thousand PPP were announced for completion in 2007. These would house an estimated twelve thousand officers. The object of the PPP was "to be as close as possible to the citizen on the neighborhood scale and to express visibly the presence of the state in order to reassure the citizen . . . as well as to intervene in all circumstances and to operate within the heart of the social fabric."[9] Each PPP would be open twenty-four hours a day and was intended to be a small-scale operation with at least fourteen men. In direct contrast to the large and intimidating police stations, the PPP were set up to create a sense of intimacy between the security forces and the citizen.

Putting his emphasis on visibility to work, Laânigri created the GUS to be as striking as possible. The men were all clean cut, tall, athletic, and handsome. As seen in figures 15, 16, and 18, they wore impressive blue uniforms—unlike any seen previously in Morocco—that looked like a fusion of police and military fatigues. The eye-catching nature of the uniform was intentional. As the police explained in their own internally produced magazine, "It's the uniform that reassures, not the trench coat of Columbo."[10] At first glance, the GUS was intended to be an entirely different kind of police, one that had severed its ties with the past. The detective of the true-crime articles and police téléfilms, who investigated cases through legwork and interrogation, was no longer sufficient for the new era. Symbolized by his trench coat and the actor Peter Falk, this detective was now a relic of the past. Today's police, with their highly visible uniforms, sporty good looks, and shining new SUVs, were intended to stand out proudly among street crowds for the entire public to see. As one journalist wrote, "The GUS attracted the admiration of a population charmed by their dynamic and pleasant appearance. It wasn't rare for passers-by to call out to GUS agents to thank and encourage them."[11]

The ultra-modern equipment of the GUS was intended to be as striking as the officers' appearance. Gone were the old cruisers, unmarked police cars, and dirty vans associated with the Years of Lead. The GUS drove brand new blue Toyota SUVs and motorcycles that clashed with the typical cars on the streets of the major cities. In these vehicles and uniforms, the GUS were meant to be "the visible part of the iceberg of reforms that the police has instituted recently in order to resituate the police in the role of protecting and serving citizens."[12] The GUS represented an entirely new police for the new Morocco, a Moroccan localization of a Western policing apparatus in both equipment and style. According to a young student quoted in the previous article, "With young and dynamic members and brand new means of transportation, the GUS reflected the symbol of modernity on the police, the same quality as their counterparts in the developed countries." Their cars, clothing, appearance, and equipment sent a message to the public about not only the police but also the country. The modernity and youthfulness of the GUS was intended both to draw the attention and admiration of the public and to reflect the state of policing in the new era.

Nonetheless, Laânigri faced a significant challenge to the success of his reforms. The mass media during the previous decade had disseminated a variety of fictional narratives of the police. Like the police procedural, these narratives positioned readers and viewers as the double of the police, encouraging them to participate in the process of investigating and solving crime. Moreover, these media sources—through their collaboration with the state—worked to blur the lines between police fact and fiction, seeking to improve the image of the real-world police and erase the public's associations of the police from the Years of Lead. In addition, the mass media and state collaborated to produce an image of the new Scientific Police as CSI: Casablanca in an attempt to convince the public that the country was able to match terrifying new kinds of criminality, such as the serial killer. Despite the highly innovative nature of these images, they worked by suggestion and persuasion, pushing the public to see the real-world police in the guise of their fictional double. While they encouraged the public to see state authority through the lens of the aspirations of the new era, these images did not require a specific response or reaction from the public.

Laânigri's plans in general—and his community policing program in particular—were dependent on the public's sympathizing with the real-world police to the point of communicating with them voluntarily. In this, he needed to change not only how the public saw the police but also how they interacted with them, not while reading the newspapers or watching television but on the streets. Unlike the Years of Lead, the state would need to achieve this through persuasion and not force. Louis Althusser offers an important perspective on the role of ideology in the mechanics of state power. In particular, he defines ideology as "the imaginary relationship of individuals to the real conditions of existence."[13] For Althusser, ideology turns individuals into subjects of the state. He calls this process interpellation, when the state engages the individual citizen directly and forces them to respond to its power. Althusser uses the example of the policeman addressing an individual on the street. The policeman calls out to the individual, who becomes a "subject" when they acknowledge, acquiesce, and respond to the call. Althusser argues that it is in this process of hailing—or interpellating—that the individual becomes a subject or citizen.

Althusser provides a valuable framework for understanding Laânigri's strategy for creating a new citizen for the community policing project. Laânigri understood from the beginning that he needed more than handsome cops who spoke English, drove new cars, and wore striking uniforms. As in Althusser's model, he had to hail the individual and make them respond to state power, interpellating a new kind of citizen in the process. Faced with perhaps the most important obstacle to the success of his reforms—and of preventing another terrorist attack—Laânigri made the decision to involve the state significantly more than ever before in the construction of the image of the police for the broader public. Like J. Edgar Hoover before him, Laânigri would intentionally blur the lines between the popular culture images of the police and the flesh-and-blood cop on the street, making the mass media a direct arm of policing in Morocco. Through this campaign, he would attempt not only to transform how the public saw the police but also to interpellate a new citizen for the era of community policing.

These Men We Fear

The new images of the police that circulated in society after the Tabit Affair were largely the product of nonstate actors, such as journalists, filmmakers, and writers, a phenomenon that pointed to a paradox of agency. While these nonstate sources hinted at the ambiguous and hybrid nature of their composition, they also gave the new images of the police a strong level of credibility. Even though the state wanted to take over the production of these images for the GUS, it still needed a nonstate source to lead the campaign. Laânigri understood from the beginning that the project would appear more credible if it did not look like old forms of state-produced propaganda. He therefore took the highly unusual step at the time, within Morocco at least, of hiring the local branch of an international advertising firm, Boomerang, to produce an advertising campaign unlike any seen before in the Middle East or North Africa. In order not simply to make the police more visible, but also to change fundamentally how the Moroccan citizen viewed and responded to them, Boomerang launched a multipronged campaign to win the hearts and minds of the Moroccan public for their police.

The first step in this campaign came in January 2005 when a number of nonstate commercial publications reported that there was a revolution taking place within the police establishment. The cover of the January 15–21, 2005, issue of the well-known Moroccan Francophone magazine *Tel Quel*, for example, features two police officers with a small shot of Laânigri's head peering in from the bottom, together with the bold headline "The Police That Wish You Well." The subheadline on the cover explains further: "GUS, Posts of Proximity, and a Trendy Publicity Campaign . . . Laânigri Makes a Great Effort to Seduce Us. Let's Give Him the Chance." The cover story in the issue points to a fundamental break that has taken place between the police of the past and of the present. "It's the story of an old girl, broke and dragging around a dirty reputation, who tries to restore her virginity to remake her life. That's the bet that the police have just made. With a publicity campaign and the launch of new corps, the cops want to convince us that they've changed. Why not?"[14] While *Tel Quel* typically takes a provocative and skeptical perspective on state initiatives, in this case it supports the police agenda. These words, which introduce the article on the new police, appear above a large color photograph of some two hundred GUS in perfectly shaped groups. These officers, dressed in their striking blue uniforms and hats, stand in formation among thirty new Toyota SUVs, motorcycles, and police vans. The men are positioned outside the Hassan II Mosque in Casablanca, standing on cream-colored tiles that contrast starkly with the dark blue of their uniforms and vehicles. This image, a version of which can be seen in figure 18, was the first of hundreds to appear as part of the new PR campaign. Instead of questioning the new police campaign, here *Tel Quel* disseminates the manufactured images of the advertising firm as if the magazine's staff had taken them, addressing readers directly to support the initiative.

The *Tel Quel* cover story details the creation of the publicity campaign and interviews the deputy director of Boomerang, Miryam Sebti. She explains that the goal of the media campaign is to "return pride to a police that will be visible from now on and will no longer make the citizen feel afraid."[15] The authors of the article also present Laânigri as a new kind of police chief, one who has severed ties with the past. According to the authors, Laânigri's top priorities are not simply restructuring the police in order to prevent another terrorist attack but transforming the image of the real-world police among the public. The striking photograph of the perfectly formed police, together with their modern uniforms and vehicles, served as an introduction to the way Laânigri would attempt to create a new kind of police in society.

Another typically confrontational weekly, *al-Baydawi* (the Casablancan), presented a similar depiction of the change that was taking place within the police. On January 26, 2005, the *Casablancan* printed a cover story with the headline "Laânigri Leads Coup d'État within Security Services."[16] The authors present the police as an institution that had been largely immune from change since it was founded in 1956. Nonetheless,

> the political transformations that Morocco has been experiencing since the launch of what is called the "democratic transition" has imposed a radical change on the national security services, which are now calling for restructuring along the lines of the new demands of society. The police are no longer considered oppressors, instruments used in confrontations between the various sides of the political terrain, as much as they are now technical instruments in the hands of the state to achieve security in society.[17]

While the authors do not discuss the publicity campaign in detail, they do point to a radical change in the police and a fundamentally new relationship between the police and society. They state that the police had resisted change for decades but have finally opened up under the influence of the political transition—the new era of openness—that has been taking place in the country during the past decade. Once an arm of repression, their mission is now to provide security for the public. The authors then discuss the various elements of what they call the "coup d'état" within the police. These include a restructuring of police divisions throughout the country as well as the launch of the GUS and community policing. As with the cover story in *Tel Quel*, the *Casablancan*, while typically confrontational with state policies, heralds the fundamental break within the police, presenting the public with the idea that the police of the past are gone forever.

On January 31, 2005, *Moroccan Events* joined in the chorus with a front-page article on a "historic" conference that took place that month in Marrakech.[18] The conference was called "study days" and, according to the article, centered around the question, "What kind of police do we want for today's Morocco?" While this topic suggested that a human rights organization or academic group was holding the conference, it turns out that it was the DGSN. High-level security officials from all over the country attended the sessions that Hamidou Laânigri led and discussed the new philosophy of the police, with its focus on the citizen. According to the article, the conference focused on the fundamental restructuring and reforms taking place "in the scope of arriving at an effective police that is focused on the citizen." The article reviewed the new philosophy of the "Police of Proximity" and the new role of the police for today's Morocco, explaining, "The nature of the relationship between the policeman and the citizen—during the past four decades—has created psychological impediments that have caused a separation between the two. The study conference tried to create new paths to eliminate these impediments." For the first time, the police openly discussed how the public distrusted them. Moreover, they admitted that they were actively seeking ways to create a close relationship with the public. The message to the public was clear—there was a new police on the scene.

It was in the context of these reports in the independent press that the first stage in Boomerang's direct campaign emerged. On February 1, 2005, a striking new form of media appeared on newsstands across the county, the glossy and colorful *Police Magazine*. The police had previously issued a periodical, the *Police Journal of National Security*, between 1961 and 2004. This earlier publication, which was discussed briefly in chapter 1 in the aftermath of the Tabit Affair, was issued quarterly and was available at the odd newsstand, typically buried under other publications. Instead of focusing on the public, it was largely intended for its internal police audience. The *Journal* was written in what is called *lughat al-khashab*, "the language of wood," a heavy and dense propagandistic style made up largely of formulaic praise for the palace, government, and the police as an institution. It was of low production quality and typically included coverage of internal police news and events, articles on juridical matters, advertisements, excerpts from the criminal code, early attempts at writing police short stories, and even crossword puzzles and special advertisements aimed largely at a police clientele. Considering the language, form, and content of the old *Journal of National Security*, the new *Police Magazine* represented a radical break with the past. Boomerang transformed what was the epitome of state propaganda into a stylish glossy magazine that looked at first as if it had nothing to do with the state.

As seen in figure 15, the cover of the first issue of *Police Magazine* featured a full-page color photograph of a handsome and youthful GUS officer. Dressed in the new uniform and special hat of the GUS, equipped with a thick leather belt boasting a gun, he stands in front of a new Toyota SUV with his modern walkie-talkie in hand, presumably receiving instructions for a rapid intervention. The concerned look on his face, together with his hands in motion, demonstrate his readiness to serve the public. This image, however, is set next to these words in bold yellow letters: "These Men We Fear." This cover therefore juxtaposes the image of the modern cop with an admission of the public's long-standing and widespread fear of the police. This striking cover suggests a total break with the police of the past. The police are not only as modern and effective as the handsome officer on the cover, but they also now explicitly mock their former image, all in the guise of a glossy media product. While the police had become increasingly open to the public in the mass media during the past decade, *Police Magazine* marked a decisive turning point. The police now enthusiastically communicated directly with the public about their inner workings, revealing all in the form of a magazine that had the veneer of a nonstate commercial media source.

Laânigri's emphasis on visibility, communication, and closeness to the citizen can be seen on nearly every page of the first issue of *Police Magazine*. In the opening editorial, entitled "Re-foundation," Laânigri enthusiastically announces the Marrakech "study days," which he explains were inspired by the king's "new concept of authority." Laânigri claims that the police no longer function to reinforce authority in society but to protect the citizen. The DGSN, he explains, "is trying to return the word 'police' to its etymology—a police at the service of the public, close to the citizen, professional, effective, respecting others just as others respect them."[19] He claims that the meeting in Marrakech "validated the configuration of the new technical and informational tools and the new structure of the DGSN . . . in the sense of modernity. We want a police close to the citizen and at his service." The police were founded in Morocco immediately after independence in 1956, and in this opening editorial, Laânigri wipes away the previous forty-nine years of history, starting the police over for the public and returning them to their origins not simply in meaning but also in public mission. At the same time, he ties this modern and technologically savvy cop to the transformations taking place in society under the new king. This new police is therefore the concrete result of the king's "new concept of authority," one of the pillars of the country's experience of political transition.

The main article of the issue, entitled "These Men We Fear," covers in detail the "new face of the police," including the role of the GUS, the Police of Proximity, and the new philosophy of visibility, communication, and closeness to the citizen.[20] The authors begin by discussing the rise of religious extremism in Morocco thanks to rural migration. They blame the May 16 attacks, however, on the laxness that the new era had ushered in:

> The new reign, essentially centered on the new notions of openness, respect for human rights, liberty of expression, the new concept of authority, and the consolidation of the state of law and institutions, went on to create, above all, among the cadres charged with security, what resembled hesitation—not to speak of passivity—in the face of civil society.[21]

In other words, the state attributes the inability to prevent the Casablanca attacks to a kind of complacency that set in because of the permissiveness of the new era. Nonetheless, according to the authors, the May 16 bombings "called the state back to reality" and forced the police to undergo a complete transformation. Among the most important aspects of this fundamental change, the authors explain, is an admission that the old image of the police is no longer suitable for the demands of today: "Who among us has not been disgusted at one time or another by the state of the typewriter used to take a complaint at the police station? Who hasn't been shocked by the condition of the police buildings and their exteriors? Who hasn't been stunned by the kinds of run-down cars that show up after someone calls for an emergency?"[22] The authors explain that the shiny new cars of the GUS and their PPP have replaced these elements of the past: "The ultimate goal is to reconcile the Moroccan citizen with their police."[23] The authors therefore admit the work that image does for policing. Officers on the streets and manning desks at the entrances to the police stations are the first contact that the public has with state authority. They are the direct symbol of the state for the public. The advertising campaign shows a striking transformation in the way the state wanted to project this image to the public. In police téléfilms like *Sofia's Restaurant*, among others, there had been a clear attempt to present the public with the newest and cleanest of police stations. Now, the state moved to transfer this emphasis on public image from the depiction of police stations on television to every officer on the street. Each individual cop now represented the front line in the construction of the image of the police.

The first issue of *Police Magazine* also features a commentary by the editor-in-chief, Younès Jaouhari, entitled "I'm Afraid of the Police." Jaouhari is not a police officer, but came to the project after a long career in the Moroccan mass media, including with the well-known weekly *Le Journal*, showing how the police employed credible nonstate journalists to produce their magazine.[24] He wrote that he was always afraid of the police and that they were present in Morocco "only to reprimand or punish." Nonetheless, he continues, "the police are changing. They are reconciling themselves with the citizen." At the same time, Jaouhari admits that this is hard for the ordinary citizen to believe, especially considering the police's history of torture, abductions, and human rights abuses. He explains:

> The recent past remains very much present in our minds. We all just participated in the stories of people murdered by the actions of the same police. Random abductions and families struck by the unknown. All that in the name of order and security? Hard to believe today that things have really changed and that the actions of the past have become a part of history.

Here, Jaouhari points to the recently mass-mediated sessions of the Equity and Reconciliation Commission, the first of its kind in the Arab world. By setting up the Equity and Reconciliation Commission, the state looked to turn the page on the decades of torture and abuse by the police and security services during the Years of Lead. While there is plenty to criticize about these sessions—including the fact that victims were not permitted to name names, no arrests would result from the testimonies, and the purview of the Commission did not go beyond 1999—they represented a significant step forward in freedom of speech in society.[25]

These sessions formed the immediate backdrop for the campaign to transform the image of the police. At exactly the time that the media dug up the abuses of the Years of Lead for the public, the police were busy constructing an entirely new image of themselves that was utterly disconnected from the past. The new image therefore served as another way of turning the page on the Years of Lead. Although much has been written about the Moroccan Equity and Reconciliation Commission, the role of the GUS in this process has been completely overlooked by scholars. The appearance of the advertising campaign for the new police at exactly the same time as the televised sessions—coupled with the way the editor of *Police Magazine* directly links the two events—demonstrates how the "refounding" of the police was also meant to complement the state's attempt to move beyond the Years of Lead. For the state, the old abusive police apparatus that was on trial in sessions of the Equity and Reconciliation Commission no longer existed. It had been replaced by the modern, Westernized, and technologically savvy police who were now highly visible throughout society.

In his editorial, Jaouhari breaks several taboos. He admits that the public suffers from a deep-seated fear of the police, one based on years of systematic human rights violations. He also admits that the experience of the Years of Lead makes it difficult to believe that the police are really changing. These positions reflect a critical stance on the police from within the establishment. The Tabit Affair—as well as the press—broke the taboo of criticizing the police in the nonstate mass media, but the establishment had continued to communicate with the public in its own sources, such as the *Journal of National Security*, in the same language as the Years of Lead. *Police Magazine* destroyed that practice. With editorials like Jaouhari's, the magazine hoped to show that the police now communicated directly with the public in the same style and with the same credibility as nonstate media sources.

The force of *Police Magazine* is not in simply the way its authors describe the new police. It is also in the striking visual elements of the magazine, which features professional photographs of the GUS in various formations that make them look organized, efficient, and responsive. Each issue also features a "Photo of the Month," a centerfold-type spread, typically of the police smiling and holding various pieces of modern equipment. In the magazine's first issue, the photo of the month—as seen in figure 16—shows a handsome and smiling GUS officer who resembles Rachid El Ouali, an actor who appeared in more police téléfilms than any other, leaning over the homework of three smiling children, who look up at him for help. The image is powerful—the police may have been torturers until only recently but now they are so friendly and sympathetic that they happily help kids with their homework. The scene also reflects a strong level of security: three young children are able to sit in a public park by themselves unthreatened. Moreover, the police have enough time on their hands to help them with their homework. An image like this of complete safety and security clashed with that of media sources like the crime tabloids. Other "Photos of the Month" depict a bold police force in their striking blue uniforms, equipped with modern radios, standing by shining four-by-fours or sitting in front of new computers. Gone are the old typewriter, beat-up car, shabby clothes, and scowl of the corrupt detective, the one condemned during the sessions of the Equity and Reconciliation Commission, which were broadcast live across the country on radio and television.

The language and images of the magazine represented innovative techniques for reforming the image of the new police. These strategies continued in the following issues as well. The second issue, for example, features a picture of a female officer in fatigues holding a handgun in front of her, taking target practice. This cover photograph—featured in figure 17—is accompanied by the title of the issue's main story: "Women in the Police Establishment."[26] The dossier boasts many photographs of women officers holding guns, driving police cars, and marching together. It explains that these are trainees for the police, indicating that the woman on the cover of the magazine is the face of the next generation of the police. The magazine also features an interview with a female police commissioner and photographs of her on the streets leading men making arrests at night.

Just as the téléfilm *White Nights* presented the Moroccan public with images of a female detective drawing her gun as she raided a house—even if these were far from reality—*Police Magazine* disseminated images of female officers in order to show that gender equality had arrived in the police establishment thanks to the inclusion of women. Respect for human rights demonstrated the globalized and modern nature of the police. The promotion and support for career equality not only broke a taboo about gender rights within the ranks of the security services but also displayed the fundamentally new character of the Moroccan police. The spirit of improved women's rights emerged in the Morocco of Mohamed VI with increased parliamentary representation and the new family code. According to *Police Magazine*, it had now reached even the core of the police.[27]

In the following issues, *Police Magazine* boasted many elements that sought to educate the public about the police. Regular features included the section "Life of an Arrondissement," which covered the news of a given section of a city; "A Night with the Police," which included photographs of the police on the beat, showing in detail how they work and respond to crime, emphasizing proper police procedure; "Words of the Cops," which quoted ordinary officers recalling particular events that "marked their police life"; interviews with police chiefs from different cities; and crime reports and specials on the country's various serial killers. Each issue also highlighted the work of an individual detective in a section entitled "A Cop Unlike Any Other." In a style similar to the true-crime articles that encouraged audience identification with an individual detective, this section allowed the public to see the entire institution of the police through the hard work of a single detective.

The subjects of the magazine were varied and included modern crime-fighting techniques, the challenges of the border police, the prison system, crime-scene processing, police training, and cybercrime. Each issue featured a "lexicon" of police terminology, to teach the public to speak like the police. Other elements included professionally staged photographs, and interviews with high-ranking officials within the police, in addition to officials from outside the police establishment, including ministers, film directors, NGO workers, and writers. The magazine also prominently featured fictional elements, from sensationalized retellings of notorious crimes and even a series of police short stories written by Fadel Ataâllah, a police commissioner who has won a literary prize for his fiction.

In his editorial on the first anniversary of *Police Magazine*, Abdelaziz Samel, the director of human resources at the DGSN, celebrated how the police now communicated with the public about all aspects of their work. He explains,

> *Police Magazine* has rejected the "language of wood." From this point of view, the magazine of the police has transcended certain taboos. It hasn't hesitated to dissect the principle institutions that watch over the security of the country and which, until recently, were not made the object of any media treatment. Whether it be the Scientific Police, the Criminal Police, the general inspections of the DGSN, or charged moments of police training, *Police Magazine* has not stopped to make the security apparatus something banal.[28]

In this editorial, Samel shuns the old form of police communication—typified by the phrase "the language of wood"—and juxtaposes it with the way the magazine presents the public with the new image of the police. The subject of the police had been a major taboo in the past. Now, the police communicate directly and voluntarily with the public in what appears to be complete and total openness. In the process, the police attempt to make themselves something common and ordinary for the public. There is so much communication now, claims Samel, that the topic of the police has become banal. Just as the new mass media, with daily true-crime articles and regular police téléfilms, began making the image of crime and punishment something commonplace and repetitive for the public, the police adopted the same goal with their own direct sources. This banalization was an attempt to transform the symbolic value of the real-world police from authoritarian, brutal, and corrupt—something striking and terrifying—to a common and natural part of the social fabric, something barely noticed.

While *Police Magazine* was highly visible to anyone passing by the newsstands across the country, magazines in Morocco have limited impact on the public. They have much smaller circulations than daily newspapers, target an educated audience, and are expensive for the majority of the public. Boomerang, in its advertising campaign, recognized this from the start. In order to disseminate its message of a new police that has broken with the past, the advertising firm also turned to much more popular forms of communication, including billboards, radio, and, above all, television. In the process, it brought its message of a new police and citizen to the entire public, elite and non-elite alike.

The Police Are Close to You for Your Security

Just as *Police Magazine* hit the newsstands, an advertisement for the new police began airing on the two television stations. As with other forms of Boomerang's campaign, this advertisement skillfully combined Laânigri's strategy of visibility, communication, and closeness to the citizen. Overall, the clip resembled the military recruitment advertisements that aired on television in the United States during the mid-2000s. The key difference, however, is that the GUS advertisement did not seek to increase applications to the police. Instead, it aimed to transform the image of the police and convince the public to participate in the process of community policing and establish a new police-citizen relationship for the post–May 16 era.

Produced in French and a version that mixed both Standard and Moroccan Arabic so that it reached the entire public regardless of education, the ad ran multiple times a day for months during prime-time hours. Washed in a rich blue color, the minute-long clip begins with a quick montage of city scenes accompanied by dramatic cutting music. Two young businessmen walk next to a glass building, holding their briefcases, smiling as two policemen on motorcycles are seen in the reflection on the window. Next, a smiling couple walks on the street holding their daughter's hand. A beautiful young woman then gets out of her car holding her cell phone, smiling and laughing as two policemen on motorcycles pass by. The scene shifts to the old city as rapid shots show young people walking around, talking and smiling. In these introductory sequences, the public is simply moving safely and happily through the urban terrain unaware that the police are constantly present on the margins, barely visible in the reflections in the modern glass buildings.

The scene then shifts to a large park in the center of the city as people walk through, talking and laughing, cut with rapid shots of the GUS driving by in an SUV, accompanied by quick wave sounds. Three children sit on a park bench doing their homework and a handsome GUS officer with his hand on his hip slowly approaches and leans over their books, smiling and offering help. The three schoolkids look up at the officer with broad smiles. An image from this sequence appeared as the "Photo of the Month" of the first issue of *Police Magazine*, as seen in figure 16. A quick cut then follows, accompanied by the same wave sound, and two GUS officers appear, holding their handheld radios, standing next to a couple. The man and woman are lost but the GUS show them their location on a tourist map. The woman then looks up at one of the officers with a broad smile, showing her surprise, gratitude, and admiration for their help. This shot records the moment of realization in the couple's eyes that these are new police who bear little resemblance to the brutal security services of days past. This couple, who are happy to communicate with the new police and ask them for help, is intended to serve as a double for the public.

At the same time, the advertisement shows how the GUS respond to emergencies rapidly and effectively. The ad quickly cuts to a GUS officer standing beside his blue SUV, talking on his hand-held radio, accompanied by the sound of a walkie-talkie clicking on and off. An image from this scene was used as the cover photograph for the first issue of *Police Magazine*, as seen in figure 15. The music becomes more rapid as the officer suddenly rushes around the car and waves to the other GUS in his squad. They run to their cars and motorcycles and drive off, accompanied by police sirens, which emphasizes their ability to intervene instantly to avert crime. Their sirens and flashing blue and red lights are mixed with sounds of the GUS driving quickly through the streets at night, as if on a Hollywood-style chase. Accompanied by exciting and rapid music and quick white flashes, the squad passes a middle-aged man who stands on the street admiring them as they speed by. This scene fades to a GUS officer standing proudly with his hands grasping his thick leather belt, positioned in the center of the shot with two GUS SUVs to the left and four GUS officers in formation on their motorcycles to the right.

Police sirens blare again and there are shots of the GUS riding their motorcycles and SUVs speeding through winding city streets on their way to intervene in a crime, followed by more exciting rapid white flashes. Finally, these images fade into a low-level shot of a row of GUS officers standing in formation on the cream-colored marble outside the Hassan II Mosque in central Casablanca. After a white flash, the image shifts to an overhead shot of the same scene as some two hundred GUS officers can now be seen in formation around motorcycles, cars, and vans, suggesting that behind a simple row of police stands the entire force. As seen in figure 18, an image from this scene was used as the publicity shot for both the January 15, 2005, *Tel Quel* article and the cover of an issue of *Police Magazine*.

As the ad comes to a close, the sound shifts from rapid and exciting beats to rich violin chords and isolated drumbeats just as the overhead shot continues up and becomes blurred. A sharply focused bright red, white, and green shield of the police appears in the center of the shot and becomes larger as the image of the GUS in formation continues to blur. Underneath the shield are the words, "The Police Are Close to You for Your Security." A still from this scene appears in figure 19. These words appeared in the first articles on the GUS and served as the slogan for the publicity campaign. The ad ends as the shield and words enlarge to take up the size of the screen.

Throughout the advertisement, a man with a striking rich voice enthusiastically narrates the following script:

> Because security and safety are fundamental
> Because it's every citizen's right to live in a safe city
> Because the city must be totally secure
> Because our security is a safeguard for our freedom
> Today, you'll find beside you the GUS
> They're up all night for our comfort and safety
> In every place and in everything we do
> In our city, day and night
> The GUS are equipped with all the necessary means
> To strengthen security in all the urban areas
> The police are close to you for your security

These words reinforce the images and action. The young middle-class people depicted in the advertisement rely on the police to secure the city so that they can go about their daily activities. The freedom that the public enjoys, the narrative underscores, is based on the police working in the background to ensure their safety, twenty-four hours a day. The narrative also stresses how the GUS are outfitted with the technological tools necessary for their mission, including walkie-talkies, SUVs, motorcycles, and guns. Finally, the slogan for the GUS—"The police are close to you for your security"—is emphasized at each turn in the advertisement. Whether working unnoticed in the background, as seen in the beginning of the clip, or in full view helping children with their homework or tourists find their way, the police are always beside the public in order to ensure their safety and comfort. This is a police that merits the admiration of the public, as seen in the smiles of the various people in the advertisement. At the same time, the rapid mobilization depicted in the clip demonstrates how this is a police ready for action at any moment.

To the Moroccan public, this television advertisement would have seemed very familiar. First, there was the intertextuality between the television clip and other aspects of the advertising campaign. Boomerang arranged for radio advertisements for the GUS that played regularly and featured the audio elements from the television clip. Moreover, the television ad served as the foundation for the most prominent images of the campaign, such as the shots of the GUS officer holding a walkie-talkie, the officer helping the children with their homework, and the formation of some two hundred men beside their vehicles. These images appeared not only in *Police Magazine* and nonstate media sources like *Moroccan Events* and *Tel Quel* but also on billboards that Boomerang rented throughout the major cities. Boomerang therefore used not only magazines, television spots, and radio ads, but also public spaces to disseminate the campaign to the public, seeking the widest possible audience. These billboards presented the image of the new police outside of the mass media and also served to reinforce the widespread nature of the campaign, making it seem banal and natural. Just as the cop on the street in his new uniform and SUV served as mobile advertisement for the new police, billboards across the major cities presented another opportunity for reinforcement and intertextuality for the broader public.

Another reason why the television advertisement would have seemed familiar was because of its relationship with the police téléfilms. In order to produce the advertisement, Boomerang turned to Sigma, the Moroccan audiovisual company that produced Noureddine Lakhmari's *The Case* téléfilms. The GUS advertisement reflects the look and feel of Lakhmari's work thanks to the use of rich colors, rapid scene cuts, striking camera angles, sharp images, jarring sounds, and exciting music. This helped to emphasize the fictional quality of the television advertisement, giving it the feel of police téléfilms like *The Case* and even *White Nights*, establishing an intertexual link with the most modernist work on Moroccan television. This style and technique of the advertisement also cast it as a nonstate media form, resembling programming on MTV more than an advertisement for the real-world police.

Yet there is a more important connection between *The Case* and the GUS advertisement. Through *The Case* films, Sigma had proven itself particularly adept at producing audiovisual images of the Moroccan police in the trappings of their Western counterparts. As chapter 5 showed, *The Case* presented the public with highly misleading representations of the Scientific Police in Morocco in an attempt to improve their real-world image for the public. The series depicts Zeineb and Meryem leading investigations into cases like the American television criminalists of *CSI*, not their counterparts in Morocco, where the Scientific Police simply serve the Criminal Police by analyzing crime scene evidence. In creating the GUS, Laânigri sought to localize a Western policing model, one that was highly foreign in Morocco. Sigma therefore was hired not simply to produce images of the GUS but also to cast them in the media into the role of community police forces in the United States or France. For many, the television advertisement was their first contact with the GUS. Sigma therefore intended to establish an image of the GUS as exciting, effective, and modern—a Moroccan localization of Western community police—before the public encountered them on the streets. In doing so, the Boomerang campaign sought to position the public to see the real-world GUS as their mass-mediated counterparts.

The Boomerang campaign was therefore based on the strategies and mechanics of the state-media interface that developed during the previous decade. The true-crime articles and téléfilms encouraged the public to accompany the police as they solved crime, establishing the police as their double and giving the public the experience of exercising state authority in the process. Boomerang sought to extend the experience of participating in state authority from popular culture texts in newspaper and television to cooperating with the real-life community police. Moreover, the advertising campaign—like the state-media interface during the previous decade—increasingly blurred the lines between the real-world police and their fictionalized image, encouraging the public to see the real-world police through the lens of their mass-mediated counterparts.

Finally, the concluding slogan for the television advertisement—"The police are close to you for your security"—is highly revealing. Even though Boomerang focused on the GUS, these words demonstrate that the campaign was aimed at transforming the image of the police as a whole and not simply the GUS of the community policing program. This is also apparent in the final seconds of the television advertisement, which feature the shield of the police, not a symbol particular to the GUS, growing larger and expanding to cover the GUS officers standing in formation, showing how the DGSN embodies the new community policing program. The GUS may be the centerpiece of the new reforms, but the advertisement targets the public's image of the police as a whole. According to the campaign, the GUS signify the present and future of the changing police, a police that is both visible and close to the ordinary Moroccan citizen.

To accompany this advertising campaign, Boomerang produced thousands of staged photographs of the GUS, not only for *Police Magazine* and billboard advertisements but also for broad dissemination in the commercial mass media. These photographs were given to the Moroccan press and soon appeared in newspaper pages, accompanying stories about the police, the GUS, or even average crime articles. These strikingly professional images first appeared when the police began inviting journalists into the police station and to go out on the beat with them. *Moroccan Events* embedded a journalist with the GUS and he wrote a detailed full-page account of his experience on the streets that featured the Boomerang-produced photographs.[29] The author individualized each cop, detailing the various routes that they took through the city and several arrests they made to protect the public from crime. Not surprisingly, the image of the GUS is highly positive as the author describes how ordinary citizens on the streets wave at them in admiration. The police even invited the editors from the *Casablancan*, the investigative weekly known for its opposition to state policies, for a round table discussion at the main police station in Casablanca about reforms in the city.[30] Through the campaign, the state managed to co-opt some of its fiercest adversaries as well as the independent daily press in order to disseminate its message of the new police. As during the serial killer panic, bringing the press out on patrols and into the police stations not only demonstrated both openness and communication with the public, but also that the state sought to engage the media in order to manage public opinion and influence perceptions.

The daily and weekly press therefore formed yet another layer for the rich background of the advertising campaign. The public saw the new face of the police when they passed by the newsstands, turned on the radio or television, looked up at the billboards on the streets, watched GUS pass by in their cars, or opened the daily newspaper. The new police—a foil for the image of the police from the Years of Lead that appeared to be on trial during the hearings of the Equity and Reconciliation Commission—aimed to be everywhere, a natural part of the social fabric. Through this new campaign, the state sought to establish the public's relationship with the GUS through their mass-mediated image, dialoguing with the other forms of police media that had been circulating in society during the previous decade. By calling for the public to respond, they attempted to interpellate a new Moroccan citizen, one who would self-identify with this new image to the point of participating in the policing process.

Like the Police of a Foreign Country

It was perhaps because of this insistence that many recoiled from the campaign, rejecting the way it urged a public response and reacting with skepticism, sarcasm, and even mockery. Within one month of the launch of the GUS, the *Casablancan* published a feature story on the new police units, calling them "moving décor" and "parade units" that "are far from reality."[31] The authors interviewed a number of police officers about the GUS and one explained, "We're not in America or France. We Moroccans don't need police as decoration."[32] The authors emphasized that, despite the efforts of the state, it was obvious that the new police were simply a copy of an international model. They reported how the public saw the new police as something imported from abroad, a security unit with no connection to local reality. For the authors, the GUS served solely as an image that would please Western observers monitoring civil rights in the country, but would have no effective role in the local environment.

Several days after the appearance of *Police Magazine,* one of the new independent dailies, *al-Nahar al-Maghribiyya* (Moroccan Day) published a picture of Laânigri with the headline, "Welcome, Colleague, to the Profession of Hardships."[33] The newspaper printed an open letter by Khalid Jamaï, the former editor of *L'Opinion,* to Laânigri, sarcastically expressing his enthusiasm and happiness when he saw the first issue of *Police Magazine* and discovered that Laânigri was its director. Jamaï mocks Laânigri, claiming that he feels calm about the future of freedom of expression in the country since Laânigri, the former head of intelligence and current chief of the police, is now also a man of the press. He tries to imagine Laânigri, on the one hand, arresting journalists and, on the other, protesting alongside other journalists against the way the security forces abuse them. Jamaï mockingly proposes that he will stand beside Laânigri in solidarity when the state shuts down his magazine and seizes its issues or when the police arrest and interrogate him for breaking a taboo.

Other forms of criticism began appearing. One front-page article in *Moroccan Events* cited well-placed sources who claimed, "The structure of the police in our country has relied on copying foreign experience, to a T, without consideration for objective conditions."[34] The author of this article points to a number of PPP that have been constructed but remain vacant, suggesting that the execution of the community policing program on the ground was a failure. The reason, the author explains, is that the state has copied the external trappings of a community policing program without taking the time to localize it to the demands of the Moroccan environment. This explains, according to the authors, why the public could see through this direct attempt to manipulate their perceptions of reality.

True to form, the *Casablancan* took aim at the image of the new police. As seen in figure 20, the cover of the October 24, 2005, issue features a highly provocative photograph of a GUS officer. Wearing sunglasses and black leather gloves, the handsome GUS officer leans his elbow forward and rests his chin on his wrist, striking a pose for the camera. The director of the *Casablancan,* Abderrahim Ariri, explained to me that this is one of his favorite cover images because the officer was posing as a way to make fun of the image of the GUS constructed in the media as glamorous, stylish, and even having a star quality on the streets. This perception of the GUS was echoed elsewhere in the press: "Black sunglasses, gleaming racing cars, and disdainful struts, some took themselves seriously as show-biz stars in the middle of filming an American TV show in the style of *Baywatch.* Others devoted themselves to picking up girls in the middle of the street."[35] While actors like Younès Migri played cops on television, it now appeared that the GUS conducted themselves on the streets as if they were playing the role of detectives on American television. It seemed that the GUS—and not the public—had been seduced by the advertising campaign and were acting as if they were living in a television movie.

The main article in the October 24, 2005, issue of the *Casablancan*, however, hits hard at the GUS. The authors begin by comparing the recent police reforms to the David Cronenberg film *The Fly*. In this analogy, Laânigri is someone who has experimented with the police and created the GUS in the process. Now, however, his creation has turned into a monster that he could not have imagined and that he has no power to control. The authors interview a number of people who give their opinions on the GUS. One explains that the GUS did nothing except "walk around and show off their muscles."[36] A later article by the editors of the *Casablancan* would state that GUS were "like a police belonging to a foreign state, being appointed in Morocco like a colonized land to 'tame' the people and make them kneel down."[37] The disconnect between the mass-mediated image of the GUS and their reality on the streets was presenting significant challenges for the credibility of the project and its ultimate success. It soon became obvious to the entire public the extent to which the GUS on the streets clashed with their mass-mediated image.

The Police of Murder

During their first year, the GUS appeared to have reduced crime. Multiple newspaper articles praised them and the community policing program for lowering incidents of violence and theft in the major cities and suggested that the public felt a sense of relief now that the GUS were on the scene. Not surprisingly, *Police Magazine* published crime statistics to demonstrate the success of the GUS. According to these numbers, in the first year after the GUS went into operation, attacks against individuals declined by 81 percent, theft declined by 85 percent, and arrests related to illegal immigration declined by 64 percent.[38] The presence of the GUS also led to rising arrest rates for other crimes, including a 150 percent increase in incidents of public disturbance, a 142 percent increase in drug-related cases, and a 50 percent increase in public complaints that were acted upon. These rising statistics suggested not the ineffectiveness of the GUS, but rather that the presence of the GUS had allowed the state to get infractions like drugs and public disturbances under control. This can also be seen in the large increase in the number of cases investigated by the police. *Police Magazine* printed statistics showing that crime declined in nearly all of the major cities during 2005 thanks to the GUS and that the police had an arrest rate of nearly 87 percent.[39]

Despite this success, complaints about GUS corruption and brutality—and not simply their arrogance or disconnect from reality—began appearing within two months after their appearance on the streets. In December 2004, *Morning* published a report that the public already saw the GUS as a failure, largely because of the bribes that they were apparently demanding.[40] At the same time, a dark reality about the GUS began to emerge. The heroic and modern image that circulated in Moroccan society had become so convincing that the GUS clearly believed it too. The advertising campaign was not simply for the public at large; it was also for the police to embody these new images. The problem was that they began to see themselves as supercops and took this image too far in the way they engaged citizens. Newspapers began reporting about "Hollywood" chases as well as "spectacular" interventions of the GUS to restore order, all with accusations of police misconduct and excesses.

The first instance of reports of this overzealousness appeared in the December 20, 2004, front-page story in *Moroccan Events*, with the following headline: "The Police Insult Citizens and Yell in Their Faces: 'The Street Is Ours!'"[41] The article emphasizes how the GUS cursed at people, insulting them for no apparent reason and screaming at them to get off the streets. The article also reports that the GUS were patrolling wealthy districts and ignoring the working-class areas where street crime was prevalent. The implication was that the GUS spent their time among the wealthy so that they could collect bribes and make money, much like Aziz's character in the téléfilm *The Witness*. The article stresses that despite the intention of the new police program, fear and anger were once again returning to the streets thanks to this aggressive treatment.

News also spread that the GUS were provoking people and brutalizing suspects in the process of making an arrest. One article in January 2005 described how an intoxicated homeless man was yelling in front of the well-known café La Choppe in central Casablanca.[42] A group of seven GUS arrived, restrained the man, and kept him on the ground with their boots. Another unit of GUS on motorcycles then arrived to "secure the scene." As for the crowds watching, the article reported that they were appalled that the GUS gave so much attention to an unarmed homeless man simply making noise. This huge show of force seemed to onlookers more appropriate for a television movie or the arrest of a dangerous criminal than for a defenseless man.

The same article explained that these kinds of scenes were happening across the country. A Moroccan man visiting Meknès, for example, briefly drove down a one-way street by accident and was quickly tailed at top speed by a unit of GUS "like high-speed chases in police movies." The police proceeded to pull the man out of the car, lean him across his hood, and cuff him, despite committing only a simple traffic violation. The anonymous author used these cases to claim that the GUS were failing at their mission to change the image of the police: "Some of the officers of this unit feel that they are made from a different clay and instead of undertaking their obligations, they are intent on putting on a show of force, terrifying citizens, and provoking them." All of this was happening, according to the article, as the GUS were ignoring the crime-infested areas that they should have been patrolling.

More reports that clashed with the advertising campaign continued to mount in 2005 as the press printed news of overzealous GUS officers arresting people like ambulant cigarette sellers in seemingly safe urban areas, using excessive force against innocent people, and detaining young men and women under morals charges. "I don't know if we're in Morocco, a country of liberalization, modernity, and general freedoms or in the mountains of Afghanistan during the Taliban, a fortress of extremism, religious intolerance, and repression," a man told the press after the GUS arrested him and a female neighbor while walking in the streets after breaking the Ramadan fast.[43] Even though the two were childhood friends—and the women in the neighborhood rushed out of their houses to defend them—the GUS presumed that the woman was a prostitute and arrested them in a "Hollywood style" by insulting them and beating them with clubs. These reports emphasized how the GUS treated people in working-class neighborhoods. Instead of the GUS winning the hearts and minds of the public, more and more articles of this type began appearing in the press, typically taking jabs at the police, claiming that despite all of their efforts, the police still had a highly negative image in society.

This perception of the GUS as brutal and overzealous, however, was solidified on October 30, 2005, in the southern city of Laâyoune. As the GUS tried to disperse a group of protestors, they reportedly savagely attacked and beat a man named Hamdi Lambarki. According to eyewitnesses, the GUS provoked the protestors and, after emerging from their vehicles to confront the crowd, beat and kicked Lambarki in the stomach and groin, hitting his head against a wall until he passed out, hemorrhaging large quantities of blood. As soon as the GUS left the scene, onlookers took Lambarki to the hospital, where he eventually died of his wounds. The official version of the event, however, was that Lambarki died as the result of being struck by a rock that a protestor threw at him. The incident sparked more rioting in the city by a public that was already furious at their mistreatment at the hands of the GUS. This further inflamed fears about the region, which has been witnessing a rise in clashes with separatists who were fighting for the independence of Western Sahara. The two officers who attacked Lambarki would later be put under investigation but would not serve jail time.

The next incident occurred in Salé, which is situated across the Bouregreg River from the capital city Rabat. The GUS posted in Salé had developed a particularly negative reputation for randomly searching people, demanding bribes, and provoking citizens. On December 31, 2005, only two months after the murder of Hamdi Lambarki in Laâyoune, GUS excesses claimed the life of another person. The incident began on December 13, when a thirty-year-old man named Adil Ziati had a confrontation with a unit of the GUS. According to the official version, the GUS approached Ziati for public intoxication. When he fled from them, the GUS chased him and one of the men accidentally hit Ziati with his motorcycle, causing him to fall into a wall. Ziati's family took him to the hospital but he eventually died after an eight-hour operation on his spine.

Ziati's statement before he died sharply contradicted the official version of events. Ziati said that he refused to give the GUS a bribe of three hundred dirhams. When the GUS officers became aggressive, Ziati explained that he fled from them. The GUS chased him down on their motorcycles, ran him over, and then beat him with their clubs and kicked him on the ground until they broke his neck and back. Photographs of Ziati's corpse were printed on the front pages of the press and the incident inflamed a city that was already furious at the GUS, sparking widespread protests in Salé. The lead officer was arrested but reports later surfaced that Ziati's family had been pressured to withdraw their complaint, a turn of events highly reminiscent of the Years of Lead. The officer would therefore never serve jail time. As the press attempted to digest Ziati's death, it soon became clear that he was the fifth person to die during the previous four months either in police custody or because of police intervention. Despite the new image of the police circulating in society, these events suggested systematic violence and reminded the public of the Years of Lead, when people died regularly in police custody because of "natural causes," "heart attack," or "suicide." Anger at the police grew steadily during this period as one weekend special in the press made the accusation that the slogan "Police at the Service of the People," which now appeared at the entrance of every police station, was "simply a sign for foreign consumption."[44]

A third murder attributed to the GUS occurred once again in Salé, this time on May 31, 2006. As before, there were two versions of events. In the official version, a young man named Abdelghafour Haddad was sitting in a café near his home when the GUS entered to conduct a random ID check. He fled from the GUS and threw himself into the front window of an Internet café, causing extensive lacerations and hemorrhaging. The GUS called for an ambulance, which transported Haddad to the hospital, where he died. The eyewitness version, however, differed significantly. According to people at the scene, after the GUS looked at Haddad's ID and searched his pockets, they told him to come with them to the police station. Haddad refused to leave unless they gave him a reason. The GUS then grabbed Haddad and began to force him into their car, clubbing him in front of his parents. When his father tried to intervene, a GUS officer pushed him back violently. Haddad became enraged but the GUS continued to beat his father, causing Haddad to flee. The GUS chased after him with their clubs and Haddad accidentally crashed into the window of the internet café, hemorrhaging badly as the GUS left the scene. Reporters arrived quickly and took pictures of Haddad's bloodied body, which appeared on the front pages of the daily press the next day. The incident sparked a protest march in the neighborhood to the local police station as people chanted phrases about GUS corruption and abuse of power. Hundreds more would march during Haddad's funeral on June 5. Despite the police's denials of wrongdoing, a report that the Moroccan Organization of Human Rights later issued found that Haddad was the victim of violence and cruel and degrading treatment by the GUS.

Haddad's murder was the beginning of the end for Laânigri and the GUS. Just as the press participated in the celebration and publicity of the GUS, it would attack them for their brutality. The front page of the June 16, 2006, issue of the well-known weekly *al-Sahifa* (the Journal) featured a photograph of Laânigri with the bold headline "The Police of Murder." On the one hand, this drew attention to the close Arabic phrase "The Police of Proximity."[45] On the other, it stood in stark contrast with the cover of the first issue of *Police Magazine,* which mocked the image of the police in Moroccan society as something to be feared. The editorial of this issue pointed to the systematic nature of their abuses, explaining, "It's gotten to the point that the GUS are bringing repression and fear, even death. That's why they deserve that we call them the 'police of death.'"[46] The editorial compared the recent murders to the Years of Lead, explaining that the cases of GUS violence are even worse. "[Police violence] took place during the Years of Lead inside basements and secret prisons. Here it is today out in the open, in the streets in front of crowds. This is the new 'transparency' that the GUS have brought with them, one of the most important achievements of 'the new era' in the security services." This stinging criticism therefore suggested that police openness during the new era simply meant that they were now emboldened to commit their violations of human rights and civil liberties in public with impunity.

The public's nicknames for the GUS also changed during this period to reflect their evolving image. The first name the public gave the GUS was the humorous "Croatians," because the colors of their hat matched those of the Croatian flag. Next, the public started calling them *lahdiya,* meaning "gift," referring to the fact that people saw them as seeking bribes. The next name took a decidedly darker turn as the public began calling the GUS *Zarqawi,* referring to the brutality of the units committing violence in the name of Abu Musab Zarqawi in Iraq. Finally, once the GUS started killing citizens, the public began calling them *Firaq al-mawt,* or "Units of Death," after the Latin American killing squads of the 1970s, bringing their public image as low as possible.

With rumors spreading that other cases of abuse did not even make it to the press, observers expected that Laânigri would be fired during the summer of 2006. It did not happen until September of that year, and for completely unexpected reasons. On September 13, the king relieved Laânigri of his duties as director general of the DGSN and placed him in charge of the Auxiliary Forces, widely seen as a humiliating demotion. It turns out that a man named Mohamed Kharraz, known as Sherif Bin Ouidane, was arrested for directing a massive drug network in the north of Morocco. He told authorities that he worked with a man named Abdelaziz Izzou, who had been the chief of police in Tangier between 1996 and 2003 and was then put in charge of palace security, based on the recommendation of Laânigri, Izzo's mentor. It did not sit well with King Mohamed VI that the man principally responsible for his security was deeply involved in a drug-dealing network. He had Izzo arrested and fired Laânigri, holding him partly responsible for Izzo's activities. In Laânigri's place, the king named the governor of Laâyoune, Charki Draiss.

In the following month, Draiss conducted a full review of the GUS. On October 16, 2006, exactly two years after their launch, Draiss decided to cancel the GUS and integrate its five thousand men into other police units.[47] The press declared the experiment of presenting the public with a new image of the police a failure. News also quickly emerged about the massive amount of money Laânigri had spent on the GUS: over twenty-five million dollars in total, a staggering sum of money for Morocco, including millions on the flashy vehicles, advertising campaign, and Police of Proximity Posts, many of which remained empty and unused.[48] Over two and a half million dollars were spent on their clothes, boots, and belts alone. The cost of each uniform was fifteen hundred dirhams, the equivalent of one hundred eighty dollars, an enormous amount by local standards. Now that the GUS were canceled, however, the uniforms would all be burned. One article detailed in particular the tremendous financial expenses of *Police Magazine*, which was "run like an American magazine."[49] Among other figures, the editor of the magazine reportedly made an annual salary that was the equivalent to the pay of twelve police commissioners. According to *al-Watan* (the Nation), the new name of the weekly *Casablancan*, the GUS project was the "biggest act of taxation piracy in the history of Morocco."[50] Despite these excesses, the salaries for the GUS officers were extremely low. The average GUS made around two thousand five hundred dirhams per month, approximately three hundred dollars. Many speculated that the low salaries and placement in difficult neighborhoods encouraged the anger and aggression of the average GUS officer. The revelation of the financial figures behind the GUS only condemned the project further. By the end of October 2006, the GUS and Laânigri's community policing program seemed as if it had not only produced few results but also wasted an enormous amount of precious financial resources.

The brutality and financial waste of the GUS only made the disconnect between their mass-mediated image and the reality on the streets more pronounced. And that was the reason the project failed. As soon as the state required the public to look back at the GUS, they appeared too clearly as a fabrication of a community policing program that existed elsewhere, not in Morocco. Téléfilms like *White Nights* and *The Case*, which presented the public with a Moroccan police that did not exist in reality, did not require the public to look too closely at their cops. The advertising campaign, however, demanded that the public interact with the GUS and compare them to their mass-mediated image. And reality clashed too strongly with simulation for the project to be successful. The state was unable to direct how the public saw the GUS, despite the widespread nature of the advertising campaign. The excesses of the GUS only reinforced for the public how the mass-mediated image was not something connected to Moroccan reality. In his discussion of the simulacrum, Baudrillard suggests that we feel the loss of the real, the absence of the thing signified. This, in turn, makes us panicked over that loss and reveals that there is nothing behind the simulacrum. While Baudrillard is writing about a highly different socioeconomic environment, it is clear that the public sensed the simulated nature of the GUS from the beginning. The abuses of the GUS only served to reinforce that sentiment, condemning the project to failure.[51]

Police Simulation Continues

Despite their ignominious end, the GUS remained very much in the public's mind. By December 2006, less than two months after their cancellation, GUS nostalgia emerged among the public and press. In addition to a number of articles calling for the return of the GUS in the face of apparently rising crime, one weekly newspaper published a full-page image of the GUS on its cover with the word "Crisis."[52] The message was clear—without the GUS, crime was once again rearing its ugly head. The main article in this issue declared the cancellation of the GUS "a grave mistake" and demanded that the state return them to the streets.[53] These public calls demonstrate that despite their failings, the GUS did establish a bridge between the state and the public, allowing some to see themselves in the guise of the police.

The public desire for a modern, effective, and sympathetic police became even more pronounced when more terrorists attacked Casablanca in the first half of 2007. During their time at the DGSN, Laânigri and the GUS had managed to prevent another attack. Now that he and the GUS were gone, suicide bombers struck again. On March 11, 2007, less than five months after the cancellation of the GUS, a man detonated a bomb at an Internet café in the Sidi Moumen district of Casablanca, wounding his partner, who also carried an explosive, and three others. On April 10, 2007, after nearly a month of investigations, the police arrived at the house of four suspects. Three blew themselves up with explosives while the police shot and killed a fourth. One police officer died in the operation. On April 14, 2007, two brothers blew themselves up near the U.S. consulate in Casablanca. One woman was wounded in this attack.

Even though the GUS were gone, the state picked up on the public's desire for a Moroccan police force that mimicked their counterparts on American or French television. As they investigated the bombing, the new antiterrorism brigade continued the function of blurring police fact and fiction in order to manage public opinion. The press printed images of muscular plainclothes cops of the antiterrorism brigade wearing black leather jackets and black ski masks brandishing large machine guns, securing the crime scenes and protecting the public. Uniformed cops held pistols and served as backup. Other men wearing bulletproof vests smashed their way through a front door with a battering ram. Crowds watched as the men with machine guns arrested suspects and kept them spread on the ground. Photographs of the Scientific Police also appeared as they collected crime-scene evidence. Other officers wore blue vests with the French words "Police Scientifique," official uniforms that had become popularized thanks to Noureddine Lakhmari's television series *The Case*. Yellow tape with the English words "Crime Scene Do Not Cross" also appeared in the press, clearly demarcating areas for analysis and making them look like they were part of an American crime scene. The media praised the police for securing the area, arresting suspects, and processing evidence.

The police had not been able to prevent these attacks, despite the widespread crackdown on Islamic radicals that took place after the May 16, 2003, bombings. Nonetheless, the state stood ready, as it had since after the Tabit Affair, to use the sensational mass media to disseminate commanding images of the police in an attempt to influence public opinion. This time, the police appeared as muscular plainclothes men, wearing black ski masks and carrying machine guns, supported by both the Criminal and Scientific Police. Thanks to large color images on the front pages of the press and the evening news, the police appeared as modern and effective as the cops on American television. The images that had been circulating through society for over a decade allowed the media to celebrate once again the new face of the police, a police that was ready to act to avert crisis and encourage public acceptance of state authority in the new era.

Epilogue

"The Police Are at the Service of the People"

THE SAME WORDS, prominently displayed on a banner or plaque, can be seen at the main entrance of police stations across Morocco: *al-Shurta fi khidmat al-sha'ab*, or, "The Police Are at the Service of the People." Every time I see this slogan, I ask myself how many different meanings it could have. How can we understand not just the phrase but also the key terms "police," "service," and "people"? How do these words relate to the past twenty years in the country? What does this slogan reveal about the nature of state authority and power in Morocco? And what does it suggest about the future, especially in the wake of the Arab Spring?

The slogan fronts the police. As this alternative history of the contemporary period in Morocco has shown, the police have acted as the linchpin for state power, authority, and legitimacy since independence. During the Years of Lead, they served as the direct symbol of state authoritarianism, using fear, repression, and violence to maintain the regime. Once the Years of Lead came to a close in the early 1990s, the state continued to turn to the police as a means to solidify its position. Unlike in previous decades, it was the image of the police in the mass media that demonstrated the changing nature of authoritarianism in the country. Before, the police operated by force and coercion, both symbolic and physical. Now, they served as a symbol to show the wider public that the state was committed to human rights, freedom of speech, rights of the individual, and the rule of law in the new era.

Thanks to the interface with the sensational and commercial mass media, the state became more and more involved in generating new representations of the police, seeking to direct these images in order to ensure that they conveyed the desired message of responsiveness and change in the new era. These images were intended to reflect a transformed police, encouraging the public to see the real-world cops in the guise of their mediated counterparts. The various forms covered in this book worked through repetition, intertextuality, suggestion, and encouragement, pointing to the way the mass media worked to make the once feared and taboo police something human, identifiable, and even banal. While Morocco featured an environment in which the authoritarian state interfaced with nonstate sensational mass media to produce new symbols of power and authority, the images of the police also reflect the globalization of American culture and media mechanics and their adaptation in a new political, cultural, and socioeconomic environment. Nonetheless, this book does not trace a story of cultural imperialism. Rather, it shows how global imagery is transformed and appropriated for highly local purposes.

"Service," the second key term in the slogan, points to the way the police performed a critical role for both the state and the people. As the Years of Lead came to a close, the state turned to attempting to manufacture public opinion in order to maintain its position. The state worked with the increasingly commercial mass media—collaboratively at times and contentiously at others—to produce images of the police that demonstrated the changing nature of authority in the country. The state paid increasing attention to public opinion, seeking to transform its brand of authoritarianism and making it responsive to public demands for change. It was the police, through their image in the mass media, who performed this service. The media used these police images in order to blur the lines between fact and fiction, creating and disseminating fictional images and mapping them onto the real-world police. These images worked to redefine the real-world police of the new era for the wider public through the characteristics of their fictional counterparts.

Nonetheless, it is possible to read the state-media interface traced in this book from a different perspective. The images of the police in the mass media were intended to demonstrate to the public that the police embodied the democratic principles and aspirations of the state in the new era. These images were also disseminated to encourage continued acceptance of state authority in an evolving political, cultural, and socioeconomic environment. Instead of celebrating reform and demonstrating that the state was responsive to change, the state-media interface could be seen as stalling democratic transition and preventing the far-reaching changes called for in the aftermath of the Tabit Affair. The process covered in this book could therefore be read as a transition in image form, content, and management, not reality, in order to maintain the authoritarian state, albeit in new external appearances.

The last element of the slogan is the people. This book tells the story of the rise of a mass media that used sensationalism and commercialism to include the broader public and cater to their interests and concerns. It shows how the public, elite and non-elite alike, formed the site for changing strategies of state control, as media industries, thanks to mutually aligned interests in the new era, indirectly performed the disciplining work that the violence of the police and security forces used to carry out in the old era. Nonetheless, as both the emergence of the serial killer and the failure of the GUS demonstrated, the public was not simply a pliable mass, easily manipulated by the state. This book points to the ambiguous, ambivalent, and contestatory role that the public played in the transformation of police images in society. Even though it is not possible to trace the reception of these new representations of the police as they emerged and circulated in society, it is undeniable that the image of the police has changed radically in Moroccan society since the early 1990s. Fear of the police and torture has largely disappeared. No longer do the real-world police inspire terror. While human rights abuses still occur in the country, the image of the police today is far removed from that of the Years of Lead. This is indisputably a significant achievement of the state-media nexus during the past twenty years.

Finally, the position of the slogan "The Police Are at the Service of the People" needs to be taken into account. While the words have been part of state propaganda since the formation of the Moroccan police after independence, they made their appearance as advertising in the entrance of police stations only in the late 1990s and early 2000s. The position of this slogan—and its words—points to the real-world interaction between state authority and the public that has taken place since the early 1990s, crystallized in the act of entering a police station. The media may have served as the vehicle for this process but it was the attempt to transform the image of the police and produce a new citizen that articulates the changing nature of state authority in the country. The location of the slogan—and its intertextuality with mass-mediated images of the police circulating throughout society—demonstrates the importance of popular culture for understanding widespread cultural and political transformations in the contemporary period and the way the state sought to bring the public into the previously taboo world of the police station through a variety of media forms to achieve change.

As of mid-2013, the Moroccan state appears to have staked its future on the ability to transform its brand of authoritarianism through mediated imagery to match the demands of the public for change. This is still an ongoing process. Many of the images of the police that I discuss in this book continue to circulate in society, including the crime tabloids, true-crime articles, police téléfilms, and mass-mediated representations of CSI: Casablanca and antiterrorism brigades. New forms of police media have also emerged. In addition to a variety of documentary programs on the police, such as the series on Moroccan serial killers on 2M, Medi1 has produced a series entitled *Milaffat bulisiyya* (Cop Files), bringing police fiction to the radio. The new nonstate Medi1 satellite channel now airs a strongly modernist crime documentary in high-definition entitled *Masrah al-jarima* (Crime Scene).[1] There remains a strong overlap between these different media forms in constructing and disseminating images of the police—and the public's relationship with state authority—in society. The wide-ranging and persistent nature of the state-media interface in Morocco suggests how the nature of authoritarianism may be changing in other countries in the region as well, highlighting the use of nonstate imagery to manage public opinion across the social spectrum to cast the state as responsive to widespread demands for change.

The verdict on whether this will prove to be an effective strategy for navigating the future is still out. The Moroccan state may move through the regional challenges of the Arab Spring intact, demonstrating that its effort to create and circulate new images of the police was successful in persuading the broader public to continue accepting the authority of the ruling system. On the other hand, it is quite possible that these attempts to transform the nature of the state and its connection with the people through the image of the police will prove powerless to prevent the same fate as Tunisia, Egypt, and Libya. From this perspective, it remains to be seen what the epilogue will be for the slogan "The Police Are at the Service of the People."

Notes

Introduction

1. Peter K. Manning, *Policing Contingencies* (Chicago: University of Chicago Press, 2003), 27.

2. For an overview of this period, see Susan Slyomovics, *The Performance of Human Rights in Morocco* (Philadelphia: University of Pennsylvania Press, 2005).

3. Abdellah Hammoudi, *Master and Disciple: The Cultural Foundations of Moroccan Authoritarianism* (Chicago: University of Chicago Press, 1997).

4. For more on the organization of the Moroccan police, see Miloudi Hamdouchi, *Le régime juridique de l'enquête policière: Étude critique* (Rabat: Renald, 1999).

5. I use the terms "state" and "regime" in this book to refer to the constellation of power brokers in Morocco, known in Moroccan Arabic as the *makhzen*. Although the term literally means "storehouse," the *makhzen* implies the economic, political, security, and royal elite that control the country. In many cases, it is impossible to differentiate these players, although it is widely assumed that power emanates from the palace in general and the king in particular. For more on the relationship between the terms "state" and *makhzen*, see Rahma Bourqia, "The Cultural Legacy of Power in Morocco," in *In the Shadow of the Sultan*, ed. Rahma Bourqia and Susan Gilson Miller (Cambridge, MA: Harvard University Press, 1999), 243–258; Alain Claisse, "Makhzen Traditions and Administrative Channels," in *The Political Economy of Morocco*, ed. I. William Zartman (New York: Praeger, 1987), 34–58.

6. See, respectively, Stephen J. King, *The New Authoritarianism in the Middle East and North Africa* (Bloomington: Indiana University Press, 2009); Jason Brownlee, *Authoritarianism in an Age of Democratization* (Cambridge: Cambridge University Press, 2007).

7. Antonio Gramsci, *Selections from the Prison Notebooks of Antonio Gramsci*, trans. Quintin Hoare and Geoffery Nowell Smith (New York: International, 1971). 57–58; Louis Althusser, "Ideology and Ideological State Apparatus (Notes Towards an Investigation)," in *Lenin and Philosophy and Other Essays* (New York: Monthly Review Press, 2001 (1971), 98–99.

8. See, for example, Melani Claire Cammett, *Globalization and Business Politics in Arab North Africa: A Comparative Perspective* (New York: Cambridge University Press, 2007); Anouar Boukhars, *Politics in Morocco: Executive Monarchy and Enlightened Authoritarianism* (London: Routledge, 2011); Pierre Vermeren, *Le Maroc de Mohammed VI: La transition inachevée* (Paris: La Découverte, 2011); Slyomovics, *The Performance of Human Rights in Morocco*.

9. For a discussion of the Francophone press after the Years of Lead, see Valérie K. Orlando, *Francophone Voices of the "New Morocco" in Film and Print: (Re)presenting a Society in Transition* (New York: Palgrave Macmillan, 2009).

10. For more on literacy in Morocco, see Daniel A. Wagner, *Literacy, Culture, and Development: Becoming Literate in Morocco* (New York: Cambridge University Press, 1993).

11. See Zakya Daoud, *Maroc: Les années de plomb, 1958–1988: Chroniques d'une résistance* (Houilles: Manucius, 2007); Mustafa al-'Alawi, *Mudhakkirat sahafi wa-thalathat muluk* [Memoirs of a Journalist and Three Kings] ([al-Dar al-Bayda'?]: Manshurat Akhbar al-Yawm, 2011).

12. For more on Filali, see Chafik Laabi, "Une réussite controversée," *Maroc Hebdo International*, 1997.

13. For a history of RTM, see 'Abd Allah Shuqrun, *al-Idha'a wa-al-talfaza al-maghribiyya* [Moroccan Radio and Television] (al-Dar al-Bayda': Matba'at al-Najah al-Jadida, 1999). For a popular treatment, see Hassan Hamdani and Ayla Mrabet, "Hassan TV: 50 ans de propagande," *Tel Quel*, April 18–24, 2009. Before satellite dishes appeared in the late 1990s, people who lived in the north of the country could watch Spanish television. Radio was widespread during the Years of Lead, but it too fell under the supervision of the Ministry of the Interior and producers were careful not to cross any "red lines" during these years. For a brief history of Moroccan radio, see Douglas A. Boyd, *Broadcasting in the Arab World: A Survey of the Electronic Media in the Middle East*, 3rd ed. (Ames: Iowa State University Press, 1999), 253–257.

14. Gramsci, *Selections from the Prison Notebooks of Antonio Gramsci*, 210.

15. I use the word "cop" in this book without any pejorative connotations.

16. Althusser, "Ideology and Ideological State Apparatus (Notes Towards an Investigation)," 117–120.

17. Max Horkheimer and Theodor W. Adorno, *Dialect of Enlightenment: Philosophical Fragments*, trans. Edmund Jephcott (Stanford, CA: Stanford University Press, 2002). 94–136.

18. Ibid., 115.

19. Jürgen Habermas, *The Structural Transformation of the Public Sphere: An Inquiry into a Category of Bourgeois Society*, trans. Thomas Burger with the assistance of Frederick Lawrence (Cambridge, MA: MIT Press, 1989 [1962]). Habermas has been criticized widely for his description of the public sphere, especially in environments outside of Western Europe and the United States. See, for example, Ursula Rao, "Empowerment through Local News Making: Studying the Media/Public Interface in India," in *The Anthropology of News and Journalism: Global Perspectives*, ed. S. Elizabeth Bird (Bloomington: Indiana University Press, 2010), 100–115.

20. John Fiske, *Understanding Popular Culture* (Boston: Unwin Hyman, 1989).

21. Lila Abu-Lughod, *Dramas of Nationhood: The Politics of Television in Egypt* (Chicago: University of Chicago Press, 2005).

22. Fiske, *Understanding Popular Culture*, 21.

23. Yuezhi Zhao, *Media, Market, and Democracy in China: Between the Party Line and the Bottom Line* (Urbana: University of Illinois Press, 1998), 2.

24. Ibid., 149.

25. Michael Schudson, *The Sociology of the News*, 2nd ed. (New York: W. W. Norton, 2011), 123.

26. Marwan Kraidy, *Reality Television and Arab Politics: Contention in Public Life* (Cambridge: Cambridge University Press, 2010), 200.

27. Hammoudi, *Master and Disciple: The Cultural Foundations of Moroccan Authoritarianism*, 9.

1. Police on Trial

1. "al-Jarima allati hazzat bi-'umq al-mujtama' al-maghribi bi-kull mukawwinatihi" [The Crime That Profoundly Shook Moroccan Society in All Its Foundations], *al-'Alam*, March 17, 1993.

2. 'Abd al-Latif Jabru, "Suqut judran Barlin wa-nihayat al-khawf" [Fall of the Berlin Wall and the End of Fear], *al-Ittihad al-Ishtiraki*, March 17, 1993.

3. "Hadha al-khabar [This News]," *al-Ittihad al-Ishtiraki*, February 6, 1993.

4. "Hala tu'arri waqi'an" [A Situation That Lays Bare a Reality], *al-'Alam*, February 28, 1993.

5. For more on court reporting during the Years of Lead, see Jonathan Smolin, "Aïcha Mekki," in *Dictionary of African Biography*, ed. Henry Louis Gates and Emmanuel Akyeampong, vol. 4 (Oxford: Oxford University Press, 2011), 180–181.

6. In his short book on the Tabit Affair, Abdelkader Chaoui traces the evolving coverage of the scandal in the *Socialist Union* and *al-'Alam* (the *Banner*.) While he mentions the sensationalism of the press, he never explains how it was developed or what role it played in transforming the mass media or the image of the police. See 'Abd al-Qadir al-Shawi, *al-Shaytan wa-al-zawba'a: Qadiyat al-'Amid Thabit fi al-sihafa* [Satan and the Storm: The Affair of Commissioner Tabit in the Press] (Rabat: al-Mawja, 1995).

7. "Ihalat al-mas'ul al-amni 'ala ghurfat al-jinayat bi-l-Dar al-Bayda'" [Transfer of Security Official to Criminal Chamber in Casablanca], *al-Ittihad al-Ishtiraki*, February 10, 1993.

8. Because the Socialist Union and the Independence Party were the two main political parties in Morocco at the time of the trial and their newspapers had the highest circulations in the country, this chapter is based on their Arabic press coverage of the case, supplementing them with the Francophone newspapers from both parties. For more on the initial *Banner* coverage of the case, see al-Shawi, *al-Shaytan wa-al-zawba'a: Qadiyat al-'Amid Thabit fi al-sihafa* [Satan and the Storm: The Affair of Commissioner Tabit in the Press], 45.

9. "'Amid shurta mumtaz fi qadaya akhlaqiyya: Hajz ashritat al-fidiyu tatadamman suwaran hayya khali'a" [High-Ranking Commissioner in Moral Affairs: Seizure of Videotapes Containing Live Depraved Images], *al-'Alam*, February 11, 1993.

10. Abdelmoula Tawhidi, "Affair de l'officier supérieur de police," *L'Opinion*, February 13, 1993.

11. Nabil Arabi, "Un médecin, un propriétaire immobilier et d'autres complices inculpés," *L'Opinion*, February 16, 1993.

12. Now that Tabit's name and position went public, the press quickly printed more information about his life and personal background. He was born in 1939 in Casablanca and joined the police force in the early 1960s. He became a detective in the early 1970s, a commissioner in 1976, and, finally, 'amid mumtaz (first-rank commissioner) in 1985. Tabit had two wives and five children. He married his first wife in 1964, but by the 1980s she lived with his parents in the Derb Ghellef neighborhood of Casablanca. In 1986, Tabit married his much younger second wife and lived with her in a villa in the same area.

13. One of the most popular films in the history of Moroccan cinema is based on the Tabit Affair: Nabil Ayouch's *Mektoub* (Morocco: Ali n' Productions, 1997).The film depicts not only how the Tabit character and his men videotape themselves sexually assaulting women, but also how his driver abducts a victim from the street. For more on this film, see Jonathan Smolin, "Nabil Ayouch," in *Contemporary Arab Filmmakers: Political Protest and Social Critique*, ed. Josef Gugler (Bloomington: Indiana University Press, forthcoming).

14. "Milaff 'amid al-shurta al-mumtaz wa-man ma'ahu amam ghurfat al-jinayat bi-l-Dar al-Bayda'" [File of First-Rank Police Commissioner and Those with Him before Criminal Court in Casablanca], *al-Ittihad al-Ishtiraki*, February 19, 1993.

15. "Ba'd infidah qadiyat rajul al-amn bi-l-Dar al-Bayda' . . ." [After Exposing Case of Security Official in Casablanca . . .], *al-Ittihad al-Ishtiraki*, February 20, 1993.

16. Nabil Arabi, "Le procès de la débauche," *L'Opinion*, February 20, 1993.

17. Nabil Arabi, "L'assainissement a-t-il commencé?," *L'Opinion*, February 21, 1993.

18. "Hunaka mas'ulun amniyyun kanu 'ala 'ilm bi-l-af'al al-shani'a al-mansuba ila al-mudda'u Thabit" [There Are Security Officials Who Knew about Abominable Acts Attributed to Tabit], *al-Ittihad al-Ishtiraki*, February 22, 1993.

19. "al-Taghayyub al-da'im li-aswat wa-suwar al-mujtama'" [Enduring Absence of Sounds and Images of Society], *al-'Alam*, March 14, 1993.

20. Abdel Wahab Chaoui, "Tabit connection," *Maroc Hebdo International*, March 5–11, 1993.

21. "Hunaka taghtiya kan yahza biha Thabit . . . min fawq!" [Tabit Was Enjoying Cover-Up . . . from Above!], *al-'Alam*, March 12, 1993.

22. For more information on newspaper circulations during the trial, see al-Shawi, *al-Shaytan wa-al-zawba'a: Qadiyat al-'Amid Thabit fi al-sihafa* [Satan and the Storm: The Affair of Commissioner Tabit in the Press], 10, 25, 46. See also Samir El Ouardighi, *l'Affaire Tabit et la presse marocaine* (Rabat: Arrisala, 1997), 14. For more on newspaper circulations in Morocco, see Muhammad 'Abd al-Rahman Barrada, *al-Sihafa al-maktuba bi-l-Maghrib: al-Tawzi' wa-al-intishar* [The Written Press in Morocco: Distribution and Dissemination] (al-Dar al-Bayda': Matba'at Dar al-Nashr al-Maghribiyya, 2002).

23. Abdellah Chankou, "Donnez-nous du sensationnel!," *Maroc Hebdo International*, March 26–April 1, 1993.

24. Nabil Arabi, "Histoire des deux étudiantes qui on fait éclaté le scandale," *L'Opinion*, February 19, 1993.

25. The identities of Tabit's final two victims were never released, but the fact that the police acted on their complaints suggested that they were members of wealthy Casablanca families. The public was outraged over this detail because, as became clear from the press coverage of the case, the majority of Tabit's victims came from financially impoverished backgrounds and did not have the means or social standing to compel the authorities to act on their complaints.

26. Arabi, "Le procès de la débauche."

27. For more on the relationship between the William Kennedy Smith trial and the growing tabloidization of the U.S. mainstream mass media, see Richard Logan Fox, Robert W. Van Sickel, and Thomas L. Steiger, *Tabloid Justice: Criminal Justice in an Age of Media Frenzy*, 2nd ed. (Boulder, CO: Lynne Rienner, 2007), 25–35.

28. David J. Krajicek, *Scooped!: Media Miss Real Story on Crime while Chasing Sex, Sleaze, and Celebrities* (New York: Columbia University Press, 1998), 57.

29. David Kamp, "The Tabloid Decade," *Vanity Fair*, February 1999.

30. Eliot Borenstein, *Overkill: Sex and Violence in Contemporary Russian Popular Culture* (Ithaca, NY: Cornell University Press, 2008).

31. Herman Wasserman, *Tabloid Journalism in South Africa* (Bloomington: Indiana University Press, 2010).

32. Early in the trial, news spread that the opposition newspaper *al-Muharrir* (the Liberator) accused Tabit as early as 1980 of abducting and sexually abusing teenage girls when he was a police commissioner in the town of Beni Mellal. Despite the damning nature of this daring accusation, the police responded at the time by giving Tabit a promotion and transferring him to a new position in Rabat. This indicated that Tabit, at the time of his arrest, had not only been committing his crimes for at least thirteen years but also had been enjoying protection from the police establishment during this entire period. For the original article, see "Haditha khatira bi-l-nisba li-wad'iyya murtakibiha wa-li-'alaqatiha bi-a'rad al-muwatinin" [Grave Incident in Terms of Status of Perpetrator and Connection to Citizens' Honor], *al-Muharrir*, July 16, 1980.

33. Nabil Arabi, "Tabit encourt désormais la peine de mort," *L'Opinion*, March 7, 1993.

34. Nabil Arabi, "L'affaire du commissaire Tabit: Un médecin, un propriétaire immoblier et d'autres complices inculpés," *L'Opinion*, February 16, 1993.
35. Nabil Arabi, "La défense de l'accusé demande une expertise psychiatrique," *L'Opinion*, February 27, 1993.
36. "Bidayat istintaq al-Kumisir Thabit min taraf al-mahkama" [Beginning of Interrogation of Commissioner Tabit by the Court], *al-Ittihad al-Ishtiraki*, March 4, 1993.
37. Nabil Arabi, "Tabitgate: Les indiscrétions d'un huis clos," *L'Opinion*, March 5, 1993.
38. For more on psychology in Morocco, see the work of Rita El Khayat, including Rita El Khayat, *La folie: El Hank-Casablanca* (Casablanca: EDDIF, 2000).
39. Maktab al-Bayda', "Jull al-tasrihat fi al-bahth al-tamhidi li-rijal al-darak 'akkadat istighlal al-nufudh" [All Statements in Preliminary Investigation of Gendarmerie Confirmed Abuse of Power], *al-'Alam*, February 27, 1993.
40. "al-Kumisir Thabit amam al-mahkama: "La tujad faqat shaqqati, hunak aydan filat" [Commissioner Tabit before Court: "There's Not Only My Apartment But Also Villas"], *al-'Alam*, March 5, 1993.
41. Nur al-Din Miftah, "Qadiyat al-Kumisir "Thabit" tusta'naf yawm al-ithnayn al-qadim" [Affair of Commissioner Tabit Will Resume Next Monday], *al-Ittihad al-Ishtiraki*, March 6, 1993.
42. "Hunaka mas'ulun amniyyun kanu 'ala 'ilm bi-l-af'al al-shani'a al-mansuba ila al-mudda'u Thabit" [There Are Security Officials Who Knew about Abominable Acts Attributed to Tabit].
43. "Thalath dahaya kull yawmayn" [Three Victims Every Two Days], *al-Ittihad al-Ishtiraki*, February 26, 1993. According to this article, the police report on Tabit begins in 1989 and the official number of 518 victims was established after watching only 34 of the 118 videotapes.
44. Nabil Arabi, "Tabit à la cour: 'Il n'y a pas que ma garçonnière, il y a aussi des villas et on fait partout ce qu'on me reproche!,'" *L'Opinion*, March 4, 1993.
45. Nabil Arabi, "Tabitgate: Ce que Tabit, Dou Naïm, Rabii et Boussairi ont déclaré devant la Cour," *L'Opinion*, March 10, 1993.
46. Although Tabit's purported sexual abilities were an object of fascination, the press still held him accountable for his actions. Don Conway-Long, in an article on the case, misreads the sexual sensationalism of the press coverage when he claims that journalists blamed the victims for Tabit's crimes. See Don Conway-Long, "Sexism and Rape Culture in Moroccan Social Discourse," *Journal of Men's Studies* 10, no. 3 (2002): 361–371.
47. Nur al-Din Miftah, "Rafa' sirriyyat al-jalasat 'and bidayat al-murafa'at" [Lifting Secrecy of Sessions at Start of Defense Arguments], *al-Ittihad al-Ishtiraki*, March 12, 1993.
48. "Des extraits des cassettes visionnées: Inceste, défloration, sadisme à l'état brut," *Libération*, March 14–15, 1993.
49. Nur al-Din Miftah, "al-Jalasat al-akthar basha'a wa-maratuniyya fi milaff al-Kumisir Thabit" [Most Disgusting and Longest Sessions in File of Commissioner Tabit], *al-Ittihad al-Ishtiraki*, March 13, 1993.
50. "Après le visionnage des cassettes: Nuit d'horreur à la cour d'appel!," *Libération*, March 13, 1993.
51. Nabil Arabi, "Cauchmardesque: Projection d'un résumé des cassettes traumatisantes," *L'Opinion*, March 13, 1993.
52. Nabil Arabi, "Peine de mort requise contre Tabit," *L'Opinion*, March 14, 1993.
53. "Des extraits des cassettes visionnées: Inceste, défloration, sadisme à l'état brut."
54. Jabru, "Suqut judran Barlin wa-nihayat al-khawf" [Fall of the Berlin Wall and the End of Fear].

55. "Min yawm li-akhar" [From Day to Day], *al-Ittihad al-Ishtiraki*, March 15, 1993.

56. "Awwal tasrih hukumi hawl qadiyat Thabit" [First Government Statement about Tabit Affair], *al-'Alam*, March 12, 1993.

57. When confronted with charges of brutality, it is common for police departments in the United States to claim that the actions were those of individuals and in no way reflect a systematic problem. See Regina G. Lawrence, *The Politics of Force: Media and the Construction of Police Brutality* (Berkeley: University of California Press, 2000), 36–43.

58. Nur al-Din Miftah, "Tariqan dayyiqan li-istimrar al-milaff maftuhan" [Two Narrow Paths for Continuing the File Are Open], *al-Ittihad al-Ishtiraki*, March 27, 1993.

59. "Jalalat al-Malik yu'lin fi khitabihi ba'd hafl al-wila' awwal ams . . . " [His Majesty the King, in His Speech after Celebration of Allegiance Yesterday, Announces . . .], *al-Ittihad al-Ishtiraki*, March 29, 1993.

60. "Halaqat musalsal al-fada'ih mutawasila" [Episodes of Series of Scandals Are Continuing], *al-Ittihad al-Ishtiraki*, April 1, 1993.

61. Driss Hanbali, "Azemmour: Affaire de viol de mineurs," *L'Opinion*, April 15, 1993.

62. Driss Hanbali, "Affaire de viol de mineurs: La parole aux citoyens," *L'Opinion*, April 27, 1993.

63. "Tasaqut al-aqni'a ba'd inhiyar "al-Thabit" [Fall of Veils after Collapse of Tabit], *al-Ittihad al-Ishtiraki*, April 10, 1993.

64. MAP, "Sahib al-Jallala yu'ayyin al-Sayyid Ahmad al-Midawi mudiran 'amman jadidan li-l-amn al-watani" [His Majesty Announces Mr. Ahmad Midaoui as New General Director of National Security], *Majallat al-Amn al-Watani*, no. 173 (1993).

65. "al-Amn wa-al-qanun" [Security and Law], *al-'Alam*, April 15, 1993.

66. Abdelmajid Smaili, "La press et le procès des commissaires," *Maroc Hebdo International*, March 5–11, 1993.

67. Chankou, "Donnez-nous du sensationnel!"

68. Abdelmajid Smaili, "Un distributeur en colère: Mohammed Berrada, directeur général de Sapress," *Maroc Hebdo International*, March 26–April 1, 1993.

69. Because of widespread distrust of the authorities, many believe that Tabit was not actually put to death, especially since his execution was not made public. Since the trial, Tabit has continued to fascinate the public and has been the subject of dozens of articles in the press and at least four extended newspaper serials and three films.

2. "He Butchered His Wife Because of Witchcraft and Adultery"

1. Stuart Hall et al., *Policing the Crisis: Mugging, the State, and Law and Order* (London: Macmillan, 1978); Philip Jenkins, *Using Murder: The Social Construction of Serial Homicide* (New York: Aldine de Gruyter, 1994). Hall et al. analyzed a series of muggings in 1970s Great Britain to demonstrate the way various interests groups define and construct problems in the media. As they showed, these constructions are not for their own sake. Rather, interest groups define a given problem in an attempt to shape public perceptions and compel the public to act in a particular way, such as supporting tough-on-crime policies, increased police funding, or particular political agendas. Scholars have used a similar approach to analyze a variety of social problems, such as child abuse, crack cocaine, satanic rituals, and serial murder, among others. See, for example, Philip Jenkins, *Moral Panic: Changing Concepts of the Child Molester in Modern America* (New Haven, CT: Yale University Press, 1998); Jimmie L. Reeves and Richard Campbell, *Cracked Coverage: Television News, the Anti-Cocaine Crusade, and the Rea-*

gan Legacy (Durham, NC: Duke University Press, 1994). I am indebted to social construction theory in my treatment of the crime tabloids in this chapter.

2. While I use the term "state" here, police officials provided this material directly to the tabloids. Nonetheless, they would not have made this sensitive information public without the approval of officials in the Ministry of the Interior.

3. Shaun T. Lopez, "Madams, Murders, and the Media: *Akhbar al-Hawadith* and the Emergence of a Mass Culture in 1920s Egypt," in *Re-Envisioning Egypt: 1919–1952*, ed. Arthur Goldschmidt, Amy J. Johnson, and Barak A. Salmoni (Cairo: American University in Cairo Press, 2005), 373–397.

4. Muhammad al-Baz, *Sihafat al-ithara: al-Siyasa wa-al-din wa-al-jins fi al-suhuf al-misriyya* [The Press of Sensationalism: Politics, Religion, and Sex in Egyptian Newspapers] (al-Qahira: Maktabat Jazirat al-Ward, 2010), 335–337; Naguib Mahfouz, *The Thief and the Dogs*, ed. and rev. John Rodenbeck, trans. Trevor Le Gassick and M. M. Badawi (New York: Doubleday, 1989 [1961]).

5. For more on this tabloid, see Asma Husayn Hafiz, *Nashr hawadith wa-jara'im al-mar'a: Dirasa tahliliyya maydaniyya bi-l-tatbiq 'ala jaridat Akhbar al-Hawadith khilala 'am* [Publishing Women's Crimes: An Analytical Field Study Applied to the Newspaper *Crime News* during a Year] (al-Qahira: Sharikat al-Faris li-l-Nashr al-Maktabi, 1993). I would like to thank Paul Heck for helping me access this text.

6. Wahid Tahi, *Jumhur sihafat al-ithara fi al-Jaza'ir: al-Simat al-'amma wa-'adat al-qira'a* [The Audience of the Sensational Press in Algeria: General Features and Practices of Reading] (Bayrut: Muntada al-Ma'arif, 2011), 129. Tahi does not specify when in 1993 the first Algerian crime tabloid was published.

7. Despite his important role in the development of the Moroccan press, little has been written on Alaoui's career. The Bibliothèque Nationale de Royaume du Maroc (BNRM) in Rabat has copies of Alaoui's earliest newspapers in its collection, including *Akhbar al-Duniya* (News of the World), *al-Duniya bi-Khayr* (Everything's Good), and *al-Usbu' al-Siyasi* (Political Week). For Alaoui's memoirs, see Mustafa al-'Alawi, *Mudhakkirat sahafi wa-thalathat muluk* [Memoirs of a Journalist and Three Kings] ([al-Dar al-Bayda'?]: Manshurat Akhbar al-Yawm, 2011).

8. Najib Skir, "al-Jara'id al-mustaqilla fi ufuq niqaba mustaqilla" [Independent Newspapers in Horizon of Independent Union], *al-Maw'id al-Siyasi*, May 15, 1993.

9. Since crime tabloid titles appeared and disappeared with such regularity—and most were makeshift publications that sought to turn a quick profit from the phenomenon—it is impossible to track the industry as a whole. Due to the fact that Najib Skir launched crime tabloids in the country and his titles were the most popular of their kind, this chapter focuses exclusively on his experience.

10. During the late 1950s and early 1960s, the *National Enquirer* capitalized on the visibility of the newsstand by featuring elements that attracted an enormous audience of readers, such as gruesome crime-scene photographs and headlines like "I Put My Baby in a Wastebasket and Poured Concrete Over Her" and "I Cut Out Her Heart and Stomped on It!" Like Skir's newspapers, the *National Enquirer* voiced a strong conservatism and outrage at what appeared to be society's rapidly declining morals and increasing levels of crime. By 1967, however, as the number of newsstands dwindled in the major cities thanks to suburban expansion, the owner of the *Enquirer*, Generoso Pope, decided to shift the focus of the tabloid from crime to celebrity tales, human-interest stories, and reports of unexplained phenomena such as UFOs in order to sell the newspaper in supermarkets and drugstores. Among the many writings on the *National Enquirer*, see David Paul Pope, *The Deeds of My Fathers: How My Grandfather and Father Built New York and Created the Tabloid World of Today* (New York: Philip Turner, 2010).

11. For more on the importance of tabloid covers, see Bill Sloan, "*I Watched a Wild Hog Eat My Baby!*": *A Colorful History of Tabloids and Their Cultural Impact* (Amherst, NY: Prometheus Books, 2001), 229.

12. See S. Elizabeth Bird, *For Enquiring Minds: A Cultural Study of Supermarket Tabloids* (Knoxville: University of Tennessee Press, 1992), 107–139.

13. For more on this phenomenon within tabloid culture, see ibid., 204–205.

14. For common tabloid themes, see ibid., 39–64.

15. In studies of tabloids in the United States, these kinds of tales are commonly called "gee-whiz" or "Hey, Maude" stories because they elicit surprise and encourage people to recount them to their friends. See, for example, ibid., 63–64.

16. Ibid., 67–78.

17. "Thariyya fi ghiyab zawjiha fi al-hajj tulzim sa'iqaha bi-mumarasat mashahid burnujarafiyya 'alayha" [While Husband Was Away on Hajj, Rich Woman Forces Driver to Act Out Pornographic Scenes with Her], *al-Mi'ad al-Siyasi*, June 8, 1994.

18. Tabloids that emerged in South Africa after apartheid also used news of magic and witchcraft to attract a large working-class audience. See Herman Wasserman, *Tabloid Journalism in South Africa* (Bloomington: Indiana University Press, 2010), 142–148.

19. For more on magic in Morocco, see Mustafa Wa'rab, *al-Mu'taqadat al-sihriyya watuqusuha fi al-Maghrib* [Magic Beliefs and Their Climate in Morocco] (Casablanca: Dar al-Haraf, 2007); Mustapha Akhmisse, *Médecine, magie et sorcellerie au Maroc, ou, l'Art traditionnel de guérir* (Casablanca: BENIMED, 1985).

20. Najib Skir, "Kathrat al-ta'ati li-l-'ilaj al-ruhani maradduhu qusur al-tibb al-'adwi wa-al-tibb al-nafsani" [Underlying Reason for Great Frequency Spiritual Treatment Is Deficiency of Medical and Psychological Medicine], *Akhbar al-Hawadith*, January 16, 1996.

21. "Shabb min Sidi Qasim yamtalik qudra khariqa fi sir' al-jann wa-ibtal al-sihr wa-al-taqaf wa-amrad ukhra" [Young Man from Sidi Qasim Has Unheard-of Ability in Fighting Demons and Thwarting Black Magic, Thaqqaf, and Other Illnesses], *al-Mi'ad al-Siyasi*, December 21, 1994.

22. "Jumu' ghafira min al-muwatinin yatawafidun 'ala zawiyat al-Sharif Ridwan bi-Sidi Qasim" [Large Groups of Citizens Flock to Shrine of Sherif Redwan in Sidi Qasim], *al-Mi'ad al-Siyasi*, December 28, 1994.

23. "Mashhad rahib bi-zawiyat al-Sharif Ridwan" [Frightening Scene at Shrine of Sherif Redwan], *al-Mi'ad al-Siyasi*, January 18, 1995.

24. "Fata ittafaqat ma'a akh khatibiha 'ala qatl ummiha min ajli ikhfa' fadihat al-haml bi-Wujda" [Girl in Oujda Killed Mother with Fiancé's Brother to Hide Scandal of Her Pregnancy], *al-Yawm al-Siyasi*, June 19, 1994.

25. Najib Skir, "Zahirat hawadith al-'unf al-muwajjih didd al-walidin bi-l-Maghrib fi tazayud mustamirr!" [Phenomenon of Crimes of Violence against Parents in Morocco Is Continuously Escalating!], *al-Yawm al-Siyasi*, December 17, 1994.

26. Ibid.

27. Even Moroccan law makes a special exception for matricide or patricide. While murder is punished by imprisonment, killing a parent is punished by death.

28. Skir, "Zahirat hawadith al-'unf al-muwajjih didd al-walidin bi-l-Maghrib fi tazayud mustamirr!" [Phenomenon of Crimes of Violence against Parents in Morocco Is Continuously Escalating!].

29. "Sayyida mutazawwija taqtul 'ashiqaha al-shurti bi-tariqa fazi'a bi-madinat Khuribga" [Married Woman Kills Her Cop Lover in Abominable Way in Khouribga], *al-Mi'ad al-Siyasi*, January 18, 1995.

30. "Shabb yuhawil al-intihar fawq 'amud kahraba'i bi-Maknas" [Youth Attempts Suicide on Top Electric Pole in Meknès], *al-Yawm al-Siyasi*, November 22, 1993.

31. Najib Skir, "Wujud al-intibah li-hadhihi al-zahira al-khatira" [The Necessity of Heeding This Dangerous Phenomenon], *al-Muwasil al-Siyasi*, November 6, 1993.

32. "Tam'an fi al-mal qatala umm khatibatihi wa-rama bi-juththatiha fi al-ghaba bi-Fas" [Greedy for Money, He Killed His Fiancée's Mother and Tossed Her Body in Fez Woods], *Akhbar al-Hawadith*, November 16, 1997.

33. "Dhabah al-'ajuz alladhi kan yumaris 'alayhi al-jins tiwal 19 sana li-'annahu talabahu bi-istimrar al-shudhudh al-jinsi baynahuma raghma annahu tab min dhalika" [He Butchered Old Man Violating Him for 19 Years Because He Asked Him to Continue Sexual Deviance between Them, Even Though He Renounced It], *al-Muwasil al-Siyasi*, September 15, 1995.

34. "Fi lahzat taysh wa-nazwa, shabb wadi' yatahawwal ila qatil" [In Moment of Recklessness and Capriciousness, Mild-Mannered Young Man Turns into Killer], *al-Yawm al-Siyasi*, December 31, 1995.

35. "Min al-hubb ma qatal" [It's Love That Kills], *al-'Alam*, December 27, 1995.

36. "Dabt imbratur al-mukhaddi wa-bi-hawzatihi amwal wa-asliha nariyya" [Arrest of Drug Emperor with Cash and Firearms], *al-Yawm al-Siyasi*, September 27, 1993.

37. For more on illegal immigration in Morocco, see Jonathan Smolin, "Burning the Past: Moroccan Cinema of Illegal Immigration," *South Central Review* 28, no. 1 (2011): 74–89.

38. "Fata ittafaqat ma'a akh khatibiha 'ala qatl ummiha min ajli ikhfa' fadihat al-haml bi-Wujda" [Girl in Oujda Killed Mother with Fiancé's Brother to Hide Scandal of Her Pregnancy].

39. "Dhabah al-'ajuz alladhi kan yumaris 'alayhi al-jins tiwal 19 sana li-'annahu talabahu bi-istimrar al-shudhudh al-jinsi baynahuma raghma annahu tab min dhalika" [He Butchered Old Man Violating Him for 19 Years because He Asked Him to Continue Sexual Deviance between Them, Even Though He Renounced It].

40. "Shabb dhu sawabiq yaqtul abahu wa-akhahu bi-sabab niza' hawla barrad shayy bi-Sidi Musa fi Sala" [Young Man with Priors Kills Father and Brother in Fight Over Pot of Mint Tea in Sidi Musa in Salé], *al-Muwasil al-Siyasi*, November 30, 1996.

41. "al-Mujrim 'Shatir' hawala ightisab imra'a bi-Asfi fa-wajada nafsahu dakhil al-sijn" ["Clever" Criminal Tried to Rape Woman in Asfi and Found Himself in Jail], *al-Yawm al-Siyasi*, June 19, 1994.

42. "al-Shurta bi-Maknas tada' haddan li-'isaba taqum bi-sariqat al-sayyarat" [Police in Meknès Put End to Gang Stealing Cars], *al-Mi'ad al-Siyasi*, November 2, 1994.

43. "Ilqa' al-qabd 'ala 'isaba ta'tarid sabil al-muwatinin wa-tastawla 'ala bata'iqihim al-wataniyya li-tunsib bi-ha 'ala al-akharin bi-l-Dar al-Bayda'" [Arrest of Gang That Obstructed Path of Citizens and Took Their National ID Cards to Swindle Others with Them in Casablanca], *al-Mi'ad al-Siyasi*, November 2, 1994.

44. "Qatalahu bi-sikkin wa-irtada sirwalahu wa-hadha'ahu thumma ladhdh bi-l-firar bi-Maknas" [He Stabbed Him to Death, Put on His Pants and Shoes, and Tried to Flee in Meknès], *al-Muwasil al-Siyasi*, March 24, 1995.

45. "Qatal 'dabit shurta' wa-fasal juththatahu ila atraf wa-rama bi-ha fi bi'r bi-'Ayn al-Shaqq bi-l-Dar al-Bayda'" [He Killed a "Police Detective," Cut Up His Body, and Threw It in a Well in Aïn Chok in Casablanca], *al-Muwasil al-Siyasi*, March 17, 1995.

46. al-Hajj 'Ali, "'Uqubat al-jara'id al-mukhtalla bi-l-akhlaq" [Punishment of Immoral Newspapers], *al-Ittihad al-Ishtiraki*, October 31, 1993.

47. Hadin Saghir, "Mulahazat 'ala al-hamish [Side Notes]," *al-Ittihad al-Ishtiraki*, December 19, 1993.

48. 'Abd al-Hamid Bin Da'ud, "Sihafat al-arsifa: al-irtizaq, al-muyu'a, wa-al-tashwish" [The Sidewalk Press: Profiteering, Dissolution, and Derangement], *al-Ittihad al-Ishtiraki*, June 17, 1995.

49. Najib Skir, "Li-kull hurriyya hudud" [Every Freedom Has Limits], *al-Muwasil al-Siyasi*, October 23, 1993.

50. Najib Skir, "Dawr wasa'il al-i'lam fi al-ta'rif bi-mazahir al-jarima dakhil al-mujtama'" [Role of Media in Making Phenomena of Crime inside Society Known], *Akhbar al-Hawadith*, March 13, 1996.

51. David J. Krajicek, *Scooped!: Media Miss Real Story on Crime while Chasing Sex, Sleaze, and Celebrities* (New York: Columbia University Press, 1998), 196.

52. Richard Gid Powers, *G-Men: Hoover's FBI in American Popular Culture* (Carbondale: Southern Illinois University Press, 1983), 110.

53. Reeves and Campbell, *Cracked Coverage: Television News, the Anti-Cocaine Crusade, and the Reagan Legacy*.

54. David L. Altheide, *Creating Fear: News and the Construction of Crisis* (New York: Aldine de Gruyter, 2002).

3. Crime-Page Fiction

1. Gilles Perrault, *Notre ami le roi* (Paris: Gallimard, 1990).

2. Salah al-Wadi', *al-'Aris* [The Bridegroom] (Casablanca: Matba'at al-Najah al-Jadida, 1998). For more on these prison narratives, see Susan Slyomovics, *The Performance of Human Rights in Morocco* (Philadelphia: University of Pennsylvania Press, 2005).

3. Muhammad al-Barini, "Hadhihi al-jarida" [This Newspaper], *al-Ahdath al-Maghribiyya*, October 22, 1998.

4. In this, *Moroccan Events* paralleled the influence of tabloid reporting on the mainstream media in the United States during and after the 1980s. See David J. Krajicek, *Scooped!: Media Miss Real Story on Crime while Chasing Sex, Sleaze, and Celebrities* (New York: Columbia University Press, 1998).

5. For a general survey, see George N. Dove, *The Police Procedural* (Bowling Green, OH: Bowling Green University Popular Press, 1982).

6. The work of Georges Simenon stands as an intermediate step between the intelligent detective and the police procedural hero. Simenon's fictional Commissaire Maigret is a police official and works within a team of detectives but operates like Sherlock Holmes in the way he solves cases through intuition and carefully questioning suspects. While forensic science and other forms of modern police work appear in Simenon's novels, they rarely if ever play a pivotal role in cracking Maigret's cases.

7. Christopher P. Wilson, *Cop Knowledge: Police Power and Cultural Narrative in Twentieth-Century America* (Chicago: University of Chicago Press, 2000), 58.

8. Ibid., 61.

9. Ibid., 60–61.

10. Leroy Panek, "Post-War American Police Fiction," in *The Cambridge Companion to Crime Fiction*, ed. Martin Priestman (Cambridge: Cambridge University Press, 2003), 78.

11. For such a reading of the police procedural, see Robert Paul Winston and Nancy C. Mellerski, *The Public Eye: Ideology and the Police Procedural* (New York: St. Martin's Press, 1992). For a Foucauldian reading of the novel as a vehicle for internalizing discipline, see D. A. Miller, *The Novel and the Police* (Berkeley: University of California Press, 1988).

12. See, respectively, the work of Leonardo Padura, Henning Mankell, Pepetela, and Batya Gur.

13. For more on the history of Arabic police fiction, see Jonathan Smolin, "Anxious Openings: Globalization in the Arabic Police Novel" (unpublished manuscript, November 29, 2012), Microsoft Word file. Before the 1990s, there was a single early attempt to write an Arabic police novel in 1963 in Morocco: Muhammad Ibn Tuhami, *Dahaya Hubb* [Victims of Love] (al-Muhammadiyya: Matba'at al-Fadala, 1963). While Arabic police fiction was absent elsewhere in the region, crime and detective fiction that privileged a rogue hero was extremely popular in the Middle East during the early twentieth century. See Elliott Colla, "Anxious Advocacy: The Novel, the Law, and Extrajudicial Appeals in Egypt," *Public Culture* 17, no. 3 (2005): 417–423.

14. Miludi Hamdushi and 'Abd al-Ilah al-Hamdushi, *al-Hut al-a'ma* [The Blind Whale] (al-Rabat: 'Ukaz, 1997). Miloudi Hamdouchi, a legendary former police commissioner widely known in Morocco as "Columbo," has written a number of police novels in Arabic and French as well as several studies on the Moroccan police and legal system. Abdelilah Hamdouchi, a screenwriter and novelist, has published five police novels, including *The Final Bet*, trans. Jonathan Smolin (Cairo: American University in Cairo Press, 2008). For more on his work, see Jonathan Smolin, "Political Malaise and the New Arabic Noir," *South Central Review* 27, no. 1 & 2 (2010): 82–90. There is no family relation between Miloudi Hamdouchi and Abdelilah Hamdouchi.

15. Hamdushi and al-Hamdushi, *al-Hut al-a'ma* [The Blind Whale], 9–10.

16. Ibid., 12.

17. Ibid., 13.

18. Ibid., 117.

19. Ibid., 128.

20. Ibid., 15.

21. Ibid., 105.

22. See Henning Mankell, *Faceless Killers*, trans. Steven T. Murray (New York: New Press, 1997). L. A. García-Roza, *A Window in Copacabana*, trans. Benjamin Moser (New York: Henry Holt, 2005). Miyuki Miyabe, *All She Was Worth*, trans. Alfred Birnbaum (Tokyo: Kodansha America, 1996).

23. See Smolin, "Anxious Openings: Globalization in the Arabic Police Novel."

24. Anita Biressi, *Crime, Fear, and the Law in True Crime Stories* (New York: Palgrave, 2001), 1.

25. Ibid., 17.

26. Wilson, *Cop Knowledge: Police Power and Cultural Narrative in Twentieth-Century America*, 134, 135.

27. Mark Seltzer, *True Crime: Observations on Violence and Modernity* (New York: Routledge, 2007), 2.

28. Jean Murley, *The Rise of True Crime: Twentieth Century Murder and American Popular Culture* (Westport, CT: Praeger, 2008), 54–55.

29. Seltzer, *True Crime: Observations on Violence and Modernity*, 9.

30. Karen Halttunen, *Murder Most Foul: The Killer and the American Gothic Imagination* (Cambridge, MA: Harvard University Press, 1998).

31. Muhammad Yasin, "Man qatala al-ustaz?!" [Who Killed the Teacher?!], *al-Ahdath al-Maghribiyya*, March 12, 1999.

32. 'Abd al-Majid Hashadi, "Qatil dhaki waqa'a fi shirr a'malihi!" [A Smart Killer Who Fell in the Evil of His Deeds!], *al-Ahdath al-Maghribiyya*, February 11, 2000.

33. Wilson, *Cop Knowledge: Police Power and Cultural Narrative in Twentieth-Century America*, 62.

34. Muhammad al-Zawhari, "Tamada fi ihanatihim bi-shudhudhihi fa-'amadu ila qatlihi harqan!" [He Kept Abusing Them with His Deviance So They Proceeded to Kill Him by Fire!], *al-Ahdath al-Maghribiyya*, December 5, 2003. Nabil Ayouch's well-known film, *Ali Zaoua*, also depicts the violent world of street children in Casablanca.

35. Richard Victor Ericson, Patricia M. Baranek, and Janet B. L. Chan, *Representing Order: Crime, Law, and Justice in the News Media* (Toronto: University of Toronto Press, 1991).

36. 'Abd al-Majid Hashadi, "Qadaya taht al-mijhar (6): Wazir al-'adl yuqabbir al-milaff wa-al-'adala tudin al-mutawarritin" [Cases under the Microscope (6): Minister of Justice Buries the File but Justice Convicts Those Involved], *al-Ahdath al-Maghribiyya*, December 2, 2000.

37. Abdelilah Hamdouchi did publish a new Arabic police novel in 2009. See 'Abd al-Ilah al-Hamdushi, *al-Mustanzafun* [Bled Dry] (al-Qunaytara: al-Buliki, 2009). For more on this novel, see Smolin, "Political Malaise and the New Arabic Noir."

38. 'Abd al-Majid Hashadi, "Mish'awidh min Maknas: Rihla min al-nasb ila al-qatl!" [Magician from Meknès: Journey from Swindling to Murder!], *al-Ahdath al-Maghribiyya*, November 6–December 5, 2002.

39. 'Abd al-Majid Hashadi, "Mish'awidh min Maknas: Rihla min al-nasb ila al-qatl! (1): Taqrir 'ala maktab al-'amid" [Magician from Meknès: Journey from Swindling to Murder! (1): Report on Commissioner's Desk], *al-Ahdath al-Maghribiyya*, November 6, 2002.

40. 'Abd al-Majid Hashadi, "Mish'awidh min Maknas: Rihla min al-nasb ila al-qatl! (7): Fi muwajaha ma'a al-mish'awidh 'Qasim'" [Magician from Meknès: Journey from Swindling to Murder! (7): Confrontation with Magician Qasim], *al-Ahdath al-Maghribiyya*, November 12, 2002.

41. Regina G. Lawrence, *The Politics of Force: Media and the Construction of Police Brutality* (Berkeley: University of California Press, 2000), 91.

42. Richard Victor Ericson, Patricia M. Baranek, and Janet B. L. Chan, *Negotiating Control: A Study of News Sources* (Toronto: University of Toronto Press, 1989), 150.

4. Prime-Time Cops

1. Since the emergence of *Moroccan Events*, the highest-circulation newspapers in the country have all been independent. At the time of writing, *Moroccan Events* has declined significantly in circulation but the most popular newspaper in the country is the independent *al-Masa'* (Evening), edited by Rachid Nini. While Nini does not rely on crime as much as *Moroccan Events*, his newspaper employs a highly sensational and populist perspective on social issues and politics.

2. For more on the history of 2M, see Meryem Saadi and Karim Boukhari, "2M l'histoire secrète," *Tel Quel*, March 7–13, 2009.

3. *Events* was a highly popular documentary series which narrated infamous crimes that took place in Morocco during the 1970s and 1980s. The first episode appeared in December 1993, only months after the Tabit Affair and during the frenzy of the new crime tabloids.

4. Although well known for his films, such as *al-Bahth 'an zawj imra'ati* (In Search of My Wife's Husband), Tazi has left a permanent influence on the development of Moroccan television production. He has also produced and directed a number of téléfilms. For a discussion of his cinema, see M. A. Tazi and Kevin Dwyer, *Beyond Casablanca: M. A. Tazi and the Adventure of Moroccan Cinema* (Bloomington: Indiana University Press, 2004).

5. Sail's other initiatives include restructuring the station's news department, increasing the number of news broadcasts per day, creating an international satellite version of 2M, and launching the station's first website. In general, he helped spread a youth culture at the station that continues to this day.

6. Hasan Rhanja, *al-Hut al-a'ma* [The Blind Whale] (Morocco: 2M, 2001).

7. Yusuf Hanani, "Ayy afaq li-l-film al-bulisi bi-l-Maghrib?" [What Horizon Is There for Police Film in Morocco?], *al-Ittihad al-Ishtiraki*, April 30, 2001.

8. Abu Ayman, "al-Muqarana bayna al-qanatayn al-ula wa-al-thani" [Comparing First and Second Channels], *al-Ahdath al-Maghribiyya*, February 19, 2001.

9. Hasan al-Wahidi, *Mat'am Sufiya* [Sofia's Restaurant] (Morocco: RTM, 2001).

10. Some RTM miniseries during the mid-1990s—such as *La tabhathu 'ani* (Don't Look for Me) and *al-Wasiya* (The Will)—include subplots of police investigations but were not filmed in police stations and did not use real police props, such as cars, vans, and holsters.

11. Abdelilah Hamdouchi, *The Final Bet*, trans. Jonathan Smolin (Cairo: American University in Cairo Press, 2008).

12. For more on garde à vue, see Susan Slyomovics, *The Performance of Human Rights in Morocco* (Philadelphia: University of Pennsylvania Press, 2005), 14–19.

13. In the novel, Othman claims that when he returned to the house, Sofia was still barely alive. He found the knife buried in her stomach and she begged him with her eyes to take it out. In a moment of panic, he grabbed onto the handle and pulled the knife from her stomach, accidentally leaving his fingerprints on the murder weapon.

14. During Ramadan 2001, several months after the release of *The Final Bet*, *Moroccan Events* published a serial entitled "Abriya' khalfa al-qudban" (Innocents behind Bars) that detailed cases in which the judicial system convicted men of crimes they did not commit.

15. Hamdouchi, *The Final Bet*, 16.

16. As Joseph Braude has shown, even the Moroccan police have a great love for Falk's character. See Joseph Braude, *The Honored Dead: A Story of Friendship, Murder, and the Search for Truth in the Arab World* (New York: Spiegel & Grau, 2011).

17. "Mat'am Sufiya wa-al-hut al-a'ma sharitan talfizyan jadidan" [*Sofia's Restaurant* and *The Blind Whale*, Two New Téléfilms], *al-Ahdath al-Maghribiyya*, March 4, 2001.

18. Adil Fadili, *al-Shahida* [The Witness] (Morocco: 2M, 2003). Fadili has directed a number of téléfilms for both RTM and 2M, including *al-Muhamma* [The Mission] and *Wald al-Hamariyya*, as well as the police series *La Brigade*.

19. M. L., "al-Raqaba wa-shahadat al-zur fi 'Duziyim'" [Censorship and False Testimony at 2M], *al-Ahdath al-Maghribiyya*, September 29, 2003.

20. Jamal Belmajdoub, *Layali bayda'* [White Nights] (Morocco: 2M, 2005). The title is a play on the Arabic name of Casablanca, Dar al-Bayda'. Belmajdoub has directed numerous works, including the film for cinema *al-Hulm al-maghribi* (Moroccan Dream), the téléfilm *Classe 8*, and the twenty-five-part television series *Khalkhalat Batul* (Batul's Anklet).

21. Jean Baudrillard, *Simulacra and Simulation* (Ann Arbor: University of Michigan Press, 1994), 2.

22. For more on the growth of fictional images of crime and punishment in the United States after 2000, see Richard Logan Fox, Robert W. Van Sickel, and Thomas L. Steiger, *Tabloid Justice: Criminal Justice in an Age of Media Frenzy*, 2nd ed. (Boulder, CO: Lynne Rienner, 2007).

5. The Moroccan "Serial Killer" and CSI: Casablanca

1. See Philip Jenkins, *Using Murder: The Social Construction of Serial Homicide* (New York: Aldine de Gruyter, 1994), 49–80. David Schmid, *Natural Born Celebrities: Serial Killers in American Culture* (Chicago: University of Chicago Press, 2005), 66–101.

2. Robert K. Ressler and Tom Schachtman, *Whoever Fights Monsters: My Twenty Years Tracking Serial Killers for the FBI* (New York: St. Martin's Press, 1993), 3.

3. For more FBI criminal profiling, see ibid.; John Douglas and Mark Olshaker, *Mind Hunter: Inside the FBI's Elite Serial Crime Unit* (New York: Pocket Books, 1996); Robert K.

Ressler, Ann Wolbert Burgess, and John E. Douglas, *Sexual Homicide: Patterns and Motives* (Lexington, MA: Lexington Books, 1988).

4. Ressler and Schachtman, *Whoever Fights Monsters: My Twenty Years Tracking Serial Killers for the FBI*, 48.

5. Richard Gid Powers, *G-Men: Hoover's FBI in American Popular Culture* (Carbondale: Southern Illinois University Press, 1983).

6. Schmid, *Natural Born Celebrities: Serial Killers in American Culture*, 72.

7. Jenkins, *Using Murder: The Social Construction of Serial Homicide*, 63–68.

8. Ressler and Schachtman, *Whoever Fights Monsters: My Twenty Years Tracking Serial Killers for the FBI*, 228–229.

9. For more on the relationship between Harris and the media construction of the serial killer, see Schmid, *Natural Born Celebrities: Serial Killers in American Culture*; Philip L. Simpson, *Psycho Paths: Tracking the Serial Killer through Contemporary American Film and Fiction* (Carbondale: Southern Illinois University Press, 2000).

10. The notorious Soviet serial killer Andrei Chikatilo was free to kill some fifty victims between 1978 and 1990 partly because the Russian press did not report on crime at the time. See Mikhail Krivich and Ol'gert Ol'gin, *Comrade Chikatilo: The Psychopathology of Russia's Notorious Serial Killer*, trans. Todd P. Blundeau (Fort Lee, NJ: Barricade Books, 1993).

11. "I'tiqal shakhs qatala khams nisa' bi-l-Jadida" [Arrest of Person Who Killed Five Women in El Jadida], *al-Ahdath al-Maghribiyya*, June 9, 2001.

12. "al-Nass al-kamil li-mahdar al-shurta al-qida'iyya alladhi tudammin al-i'tirafat al-awwaliyya li-'saffah al-Jadida'" [Complete Text of Police Report That Contains Preliminary Confessions of "Killer of El Jadida"], *al-Sabah*, June 14, 2001.

13. 'Abd al-Majid Hashadi, "Dahayahu min al-nisa' wa-uslububu fi al-qatl wahid wa-dhika'uhu ja'alahu bi-man'an 'an al-'iqab!" [His Victims were Women, His Method in Killing Was the Same, and His Intelligence Kept Him Away from Punishment!], *al-Ahdath al-Maghribiyya*, June 15, 2001.

14. "I'tiqal shakhs qatala khams nisa' bi-l-Jadida" [Arrest of Person Who Killed Five Women in El Jadida].

15. 'Abd Allah Ghaytumi, "Qatil zall taliqan wa-bari'an fi al-sijn" [Killer Remained Free While Two Innocent Men Were in Jail], *al-Sabah*, June 11, 2001.

16. 'Abd Allah Ghaytumi, "Saffah al-Jadida i'tarafa wa-'bi-damm barid' bi-jara'imihi" [Killer of El Jadida Confessed to His Crimes "In Cold Blood"], *al-Sabah*, June 20, 2001.

17. Ghaytumi, "Qatil zall taliqan wa-bari'an fi al-sijn" [Killer Remained Free While Two Innocent Men Were in Jail].

18. 'Umar Jari and 'Abd Allah Ghaytumi, "Tafasil muthira hawla qadiyat 'Saffah Nisa'" al-Jadida" [Sensational Details about Case of "Killer of Women" of El Jadida], *al-Sabah*, June 12, 2001.

19. See, for example, 'Abd Allah Ghaytumi, "al-Mahdar al-kamil li-i'tirafat saffah al-Jadida" [Complete Police Report of Confessions of Killer of El Jadida], *al-Sabah*, June 14, 2001.

20. 'Abd Allah Ghaytumi, "'Saffah al-nisa' bi-l-Jadida yaqul inna dafi' irtikab al-jara'im lam yakun al-sariqa bal al-'ajz al-jinsi" ["Killer of Women" in El Jadida Says Motive for Committing Crimes Wasn't Theft But Impotence], *al-Sabah*, October 2, 2001.

21. "al-'Uthur 'ala juththa mushawwaha li-rajul bi-l-Dar al-Bayda'!" [Discovery of Man's Mutilated Body in Casablanca!], *al-Ahdath al-Maghribiyya*, May 28, 2002.

22. al-Husayn Yazi, "Lughz nisf juththat al-Ma'arif lam yuhal ba'd" [Puzzle of Half Body of Maârif Hasn't Been Solved Yet], *al-Sabah*, May 29, 2002.

23. Radwan Hafyani, al-Husayn Yazi, and Abd al-'Ali Tujid, "al-'Uthur 'ala juththat shabba muqatta'a wa-mu'abba'a fi akyas bi-l-Dar al-Bayda'" [Discovery of Young Woman's Body Cut Up and Packed into Bags in Casablanca], *al-Sabah*, August 16, 2002.

24. "al-Tashrih al-tibbi yufid anna al-qatala muhtarifun" [Autopsy Shows Killers Are Professionals], *al-Ahdath al-Maghribiyya*, August 19, 2002.

25. Duha Zayn al-Din, "Dahiyat jarimat Diyur Hantat ikhtafat baʿd al-munada ʿalayha min taraf fatah" [Victim of Diyur Hantat Crime Disappeared after She Was Called on by Girl], *al-Sabah*, August 19, 2002.

26. "Taharriyat mukaththafa bahthan ʿan al-fatah al-majhula" [Intensive Investigations Looking for Anonymous Girl], *al-Ahdath al-Maghribiyya*, August 22, 2002.

27. Khalid al-ʿAtawi, "Baʿd jarimat al-shahr al-madi bi-l-Dar al-Bayda', al-ʿuthur ʿala juththat fatah muqattaʿa ila thalathat ajza' bidun ra's!" [After Last Month's Crime in Casablanca, Discovery of Young Woman's Body Cut up into Three Parts with No Head!], *al-Ahdath al-Maghribiyya*, September 11, 2002.

28. al-Husayn Yazi, "al-ʿUthur ʿala al-atraf al-sufla li-fatah fi kis balastiki bi-l-Dar al-Bayda'" [Discovery of Girl's Lower Limbs in Plastic Bag in Casablanca], *al-Sabah*, September 11, 2002.

29. "Qatilat "Lajirund" la tazal majhulat al-huwiya" [Woman Killed in La Gironde Still Unidentified], *al-Ahdath al-Maghribiyya*, September 13, 2002.

30. "Khawf yusaytir ʿala fatayat al-Dar al-Bayda' min an yatahawwalna ila kumat lahm fi kis balastiki aswad" [Fear of Turning Into Pile of Flesh in Black Plastic Bag Seizes Young Women of Casablanca], *al-Sabah*, September 14–15, 2002.

31. Samir Achehbar, "Serial killer à Casablanca?," *Tel Quel*, September 21–27, 2002.

32. "Masdar amni mus'ul . . . dawafiʿ al-jarimatayn akhlaqiyya wa-la-majal li-l-rabt baynahuma" [Security Official Source . . . Motives for Two Crimes Are Moral and There Is No Way to Link Them], *al-Ahdath al-Maghribiyya*, September 16, 2002.

33. al-Husayn Yazi, "al-Tibb al-sharʿi yadrus sinn wa-qamat wa-kull atraf al-juththa al-mumaththal bi-ha" [Forensic Medicine Studies Age, Build, and All Limbs of Mutilated Body], *al-Sabah*, September 17, 2002.

34. ʿAbd al-Majid Hashadi, "Fi hiwar maʿa al-tabib al-sharʿi Saʿid al-Wahliyya" [Interview with Medical Examiner Saeed Louahlia], *al-Ahdath al-Maghribiyya*, September 25, 2002.

35. "Aghlab al-mujrimin taʿarradu li-hazzat ʿanifa fi marhalatay al-tufula wa-al-murahaqa" [Most Criminals Face Violent Shocks in Periods of Childhood and Adolescence], *al-Sabah*, September 30, 2002.

36. "Halqa jadida min silsilat qatl shabbat wa-taqtiʿ juthathihinna bi-l-Dar al-Bayda'" [New Part in Series of Murdering Young Women and Cutting Up Their Bodies in Casablanca], *al-Ahdath al-Maghribiyya*, December 4, 2002.

37. "Taharriyat mukaththafa li-masalih al-amn wa-tahdid huwiyat al-dahiya qad yusaʿid fi al-tahqiq" [Intensified Police Investigations; Identifying Victim Might Help Investigation], *al-Ahdath al-Maghribiyya*, December 5, 2002.

38. ʿAbd al-Majid Hashadi, "Taqrir al-tabib al-sharʿi yujad fi marahil mutaqaddima li-tahdid huwiyat al-dahiya" [Medical Examiner's Report in Advanced Stages to Identify Victim], *al-Ahdath al-Maghribiyya*, December 15, 2002.

39. ʿAbd al-Majid Hashadi, "al-Dar al-Bayda' tafrid taʿamulan istithna'iyyan wa-al-jarima tashhad tahawwulan nawʿiyyan" [Casablanca Imposes Exceptional Treatment as Crime Is Witnessing Qualitative Transformation], *al-Ahdath al-Maghribiyya*, January 4, 2003.

40. Khalid al-ʿAtawi and ʿAbd al-Majid Hashadi, "Hal yumkin tasnif qatl wa-tashwih juthath al-fatayat bi-l-Bayda' fi khanat al-jara'im al-kamila?" [Is It Possible to Classify Killing and Mutilating of Young Women's Bodies as Perfect Crimes?], *al-Ahdath al-Maghribiyya*, January 4, 2003.

41. "Ila mata tastamirr silsilat al-juthath al-muqattaʿa bi-l-Bayda'?" [How Long Will Series of Cut Up Bodies Continue in Casa?]" *al-Ahdath al-Maghribiyya*, January 27, 2003.

42. "Lughz al-juththa al-rabi'a fi tariqihi ila al-hall ba'd i'tiraf al-muttahima!" [Puzzle of Fourth Body on Its Way to Being Solved after Female Suspect's Confession!], *al-Ahdath al-Maghribiyya*, January 28, 2003.

43. "Fi tahaddi jadid li-amn al-Bayda': juththa jadida muqatta'a ila juz'ayn wa-bi-dun malamih wa-basamat!" [New Challenge to Casa Police: New Body Cut in Two without Features or Fingerprints!], *al-Ahdath al-Maghribiyya*, February 13, 2003.

44. Muhammad al-Rami, "al-'Uthur 'ala juththa jadida mujazza'a wa-muwazza'a bi-shawari' al-Dar al-Bayda'" [Discovery of New Body Mutilated and Distributed in Casablanca Streets], *al-Ittihad al-Ishtiraki*, February 13, 2003.

45. Muhammad Belftuh, "al-Dha'ar yatamallak al-sukkan" [Fear Seizes Residents], *al-'Alam*, February 15, 2003.

46. al-Husayn Yazi and Radwan Hafyani, "Murtakibu al-jara'im al-khams al-ghamida fi al-Bayda' muhtarifun fi taqti' al-juthath wa-laysa al-qatl" [Perpetrators of Five Mysterious Crimes in Casa Are Professionals at Cutting Up Bodies but Not at Killing], *al-Sabah*, February 15–16, 2003.

47. 'Abd al-Majid Hashadi, "Risala min imra'a majhula tujri al-tahqiq bi-sha'niha tuhaddid 'dawafi'' al-qatl" [Investigation Moves concerning Letter from Unknown Woman That Establishes "Motives" of Murder], *al-Ahdath al-Maghribiyya*, February 15, 2003.

48. Muhammad Abu Yahda, "Kayfa fakka amn al-Dar al-Bayda' lughz taqti' juththatayn ba'd al-ihtida' li-l-haris al-muntahar" [How Casablanca Police Cracked Puzzle of Dismembering Two Bodies after Discovering Guard Who Committed Suicide], *al-Ahdath al-Maghribiyya*, March 4, 2003.

49. S.A., "Le gardien suicidé était probablement un tueur en série," *L'Opinion*, March 5, 2003.

50. "al-'Uthur 'ala baqaya wajh juththat al-Ma'arif qad yaqud li-tarkib sura taqribiyya li-l-dahiyya" [Discovery of Remains of Maârif Body's Face Might Lead to Constructing Approximate Picture of Victim], *al-Ahdath al-Maghribiyya*, March 5, 2003.

51. Muhammad Abu Yahda, "al-Jani kana musaban bi-hawas jinsi wa-tasarrufatuhu lam takun da'iman tabi'iyya" [Criminal Was Struck by Sexual Madness and His Actions Were Not Always Natural], *al-Ahdath al-Maghribiyya*, March 7, 2003.

52. al-Husayn Yazi and Mustafa Hurmat Allah, "Zuwita al-mushtabih fi irtikab jarimatay al-Ma'arif wa-La Jirund da'a al-shurta ila al-bahth 'anhu" [Zouita, Accused of Committing Maârif and La Gironde Crimes, Called Police to Search for Him], *al-Sabah*, March 8–9, 2003.

53. 'Abd al-Majid Hashadi, "al-Sura al-tarkibiyya li-dahiyat al-Ma'arif tu'akkid al-tuhma 'ala haris al-'imara al-muntahar" [Constructed Image of Maârif Victim Confirms Charge against Building Guard That Committed Suicide], *al-Ahdath al-Maghribiyya*, March 15, 2003.

54. See Schmid, *Natural Born Celebrities: Serial Killers in American Culture*, 209–242.

55. 'Abd al-Majid Hashadi, "al-Risala al-tamwihiyya tuhaddid dawafi' al-jarima al-muzdawija wa-sariqat al-dahiya ja'at aradan" [Feigned Letter Confirms Motives of Double Crime and Theft from Victim Happened by Chance], *al-Ahdath al-Maghribiyya*, March 16, 2003.

56. This characterization, however, was clearly a fabrication. On April 28, after the case had disappeared from public attention, the press reported that the motive for Zouita's murdering both the Maârif victim and the prostitute was that they had a son together. It had been presumed all along that Zouita was the father of the boy. Now, DNA proved that the last victim was the father and the press subsequently presumed that Zouita killed him in revenge. This discredited the police and media theory that the murder was the result of a homosexual relationship between the two.

57. Hashadi, "al-Sura al-tarkibiyya li-dahiyat al-Ma'arif tu'akkid al-tuhma 'ala haris al-'imara al-muntahar" [Constructed Image of Maârif Victim Confirms Charge against Building Guard That Committed Suicide].

58. Aaron Doyle, *Arresting Images: Crime and Policing in Front of the Television Camera* (Toronto: University of Toronto Press, 2003). For more on public relations between the police and the media, see Richard Victor Ericson, Patricia M. Baranek, and Janet B. L. Chan, *Negotiating Control: A Study of News Sources* (Toronto: University of Toronto Press, 1989).

59. The press made much of the coincidence that the city name Taroudant in Berber means "the child is missing."

60. 'Abd al-Majid Hashadi, "Baqaya al-juthath al-thamani allati 'uthira 'alayha li-atfal dhukur tatarawah a'maruhum bayna 13 wa-17 sana" [Age of Remains of Eight Bodies of Male Children That Were Discovered Ranges between 13 and 17 Years], *al-Ahdath al-Maghrbiyya*, August 24, 2004.

61. Radwan Hafyani, "Dahaya al-Wad al-Wa'ir yabhathun 'an qatilihim" [Victims of Wad Waeer Search for Their Killer], *al-Sabah*, August 30, 2004.

62. 'Abd al-Majid Hashadi, "Masadir tarjah an yakun 'adad dahaya mudhbahat al-atfal bi-Tarudant akbar bi-kathir min al-halat al-muktashafa" [Sources Find It Likely That Number of Butchered Child Victims in Taroudant Is Much Higher Than Reported Cases], *al-Ahdath al-Maghribiyya*, August 26, 2004.

63. Hafyani, "Dahaya al-Wad al-Wa'ir yabhathun 'an qatilihim" [Victims of Wad Waeer Search for Their Killer].

64. 'Abd al-Majid Hashadi, "al-Tahqiq ma'a 'adad min al-ashkhas dhawi al-miyulat al-jinsiyya al-shadhdha" [Investigating Number of People with Sadistic Sexual Predilections], *al-Ahdath al-Maghribiyya*, September 1, 2004.

65. Mustafa Sufr, "al-Tibb al-shar'i yastantiq 'idham juthath Tarudant" [Forensic Medicine Makes Bones of Taroudant Bodies Speak], *al-Sabah*, August 26, 2004.

66. 'Abd al-Majid Hashadi, "Akthar min tis'in unsuran min ajhizat al-amn al-mukhtalifa tata'aqqab saffah Tarudant" [Over Ninety Investigators from Different Security Branches Tracking Killer of Taroudant, *al-Ahdath al-Maghribiyya*, August 27, 2004.

67. 'Abd al-Majid Hashadi, "al-Tahdid al-niha'i li-a'mar al-dahaya yu'akkid 'ala tarawuhiha bayna 10 wa-15 sana" [Final Determination of Victims' Ages Confirms Range between 10 and 15 Years], *al-Ahdath al-Maghribiyya*, August 31, 2004.

68. 'Abd al-Majid Hashadi, "Tamshit manatiq jadida bi-Tarudant bina' 'ala nata'ij al-khibra al-mujra 'ala al-turab al-'aliqa bi-l-rifat" [Combing New Regions of Taroudant Based on Results of Test Conducted on Soil Attached to Remains], *al-Ahdath al-Maghribiyya*, September 2, 2004.

69. Despite this sensational coverage of the DNA tests, it would be several months before the results were known.

70. Mustafa Sufr and Muhammad al-Ibrahimi, "Mujrim Tarudant kan yanam fawq rufat dahayahu" [Criminal of Taroudant Was Sleeping on Top of Remains of His Victims], *al-Sabah*, September 9, 2004.

71. Mustafa Azukah, "Ism al-muttaham al-mudawwan 'ala risala 'uthira 'alayha ma'a al-riffat qada ila i'tiqalihi" [Name of Accused Written on Letter Found with Remains Led to His Arrest] *al-Ahdath al-Maghribiyya*, September 9, 2004.

72. Mustafa Azukah, "al-Muttaham ta'arrad li-i'tida' jinsi fi tufulatihi fa-sa'a li-'l-intiqam'!" [Suspect Faced Sexual Assault in Childhood and Sought "Revenge"!], *al-Ahdath al-Maghribiyya*, September 11, 2004.

73. Duha Zayn al-Din, "al-Jara'im al-jinsiyya tajtah al-mujtama' al-maghribi" [Sexual Crimes Strike Moroccan Society], *al-Sabah*, September 15, 2004.

74. Mustafa Sufr, "al-Mujrim al-sadi kan wara' juthath Tarudant" [Sadistic Criminal behind Bodies of Taroudant], *al-Sabah*, September 15, 2004.

75. 'Abd Allah Ghaytumi, "I'tirafat 'saffah' Tarudant (5/5)" [Confessions of "Killer" of Taroudant, Part 5], *al-Sabah*, October 16–17, 2004.

76. "'Abd al-'Ali al-Hadi: 'Hina umaris al-jins 'ala al-dahiya wa-aqtuluhu ash'ur bi-l-nashwa wa-al-farha!'" [Abdelali Hadi: "When I Have Sex with the Victim, I Kill Him and Feel Elation and Joy!"], *al-Ahdath al-Maghribiyya*, December 4, 2004.

77. Ahmad Ayit al-Talib, "Fi hadith khass li-majallat al-shurta qatil Tarudant yahki 'an nafsihi wa-'an tafasil jara'imihi" [Exclusive Discussion with *Police Magazine*: Killer of Taroudant Talks about Himself and Details of His Crimes], *Majallat al-Shurta*, February 2005.

78. See, for example, Mustafa Sufr, "Tafasil nihayat kabus ashla' juththat al-Hayy al-Hasani" [Details of End of Nighmare of Remains of Hay Hassani Body], *al-Sabah*, June 3, 2005; "Tafasil suqut al-muttahimin fi maqtal muhami Maknas wa-zawjatihi" [Details of Suspect's Arrest in Killing of Meknès Lawyer and His Wife], *al-Ahdath al-Maghribiyya*, June 21, 2006.

79. Awsi Muh Lahsan, "Yawm ma'a al-markaz al-watani li-l-shurta al-'ilmiyya: Khubara' musallihun bi-l-taqniyya li-kashf alghaz al-jara'im" [Day with National Center for Scientific Police: Experts Armed with Technique for Uncovering Puzzles of Crimes], *al-Ahdath al-Maghribiyya*, April 3, 2005.

80. See, for example, al-Sadiq Bukzul, "al-Muktabar al-watani li-l-shurta al-'ilmiyya bi-l-Dar al-Bayda' yanfatah 'ala al-sihafa: 'Ulama' warrathiyyun wa-biyulujiyyun yata'aqqabun al-mujrimin" [National Headquarters of Scientific Police in Casablanca is Opened to the Press: DNA and Bio-Scientists Track Down Criminals], *al-Ahdath al-Maghribiyya*, February 15, 2007; Amélie Amilhau, "Les 'Experts' de Casa: Descente dans les labos de la police scientifique," *Le Journal*, February 17–23, 2007.

81. Noureddine Lakhmari, "al-Qadiya" [The Case], (Casablanca: 2M, 2006). Lakhmari is best known for his film *Casanegra*, which first appeared in the cinema in December 2008. For more on his work, see Valérie K. Orlando, *Screening Morocco: Contemporary Film in a Changing Society*, Ohio University Research in International Studies (Athens: Ohio University Press, 2011), 76–82.

82. As in the United States, the Moroccan media produced special reports and programs about local serial killers as entertainment. By 2011, 2M even began producing a series of documentaries about Moroccan serial killers, including Zouita and Hadi, called *Akhtar al-Mujrimin* [The Most Dangerous Criminals]. For online episodes, see http://www.2m.ma/Programmes/Magazines/Societe/node_26249.

6. From Morocco's 9/11 to Community Policing

1. The only exception to this was when Algerian gunmen killed two Spanish tourists in a Marrakech hotel in 1994.

2. It should be mentioned that many of the facts behind the bombings remain murky. After their arrest, Omari claimed that Moroccan secret services provided him with the bombs while Jalil said that the group was manipulated by the secret services.

3. See http://www.hrw.org/reports/2004/10/20/morocco-human-rights-crossroads-0.

4. For more on Laânigri's time at the DST, see 'Abd al-Hamid al-'Awni, *al-Janral al-qawi: La'nikri* [The Strong General: Laânigri] (Fas: Manshurat 'Arabiyya, 2003).

5. Driss Bennani, "Laânigri, un destin marocain," *Tel Quel*, September 16–22, 2006, 43.

6. 'Abd al-Latif Aknush and 'Aziz Samil, "Ha'ula'i al-rijal alladhina nukhafuhum" [These Men We Fear], *Majallat al-Shurta*, February 2005, 13. In their own publications, the police cite the work of Jean-Jacques Gleizal and Jean-Charles Froment, Sebastian Roché, and Wesley G. Skogan. See Youssef Chami, "Qu'est-ce que la police de proximité?," *Police Magazine*, September 2005. For more on community policing, see William Lyons, *The Politics of Community Policing: Rearranging the Power to Punish* (Ann Arbor: University of Michigan Press, 1999).

7. For an extensive history of Hoover's collaboration with American popular culture industries, see Richard Gid Powers, *G-Men: Hoover's FBI in American Popular Culture* (Carbondale: Southern Illinois University Press, 1983). Collaboration between American security agencies and popular culture is still widespread today.

8. '. K., "al-Idara al-'amma li-l-amn al-watani tuwajih tafashshiyan mulahizan li-l-inhiraf" [DGSN Faces Noticeable Spread of Criminality], *al-Sabah*, October 23–24, 2004.

9. Aknush and Samil, "Ha'ula'i al-rijal alladhina nukhafuhum" [These Men We Fear], 18.

10. Ibid., 19.

11. Majdoulein El Atouabi, "La fin du carnaval," *Maroc Hebo International*, October 20–26, 2006, 29.

12. Aknush and Samil, "Ha'ula'i al-rijal alladhina nukhafuhum" [These Men We Fear], 18.

13. Louis Althusser, "Ideology and Ideological State Apparatus (Notes Towards an Investigation)," in *Lenin and Philosophy and Other Essays* (New York: Monthly Review Press, 2001 [1971]), 109.

14. Driss Bennani and Abdellatif El Azizi, "Cette police qui vous veut du bien," *Tel Quel*, January 15–21, 2005, 22.

15. Ibid., 25.

16. 'Abd al-Rahim Ariri and Mustafa Hurmat Allah, "al-'Anikri yaqud inqilaban dakhil jihaz al-amn" [Laânigri Leads Coup d'État within Security Services], *al-Baydawi*, January 26, 2005.

17. Ibid., 4.

18. 'Aziz Batrah, "Qararat amniyya jadida tuhaddid tuwajjuhat al-idara al-'amma li-l-amn al-watani" [New Security Decisions Set Directions of DGSN], *al-Ahdath al-Maghribiyya*, January 31, 2005.

19. Hamidu al-'Anikri, "I'adat al-ta'sis [Re-Foundation]," *Majallat al-Shurta*, February 2005.

20. Aknush and Samil, "Ha'ula'i al-rijal alladhina nukhafuhum" [These Men We Fear], 11.

21. Ibid., 13.

22. Ibid., 14.

23. Ibid., 16.

24. Yunis al-Jawhari, "Akhaf min al-shurta" [I'm Afraid of the Police], *Majallat al-Shurta*, February 2005.

25. For more on these sessions, see http://www.ier.ma. It is significant that that the commission is not named a "Truth and Reconcilliation Commission." The fact that victims were not allowed to name their torturers and that the commission did not have any prosecutorial powers suggest that the state was not seeking truth in setting up the sessions.

26. 'Abd al-Latif Aknush, Muhammad Bin Khuluq, and Nawal al-Mansur, "al-Mar'a dakhil mu'assasat al-shurta" [Women in the Police Establishment], *Majallat al-Shurta*, March 2005.

27. Nonetheless, despite this celebrated image of female police commissioners and officers taking target practice, women were not allowed to carry guns without prior authorization.

28. 'Abd al-'Aziz Samil, "al-Tawasul dakhil mu'assasat al-shurta" [Communication in the Police Establishment], *Majallat al-Shurta*, January 2006. Several phrases in this translation appear in the French version of the editorial and not the Arabic.

29. Khalid al-'Atawi, "Kayfa yahrus rijal al-amn shawari' al-Dar al-Bayda'!" [How Police Protect Streets of Casablanca!], *al-Ahdath al-Maghribiyya*, February 12, 2005.

30. 'Abd al-Rahim Ariri and Mustafa Hurmat Allah, "Khuttat al-shurta wa-al-muntakhibin li-fakk al-hisar" [Plan of Police and the Elected to Break Blockade], *al-Baydawi*, February 23, 2005. Both Ariri and Hurmat Allah would later be arrested and interrogated at the same police station in 2007 for leaking military documents.

31. 'Abd al-Rahim Ariri, Fatima Yasin, and Ahmad Busitta, "Qarasanat al-'Anikri amam al-barlaman" [Laânigri's Piracy before Parliament], *al-Baydawi*, November 17, 2004, 4, 5.

32. Ibid., 5.
33. Khalid al-Jama'i, "Risala maftuha ila zamili al-'Anikri" [Open Letter to My Colleague Laânigri], *al-Nahar al-Maghribiyya*, February 4, 2005.
34. "Marakiz amn al-qurb ma zalat khaliyya" [PPPs Still Vacant], *al-Ahdath al-Maghribiyya*, September 11, 2005.
35. El Atouabi, "La fin du carnaval," 31.
36. Tawfiq Misbah, Yusif Khatib, and Mustafa Hurmat Allah, "Fara'inat al-'Anikri" [Laânigri's Pharaohs], *al-Baydawi*, October 24, 2005.
37. 'Abd al-Rahim Ariri and Mustafa Hurmat Allah, "Asrar inhiyar imbraturiyyat al-'Anikri" [Secrets of Fall of Laânigri's Empire], *al-Watan*, October 21, 2006, 9.
38. "Hasilat al-tadakhkhulat al-midaniyya li-l-majmu'at al-hadariyya li-l-amn" [Results of GUS Field Interventions], *Majallat al-Shurta*, November 2005.
39. "al-Ittijahat al-'amma li-l-ijram khilal sanat 2005" [General Directions of Criminality during 2005], *Majallat al-Shurta*, July–August 2006.
40. Duha Zayn al-Din, "al-Majmu'at al-hadariyya fashilat hasb al-muwatinin wa-mas'ul amni yara anna al-waqt mubakkir li-l-taqyim" [GUS Have Failed according to Citizens But Security Official Thinks It's Too Early to Judge], *al-Sabah*, December 20, 2004.
41. Mustafa Azukah, "Rijal amn yuhinun al-muwatinin wa-yusarrikhun fi wujuhihim 'al-shari' diyalna!'" [Policemen Insult Citizens and Scream in Their Faces "The Street Is Ours!"], *al-Ahdath al-Maghribiyya*, December 20, 2004.
42. "I'tida' 'ala muwatin bi-l-Dar al-Bayda' wa-akhar bi-Maknas wa-al-nuqat al-sawda' taht rahmat al-munharifin" [Aggression against Citizen in Casablanca and Another in Meknès, Black Spots at Criminals' Mercy], *al-Ahdath al-Maghribiyya*, January 17, 2005.
43. Muhammad al-Budali, "Tajawuzat shurtat al-qurb tahzur al-samar wa-al-tajawwul fi Radaman bi-Sala" [Excesses of Police of Proximity Prohibit Evening Chats and Strolls during Ramadan in Salé], *al-Ahdath al-Maghribiyya*, October 20, 2005.
44. Khalid al-'Atawi, "al-Bulis matjish hatta yakun al-dam!" [Cops Don't Come Unless There's Blood!], *al-Ahdath al-Maghribiyya*, April 22, 2006.
45. Muhammad Hafidh, "Shurtat al-mawt" [Police of Death], *al-Sahifa*, June 9–15, 2006.
46. Ibid., 3.
47. Other explanations for the end of the GUS circulated in the press. These included the king's displeasure at the way the GUS were booed during a parade for the fiftieth anniversary of the police and that the king became angry when he saw a unit of the GUS playing soccer instead of serving the royal motorcade. Another explanation was that the decision was simply political and that Draiss wanted to wipe away as many traces of his predecessor as possible.
48. For a full accounting, see Ariri and Hurmat Allah, "Asrar inhiyar imbraturiyyat al-'Anikri" [Secrets of Fall of Laânigri's Empire], 8. See also 'Abd al-Haqq Belshukr, "Akhta' al-'Anikri allati qadat ila nihayat shurtat 'Karwatiya'" [Laânigri's Mistakes That Led to End of "Croatians"], *al-Masa'*, October 28–29, 2006.
49. Khalid al-'Atawi, "Majallat al-shurta tastanzif juyub rijal al-shurta" [*Police Magazine* Drains Policemen's Pockets], *al-Sabah*, October 23–24, 2006.
50. Ariri and Hurmat Allah, "Asrar inhiyar imbraturiyyat al-'Anikri" [Secrets of Fall of Laânigri's Empire], 8.
51. For a reading of the American police as a simulacrum on the television program *Cops*, see Kevin Glynn, *Tabloid Culture: Trash Taste, Popular Power, and the Transformation of American Television* (Durham, NC: Duke University Press, 2000).
52. al-Hasan Ayit Bihi, "'al-Krisaj' yaghzu shawari' al-mudun" ["Crisis" Invades City Streets], *al-Mustaqill*, December 1–7, 2006.
53. Ibid., 4.

Epilogue

1. For online episodes, see http://www.medi1.com/emissions/police and http://www.medi1tv.com/fr/investigation.

Bibliography

"'Abd al-'Ali al-Hadi: 'Hina umaris al-jins 'ala al-dahiya wa-aqtuluhu ash'ur bi-l-nashwa wa-al-farha!'" [Abdelali Hadi: "When I Have Sex with the Victim, I Kill Him and Feel Elation and Joy!"]. *al-Ahdath al-Maghribiyya*, December 4, 2004, 2.

Abu Yahda, Muhammad. "al-Jani kana musaban bi-hawas jinsi wa-tasarrufatuhu lam takun da'iman tabi'iyya" [Criminal Was Struck by Sexual Madness and His Actions Were Not Always Natural]. *al-Ahdath al-Maghribiyya*, March 7, 2003, 1.

———. "Kayfa fakka amn al-Dar al-Bayda' lughz taqti' juththatayn ba'd al-ihtida' li-l-haris al-muntahar" [How Casablanca Police Cracked Puzzle of Dismembering Two Bodies after Discovering Guard Who Committed Suicide]. *al-Ahdath al-Maghribiyya*, March 4, 2003, 8.

Abu-Lughod, Lila. *Dramas of Nationhood: The Politics of Television in Egypt*. Chicago: University of Chicago Press, 2005.

Achehbar, Samir. "Serial killer à Casablanca?" *Tel Quel*, September 21–27, 2002, 9.

"Aghlab al-mujrimin ta'arradu li-hazzat 'anifa fi marhalatay al-tufula wa-al-murahaqa" [Most Criminals Face Violent Shocks in Periods of Childhood and Adolescence]. *al-Sabah*, September 30, 2002, 7.

Akhmisse, Mustapha. *Médecine, magie et sorcellerie au Maroc, ou, l'Art traditionnel de guérir*. Casablanca: BENIMED, 1985.

Aknush, 'Abd al-Latif, Muhammad Bin Khuluq, and Nawal al-Mansur. "al-Mar'a dakhil mu'assasat al-shurta" [Women in the Police Establishment]. *Majallat al-Shurta*, March 2005, 12–18.

Aknush, 'Abd al-Latif, and 'Aziz Samil. "Ha'ula'i al-rijal alladhina nukhafuhum" [These Men We Fear]. *Majallat al-Shurta*, February 2005, 11–19.

'Alawi, Mustafa al-. *Mudhakkirat sahafi wa-thalathat muluk* [Memoirs of a Journalist and Three Kings]. [al-Dar al-Bayda'?]: Manshurat Akhbar al-Yawm, 2011.

'Ali, al-Hajj. "'Uqubat al-jara'id al-mukhtalla bi-l-akhlaq" [Punishment of Immoral Newspapers]. *al-Ittihad al-Ishtiraki*, October 31, 1993, 4.

Altheide, David L. *Creating Fear: News and the Construction of Crisis*. New York: Aldine de Gruyter, 2002.

Althusser, Louis. "Ideology and Ideological State Apparatus (Notes Towards an Investigation)." Translated by Ben Brewster. In *Lenin and Philosophy and Other Essays*, 85–126. New York: Monthly Review Press, 2001 (1971).

"'Amid shurta mumtaz fi qadaya akhlaqiyya: Hajz ashritat al-fidiyu tatadamman suwaran hayya khali'a" [High-Ranking Commissioner in Moral Affairs: Seizure of Videotapes Containing Live Depraved Images]. *al-'Alam*, February 11, 1993, 1.

Amilhau, Amélie. "Les 'Experts' de Casa: Descente dans les labos de la police scientifique." *Le Journal*, February 17–23, 2007, 36–45.

"Amn wa-al-qanun, al-" [Security and Law]. *al-'Alam*, April 15, 1993, 1.

'Anikri, Hamidu al-. "I'adat al-ta'sis" [Re-Foundation]. *Majallat al-Shurta*, February 2005, 3.

"Après le visionnage des cassettes: Nuit d'horreur à la cour d'appel!" *Libération*, March 13, 1993.

Arabi, Nabil. "l'affaire du commissaire Tabit: Un médecin, un propriétaire immoblier et d'autres complices inculpés." *L'Opinion*, February 16, 1993, 1, 3.

———. "l'assainissement a-t-il commencé?" *L'Opinion*, February 21, 1993, 1, 3.

———. "Cauchmardesque: Projection d'un résumé des cassettes traumatisantes." *L'Opinion*, March 13, 1993, 1, 3.

———. "La défense de l'accusé demande une expertise psychiatrique." *L'Opinion*, February 27, 1993, 1, 3.

———. "Histoire des deux étudiantes qui on fait éclaté le scandale." *L'Opinion*, February 19, 1993, 1, 4.

———. "Un médecin, un propriétaire immobilier et d'autres complices inculpés." *L'Opinion*, February 16, 1993, 1, 3.

———. "Peine de mort requise contre Tabit." *L'Opinion*, March 14, 1993, 1, 3.

———. "Le procès de la débauche." *L'Opinion*, February 20, 1993, 1, 5.

———. "Tabit à la cour: 'Il n'y a pas que ma garçonnière, il y a aussi des villas et on fait partout ce qu'on me reproche!'" *L'Opinion*, March 4, 1993, 1, 5.

———. "Tabit encourt désormais la peine de mort." *L'Opinion*, March 7, 1993, 1, 3.

———. "Tabitgate: Ce que Tabit, Dou Naïm, Rabii et Boussairi ont déclaré devant la Cour." *L'Opinion*, March 10, 1993, 1, 3.

———. "Tabitgate: Les indiscrétions d'un huis clos." *L'Opinion*, March 5, 1993, 1, 5.

Ariri, 'Abd al-Rahim, and Mustafa Hurmat Allah. "al-'Anikri yaqud inqilaban dakhil jihaz al-amn" [Laânigri Leads Coup d'État within Security Services]. *al-Baydawi*, January 26, 2005, 4–6.

———. "Asrar inhiyar imbraturiyyat al-'Anikri" [Secrets of Fall of Laânigri's Empire]. *al-Watan*, October 21, 2006, 6–9.

———. "Khuttat al-shurta wa-al-muntakhibin li-fakk al-hisar" [Plan of Police and the Elected to Break Blockade]. *al-Baydawi*, February 23, 2005, 5–11.

Ariri, 'Abd al-Rahim, Fatima Yasin, and Ahmad Busitta. "Qarasanat al-'Anikri amam al-barlaman" [Laânigri's Piracy before Parliament]. *al-Baydawi*, November 17, 2004, 4–7.

'Atawi, Khalid al-. "Ba'd jarimat al-shahr al-madi bi-l-Dar al-Bayda', al-'uthur 'ala juththat fatah muqatta'a ila thalathat ajza' bidun ra's!" [After Last Month's Crime in Casablanca, Discovery of Young Woman's Body Cut Up into Three Parts with No Head!]. *al-Ahdath al-Maghribiyya*, September 11, 2002, 1.

———. "al-Bulis matjish hatta yakun al-dam!" [Cops Don't Come Unless There's Blood!]. *al-Ahdath al-Maghribiyya*, April 22, 2006, 11.

———. "Kayfa yahrus rijal al-amn shawari' al-Dar al-Bayda'!" [How Police Protect Streets of Casablanca!]. *al-Ahdath al-Maghribiyya*, February 12, 2005, 6.

———. "Majallat al-shurta tastanzif juyub rijal al-shurta" [*Police Magazine* Drains Policemen's Pockets]. *al-Sabah*, October 23–24, 2006, 1.

'Atawi, Khalid al-, and 'Abd al-Majid Hashadi. "Hal yumkin tasnif qatl wa-tashwih juthath al-fatayat bi-l-Bayda' fi khanat al-jara'im al-kamila?" [Is It Possible to Classify Killing and Mutilating of Young Women's Bodies as Perfect Crimes?]. *al-Ahdath al-Maghribiyya*, January 4, 2003, 11.

'Awni, 'Abd al-Hamid al-. *al-Janral al-qawi: La'nikri* [The Strong General: Laânigri]. Fas: Manshurat 'Arabiyya, 2003.

"Awwal tasrih hukumi hawl qadiyat Thabit" [First Government Statement about Tabit Affair]. *al-'Alam*, March 12, 1993, 1.

Ayit al-Talib, Ahmad. "Fi hadith khass li-majallat al-shurta qatil Tarudant yahki 'an nafsihi wa-'an tafasil jara'imihi" [Exclusive Discussion with *Police Magazine*: Killer of Taroudant Talks about Himself and Details of His Crimes]. *Majallat al-Shurta*, February 2005, 34–41.

Ayit Bihi, al-Hasan. "'al-Krisaj' yaghzu shawari' al-mudun" ["Crisis" Invades City Streets]. *al-Mustaqill*, December 1–7, 2006, 4–7.

Ayman, Abu. "al-Muqarana bayna al-qanatayn al-ula wa-al-thani" [Comparing First and Second Channels]. *al-Ahdath al-Maghribiyya*, February 19, 2001, 5.

Ayouch, Nabil. *Mektoub*. Morocco: Ali n' Productions, 1997.

Azukah, Mustafa. "Ism al-muttaham al-mudawwan 'ala risala 'uthira 'alayha ma'a al-riffat qada ila i'tiqalihi" [Name of Accused Written on Letter Found with Remains Led to His Arrest]. *al-Ahdath al-Maghribiyya*, September 9, 2004, 1.

———. "al-Muttaham ta'arrad li-i'tida' jinsi fi tufulatihi fa-sa'a li-'l-intiqam'!" [Suspect Faced Sexual Assault in Childhood and Sought "Revenge"!]. *al-Ahdath al-Maghribiyya*, September 11, 2004, 1.

———. "Rijal amn yuhinun al-muwatinin wa-yusarrikhun fi wujuhihim 'al-shari' diyalna!' [Policemen Insult Citizens and Scream in Their Faces "The Street Is Ours!"]. *al-Ahdath al-Maghribiyya*, December 20, 2004, 1, 12.

"Ba'd infidah qadiyat rajul al-amn bi-l-Dar al-Bayda' . . ." [After Exposing Case of Security Official in Casablanca . . .]. *al-Ittihad al-Ishtiraki*, February 20, 1993, 1.

Barini, Muhammad al-. "Hadhihi al-jarida" [This Newspaper]. *al-Ahdath al-Maghribiyya*, October 22, 1998, 1.

Barrada, Muhammad 'Abd al-Rahman. *al-Sihafa al-maktuba bi-l-Maghrib: al-Tawzi' wa-al-intishar* [The Written Press in Morocco: Distribution and Dissemination]. al-Dar al-Bayda': Matba'at Dar al-Nashr al-Maghribiyya, 2002.

Batrah, 'Aziz. "Qararat amniyya jadida tuhaddid tuwajjuhat al-idara al-'amma li-l-amn al-watani" [New Security Decisions Set Directions of DGSN]. *al-Ahdath al-Maghribiyya*, January 31, 2005, 1.

Baudrillard, Jean. *Simulacra and Simulation*. Ann Arbor: University of Michigan Press, 1994.

Bayda', Maktab al-. "Jull al-tasrihat fi al-bahth al-tamhidi li-rijal al-darak 'akkadat istighlal al-nufudh" [All Statements in Preliminary Investigation of Gendarmerie Confirmed Abuse of Power]. *al-'Alam*, February 27, 1993, 1.

Baz, Muhammad al-. *Sihafat al-ithara: al-Siyasa wa-al-din wa-al-jins fi al-suhuf al-misriyya* [The Press of Sensationalism: Politics, Religion, and Sex in Egyptian Newspapers]. al-Qahira: Maktabat Jazirat al-Ward, 2010.

Belftuh, Muhammad. "al-Dha'ar yatamallak al-sukkan" [Fear Seizes Residents]. *al-'Alam*, February 15, 2003, 1.

Belmajdoub, Jamal. *Layali bayda'* [White Nights]. Morocco: 2M, 2005.

Belshukr, 'Abd al-Haqq. "Akhta' al-'Anikri allati qadat ila nihayat shurtat 'Karwatiya'" [Laânigri's Mistakes That Led to End of "Croatians"]. *al-Masa'*, October 28–29, 2006, 2.

Bennani, Driss. "Laânigri, un destin marocain." *Tel Quel*, September 16–22, 2006, 36–44.

"Bidayat istintaq al-Kumisir Thabit min taraf al-mahkama" [Beginning of Interrogation of Commissioner Tabit by the Court]. *al-Ittihad al-Ishtiraki,* March 4, 1993, 1.

Bin Da'ud, 'Abd al-Hamid. "Sihafat al-arsifa: al-irtizaq, al-muyu'a, wa-al-tashwish" [The Sidewalk Press: Profiteering, Dissolution, and Derangement]. *al-Ittihad al-Ishtiraki,* June 17, 1995, 6–8.

Bird, S. Elizabeth. *For Enquiring Minds: A Cultural Study of Supermarket Tabloids.* Knoxville: University of Tennessee Press, 1992.

Biressi, Anita. *Crime, Fear, and the Law in True Crime Stories.* New York: Palgrave, 2001.

Borenstein, Eliot. *Overkill: Sex and Violence in Contemporary Russian Popular Culture.* Ithaca, NY: Cornell University Press, 2008.

Boukhars, Anouar. *Politics in Morocco: Executive Monarchy and Enlightened Authoritarianism.* London: Routledge, 2011.

Bourqia, Rahma. "The Cultural Legacy of Power in Morocco." In *In the Shadow of the Sultan,* edited by Rahma Bourqia and Susan Gilson Miller, 243–258. Cambridge, MA: Harvard University Press, 1999.

Boyd, Douglas A. *Broadcasting in the Arab World: A Survey of the Electronic Media in the Middle East.* 3rd ed. Ames: Iowa State University Press, 1999.

Braude, Joseph. *The Honored Dead: A Story of Friendship, Murder, and the Search for Truth in the Arab World.* New York: Spiegel & Grau, 2011.

Brownlee, Jason. *Authoritarianism in an Age of Democratization.* Cambridge: Cambridge University Press, 2007.

Budali, Muhammad al-. "Tajawuzat shurtat al-qurb tazhur al-samar wa-al-tajawwul fi Radaman bi-Sala" [Excesses of Police of Proximity Prohibit Evening Chats and Strolls during Ramadan in Salé]. *al-Ahdath al-Maghribiyya,* October 20, 2005, 9.

Bukzul, al-Sadiq. "al-Muktabar al-watani li-l-shurta al-'ilmiyya bi-l-Dar al-Bayda' yanfatah 'ala al-sihafa: 'Ulama' warrathiyyun wa-biyulujiyyun yata'aqqabun al-mujrimin" [National Headquarters of Scientific Police in Casablanca Is Opened to the Press: DNA and Bio-Scientists Track Down Criminals]. *al-Ahdath al-Maghribiyya,* February 15, 2007, 19.

Cammett, Melani Claire. *Globalization and Business Politics in Arab North Africa: A Comparative Perspective.* Cambridge: Cambridge University Press, 2007.

Chami, Youssef. "Qu'est-ce que la police de proximité?" *Police Magazine,* September 2005, 70.

Chankou, Abdellah. "Donnez-nous du sensationnel!" *Maroc Hebdo International,* March 26–April 1, 1993, 15.

Chaoui, Abdel Wahab. "Tabit connection." *Maroc Hebdo International,* March 5–11, 1993, 6.

Claisse, Alain. "Makhzen Traditions and Administrative Channels." In *The Political Economy of Morocco,* edited by I. William Zartman, 34–58. New York: Praeger, 1987.

Colla, Elliott. "Anxious Advocacy: The Novel, the Law, and Extrajudicial Appeals in Egypt." *Public Culture* 17, no. 3 (2005): 417–423.

Conway-Long, Don. "Sexism and Rape Culture in Moroccan Social Discourse." *Journal of Men's Studies* 10, no. 3 (2002): 361–371.

"Dabt imbratur al-mukhaddirat wa-bi-hawzatihi amwal wa-asliha nariyya" [Arrest of Drug Emperor with Cash and Firearms]. *al-Yawm al-Siyasi,* September 27, 1993, 3.

Daoud, Zakya. *Maroc: Les années de plomb, 1958–1988: Chroniques d'une résistance.* Houilles: Manucius, 2007.
"Des extraits des cassettes visionnées: Inceste, défloration, sadisme à l'état brut." *Libération,* March 14–15, 1993, 6.
"Dhabah al-'ajuz alladhi kan yumaris 'alayhi al-jins tiwal 19 sana li-'annahu talabahu bi-istimrar al-shudhudh al-jinsi baynahuma raghma annahu tab min dhalika" [He Butchered Old Man Violating Him for 19 Years because He Asked Him to Continue Sexual Deviance between Them, Even Though He Renounced It]. *al-Muwasil al-Siyasi,* September 15, 1995, 8.
Douglas, John, and Mark Olshaker. *Mind Hunter: Inside the FBI's Elite Serial Crime Unit.* New York: Pocket Books, 1996.
Dove, George N. *The Police Procedural.* Bowling Green, OH: Bowling Green University Popular Press, 1982.
Doyle, Aaron. *Arresting Images: Crime and Policing in Front of the Television Camera.* Toronto: University of Toronto Press, 2003.
Driss, Bennani, and Abdellatif El Azizi. "Cette police qui vous veut du bien." *Tel Quel,* January 15–21, 2005, 22–27.
Dwyer, Kevin. *Beyond Casablanca: M. A. Tazi and the Adventure of Moroccan Cinema.* Bloomington: Indiana University Press, 2004.
El Atouabi, Majdoulein. "La fin du carnaval." *Maroc Hebo International,* October 20–26, 2006, 28–31.
Ericson, Richard Victor, Patricia M. Baranek, and Janet B. L. Chan. *Negotiating Control: A Study of News Sources.* Toronto: University of Toronto Press, 1989.
———. *Representing Order: Crime, Law, and Justice in the News Media.* Toronto: University of Toronto Press, 1991.
Fadili, Adil. *al-Shahida* [The Witness]. Morocco: 2M, 2003.
"Fata ittafaqat ma'a akh khatibiha 'ala qatl ummiha min ajli ikhfa' fadihat al-haml bi-Wujda" [Girl in Oujda Killed Mother with Fiancé's Brother to Hide Scandal of Her Pregnancy]. *al-Yawm al-Siyasi,* June 19, 1994, 9.
"Fi lahzat taysh wa-nazwa, shabb wadi' yatahawwal ila qatil" [In Moment of Recklessness and Capriciousness, Mild-Mannered Young Man Turns into Killer]. *al-Yawm al-Siyasi,* December 31, 1995, 2.
"Fi tahaddi jadid li-amn al-Bayda': juththa jadida muqatta'a ila juz'ayn wa-bi-dun malamih wa-basamat!" [New Challenge to Casa Police: New Body Cut in Two without Features or Fingerprints!]. *al-Ahdath al-Maghribiyya,* February 13, 2003, 1.
Fiske, John. *Understanding Popular Culture.* Boston: Unwin Hyman, 1989.
Fox, Richard Logan, Robert W. Van Sickel, and Thomas L. Steiger. *Tabloid Justice: Criminal Justice in an Age of Media Frenzy.* 2nd ed. Boulder, CO: Lynne Rienner, 2007.
García-Roza, L. A. *A Window in Copacabana.* Translated by Benjamin Moser. New York: Henry Holt, 2005.
Ghaytumi, 'Abd Allah. "I'tirafat 'Saffah' Tarudant (5/5)" [Confessions of "Killer" of Taroudant, Part 5]. *al-Sabah,* October 16–17, 2004, 5.
———. "al-Mahdar al-kamil li-i'tirafat Saffah al-Jadida" [Complete Police Report of Confessions of Killer of El Jadida]. *al-Sabah,* June 14, 2001, 1.
———. "Qatil zall taliqan wa-bari'an fi al-sijn" [Killer Remained Free While Two Innocent Men Were in Jail]. *al-Sabah,* June 11, 2001, 1.

———. "Saffah al-Jadida i'tarafa wa-'bi-damm barid' bi-jara'imihi'" [Killer of El Jadida Confessed to His Crimes "In Cold Blood"]. *al-Sabah*, June 20, 2001, 1.

———. "'Saffah al-Nisa" bi-l-Jadida yaqul inna dafi' irtikab al-jara'im lam yakun al-sariqa bal al-'ajz al-jinsi" ["Killer of Women" in El Jadida Says Motive for Committing Crimes Wasn't Theft But Impotence]. *al-Sabah*, October 2, 2001, 1.

Glynn, Kevin. *Tabloid Culture: Trash Taste, Popular Power, and the Transformation of American Television*. Durham, NC: Duke University Press, 2000.

Gramsci, Antonio. *Selections from the Prison Notebooks of Antonio Gramsci*. Translated by Quintin Hoare and Geoffery Nowell Smith. New York: International, 1971.

Habermas, Jürgen. *The Structural Transformation of the Public Sphere: An Inquiry into a Category of Bourgeois Society*. Translated by Thomas Burger with the assistance of Frederick Lawrence. Cambridge, MA: MIT Press, 1989 [1962].

"Hadha al-khabar" [This News]. *al-Ittihad al-Ishtiraki*, February 6, 1993.

"Haditha khatira bi-l-nisba li-wad'iyya murtakibiha wa-li-'alaqatiha bi-a'rad al-muwatinin" [Grave Incident in Terms of Status of Perpetrator and Connection to Citizens' Honor]. *al-Muharrir*, July 16, 1980, 4.

Hafidh, Muhammad. "Shurtat al-mawt" [Police of Death]. *al-Sahifa*, June 9–15, 2006, 3.

Hafiz, Asma Husayn. *Nashr hawadith wa-jara'im al-mar'a: Dirasa tahliliyya maydaniyya bi-l-tatbiq 'ala jaridat Akhbar al-Hawadith khilala 'am* [Publishing Women's Crimes: An Analytical Field Study Applied to the Newspaper *Crime News* during a Year]. al-Qahira: Sharikat al-Faris li-l-Nashr al-Maktabi, 1993.

Hafyani, Radwan. "Dahaya al-Wad al-Wa'ir yabhathun 'an qatilihim" [Victims of Wad Waeer Search for Their Killer]. *al-Sabah*, August 30, 2004, 5.

Hafyani, Radwan, al-Husayn Yazi, and 'Abd al-'Ali Tujid. "al-'Uthur 'ala juththat shabba muqatta'a wa-mu'abba'a fi akyas bi-l-Dar al-Bayda'" [Discovery of Young Woman's Body Cut Up and Packed into Bags in Casablanca]. *al-Sabah*, August 16, 2002, 1.

"Hala tu'arri waqi'an" [A Situation That Lays Bare a Reality]. *al-'Alam*, February 28, 1993, 1, 9.

"Halaqat musalsal al-fada'ih mutawasila" [Episodes of Series of Scandals Are Continuing]. *al-Ittihad al-Ishtiraki*, April 1, 1993, 1.

Hall, Stuart, Chas Critcher, Tony Jefferson, John Clarke, and Brian Roberts. *Policing the Crisis: Mugging, the State, and Law and Order*. London: Macmillan, 1978.

"Halqa jadida min silsilat qatl shabbat wa-taqti' juthathihinna bi-l-Dar al-Bayda'" [New Part in Series of Murdering Young Women and Cutting Up Their Bodies in Casablanca]. *al-Ahdath al-Maghribiyya*, December 4, 2002, 1.

Halttunen, Karen. *Murder Most Foul: The Killer and the American Gothic Imagination*. Cambridge, MA: Harvard University Press, 1998.

Hamdani, Hassan, and Ayla Mrabet. "Hassan TV: 50 ans de propagande." *Tel Quel*, April 18–24, 2009, 54–64.

Hamdouchi, Abdelilah. *The Final Bet*. Translated by Jonathan Smolin. Cairo: American University in Cairo Press, 2008.

Hamdouchi, Miloudi. *Le régime juridique de l'enquête policière: Étude critique*. Rabat: Renald, 1999.

Hamdushi, 'Abd al-Ilah al-. *al-Mustanzafun* [Bled Dry]. al-Rabat: al-Bukili, 2009.

Hamdushi, Miludi, and 'Abd al-Ilah al-Hamdushi. *al-Hut al-a'ma* [The Blind Whale]. al-Rabat: 'Ukaz, 1997.

Hammoudi, Abdellah. *Master and Disciple: The Cultural Foundations of Moroccan Authoritarianism.* Chicago: University of Chicago Press, 1997.

Hanani, Yusuf. "Ayy afaq li-l-film al-bulisi bi-l-maghrib?" [What Horizon Is There for Police Film in Morocco?]. *al-Ittihad al-Ishtiraki,* April 30, 2001, 6.

Hanbali, Driss. "Affaire de viol de mineurs: La parole aux citoyens." *L'Opinion,* April 27, 1993, 1, 3.

———. "Azemmour: Affaire de viol de mineurs." *L'Opinion,* April 15, 1993, 1.

Hashadi, 'Abd al-Majid. "Akthar min tis'in unsuran min ajhizat al-amn al-mukhtalifa tata'aqqab Saffah Tarudant" [Over Ninety Investigators from Different Security Branches Tracking Killer of Taroudant]. *al-Ahdath al-Maghribiyya,* August 27, 2004, 1.

———. "Baqaya al-juthath al-thamani allati 'uthira 'alayha li-atfal dhukur tatarawah a'maruhum bayna 13 wa-17 sana" [Age of Remains of Eight Bodies of Male Children That Were Discovered Ranges between 13 and 17 Years]. *al-Ahdath al-Maghrbiyya,* August 24, 2004, 1.

———. "Dahayahu min al-nisa' wa-uslububu fi al-qatl wahid wa-dhika'uhu ja'alahu bi-man'an 'an al-'iqab!" [His Victims were Women, His Method in Killing Was the Same, and His Intelligence Kept Him Away from Punishment!]. *al-Ahdath al-Maghribiyya,* June 15, 2001, 5.

———. "al-Dar al-Bayda' tafrid ta'amulan istithna'iyyan wa-al-jarima tashhad tahawwulan naw'iyyan" [Casablanca Imposes Exceptional Treatment as Crime Is Witnessing Qualitative Transformation]. *al-Ahdath al-Maghribiyya,* January 4, 2003, 10.

———. "Fi hiwar ma'a al-tabib al-shar'i Sa'id al-Wahliyya" [Interview with Medical Examiner Saeed Louahlia]. *al-Ahdath al-Maghribiyya,* September 25, 2002, 1, 12.

———. "Masadir tarjah an yakun 'adad dahaya mudhbahat al-atfal bi-Tarudant akbar bi-kathir min al-halat al-muktashafa" [Sources Find It Likely That Number of Butchered Child Victims in Taroudant Is Much Higher Than Reported Cases]. *al-Ahdath al-Maghribiyya,* August 26, 2004, 1, 12.

———. "Mish'awidh min Maknas: Rihla min al-nasb ila al-qatl! (1): Taqrir 'ala maktab al-'amid" [Magician from Meknès: Journey from Swindling to Murder! (1): Report on Commissioner's Desk]. *al-Ahdath al-Maghribiyya,* November 6, 2002, 9.

———. "Mish'awidh min Maknas: Rihla min al-nasb ila al-qatl! (7): Fi muwajaha ma'a al-mish'awidh 'Qasim'" [Magician from Meknès: Journey from Swindling to Murder! (7): Confrontation with Magician Qasim]. *al-Ahdath al-Maghribiyya,* November 12, 2002, 9.

———. "Mish'awidh min Maknas: Rihla min al-nasb ila al-qatl!" [Magician from Meknès: Journey from Swindling to Murder!]. *al-Ahdath al-Maghribiyya,* November 6–December 5, 2002, 9.

———. "Qadaya taht al-mijhar (6): Wazir al-'adl yuqabbir al-milaff wa-al-'adala tudin al-mutawarritin" [Cases under the Microscope (6): Minister of Justice Buries the File but Justice Convicts Those Involved]. *al-Ahdath al-Maghribiyya,* December 2, 2000, 7.

———. "Qatil dhaki waqa'a fi shirr a'malihi!" [A Smart Killer Who Fell in the Evil of His Deeds!]. *al-Ahdath al-Maghribiyya,* February 11, 2000, 5.

———. "Risala min imra'a majhula tujri al-tahqiq bi-sha'niha tuhaddid 'dawafi'' al-qatl" [Investigation Moves Concerning Letter from Unknown Woman That Establishes "Motives" of Murder]. *al-Ahdath al-Maghribiyya,* February 15, 2003, 1.

———. "al-Risala al-tamwihiyya tuhaddid dawafiʿ al-jarima al-muzdawija wa-sariqat al-dahiya jaʾat aradan" [Feigned Letter Confirms Motives of Double Crime and Theft from Victim Happened by Chance]. *al-Ahdath al-Maghribiyya*, March 16, 2003, 1.

———. "al-Sura al-tarkibiyya li-dahiyat al-Maʿarif tuʾakkid al-tuhma ʿala haris al-ʿimara al-muntahar" [Constructed Image of Maârif Victim Confirms Charge against Building Guard That Committed Suicide]. *al-Ahdath al-Maghribiyya*, March 15, 2003, 1.

———. "al-Tahdid al-nihaʾi li-aʿmar al-dahaya yuʾakkid ʿala tarawuhiha bayna 10 wa-15 sana" [Final Determination of Victims' Ages Confirms Range between 10 and 15 Years]. *al-Ahdath al-Maghribiyya*, August 31, 2004, 1.

———. "al-Tahqiq maʿa ʿadad min al-ashkhas dhawi al-miyulat al-jinsiyya al-shadhdha" [Investigating Number of People with Sadistic Sexual Predilections]. *al-Ahdath al-Maghribiyya*, September 1, 2004, 1.

———. "Tamshit manatiq jadida bi-Tarudant binaʾ ʿala nataʾij al-khibra al-mujra ʿala al-turab al-ʿaliqa bi-l-rifat" [Combing New Regions of Taroudant Based on Results of Test Conducted on Soil Attached to Remains]. *al-Ahdath al-Maghribiyya*, September 2, 2004, 1.

———. "Taqrir al-tabib al-sharʿi yujad fi marahil mutaqaddima li-tahdid huwiyat al-dahiya" [Medical Examiner's Report in Advanced Stages to Identify Victim]. *al-Ahdath al-Maghribiyya*, December 15, 2002, 1.

"Hasilat al-tadakhkhulat al-midaniyya li-l-majmuʿat al-hadariyya li-l-amn" [Results of GUS Field Interventions]. *Majallat al-Shurta*, November 2005, 66.

Horkheimer, Max, and Theodor W Adorno. *Dialect of Enlightenment: Philosophical Fragments*. Translated by Edmund Jephcott. Stanford, CA: Stanford University Press, 2002.

"Hunaka masʾulun amniyyun kanu ʿala ʿilm bi-l-afʿal al-shaniʿa al-mansuba ila al-muddaʿu Thabit" [There Are Security Officials Who Knew about Abominable Acts Attributed to Tabit]. *al-Ittihad al-Ishtiraki*, February 22, 1993, 1.

"Hunaka taghtiyya kan yahza biha Thabit . . . min fawq!" [Tabit Was Enjoying Cover-Up . . . from Above!]. *al-ʿAlam*, March 12, 1993, 1.

"Ihalat al-masʾul al-amni ʿala ghurfat al-jinayat bi-l-Dar al-Baydaʾ" [Transfer of Security Official to Criminal Chamber in Casablanca]. *al-Ittihad al-Ishtiraki*, February 10, 1993.

"Iʿtidaʾ ʿala muwatin bi-l-Dar al-Baydaʾ wa-akhar bi-Maknas wa-al-nuqat al-sawdaʾ taht rahmat al-munharifin" [Aggression against Citizen in Casablanca and Another in Meknès, Black Spots at Criminals' Mercy]. *al-Ahdath al-Maghribiyya*, January 17, 2005, 1.

"Iʿtiqal shakhs qatala khams nisaʾ bi-l-Jadida" [Arrest of Person Who Killed Five Women in El Jadida]. *al-Ahdath al-Maghribiyya*, June 9, 2001, 1.

"Ila mata tastamirr silsilat al-juthath al-muqattaʿa bi-l-Baydaʾ?" [How Long Will Series of Cut Up Bodies Continue in Casa?]. *al-Ahdath al-Maghribiyya*, January 27, 2003, 1.

"Ilqaʾ al-qabd ʿala ʿisaba taʿtarid sabil al-muwatinin wa-tastawla ʿala bataʾiqihim al-wataniyya li-tunsib bi-ha ʿala al-akharin bi-l-Dar al-Baydaʾ" [Arrest of Gang That Obstructed Path of Citizens and Took Their National ID Cards to Swindle Others with Them in Casablanca]. *al-Miʿad al-Siyasi*, November 2, 1994, 2.

"Ittijahat al-ʿamma li-l-ijram khilal sanat 2005, al-" [General Directions of Criminality during 2005]. *Majallat al-Shurta*, July–August 2006, 74.

Jabru, 'Abd al-Latif. "Suqut judran Barlin wa-nihayat al-khawf" [Fall of the Berlin Wall and the End of Fear]. *al-Ittihad al-Ishtiraki*, March 17, 1993, 3.
"Jalalat al-Malik yu'lin fi khitabihi ba'd hafl al-wila' awwal ams . . ." [His Majesty the King, in His Speech after Celebration of Allegiance Yesterday, Announces . . .]. *al-Ittihad al-Ishtiraki*, March 29, 1993, 2.
Jama'i, Khalid al-. "Risala maftuha ila zamili al-'Anikri" [Open Letter to My Colleague Laânigri]. *al-Nahar al-Maghribiyya*, February 4, 2005, 1.
Jari, Umar, and 'Abd Allah Ghaytumi. "Tafasil muthira hawla qadiyat 'Saffah Nisa'" al-Jadida" [Sensational Details about Case of "Killer of Women" of El Jadida]. *al-Sabah*, June 12, 2001, 1.
"Jarima allati hazzat bi-'umq al-mujtama' al-maghribi bi-kull mukawwinatihi, al-" [The Crime That Profoundly Shook Moroccan Society in All Its Foundations]. *al-'Alam*, March 17, 1993, 1.
Jawhari, Yunis al-. "Akhaf min al-shurta" [I'm Afraid of the Police]. *Majallat al-Shurta*, February 2005, 50.
Jenkins, Philip. *Moral Panic: Changing Concepts of the Child Molester in Modern America*. New Haven, CT: Yale University Press, 1998.
———. *Using Murder: The Social Construction of Serial Homicide*. New York: Aldine de Gruyter, 1994.
"Jumu' ghafira min al-muwatinin yatawafidun 'ala zawiyat al-Sharif Ridwan bi-Sidi Qasim" [Large Groups of Citizens Flock to Shrine of Sherif Redwan in Sidi Qasim]. *al-Mi'ad al-Siyasi*, December 28, 1994, 9.
K., '. "al-Idara al-'amma li-l-amn al-watani tuwajih tafashshiyan mulahizan li-l-inhiraf" [DGSN Faces Noticeable Spread of Criminality]. *al-Sabah*, October 23–24, 2004, 3.
Kamp, David. "The Tabloid Decade." *Vanity Fair*, February 1999.
"Khawf yusaytir 'ala fatayat al-Dar al-Bayda' min an yatahawwalna ila kumat lahm fi kis balastiki aswad" [Fear of Turning Into Pile of Flesh in Black Plastic Bag Seizes Young Women of Casablanca]. *al-Sabah*, September 14–15, 2002, 5.
Khayat, Rita El. *La folie: El Hank-Casablanca*. Casablanca: EDDIF, 2000.
King, Stephen J. *The New Authoritarianism in the Middle East and North Africa*. Bloomington: Indiana University Press, 2009.
Kraidy, Marwan. *Reality Television and Arab Politics: Contention in Public Life*. Cambridge: Cambridge University Press, 2010.
Krajicek, David J. *Scooped!: Media Miss Real Story on Crime while Chasing Sex, Sleaze, and Celebrities*. New York: Columbia University Press, 1998.
Krivich, Mikhail, and Ol'gert Ol'gin. *Comrade Chikatilo: The Psychopathology of Russia's Notorious Serial Killer*. Translated by Todd P. Blundeau. Fort Lee, NJ: Barricade Books, 1993.
"Kumisir Thabit amam al-mahkama: 'La tujad faqat shaqqati, hunak aydan filat', al-" [Commissioner Tabit before Court: "There's Not Only My Apartment But Also Villas"]. *al-'Alam*, March 5, 1993, 1.
Laabi, Chafik. "Une réussite controversée." *Maroc Hebdo International*, 1997, 21.
Lakhmari, Noureddine. *al-Qadiya* [The Case]. Morocco: 2M, 2006.
Lawrence, Regina G. *The Politics of Force: Media and the Construction of Police Brutality*. Berkeley: University of California Press, 2000.
Lopez, Shaun T. "Madams, Murders, and the Media: *Akhbar al-Hawadith* and the Emergence of a Mass Culture in 1920s Egypt." In *Re-Envisioning Egypt: 1919–1952*, edited

by Arthur Goldschmidt, Amy J. Johnson, and Barak A. Salmoni, 373–397. Cairo: American University in Cairo Press, 2005.
"Lughz al-juththa al-rabi'a fi tariqihi ila al-hall ba'd i'tiraf al-muttahima!" [Puzzle of Fourth Body on Its Way to Being Solved after Female Suspect's Confession!]. *al-Ahdath al-Maghribiyya*, January 28, 2003, 1.
Lyons, William. *The Politics of Community Policing: Rearranging the Power to Punish*. Ann Arbor: University of Michigan Press, 1999.
M. L. "al-Raqaba wa-shahadat al-zur fi 'Duziyim' [Censorship and False Testimony at 2M]. *al-Ahdath al-Maghribiyya*, September 29, 2003, 9.
Mahfouz, Naguib. *The Thief and the Dogs*. Edited and revised by John Rodenbeck. Translated by Trevor Le Gassick and M. M. Badawi. New York: Doubleday, 1989 [1961].
Mankell, Henning. *Faceless Killers*. Translated by Steven T. Murray. New York: New Press, 1997.
Manning, Peter K. *Policing Contingencies*. Chicago: University of Chicago Press, 2003.
MAP. "Sahib al-Jallala yu'ayyin al-Sayyid Ahmad al-Midawi mudiran 'amman jadidan li-l-amn al-watani" [His Majesty Announces Mr. Ahmad Midaoui as New General Director of National Security]. *Majallat al-Amn al-Watani*, no. 173 (1993): 2–3.
"Marakiz amn al-qurb ma zalat khaliyya" [PPPs Still Vacant]. *al-Ahdath al-Maghribiyya*, September 11, 2005, 1.
"Masdar amni mus'ul . . . dawafi' al-jarimatayn akhlaqiyya wa-la-majal li-l-rabt baynahuma" [Security Official Source . . . Motives for Two Crimes Are Moral and There Is No Way to Link Them]. *al-Ahdath al-Maghribiyya*, September 16, 2002, 1.
"Mashhad rahib bi-zawiyat al-Sharif Ridwan" [Frightening Scene at Shrine of Sherif Redwan]. *al-Mi'ad al-Siyasi*, January 18, 1995, 10.
"Mat'am Sufiya wa-al-hut al-a'ma sharitan talfizyan jadidan" [*Sofia's Restaurant* and *The Blind Whale*, Two New Téléfilms]. *al-Ahdath al-Maghribiyya*, March 4, 2001, 9.
Miftah, Nur al-Din. "al-Jalasat al-akthar basha'a wa-maratuniyya fi milaff al-Kumisir Thabit" [Most Disgusting and Longest Sessions in File of Commissioner Tabit]. *al-Ittihad al-Ishtiraki*, March 13, 1993, 1, 8.
———. "Qadiyat al-Kumisir 'Thabit' tusta'naf yawm al-ithnayn al-qadim [Affair of Commissioner Tabit Will Resume Next Monday]. *al-Ittihad al-Ishtiraki*, March 6, 1993, 1.
———. "Rafa' sirriyyat al-jalasat 'and bidayat al-murafa'at" [Lifting Secrecy of Sessions at Start of Defense Arguments]. *al-Ittihad al-Ishtiraki*, March 12, 1993, 1, 12.
———. "Tariqan dayyiqan li-istimrar al-milaff maftuhan" [Two Narrow Paths for Continuing the File Are Open]. *al-Ittihad al-Ishtiraki*, March 27, 1993, 1.
"Milaff 'amid al-shurta al-mumtaz wa-man ma'ahu amam ghurfat al-jinayat bi-l-Dar al-Bayda'" [File of First-Rank Police Commissioner and Those with Him before Criminal Court in Casablanca]. *al-Ittihad al-Ishtiraki*, February 19, 1993, 1.
Miller, D. A. *The Novel and the Police*. Berkeley: University of California Press, 1988.
"Min al-hubb ma qatal" [It's Love That Kills]. *al-'Alam*, December 27, 1995, 1.
"Min yawm li-akhar" [From Day to Day]. *al-Ittihad al-Ishtiraki*, March 15, 1993, 1.
Misbah, Tawfiq, Yusif Khatib, and Mustafa Hurmat Allah. "Fara'inat al-'Anikri" [Laânigri's Pharaohs]. *al-Baydawi*, October 24, 2005, 6–9.
Miyabe, Miyuki. *All She Was Worth*. Translated by Alfred Birnbaum. Tokyo: Kodansha America, 1996.

Muh Lahsan, Awsi. "Yawm ma'a al-markaz al-watani li-l-shurta al-'ilmiyya: Khubara' musallihun bi-l-taqniyya li-kashf alghaz al-jara'im" [Day with National Center for Scientific Police: Experts Armed with Technique for Uncovering Puzzles of Crimes]. *al-Ahdath al-Maghribiyya,* April 3, 2005, 6.

"Mujrim 'Shatir' hawala ightisab imra'a bi-Asfi fa-wajada nafsahu dakhil al-sijn, al-" ["Clever" Criminal Tried to Rape Woman in Asfi and Found Himself in Jail]. *al-Yawm al-Siyasi,* June 19, 1994, 8.

Murley, Jean. *The Rise of True Crime: Twentieth Century Murder and American Popular Culture.* Westport, CT: Praeger, 2008.

"Nass al-kamil li-mahdar al-shurta al-qida'iyya alladhi tudammin al-i'tirafat al-awwaliyya li-'Saffah al-Jadida', al-" [Complete Text of Police Report That Contains Preliminary Confessions of "Killer of El Jadida]. *al-Sabah,* June 14, 2001, 2.

Orlando, Valérie K. *Francophone Voices of the "New Morocco" in Film and Print: (Re)presenting a Society in Transition.* New York: Palgrave Macmillan, 2009.

———. *Screening Morocco: Contemporary Film in a Changing Society.* Ohio University Research in International Studies. Athens: Ohio University Press, 2011.

Ouardighi, Samir El. *L'Affaire Tabit et la presse marocaine.* Rabat: Arrisala, 1997.

Panek, Leroy. "Post-War American Police Fiction." In *The Cambridge Companion to Crime Fiction,* edited by Martin Priestman. Cambridge: Cambridge University Press, 2003.

Perrault, Gilles. *Notre ami le roi.* Paris: Gallimard, 1990.

Pope, David Paul. *The Deeds of My Fathers: How My Grandfather and Father Built New York and Created the Tabloid World of Today.* New York: Philip Turner, 2010.

Powers, Richard Gid. *G-Men: Hoover's FBI in American Popular Culture.* Carbondale: Southern Illinois University Press, 1983.

"Qatal 'dabit shurta' wa-fasal juththatahu ila atraf wa-rama bi-ha fi bi'r bi-'Ayn al-Shaqq bi-l-Dar al-Bayda'" [He Killed a "Police Detective," Cut Up His Body, and Threw It in a Well in Aïn Chok in Casablanca]. *al-Muwasil al-Siyasi,* March 17, 1995, 9.

"Qatalahu bi-sikkin wa-irtada sirwalahu wa-hadha'ahu thumma ladhdh bi-l-firar bi-Maknas" [He Stabbed Him to Death, Put on His Pants and Shoes, and Tried to Flee in Meknès]. *al-Muwasil al-Siyasi,* March 24, 1995, 8.

"Qatilat 'Lajirund' la tazal majhulat al-huwiya" [Woman Killed in La Gironde Still Unidentified]. *al-Ahdath al-Maghribiyya,* September 13, 2002, 1.

Rami, Muhammad al-. "al-'Uthur 'ala juththa jadida mujazza'a wa-muwazza'a bi-shawari' al-Dar al-Bayda'" [Discovery of New Body Mutilated and Distributed in Casablanca Streets]. *al-Ittihad al-Ishtiraki,* February 13, 2003, 1.

Rao, Ursula. "Empowerment through Local News Making: Studying the Media/Public Interface in India." In *The Anthropology of News and Journalism: Global Perspectives,* edited by S. Elizabeth Bird, 100–115. Bloomington: Indiana University Press, 2010.

Reeves, Jimmie L., and Richard Campbell. *Cracked Coverage: Television News, the Anti-Cocaine Crusade, and the Reagan Legacy.* Durham, NC: Duke University Press, 1994.

Ressler, Robert K., Ann Wolbert Burgess, and John E. Douglas. *Sexual Homicide: Patterns and Motives.* Lexington, MA: Lexington Books, 1988.

Ressler, Robert K., and Tom Schachtman. *Whoever Fights Monsters: My Twenty Years Tracking Serial Killers for the FBI.* New York: St. Martin's Press, 1993.

Rhanja, Hasan. *al-Hut al-a'ma* [The Blind Whale]. Morocco: 2M, 2001.
S. A. "Le gardien suicidé était probablement un tueur en série." *L'Opinion,* March 5, 2003, 1.
Saadi, Meryem, and Karim Boukhari. "2M l'histoire secrète." *Tel Quel,* March 7–13, 2009, 58–66.
Saghir, Hadin. "Mulahazat 'ala al-hamish" [Side Notes]. *al-Ittihad al-Ishtiraki,* December 19, 1993, 4.
Samil, 'Abd al-'Aziz. "al-Tawasul dakhil mu'assasat al-shurta" [Communication in the Police Establishment]. *Majallat al-Shurta,* January 2006, 2.
"Sayyida mutazawwija taqtul 'ashiqaha al-shurti bi-tariqa fazi'a bi-madinat Khuribga" [Married Woman Kills Her Cop Lover in Abominable Way in Khouribga]. *al-Mi'ad al-Siyasi,* January 18, 1995, 4.
Schmid, David. *Natural Born Celebrities: Serial Killers in American Culture.* Chicago: University of Chicago Press, 2005.
Schudson, Michael. *The Sociology of the News.* 2nd ed. New York: W. W. Norton, 2011.
Seltzer, Mark. *True Crime: Observations on Violence and Modernity.* New York: Routledge, 2007.
"Shabb dhu sawabiq yaqtul abahu wa-akhahu bi-sabab niza' hawla barrad shayy bi-Sidi Musa fi Sala" [Young Man with Priors Kills Father and Brother in Fight Over Pot of Mint Tea in Sidi Musa in Salé]. *al-Muwasil al-Siyasi,* November 30, 1996, 9.
"Shabb min Sidi Qasim yamtalik qudra khariqa fi sir' al-jann wa-ibtal al-sihr wa-al-taqaf wa-amrad ukhra" [Young Man from Sidi Qasim Has Unheard-of Ability in Fighting Demons and Thwarting Black Magic, Thaqqaf, and Other Illnesses]. *al-Mi'ad al-Siyasi,* December 21, 1994, 9.
"Shabb yuhawil al-intihar fawq 'amud kahraba'i bi-Maknas" [Youth Attempts Suicide on Top Electric Pole in Meknès]. *al-Yawm al-Siyasi,* November 22, 1993, 6.
Shawi, 'Abd al-Qadir al-. *al-Shaytan wa-al-zawba'a: Qadiyat al-'Amid Thabit fi al-sihafa* [Satan and the Storm: The Affair of Commissioner Tabit in the Press]. al-Rabat: al-Mawja, 1995.
Shuqrun, 'Abd Allah. *al-Idha'a wa-al-talfaza al-maghribiyya: Waqa'i' wa-dhikriyat* [Moroccan Radio and Television: Facts and Memories]. al-Dar al-Bayda': Matba'at al-Najah al-Jadida, 1999.
"Shurta bi-Maknas tada' haddan li-'isaba taqum bi-sariqat al-sayyarat, al-" [Police in Meknès Put End to Gang Stealing Cars]. *al-Mi'ad al-Siyasi,* November 2, 1994, 4.
Simpson, Philip L. *Psycho Paths: Tracking the Serial Killer through Contemporary American Film and Fiction.* Carbondale: Southern Illinois University Press, 2000.
Skir, Najib. "Dawr wasa'il al-i'lam fi al-ta'rif bi-mazahir al-jarima dakhil al-mujtama'" [Role of Media in Making Phenomena of Crime inside Society Known]. *Akhbar al-Hawadith,* March 13, 1996, 12.
———. "al-Jara'id al-mustaqilla fi ufuq niqaba mustaqilla" [Independent Newspapers in Horizon of Independent Union]. *al-Maw'id al-Siyasi,* May 15, 1993, 2.
———. "Kathrat al-ta'ati li-l-'ilaj al-ruhani maradduhu qusur al-tibb al-'adwi wa-al-tibb al-nafsani" [Underlying Reason for Great Frequency Spiritual Treatment Is Deficiency of Medical and Psychological Medicine]. *Akhbar al-Hawadith,* January 16, 1996, 12.
———. "Li-kull hurriyya hudud" [Every Freedom Has Limits]. *al-Muwasil al-Siyasi,* October 23, 1993, 2.

——. "Wujud al-intibah li-hadhihi al-zahira al-khatira" [The Necessity of Heeding This Dangerous Phenomenon]. *al-Muwasil al-Siyasi,* November 6, 1993, 2.

——. "Zahirat hawadith al-'unf al-muwajjih didd al-walidin bi-l-Maghrib fi tazayud mustamirr!" [Phenomenon of Crimes of Violence against Parents in Morocco Is Continuously Escalating!]. *al-Yawm al-Siyasi,* December 17, 1994, 10.

Sloan, Bill. *"I Watched a Wild Hog Eat My Baby!": A Colorful History of Tabloids and Their Cultural Impact.* Amherst, NY: Prometheus Books, 2001.

Slyomovics, Susan. *The Performance of Human Rights in Morocco.* Philadelphia: University of Pennsylvania Press, 2005.

Smaili, Abdelmajid. "Un distributeur en colère: Mohammed Berrada, directeur général de Sapress." *Maroc Hebdo International,* March 26–April 1, 1993, 14–15.

——. "La press et le procès des commissaires." *Maroc Hebdo International,* March 5–11, 1993, 3.

Smolin, Jonathan. "Aïcha Mekki." In *Dictionary of African Biography,* edited by Henry Louis Gates and Emmanuel Akyeampong. Oxford: Oxford University Press, 2011.

——. "Anxious Openings: Globalization in the Arabic Police Novel." Unpublished manuscript, last modified November 29, 2012. Microsoft Word file.

——. "Burning the Past: Moroccan Cinema of Illegal Immigration." *South Central Review* 28, no. 1 (2011): 74–89.

——. "Nabil Ayouch." In *Contemporary Arab Filmmakers: Political Protest and Social Critique,* edited by Josef Gugler. Bloomington: Indiana University Press, forthcoming.

——. "Political Malaise and the New Arabic Noir." *South Central Review* 27, no. 1 & 2 (2010): 82–90.

Sufr, Mustafa. "al-Mujrim al-sadi kan wara' juthath Tarudant" [Sadistic Criminal behind Bodies of Taroudant]. *al-Sabah,* September 15, 2004, 7.

——. "Tafasil nihayat kabus ashla' juththat al-Hayy al-Hasani" [Details of End of Nighmare of Remains of Hay Hassani Body]. *al-Sabah,* June 3, 2005, 1, 6.

——. "al-Tibb al-shar'i yastantiq 'idham juthath Tarudant" [Forensic Medicine Makes Bones of Taroudant Bodies Speak]. *al-Sabah,* August 26, 2004, 1.

Sufr, Mustafa, and Muhammad al-Ibrahimi. "Mujrim Tarudant kan yanam fawq rufat dahayahu" [Taroudant Criminal Was Sleeping on Victims' Remains]. *al-Sabah,* September 9, 2004, 3.

"Tafasil suqut al-muttahimin fi maqtal muhami Maknas wa-zawjatihi" [Details of Suspect's Arrest in Killing of Meknès Lawyer and His Wife]. *al-Ahdath al-Maghribiyya,* June 21, 2006, 1, 12.

"Taghayyub al-da'im li-aswat wa-suwar al-mujtama', al-" [Enduring Absence of Sounds and Images of Society]. *al-'Alam,* March 14, 1993, 2.

"Taharriyat mukaththafa bahthan 'an al-fatah al-majhula" [Intensive Investigations Looking for Anonymous Girl]. *al-Ahdath al-Maghribiyya,* August 22, 2002, 1.

"Taharriyat mukaththafa li-masalih al-amn wa-tahdid huwiyat al-dahiya qad yusa'id fi al-tahqiq" [Intensified Police Investigations, Identifying Victim Might Help Investigation]. *al-Ahdath al-Maghribiyya,* December 5, 2002, 1.

Tahi, Wahid. *Jumhur sihafat al-ithara fi al-Jaza'ir: al-Simat al-'amma wa-'adat al-qira'a* [The Audience of the Sensational Press in Algeria: General Features and Practices of Reading]. Bayrut: Muntada al-Ma'arif, 2011.

"Tam'an fi al-mal qatala umm khatibatihi wa-rama bi-juththatiha fi al-ghaba bi-Fas" [Greedy for Money, He Killed His Fiancée's Mother and Tossed Her Body in Fez Woods]. *Akhbar al-Hawadith*, November 16, 1997, 10.

"Tasaqut al-aqni'a ba'd inhiyar al-Thabit" [Fall of Veils after Collapse of Tabit]. *al-Ittihad al-Ishtiraki*, April 10, 1993, 6.

"Tashrih al-tibbi yufid anna al-qatala muhtarifun, al-" [Autopsy Shows Killers Are Professionals]. *al-Ahdath al-aghribiyya*, August 19, 2002, 1.

Tawhidi, Abdelmoula. "Affair de l'officier supérieur de police." *L'Opinion*, February 13, 1993, 1, 3.

"Thalath dahaya kull yawmayn" [Three Victims Every Two Days]. *al-Ittihad al-Ishtiraki*, February 26, 1993, 1.

"Thariya fi ghiyab zawjiha fi al-hajj tulzim sa'iqaha bi-mumarasat mashahid burnujarafiyya 'alayha" [While Husband Was Away on Hajj, Rich Woman Forces Driver to Act Out Pornographic Scenes with Her]. *al-Mi'ad al-Siyasi*, June 8, 1994, 2.

Tuhami, Muhammad Ibn. *Dahaya Hubb* [Victims of Love]. al-Muhammadiyya: Matba'at al-Fadala, 1963.

"'Uthur 'ala baqaya wajh juththat al-Ma'arif qad yaqud li-tarkib sura taqribiyya li-l-dahiyya, al-" [Discovery of Remains of Maârif Body's Face Might Lead to Constructing Approximate Picture of Victim]. *al-Ahdath al-Maghribiyya*, March 5, 2003, 1.

"'Uthur 'ala juththa mushawwaha li-rajul bi-l-Dar al-Bayda'!, al-" [Discovery of Man's Mutilated Body in Casablanca!]. *al-Ahdath al-Maghribiyya*, May 28, 2002, 1.

Vermeren, Pierre. *Le Maroc de Mohammed VI: La transition inachevée*. Paris: La Découverte, 2011.

Wa'rab, Mustafa. *al-Mu'taqadat al-sihriyya wa-tuqusuha fi al-Maghrib* [Magic Beliefs and Their Climate in Morocco]. al-Dar al-Bayda': Dar al-Haraf, 2007.

Wadi', Salah al-. *al-'Aris* [The Bridegroom]. al-Dar al-Bayda': Matba'at al-Najah al-Jadida, 1998.

Wagner, Daniel A. *Literacy, Culture, and Development: Becoming Literate in Morocco*. Cambridge: Cambridge University Press, 1993.

Wahidi, Hasan al-. *Mat'am Sufiya* [Sofia's Restaurant]. Morocco: RTM, 2001.

Wasserman, Herman. *Tabloid Journalism in South Africa*. Bloomington: Indiana University Press, 2010.

Wilson, Christopher P. *Cop Knowledge: Police Power and Cultural Narrative in Twentieth-Century America*. Chicago: University of Chicago Press, 2000.

Winston, Robert Paul, and Nancy C. Mellerski. *The Public Eye: Ideology and the Police Procedural*. New York: St. Martin's Press, 1992.

Yasin, Muhammad. "Man qatala al-ustaz?!" [Who Killed the Teacher?!]. *al-Ahdath al-Maghribiyya*, March 12, 1999.

Yazi, al-Husayn. "Lughz nisf juththat al-Ma'arif lam yuhal ba'd" [Puzzle of Maârif Half Body Hasn't Been Solved Yet]. *al-Sabah*, May 29, 2002, 1.

———. "al-Tibb al-shar'i yadrus sinn wa-qamat wa-kull atraf al-juththa al-mumaththal bi-ha" [Forensic Medicine Studies Age, Build, and All Limbs of Mutilated Body]. *al-Sabah*, September 17, 2002, 5.

———. "al-'Uthur 'ala al-atraf al-sufla li-fatah fi kis balastiki bi-l-Dar al-Bayda'" [Discovery of Girl's Lower Limbs in Plastic Bag in Casablanca]. *al-Sabah*, September 11, 2002, 1.

Yazi, al-Husayn, and Radwan Hafyani. "Murtakibu al-jara'im al-khams al-ghamida fi al-Bayda' muhtarifun fi taqti' al-juthath wa-laysa al-qatl" [Perpetrators of Five Mysterious Crimes in Casa Are Professionals at Cutting Up Bodies but Not at Killing]. *al-Sabah,* February 15–16, 2003, 1.

Yazi, al-Husayn, and Mustafa Hurmat Allah. "Zuwita al-mushtabih fi irtikab jarimatay al-Ma'arif wa-La Jirund da'a al-shurta ila al-bahth 'anhu" [Zouita, Accused of Maârif and La Gironde Crimes, Called Police to Search for Him]. *al-Sabah,* March 8–9, 2003, 4.

Zawhari, Muhammad al-. "Tamada fi ihanatihim bi-shudhudhihi fa-'amadu ila qatlihi harqan!" [He Kept Abusing Them with His Deviance So They Proceeded to Kill Him by Fire!]. *al-Ahdath al-Maghribiyya,* December 5, 2003, 9.

Zayn al-Din, Duha. "Dahiyat jarimat Diyur Hantat ikhtafat ba'd al-munada 'alayha min taraf fatah" [Victim of Diyur Hantat Crime Disappeared after She Was Called On by Girl]. *al-Sabah,* August 19, 2002, 1.

———. "al-Jara'im al-jinsiyya tajtah al-mujtama' al-maghribi" [Sexual Crimes Strike Moroccan Society]. *al-Sabah,* September 15, 2004, 6–7.

———. "al-Majmu'at al-hadariyya fashilat hasb al-muwatinin wa-mas'ul amni yara anna al-waqt mubakkir li-l-taqyim" [GUS Have Failed according to Citizens But Security Official Thinks It's Too Early to Judge]. *al-Sabah,* December 20, 2004, 4.

Zhao, Yuezhi. *Media, Market, and Democracy in China: Between the Party Line and the Bottom Line.* Urbana: University of Illinois Press, 1998.

Index

Numbers in italics refer to illustrations.

abduction, 4, 14, 21, 33–34, 86, 205, 217, 241n13, 242n32
Ablal, Ayad, 181
Abu-Lughod, Lila, 8
actors, film and television, 9, 12, 36, 126, 128, 131, 136, 155–156, 157, 159, 178–179, 201, 210, 218, 226
addiction, 70, 137, 145, 150–151
adoption, 60–61, 71
Adorno, Theodor, 7
adultery, 32–33, 47, 62, 67, 84–85, 108, *116*
advertising, 7, 10, 12–13, 53, 56, 84, 187, *196*, *198*, *199*, 212, 215–217, 220–229, 232–233, 237; advertising firms, 9, 202, 213; television, *196*, *198*, *199*, 223–224. *See also* Boomerang
Afghanistan, 203, 229
Aïn Chok, 169, 173
Alaoui, Mustapha, 5, 50–52, 245n7
alcohol, 69, 150
Algeria, 50, 245n6, 256n1
Alternance, 80–83, 89, 93, 95, 97, 99, 105, 112, 124–125, 132, 143, 148, 208
Altheide, David L., 78
Althusser, Louis, 7, 203, 211–212
apartheid, 30, 246n18
Arab Spring, 13, 235, 237
Arabi, Nabil, 22–23, 27–28, 30–32, 34, 36
Arabic language, 5, 11, 12, 40, 79, 81, 85, 88, 96, 112, 113, 126, 135, 143, 144, 155, 174, 220, 239n5, 249n14, 257n28
Arbad, Bouchaïb, 42–44, 64
Ataâlah, Fadel, 219
audience, 4, 6, 8–12, 15–16, 22, 24–25, 31–32, 37–38, 42, 44–46, 50–51, 54–57, 71, 73, 78, 80–81, 83–84, 86–89, 92, 95, 98, 100–101, 109, 214, 219, 223, 245n10; educated, 85–86, 112, 220; elite, 7, 27; illiterate, 37; semiliterate, 37, 45, 86; television, 30, 113, 124–131, 133–134, 138, 142, 145, 148–151, 153, 155, 157, 161, 178–179, 187–188; working-class, 4, 7, 11, 25, 49, 51, 54, 59–60, 62–63, 70, 75, 112, 246n18
authoritarianism, state, 2–4, 6–10, 15, 17–18, 24, 41, 70, 80, 97, 101, 131, 148, 235–236; nature of, 10–11, 16, 18, 235, 237; transformation of, 4, 6–8, 10, 13, 16, 25, 30, 38, 46, 79, 89, 125, 236–237. *See also* authority; Years of Lead, authoritarianism in
authority, 22, 40, 44, 207, 215–216; crisis of, 6, 11–12, 16, 41, 44–45, 174, 190, 201; police, 17–18, 23, 88, 93, 158, 180, 190, 204, 236; state, 2–4, 6–7, 10, 39, 41, 44–45, 60, 73, 78, 82–83, 99, 102–103, 106–107, 111–113, 124–126, 134, 140–141, 143, 147–148, 151, 155–156, 157–159, 173, 203, 208, 211, 216, 224, 234, 235–238. *See also* authoritarianism, state
autopsies, 92, 103, 107, *121*, 131–132, 149, 165, 167, 170–172, 177–178, 188, *192*
Auxiliary Forces, 3, 231
Ayouch, Nabil, 241n13, 249n34

Banner (al-'Alam), 5, 20, 25, 27, 39–41, 44–45, 67, 167, 241n6
Baranek, Patricia M., 107, 112
Barini, Muhammad al-, 82–84
Basri, Driss, 41–42, 205–206
Baudrillard, Jean, 12, 153, 233
Belharash, Mohamed, 162–164, 166, 184
Belmajdoub, Jamal, *123*, 148–153, 251n20
Ben Ali, Zine El Abidine, 1
Benhachem, Hafid, 206
Bentassir, Abdelhaq, 204
Benyaich, Hicham, 178
Berkowitz, David, 159
Berrada, Mohamed, 45
Biressi, Anita, 95
Blind Whale, The (al-Hut al-a'ma) (novel), 89–91, 93–95, 97, 100–102, 109, 111, 126, 156, 157
Blind Whale, The (téléfilm), 120, 121, *127*, 130, 132–136, 138, 140–142, 149, 151, 153, 178, 188, *192*
Boomerang, 199, 212–215, 220, 223–225
Border Police, 3, 219
Borensetin, Eliot, 30
Boston Globe, 28
Boston Strangler, 88, 161

277

Bouchta, Farida, 169–170, 173
bribery, 1, 139, 143–146, 227–231
Bundy, Ted, 159, 161–162, 185

Campbell, Richard, 78
Capote, Truman, 96
Casablanca, 2–4, 12, 14, 16, 21–22, 27, 42–43, 72, 90–91, 93, 105, 107, 109–110, *120*, *121*, 128–133, 135, 138, 142, 146, 148–154, 158–159, 164–165, 167–173, 178–181, 186–190, *192*, *193*, *194*, *198*, 201, 203–205, 207–209, 211, 213, 216, 222, 225, 228, 233, 237, 241n12, 242n25, 249n34, 251n20
Casablancan (al-Baydawi), 213–214, 225–227, 232
Case, The (al-Qadiya), 187–189, 223, 232, 234
censorship, 15–17, 30, 43, 46, 75, 141, 146–148; self-censorship, 18–19, 136
Chan, Janet B. L., 107, 112
Chandler, Raymond, 87
Chaoui, Abdelkader, 241n6
Chikatilo, Andrei, 252n10
Choukri, Mohamed, 40
Christie, Agatha, 88
circulation, 5, 11, 24, 26, 37, 45, 51–52, 75, 79, 81, 84–85, 103, 106, 112, 130, 157, 220, 241n8, 250n1
civil rights, 77, 226
class, 15, 22, 85; conflict, 55–56, 145; middle class, 87–88, 91, 128–129, 134, 141, 222; working class, 11, 48–49, 51, 53–55, 57, 59–60, 62–65, 70–71, 74–75, 78–79, 87, 112, *117*, 151, 228–229, 246n18. *See also* audience, working-class; readers, working-class
coercion, 1, 3–4, 7, 10, 15, 46, 112, 235
Cold War, 4, 18
Columbo, 138, 210, 249n14
commercialism, 11, 81–82, 112, 236. *See also* media, commercial
community policing, 12–13, 202, 207–214, 220, 224, 226–227, 232
computers, 14, 130–131, 177–178, 187, *191*, 206, 210, 218
confessions, criminal, 2, 71, 76, 98, 100–103, 135, 137, 185–186, 205
conservatism, 6, 20, 25, 54, 55, 58, 60, 87, 161, 245n10; conservative audience, 47, 65, 84, 86. *See also* television, conservatism of
Conway-Long, Don, 243n46
Cop Files (Milaffat bulisiyya), 237
Cops, 179, 208
corruption, 1, 22, 75, 108, 133, 147–148; of police, 2, 18, 23–24, 39–40, 93, 107, 132, 142–143, 146–147, 207, 218, 220, 227, 230

cover-ups, 24–26, 31–32, 34, 37–38, 43–44
Creasey, John, 87
crime, 13, 37, 47–48, 50, 53, 59–66, 68–71, 73–75, 78, 82, 84–89, 92–93, 95–98, 100–105, 111, 113, 128, 134, 137, 140–142, 148, 158–161, 166, 171, 173, 190, 202, 205, 207, 209, 228, 233, 251n14; control of, 18, 72–75, 78, 178, 186, 208, 219, 221, 225, 244n1; coverage of, 16, 18, 33, 49, 50–51, 54, 65, 68, 76, 86–87, 96, 100–101, 103, 108, 112, 151, 157, 161, 164, 167, 186, 189, 250n1, 252n10; depictions of, 4, 8–10, 45, 47–49, 70, 82, 87, 98–99, 106, 112–113, 124, 126, 156, 157, 220; labs, 12, 103, 106, 159, 169, 177, 186, 188; narratives, 11, 79, 81, 96, 103, 250n3; organized, 68–69, 134, 205; real-world, 12, 77, 81, 87, 96–99, 101, 108–110; reports, 11, 50, 53, 110, 208, 219; solving, 7, 18, 71–72, 87–92, 94, 99, 101–105, 132, 135, 149, 152, 162, 166, 168–169, 202, 211, 224; violent, 18, 45, 65, 74, 150, 160; waves, 11, 47–49, 70, 77–79. *See also* crime scenes; criminality; journalism, crime; Moroccan True Crime; narratives, true-crime; photography, crime scene; television, crime reporting
Crime Scene (Masrah al-jarima), 237
crime scenes, 48–49, 53, 64, 72, 74, 77, 86, 92, 101–103, 106, 128–131, 137, 139, 149, 159, 171, 173, 174–175, 186, 188–189, 208, 224, 234, 245n10. *See also* photography, crime scene
Criminal Police, 71–72, 164, 187, 189, 219, 224
criminality, 63, 72, 171, 207; forms, 12, 71, 88, 158–160, 163–164, 168, 172–173, 177, 184–186, 189–190, 201, 205, 209, 211; Western, 180, 201, 205
cultural production, 81, 95, 157

Dahmer, Jeffrey, 176
degradation, 68–71, 133, 231; of inner reality, 33, 64, 67, 93, 183; moral, 31, 33, 47, 49–50, 55, 64, 67, 71, 84; religious, 84; sexual, 55; social, 55
democracy, 2, 24, 39–42, 74–77, 80, 93, 101, 126, 136, 141, 213; democratic reform, 38, 40, 75, 99, 112, 152; democratic values, 82, 90, 95, 97, 105, 112, 131, 148, 153, 155, 157–158, *197*, 236
demons, 57–59, *117*; demon possession, 57, 59
depravity, 19–20, 33, 43, 62–63, 74
detention centers: Derb Moulay Chérif, 2; Tazmamart, 81; Témara, 205–206
directors, film, 9, 12, 125, 138, 141, 155, 157, 159, 201, 208, 219, 226
dissent, 1–2, 7, 9, 80, 141, 148
DNA, 159, 177–180, 182, 187, 254n56, 255n69

Draiss, Charki, 232, 258n47
drugs, 34, 49, 55, 66, 68–70, 78, 107, 148–151, 227, 231; cannabis, 150; cocaine, 78, 141, 145, 148, 150–151, 153–154, 244n1; drug dealers, 69–70, 94, 123, 148, 150–151, 153–154, 232; drug smuggling, 68, 70, 90–91, 94, 140, 205; hashish, 55, 69, 90, 94, 133, 150; *qarqubi*, 150. See also addiction

Echoes of Skhirat and Tamara (Asda' al-Skhirat-Tamara), 52
education, 15, 44, 53, 56, 80, 113, 220
Egypt, 1–2, 50, 238
elites, 1, 5, 11, 15, 26–27, 38, 41, 46, 48, 54, 73, 88, 93, 105, 112–113, 126, 145, 150, 169, 174, 207, 220, 236, 239n5. See also audience, elite; non-elites
engagements, marriage, 57, 63–64, 153
England, 77, 207
entertainment, 5, 7, 34, 81, 95–97, 104, 106, 112, 125, 133, 256n82; entertainment industry, 7, 161
Equity and Reconciliation Commission, 205, 217–218, 225
Ericson, Richard V., 107, 112
Europe, 56, 61, 68, 70, 94, 141, 158, 179, 190, 203, 240n19. See also France; Spain
Evening (al-Masa'), 250n1
Events (Waqa'i), 126, 162, 250n3
evidence, 14, 16, 19–21, 23, 26, 28–31, 35, 37, 49, 61, 71–72, 87, 90, 92–95, 100–101, 103, 106, 108, 135–137, 139–140, 146, 152, 166, 169–171, 174–175, 177–178, 180, 182, 186, 188–189, 224, 234. See also forensics, forensic evidence
extremism, religious, 2, 169, 202–207, 216, 229, 234

fabrication, 12–13, 17, 76, 93, 141, 147–153, 155–158, 161, 180, 188, 203, 232, 254n56
Fadili, Adil, 141–142, 146–148, 150, 154, 156, 251n18. See also *Witness, The (al-Shahida)*
Falk, Peter, 138, 210, 251n16. See also *Columbo*
family, 2, 24, 37, 62–64, 74, 87, 91, 111, 128–129, 154; breakdown of, 60–63, 66, 75
family code (*Mudawwana*), 80, 219
fear, 3, 7, 11, 12, 15, 19–21, 23–24, 43–45, 48, 72, 79, 158, 164, 166–173, 181, 183, 186, 189, 208, 229; of police, 2, 7, 16, 21–22, 34, 38–39, 44, 78, 215–217, 228, 231, 235, 237; as a tool, 74, 78, 97
Federal Bureau of Investigation (FBI), 78, 159–164, 175, 182, 184–186, 202, 206–207. See also Hoover, J. Edgar

Fez, 3, 63, 204
Filali, Mohamed, 5
Final Bet, The, 135–136, 140, 249n14, 251n14
Fiske, John, 8
forensics, 12, 92, 103, 106, 131–132, 139, 149, 155, 158–159, 165, 167, 169–171, 173, 175, 177, 179–180, 186, 188–190, 248n6; forensic evidence, 87, 175; forensic science, 132, 169–170, 248n6. See also Institute of Forensic Science
fortune telling, 57
France, 6, 56, 60–61, 77, 81, 168, 179, 207, 224–225
Franco, Francisco, 89–90
freedom: of expression, 1–2, 6, 8, 10, 19, 22, 25, 41, 45–46, 75–76, 80, 89, 158, 226; of the press, 23, 25, 79; of speech, 19, 30, 38–40, 64, 74, 81, 83, 173, 217, 235
French language, 5, 20, 40, 80, 85, 96, 125, 126, 155, 174, 187, 210, 220, 234, 249n14, 257n28
Froment, Jean-Charles, 256n6
fuqaha. See witch doctors

Gacy, John Wayne, 88, 159, 161–162, 176, 185
gangs, 55, 68–69, 72, 109, *116*
gangsters, 78, 160
Garcia-Roza, Luiz Alfredo, 94
garde à vue (al-i'tiqal al-ihtiyati), 136, 140
Gendarmerie, 3, 14, 21, 30
gender, 29; equality, 80, 148, 152–153, 218; relationships, 152; rights, *197*, 219
General Direction of National Security, 206
General Direction of Studies and Documentation, 206
Ghallab, Abdelkrim, 40
Gleizal, Jean-Jacques, 256n6
globalization, 29, 30, 68–70, 74, 94, 205, 218, 235
Gramsci, Antonio, 4, 6
Grand Angle, 177–179, *192*
Gulf War, 4, 203
guns, 36, 42, 49, 69, 90, 94, 123, 127, 128, 132, 133, 134, 152, 189, 205, 215, 218, 222, 234, 257n27

Habermas, Jürgen, 7, 240n19
Hachadi, Abdelmajid, 96–97, 106–109, 113, 171
Haddad, Abdelghafour, 230–231
Hadi, Abdelali, 182–186, 188–189, *195*
Hall, Stuart, 47, 158, 244n1
Hamdouchi, Abdelilah, 89, 95, 126–127, 134–136, 139–141, 249n14, 250n37. See also *Blind Whale, The (al-Hut al-a'ma)* (novel); *Final Bet, The*

Hamdouchi, Miloudi, 89, 95, 249n14. See also *Blind Whale, The (al-Hut al-a'ma)* (novel)
Hamman, Hajj, 57
Hammett, Dashiell, 87
Hammoudi, Abdellah, 3, 10
Harakat, Abubakr, 184
Harris, Thomas, 161
Hassan II (king), 2, 3, 41–42, 44, 80–81, 207
Hollywood, 73, 133, 134, 141, 149–150, 152, 160, 168, 173–174, 208, 221, 228–229
homosexuality, 65–67, 84, 159, 176, 254n56
Hoover, J. Edgar, 78, 202, 208, 212
Horkheimer, Max, 7
Hotel Farah, 203–204
human rights, 4, 6–7, 10–11, 18, 23–24, 79, 80, 82, 90, 97, 99, 101, 124, 126, 130, 135–137, 143, 157, 205, 207, 216, 218, 235; abuses, 1–2, 15, 40–41, 81, 108, 132, 134, 155, 205–206, 217, 231, 237; organizations, 81, 94, 107, 214. See also Human Rights Watch; Moroccan Organization of Human Rights
Human Rights Watch, 204–205

Ibn Rochd Hospital, 131, 149
illiteracy, 5, 46. See also literacy
immigration, 56–57, 61; illegal, 69, 89, 227
immorality, 16, 19, 32–33, 48, 56–57, 60–61, 63–65, 68, 71, 74, 77
impotence, 50, 58, 85, 163
incest, 35, 84
Incident News (Akhbar al-Hawadith), 50, 52, 63, 76
independence, Moroccan, 2–3, 6, 15, 17, 23, 27, 83, 130, 145, 215, 235, 237
Independence Party, 5, 20, 241n8
Institute of Forensic Science, 171
interface, media-state, 7, 9–11, 13, 60, 211, 224, 235–237. See also media, collaboration with state
interpellation, 7, 13, 211–212, 225
intertextuality, 8, 12, 106, 155, 178, 223, 235, 237
intimidation, 1–3, 46, 151–152
Islam, 17, 33, 59, 61, 75. See also Muslims
Izzou, Abdelaziz, 232

Jalil, Rachid, 204, 256n2
Jamaï, Khalid, 226
Jaouhari, Younès, 216–218
Jebru, Abdellatif, 38
Jenkins, Philip, 160
Jenkins, Stephen, 47, 158

Jewish Alliance Club, 203–204
Journal (al-Sahifa), 231
Le Journal, 187, 216
Journal of National Security (Majallat al-Amn al-Watani), 44, 214–215, 218
journalism: crime, 33, 50, 88, 100, 104, 186; tabloid, 30. See also journalists
journalists, 2, 4, 9, 15–19, 22–25, 27–28, 30–32, 34–46, 58–59, 74–77, 81, 84, 96–101, 106, 108–110, 112–113, *114*, 124, 159–160, 163, 165, 181, 183, 201, 206, 208, 212, 216, 224–226, 243n46. See also journalism
justice, 4, 7, 15, 21, 23, 39–41, 49, 68, 71–73, 77, 96–97, 100, 103, 105, 107–108, 132, 137, 140, 143, 145–149, 189

Kharraz, Mohamed (Sherif Bin Ouidane), 231
King, Rodney, 30
Kraidy, Marwan M., 10

Laânigri, Hamidou, *200,* 201–202, 205–215, 220, 224, 226–227, 231–233
Laâyoune, 229, 232
Lakhmari, Noureddine, 187, 189, 223, 234, 256n81. See also *Case, The (al-Qadiya)*
Lambarki, Hamdi, 229
"language of wood" (*lughat al-khashab*), 40, 214, 219
Laughing Week (al-Usbu' al-Dahik), 5
Lawrence, Regina G., 112
liberalization, 77, 229; economic, 1, 18, 94; political, 3, 18, 66, 89. See also television, liberalization of
Liberator (al-Muharrir), 5, 242n32
Libya, 238
literacy, 8, 27, 113. See also audience, semiliterate; illiteracy; readers, semiliterate
Lopez, Shaun T., 50
Louahlia, Saeed, 107–108, 170, 177, 179–182, *193*
Lubna, Sharifa, 58

magazines, 5, 10, 12, 47, 50, 78, *198,* 206, 215, 220, 223, 232. See also *Tel Quel*; *Police Magazine (Majallat al-Shurta)*
magic, 57–58, *117,* 246n18; magicians, 58, 110–111
Mahfouz, Naguib, 50
makhzen (elite power brokers), 3, 239n5
Mankell, Henning, 94
Manning, Peter K., 2
Manson, Charles, 88
Market News (Akhbar al-Suq), 5

Marrakech, 57, 204, 209, 214–215, 256n1
Mawhoub, Aziz, 136–139
McBain, Ed, 87
Medi, 1, 237
media: audiovisual, 18, 25, 37, 131, 134, 151, 206; collaboration with police, 18, 72, 160, 177, 208; collaboration with state, 7, 11, 48–49, 70, 74, 77–79, 112, 158, 209, 211, 236; commercial, 9, 49, 70, 79, 202, 209, 215, 224, 235–236; environment, 7–10, 77; forms of, 7, 47, 49, 75, 78–79, 81, 95, 113, 214–215, 237; global, 15, 29–30; and image of police, 48, 53, 72, 82, 97, 99, 126, 132–133, 141, 148, 153, 158, 180, 187, 189–190, 201–203, 208, 211, 223–224, 226, 234, 235–237; industries, 13, 236; language in, 30, 35; mass, 4–9, 12–13, 15–16, 18, 20, 28–30, 33, 38, 43, 45–46, 48, 53, 74–78, 83, 85, 88, 112, 124–125, 147, 151, 159, 161, 176–177, 180, 182, 184, 186, 207, 220, 241n6, 244n1, 256n82; nonstate, 52, 78, 157, 201, 215, 217–218, 223, 235; police media, 225, 237; police use of, 178–179, 201, 208–209, 212, 215; print, 29, 104, 113, 124, 161; sensational, 9–10, 12, 16, 38, 73, 78–79, 82, 163, 172, 234–235; sources, 7–8, 46, 52, 58, 113, 124, 157, 211, 215, 218, 223; studies, 7, 10; texts, 8, 101, 107; U.S., 29, 33, 37, 159–161, 163, 176, 185, 208, 248n4. *See also* interface, media-state; newspapers; opening, media; pluralism, media; radios; tabloids; television; Years of Lead, media in
medical examiners, 92, 106, *121*, 131–132, 138–139, 149, 165, 167, 169–173, 178, 180–181, 190, *192*, *193*
medicine, modern, 58–59
Meeting of the Political (*Liqa' al-Siyasi*), 51–52
Mekki, Aïcha, 18
Middle East, 6, 8, 24, 88, 134, 212, 249n13
Miftah, Noureddine, 35–36
migration, rural, 207, 216
Migri, Younès, 128–129, 131, 179, 226
Ministry of Culture, 5
Ministry of the Interior, 3, 5, 18–19, 75, 240n13, 245n2
Miyabe, Miyuki, 94
modernity, 151, 153–154, 211, 215, 223, 229, 237; technological, 12, 103, 141, 178, 180, 186
modernization, 83, 127, 134, 140, 155, 206–207
Mohamed VI (king), 3, 125–126, 135, 155, 205–207, 219, 232
moral panic, 11, 48, 50, 64, 70, 78

morality, 22, 47, 54, 58, 61–62, 64–65, 88, 92; moral values, 17, 60. *See also* immorality
morgues, 99, 103, 125, 131, 133, 138, 157, 164, 178, 201
Morning, 163–165, 167–169, 173, 181, 183–185, 227
Moroccan Day (*al-Nahar al-Maghribiyya*), 226
Moroccan Events (*al-Ahdath al-Maghribiyya*), 11, 79, 81–87, 95–106, 108–113, 124–125, 127, 131–133, 147, 151, 155, 157, 164–167, 169–173, 175–176, 181–183, 186–187, 190, 214, 223, 225–226, 228, 248n4, 250n1, 251n14
"Moroccan exceptionalism," 203, 205
Moroccan Organization of Human Rights, 231
Morrocan Radio and Television (RTM), 5, 134–136, 138, 140, 147, 155, 157, 251n10, 251n18
Moroccan True Crime, 11, 79, 81–82, 87, 96–97, 104, 106, 109–110, 112–113, 131, 157, 165, 187, 201. *See also* narratives, true-crime
mosques, 24, 55; Hassan II Mosque, *198*, 213, 222
Most Dangerous Criminals, The (*Akhtar al-Mujrimin*), 256n82
motorcycles, 93, 129, 209–210, 213, 220–222, 228, 230
Moumen, Mohamed, 51–52
Moutachawik, Mustapha, 161–162
Mubarak, Hosni, 1–2
murder, 13, 49–50, 60–68, 71, 73–74, 77, 84, 86, 90–91, 93–94, 98–101, 104–106, 108, 110–111, *118*, 128–131, 135–137, 139, 142–147, 149, 158, 161–167, 169–174, 176, 179, 181–183, 185–186, 188–189, 217, 246n27, 251n13, 254n56; matricide, 62, 65, 86, 139, 246n27; patricide, 85, 246n27; police, 229–231; serial, 12, 160, 163, 168, 170–171, 173, 175–177, 180, 244n1; victims, 49, 53, 86, 89, 130, 143, 145. *See also* serial killers
Murley, Jane, 96
Muslims, 24. *See also* Islam

narratives, prison, 81, 91
narratives, true-crime, 7, 11–12, 82, 95–98, 102, 104–106, 108–111, 113, *119*, 124–125, 131–133, 137, 147, 155, 157–158, 164–166, 169, 176, 190, 201–202, 209–210, 219, 224, 237. *See also* Moroccan True Crime
National Enquirer, 245n10
necrophilia, 85
New York Times, 28
newspapers, 6, 8–10, 15, 17–18, 22, 24, 26, 31, 34, 37–40, 43, 45, 50, 53–54, 59, 75–77, 81, 83, 96, 132, 155, 159, 161, 164, 169–170, 173, 211,

228, 245n7, 245n10; daily, 5, 11, 38, 67, 82–86, 106, 113, 174, 180, 183, 220; government, 25, 48–49, 82; independent, 11, 50, 51–52, 82, 124, 158, 164, 250n1; party, 17, 21, 25, 27, 35, 51, 75, 86, 112, 158, 167, 241n8; subscriptions, 53, 84; weeklies, 5, 50–52, 54, 58, 75, 76, 82. *See also individual titles;* tabloids
non-elites, 15, 38, 41, 48–49, 54, 78, 113, 126, 174, 220, 236. *See also* readers, non-elite
nongovernmental organizations (NGOs), 80–81, 219
Nini, Rachid, 250n1
North Africa, 24, 88, 212

Obihi, Hussein, 58
Omari, Mohamed, 204, 256n2
opening: of borders, 69–70, 94; economic, 68, 70; media, 50, 55; political, 50, 63, 89
L'Opinion, 20–22, 27, 36, 85, 175, 226
Ouadie, Salah El-, 40, 81
Ouahidi, Hassan El-, *122,* 138. *See also Sofia's Restaurant (Mat'am Sufiya)*
Ouali, Rachid El-, 152, 218

party press, 17, 26–27, 41, 45–46, 49–51, 53–54, 56, 64, 74–79, 81, 83–84, 100, 106, 112, 151, 167
pedophilia, 84
Perrault, Giles, 80
photography, 5, 11, 12, 26, 37, 42, 44, 50–55, 58–60, 62–64, 66, 69–73, 75, 77, 86–87, *114,* 166, 175, 180–183, 187, 204, 213, 215, 218–219, 221, 224–226, 230–231, 234; crime-scene, 47–49, 53, 64, 66, 68, 74, 86, 137, 167–168, 173, 208, 245n10
pluralism: media, 76, 206; political, 76, 83
police fiction, 95, 98–101, 106, 108–111, 113, 126–127, 153, 169, 202, 237, 249n13. *See also* police novels
Police Magazine (Majallat al-Shurta), 185, 195–198, 214–224, 226–227, 231–232
police novels, 11, 81, 87–89, 95–97, 99, 101–102, 106, 108–110, 113, 126, 128, 135, 166, 169, 172, 183, 187, 249nn13–14, 250n37
Police of Proximity program *(Shurtat al-Qurb),* 207, 210, 214, 216, 231. *See also* police stations, Police of Proximity Posts (PPP)
police officers, female, 207, 218, 257n27
police stations, 12, 39, 53, 73, 82, 92, 101, 103, 105, 107–108, 125, 130–133, 136–140, 144–146, 152, 155–156, 157, 159, 161, 170, 172–173, 187, 188, 201, 208, 210, 216, 224, 230, 235, 237, 251n10, 257n30; Casablanca, *120,* 129, 131, 142–143, 148–149, 152–153, 179, 225; Police of Proximity Posts (PPP), 210, 216, 226, 232; Salé, 138
Political Appointment (al-Maw'id al-Siyasi), 51, 62
Political Communicator (al-Muwasil al-Siyasi), 52, 57, 64
Political Day (al-Yawm al-Siyasi), 52, 60, 62, 66, 69
political parties, 5, 36, 40, 50, 52, 83, 241n8. *See also* Independence Party; newspapers, party; party press; Socialist Union Party
Political Rendezvous (al-Mi'ad al-Siyasi), 52, 57, 58–59
Pope, Generoso, 245n10
popular culture, 8, 10, 58, 78, 160, 208, 212, 224, 237, 257n7
power, 2, 8, 21–22, 25, 80, 111, 235, 239n5; abuse of, 40–42, 231; of police, 17–18, 22–24, 34, 39–40, 88, 93, 183, 201; state, 3–4, 23, 45–46, 97–98, 131, 211–212, 235
Powers, Richard Gid, 78, 160
prisoners, political, 80–81, 138
procedures, legal, 92, 108; police, 88, 95, 101, 106–107, 109, 131, 219
profiling, 153, 159–161, 169
propaganda, 9–10, 49, 124, 126, 147; state, 5–6, 75, 113, 212, 215, 237
prostitution, 31, 47, 68–69, 84; prostitutes, 32–33, 55–56, 143, 162, 175–176, 229, 254n56
psychology, 4, 32, 58, 152–153, 168, 170–171, 176, 181, 183–184, 214
psychopaths, 168, 175, 184
public opinion, 7, 9, 11, 13, 41, 46, 48–49, 52, 70, 73, 77, 79, 82, 111, 124–125, 190, 202, 225, 234, 236–237
public relations, 4, 159–160, 169, 179, 182, 202, 208–209
punishment, 4, 9–11, 16, 22, 48–49, 53, 59–60, 70, 79, 81–82, 88, 96, 98, 100, 103, 106, 124, 126, 156, 157, 183, 220

Quran, 6, 58, 61–62, 136

Rabat, 6, 12, 51, 55, 66, 138, 205, 209, 229, 242n32, 245n7
radicals, Islamist. *See* extremism, religious
radios, 8, 21, 25, 78, 160, 220, 223, 225, 237, 240n13; police, 31, 36, 206, 210, 218, 221
Ramadan, 24–26, 106, 110–111, 187, 229
rape, 19, 28–30, 33–35, 50, 55, 57, 77, 85, 105, 184–185

readers, 5, 8, 12, 27, 35–36, 45–46, 47, 49, 51, 55–61, 72, 76, 83–85, 87, 94–95, 104, 107–108, 164, 189, 213, 245n10; conservative, 65; educated, 113; non-elite, 4, 11; and relationship with police, 88–91, 93, 97–98, 100–102, 104, 109, 111–112, 211; semiliterate, 53, 86; working-class, 53, 57, 70, 75
Reagan, Ronald, 78, 160
realism, 131, 133, 149, 155–156
Redwan, Sherif, 58–59, 117
Reed, Jimmie L., 78
reform, 6–7, 18, 41, 45, 80, 90, 126, 136, 236; democratic, 38, 40, 75, 99, 112, 152; of police, 9, 42, 112, 125, 135, 206, 208
religion, 55, 61, 86, 229. *See also* extremism, religious; Islam
respectability, 21, 59, 86; appearance of, 32–33, 43, 47, 55, 64–67, 93, 183
Ressler, Robert, 159–161, 176, 184–186
Rhanja, Hassan, *120, 121,* 126, 129, 133–134, 138, 178. See also *Blind Whale, The* (téléfilm)
Rmaïl, Bouchaïb, 171, 179, 209
Roché, Sebastian, 256n6
Roughead, William, 96
Royal Police, 3
RTM. *See* Moroccan Radio and Television (RTM)
Rule, Ann, 96
rule of law, 6–7, 10, 11, 15, 24, 39, 79, 80, 82, 93, 95, 97, 99, 101, 105, 112–113, 124, 126, 135, 141, 143, 145–148, 153–154, 157–158, 205, 235
Russia, 30, 252n10

sadism, 32, 35–36, 181, 185
Saghir, Hadin, 18, 75–77, 113
Sail, Noureddine, 127
Salafiyya Jihadiyya, 204
Samel, Abdelaziz, 219–220
Saudi Arabia, 1, 27–28, 63
Schmid, David, 160
Schudon, Michael, 9
science, 92, 106–108, 132, 158–159, 168, 169, 171, 177, 179–180, 182, 186, 188. *See also* forensics, forensic science; Scientific Police
Scientific Police, 171, 175, 177–181, 186–189, *191, 192, 193, 194,* 211, 219, 223–224, 234
Sebti, Miryam, 213
Secret Police (Department of Territorial Security, DST), 3, 205–207
security, 6, 17, 47, 66, 68, 73–74, 86, 92, 112, 140, 147, 167–168, 171, 173, 179, *196,* 204, 206–207, 209, 213–214, 216–219, 222, 224

security forces, 1–3, 14, 16–19, 21–22, 38, 50, 74, 130, 165, 168, 171, 187, 201, 205, 209–210, 213–214, 217, 219, 221, 225–226, 231, 236, 239n5, 257n7
Seltzer, Mark, 96–97
sensationalism, 4–13, 15–16, 25–26, 29–30, 33–34, 38, 42, 44–46, 48–51, 73, 75, 78, 81, 84, 86, 124–125, 151, 161, 236, 241n6; sexual, 27–31, 34–35, 243n46. *See also* media, sensational
separatists, 229
September 11 attacks, 201, 203, 205, 206
serial killers, 12, 110, 158–164, 166, 168–181, 183–186, 188–190, *191, 192, 195,* 201–202, 205, 208, 211, 219, 225, 236–237, 252n10, 256n82. *See also* murder, serial
sex, 21, 25, 27, 29–30, 32, 33, 37, 60, 62, 65, 67, 84–85, 98, 124, 162–163, 182, 185. *See also* degradation, sexual; homosexuality; incest; necrophilia; pedophilia; sensationalism, sexual
Sigma, 223–224
Silence of the Lambs, The, 161
Simenon, Georges, 248n6
Sirat al-Mustaqim, 204
Skir, Najib, 51–55, 58–59, 61–63, 74–77, 205, 245n9
Skogan, Wesley G., 256n6
Smith, William Kennedy, 28–29, 31
smuggling, 68–70, 90–91, 94, 140, 205
social change, 16, 90
social cohesion, 3, 6, 16, 44, 79
Social Union, 75
Socialist Union (al-Ittihad al-Ishtiraki), 5, 16, 19–20, 22–23, 25, 35–36, 39–41, 43, 45, 51, 76, 82, 113, 167, 173, 241n6
Socialist Union Party, 5, 35, 45, 74, 80, 241n8
sociopaths, 64, 159, 163, 183, 185
Sofia's Restaurant (Mat'am Sufiya), 122, 134–136, 138–141, 151, 216
South Africa, 30, 246n18
Spain, 89–90
Strait of Gibraltar, 69, 203, 206
street children, 104–105, 249n34
suicide, 32, 62–63, 65, 86, 107, 170, 174–176, 185, 230
suicide bombers, 12, 201, 203, 233
Suleiman, Mahmoud, 50
SUVs (sports utility vehicles), 209–210, 213, 221–222

Tabit, Hajj Mustapha, 14, 21–23, 26–27, 32–34, 39–40, 42–43, 45, 52, 54, 241nn12–13, 242n32;

complaints against, 23–24, 31, 242n32; crimes of, 4, 24, 27–28, 31–32, 36–37, 243n43; execution of, 45, 244n69. *See also* Tabit Affair

Tabit Affair, 4–6, 10–11, 15–16, 24–30, 32, 38–42, 44–46, 47–49, 53–54, 56, 59, 64, 70, 77–78, 80, 84, 86, 93, 112, 124, 128, 158, 166, 174, 183, 212, 214, 217, 234, 236, 241n6, 241n13, 250n3; post-Tabit era, 64, 70–71, 73, 93; trial of, 32–33, 35, 38–39, 42, *114, 115*. *See also* Tabit, Hajj Mustapha

tabloids: collaboration with police, 49, 208, 245n2; collaboration with state, 49, 53, 77–78; covers, 50, 53, 60, 67, 69, 71, 73, 75, 113, *118*, 205; crime tabloids, 11, 16, 47–60, 65, 79, 81–82, 84–86, 89, 92–94, 97–98, *116*, 124, 128, 140, 166, 168, 174, 176, 179, 183, 218, 237, 244n1, 245n6, 245n9, 250n3; depiction of police, 48, 70, 72–73, 78, 98, 109, 112, 201; depiction of society, 61–64, 68–70, 74, 77; and party press, 74–76, 84; prose, 87, 100; revealing hidden evils, 64–67. *See also individual titles*; journalism, tabloid

Taoussi, Hassan, 204

Tawhidi, Abdelmoula, 20–21

Tazi, Mohamed Abderrahmane, 127, 250n4

teamwork, 92–93, 103, 110

technology, 12, 54, 58, 103, 141, 158, 178, 180, 186–187, 190, *191*, 206–207, 210, 215, 217, 222

Tel Quel, 169, 212–214, 222–223

téléfilms, 113, *120, 121, 122, 123,* 125–127, 134, 136, 140–141, 147–149, 151, 153–155, 157–158, 161, 169, 178–179, 187–189, *192*, 201–202, 209–210, 216, 218, 220, 223–224, 237, 250n4, 251n18. *See also Blind Whale, The* (téléfilm); *Case, The (al-Qadiya); Sofia's Restaurant (Mat'am Sufiya); White Nights; Witness, The (al-Shahida)*

television, 5–13, 25, 95, 106, 124–127, 130, 133–136, 141, 143, 147–148, 151, 153, 157, 159, 162, 178, 183, 188, 211, 216, 218, 224–226, 240n13, 250n4, 251n20; American, 12, 28–30, 87–88, 133, 141, 149–150, 152, 158, 160–161, *200*, 220, 226, 233–234; cameras, 131, 183, 201; conservatism of, 124, 126, 133–135, 140, 143, 155; crews, 156, 174, 177, 179, 208; crime reporting, 21, 25, 37, 174, 177, 186; executives, 126, 134, 156; liberalization of, 25, 206; movies, 113, *120*, 125, 127, 132, 157, 178, 187, 227–228; programming, 5, 8, 10, 113, 125, 134, 140, 155, 179, 223; stations, 124–126, 134, 136, 140, 156, 187, 220. *See also* advertising, television; Medi1; Moroccan Radio and Television (RTM); téléfilms; 2M

terrorism, 13, 158, 201–209, 212–213, 233–234, 237. *See also* suicide bombers; War on Terror

Thomas, Clarence, 29, 31

Today's News (Akhbar al-Yawm), 50

torture, 2, 3, 12, 36, 50, 101, 107, 125, 135, 137, 155, 157, 205, 217–218, 237, 257n25

transparency, 41, 48, 64, 74, 156; police, 131, 155, 206, 208, 231

Treat, Lawrence, 87

trials, criminal, 2, 25, 75

trust, 19, 43, 66–67, 82

Tunisia, 1, 238

2M, 124–127, 131, 134, 141, 146–148, 155, 157, 162, 174, 177, 179, 187, 237, 250n5, 251n18, 256n82

United Arab Emirates, 205

United States, 28–31, 53, 55, 56, 59, 61, 77–78, 87–88, 95–96, 112, 155, 158–159, 161–163, 168, 179, 185–186, 203–205, 207, 220, 224, 240n19, 244n57, 246n15, 248n4, 256n82. *See also* television, American

urban life, 8, 207–208, 221–222, 229

Urban Security Units (GUS), *195, 196, 199, 200,* 209–218, 220–233, 236, 258n47

videotapes, 4, 14, 19–21, 27–31, 33, 35–39, 42–43, 56, 241n13, 243n43

violence, 1, 4, 10, 13, 19, 27, 30, 36, 47–50, 54, 60, 64, 65, 67–70, 72–73, 77, 85, 87, 89, 95, 159, 170, 205, 227; police, 2, 6, 73, 230–231, 235–236; state, 3, 15, 79, 82, 112

visas, 68, 69

visibility, of police, 49, 96, 157, 208, 210, 215–216, 220

voyeurism, 28, 34, 37–38

War on Terror, 201, 203

Waugh, Hillary, 87

Weekly Rise, The (al-Shuruq al-Usbu'ī), 50

Western Sahara, 17, 229

White Nights, 123, 148–149, 151, 153–156, 157, 188–189, 218, 223, 232

Willets, Jeffery, 29

Willets, Kathy, 29, 31, 33

Wilson, Christopher P., 88, 96, 103

witch doctors, 32, 86. *See also* witchcraft

witchcraft, 47, 57, 58, 246n18. *See also* witch doctors

Witness, The (al-Shahida), 141, 150, 156, 228; censorship of, 146–148

women's groups, 80

women's rights, 80–81, 219

Years of Lead, 2, 5, 10, 15, 38, 43, 48, 65, 75, 81, 138, 205, 217; authoritarianism in, 17, 25, 70, 80, 112, 131; end of, 70, 205, 235–236; language of, 21, 30, 40, 48, 218; media in, 9, 18, 24, 26, 34, 43, 49–50, 68, 70, 74, 140, 147, 155, 240n13; police, 3, 11–12, 18, 21, 23, 34, 35, 39, 71, 73–75, 78, 82, 90, 92, 94–95, 101, 107, 113, 129–130, 137, 143, 145, 155, 157, 202, 210–211, 217, 225, 230–231, 235, 237; post-Years of Lead era, 6, 44, 48, 53, 60, 136; repression in, 4, 6, 45, 97; and state power, 3, 6, 46

Youssoufi, Abderrahman, 80–81
youth, 56, 61–63, 69–70, 86, 148, 150–151, 155, 250n5

Zarqawi, Abu Musab, 231
Zhao, Yuezhi, 9
Ziati, Adil, 229–230
Zouita, Mohamed, 174–182, 184–186, 188–189, *191, 192*, 209, 254n56, 256n82

JONATHAN SMOLIN is Associate Professor of Asian and Middle Eastern Languages and Literatures at Dartmouth College. His publications include a translation of Abdelilah Hamdouchi's *The Final Bet: A Modern Arabic Novel*, the first Arabic police novel translated into English.

www.ingramcontent.com/pod-product-compliance
Lightning Source LLC
Chambersburg PA
CBHW070754230426
43665CB00017B/2349